PRINCIPLES OF LEADERSHIP

What We Can Learn From the Life and Ministry of Bill Bright

Compiled and Edited by
TED MARTIN & MICHAEL COZZENS

Principles of Leadership: What We Can Learn from the Life and Ministry of Bill Bright

Published by
New*Life* Publications
A ministry of Campus Crusade for Christ
P.O. Box 620877
Orlando, FL 32862-0877

Edited by Joette Whims and Lynn Copeland

Design and production by Genesis Group

Cover by David Marty Design

Printed in the United States of America

ISBN 1-56399-174-8

Contents

PART THREE: SPECIAL ISSUES

Preface

A group of Campus Crusade for Christ staff, many of whom teach in Crusade-related schools of theology around the world, attended the annual meeting of the Evangelical Theological Society in Boston in November 1999. One of our group, Randall Gleason, made a suggestion that led to this book.

Often, when a prominent professor retires, a group of colleagues—fellow professors, former students, scholarly associates in his or her field—put together a *Festschrift* (German for "festive writing") in honor of their retiring friend. Dr. Gleason suggested that we publish a *Festschrift* in honor of Dr. Bill Bright as he steps down from fifty years of leadership of Campus Crusade for Christ. We all thought that this was a wonderful idea. The group asked me to serve as editor, probably because I have been involved in the biblical, theological, and ministry training of Campus Crusade for Christ for forty years. Although I agreed somewhat reluctantly, I view it as a sacred responsibility. I asked Dr. Michael Cozzens, who has his doctorate in communications, to be co-editor.

From the beginning, we decided that this would be a special kind of *Festschrift*. Often a *Festschrift* is a dry, dusty, scholarly tome that is read only by a few dry, dusty scholars. We wanted to produce a book that would be practical and inspiring, a book that would be widely read and applied, a book that would further Bill Bright's goal of helping to fulfill the Great Commission in this generation. We determined that the chapters of the book would deal with biblical principles which have been important to the life and ministry of Bill Bright and which, under his leadership, have become important to the worldwide ministry of Campus Crusade for Christ.

The chapters were written by a variety of people. Some are professors in our various schools of theology, teachers who have a strong practical-ministry emphasis. Other chapters were written by leaders of various ministries of Campus Crusade for Christ; many have worked closely with Bill Bright for many years. All the writers have had their personal lives and ministries greatly impacted by Campus Crusade for Christ and by the principles in this book.

The release of this book coincides with the fiftieth anniversary of Campus Crusade for Christ and with Bill's decision to step down from leadership, turning the reigns of the ministry over to Steve Douglass as the new president. It also marks the approach of Bill's eightieth birthday.

As the writers of this book, we dedicate it to Bill Bright in honor of the Christ whom he has faithfully served. We each owe much to Bill as a teacher, both by precept and by example. We owe much to the principles discussed in this book. We pray that God will use this book to further these principles throughout the ministry of Campus Crusade for Christ around the world, as well as throughout the Body of Christ. As Christians study and adapt these principles to their lives and to the various ministries of which they are a part, we pray that God will use them to win, build, and send other men and women to help fulfill the Great Commission until our Savior returns.

Although this book is a tribute to Dr. William R. Bright as he steps down from the presidency of Campus Crusade, we would be remiss if we did not mention Vonette Bright and her unique contribution to Bill's life and ministry. She has made great contributions on her own to Campus Crusade and the Body of Christ in many ways, especially in the area of prayer. But her greatest joy in ministry seems to be in helping Bill and Campus Crusade for Christ succeed. We will never know what Bill might have done without Vonette, but we are all convinced that it would have been much less than he has been able to accomplish with her help. We hope that Vonette will also feel honored by the content of this book.

Michael Cozzens and I want to express our appreciation to each writer for taking time out of busy schedules to write these chapters. We also appreciate the work of Karen Race and Stacy Thomas for contacting writers and making revisions. These two represent countless other secretaries and helpers who have assisted the individual writers, many of whom we are not even aware.

As with Campus Crusade's ministry itself, this has been a group effort. But the goal of it all is to bless and motivate you. May God use you to "come help change the world" for Christ.

TED MARTIN,
Editor

Foreword

It is awesome, as young people today might say, to be asked to write a foreword in place of Billy Graham, who would have been the logical person to do so but whose health has not allowed it. It is even more stirring because both Billy Graham and Bill Bright are being dragged down by disease, as is my wife. And I, only slightly younger than these two giants, probably don't have many more years to anticipate.

It is dire circumstances such as these that enable clearer insight into tremendous events. These two men have each led two radically different approaches to world evangelism, both with unprecedented success. In Bill Bright's case, we near not only the end of his earthly days (apart from a medical miracle), but also his eightieth birthday. In addition, we near the fiftieth anniversary of the organization he founded.

In this book, which is much more than the usual *Festschrift* composed by a professor's students, we find striking behind-the-scenes insights into the actual principles of effective witness. They are generated by his faithful, personal followers whose mighty works employ not only their special talents, but Bill's own unmistakable imprint.

No organization better displays the truth of the often-quoted observation that the business that best succeeds is not the one which works out the best plan, but the one which works its plan out the best. Bill and Vonette, and you cannot readily speak of one without the other, have for fifty years been launching one major new plan after another. Perhaps none of them has been quite perfect. But all of them have been superbly undertaken.

This is in some great part due to a third "inseparable," Steve Douglass. With a background at the Harvard Business School, he joined Bill and is now shouldering the incredible present global network representing Bill Bright's vision, his profound respect for God's leading, and his incessant concern for quality of management.

Few ministries in history have the physical proportions of Campus Crusade's global network. Few have reflected a more detailed grasp of integral, coherent strategy. For example, when the payroll enabling their Latin American staff went beyond two million dollars a year (U. S. staff were already on personal support), Crusade decisively and daringly adopted a personal support system many said would never work "on the mission field." They lost a few staff, but it worked. And the strategy has worked elsewhere. It has neatly avoided one of the most serious pitfalls in mission work—dependency.

Many much-larger examples in Crusade's work these past fifty years show the organization's flair for plans no one else thought of or could hardly believe in, typically involving many other collaborating organizations. Take the nationwide "I Found It" campaign, or the Soviet Union–wide "Co-Mission" plan in which other organizations were so fully involved that it was not simply a Crusade enterprise. The breathtaking plan to zero in on the 5,000 million-person areas of the earth's surface is another. And a crowning achievement has been the unparalleled JESUS Film Project which, though designed and led by Crusade, has enlisted literally hundreds of other organizations in its outworking.

In one sector of missions today, there has been a decrying of "Managerial Missiology." Yet, no single organization I know of has been more constantly and brilliantly successful in demonstrating the harmonious and explosive combination of management principles and evangelistic zeal. Crusade is characterized by audacity, grace, and competence in management.

One of the crucial events in Crusade's history was the watershed year during which many of Bill's regional leaders and staff walked out because they decided they wanted a different management style. Their ideas were not reprehensible at face value. They were keen-thinking and dedicated people. But Bill and Vonette chose to maintain a lean and coherent strategy of a different sort. (And they ended the year with even more staff.)

Today, it would be hard to imagine how a ministry that is one of the largest, if not the largest, in missions could have become what it is if its coherence had not been maintained. A team cannot follow every member's best ideas. A team is a team when individuals routinely give up their personal plans for enthusiastic agreement on the plan of the team. But in this area, Crusade, as well as many other mission teams, has had to go upstream, against the very grain of an American culture that seems to encourage an excessive individualism. Bill, Vonette, Steve, Paul Eshleman, and other key personalities close to Bill all have outstanding skills and abilities and ideas, and I am sure Bill has learned as well as taught within that inner circle. That is, he has been surrounded by divergent ideas. But the outworking has been linear, including coherent plans in which all have been involved heart and soul.

This book will let the reader in on some of the successful principles that underlie the truly astounding, global team which Crusade now constitutes and that will continue on vigorously and effectively after Bill's personal contribution concludes. One of the most unusual and cogent is the principle of sharing and giving to other organizations. The U. S. Center for World Mission would not even exist if not for Crusade's substantial generosity.

Where did Crusade come from? I met Bill before it existed. Dan Fuller, son of the founder of the incredibly influential *Old-Fashioned Revival Hour* of the 1930s and 1940s, the first nationwide religious broadcast in this country, went to Princeton Theological Seminary in 1946. As a high school friend and Navigator pal, I went with him. Our parents, who knew each other, thought we could keep each other true to the gospel even if 3,000 miles away from home. There we met Bill Bright. He, too, had already met both Charles E. Fuller and Dawson Trotman, founder of the Navigators. Then Dan Fuller's father decided to found Fuller Theological Seminary, where all three of us—Dan, Bill, and I—then transferred in 1947. There we met the great Bible teacher Wilbur Smith, who gave Crusade its name; church historian Harold Lindsell; New Testament scholar Everett Harrison; and theologian Carl F. H. Henry, who by now is the only one of these four still alive, nearing ninety, and who handwrote a two-page letter to me only a few days ago.

Bill and I and others have been truly blessed by and undergirded by these earlier great men: Fuller, Trotman, and these professors. However, in this book you will see totally unexpected fruits born of those earlier seed experiences, which exceeded the imagination of any of them. And this is not the end of it all. In this book, you will see more seeds of even greater things in the future. Why? In great part not because Bill and Vonette have commanded a great audience, as did D. L. Moody, but because they have forged a tightly knit community of workers, an ongoing fellowship whose principles of action clearly demonstrate ongoing viability. True to Bill and Vonette's principles, their disciples are unselfishly sharing their insights with everyone else in this book.

Thus those who hold this book in their hands hold immense wisdom and insight, as well as the clear evidences of the power and glory of the living God in our times—the One to Whom, and for Whom, and by Whom, and from Whom all this derives. Those who write these chapters all recognize Him as the One they have been ultimately following all along, and continue to follow. This is true, in good part, because Bill and Vonette themselves have also been following Him as the central reality of their lives. Clearly, more than all the plans and principles you find here is the constant God-consciousness of these two, which can be and should be for all readers the most powerful contribution of this book.

May God uphold you and bless you, Bill and Vonette, in this special time of your lives.

RALPH D. WINTER,
Founder, U. S. Center for World Mission

CHAPTER 1

A Real-Life Illustration

MICHAEL COZZENS
On Staff since 1977
Academic Dean, International School of Theology

One noteworthy threat to the success of the Church in America today is that it may be trivialized and ignored because of a perception that the historic Christian faith is fundamentally irrelevant to modern existence. When people see little or no connection between theology and real life demonstrated in followers of Christ, the power of the gospel is effectively neutralized. Thus, it is of great significance when God uses someone to help others grasp the practical implications of the great truths of revelation so that their lives come to reflect redemption and spiritual transformation. It is the Life of Christ lived by modern disciples that glorifies God, directs others to the Savior, and reveals the relevance of God's kingdom and His Church.

Few people in the history of the Christian movement have done more to encourage the practical application of simple biblical exhortations concerning personal evangelism, ministry, and a devoted life "in Christ" than Dr. Bill Bright. Throughout his fifty-plus years of ministry around the world, Dr. Bright has encouraged Christians to "walk in the Spirit" moment by moment and share God's love with those who have never "made the wonderful discovery of knowing God personally." In ever-enthusiastic fashion, Dr. Bright has challenged anyone who would listen to live differently because of truths about God: the Father, the Son, and the Holy Spirit.

This collection of essays is intended to be a tribute to someone who readily directs such honor and praise to his Lord and Master. This collection is also intended as a resource for Christians who seek to be used by God to help change their world. Each chapter examines a biblical principle of life or ministry that has been characteristic of Dr. Bright and the worldwide movement called Campus Crusade for Christ. The methods of ministry blessed by God and practiced by Bill Bright are presented here as examples. Certainly, the principles presented in this book are evident outside Campus Crusade in many biblically oriented ministries and churches around the world; and many affirm the direct and indirect influence of Campus Crusade "training." Since these principles are taken directly from the pages of Scripture, it is no surprise that many would practice them. Dr. Bright's remarkable contribution from the beginning has been finding simple ways to encourage the practical application of biblical principles.

This book, then, is a tool that may be read with several "practical" questions in mind. In fact, the reader is encouraged to repeatedly ask, "How can *I* use or adapt this principle to *my* life and ministry?" Whether you are a "professional" in ministry (pastor, missionary, full-time Christian worker) or a willing volunteer (Sunday school teacher, Bible study leader, lay minister, youth leader, or the leader of a prayer or care group at church or in your home), there is much of great value to be gleaned from this set of essays. Dr. Bright would be honored and pleased to know that God used this book to bless those who apply these principles in their lives and ministries.

You will find that some of the principles are more personal in nature, relating primarily to a Christian's walk before the Lord. Others are more focused on ministry and how one might be more effective in advancing God's kingdom. A few principles presented relate to leadership in Christian organizations.

I encourage you to ask God to direct your thinking as you reflect on the examples in this book. As you read, or perhaps at the conclusion of each chapter:

- Prayerfully write out some ways you might adapt and apply what you have read.
- Take an additional moment to identify and record *action steps*—specific things that you can do, steps toward utilizing the principles that will enhance your ministry.
- At the conclusion of the book, review and revise your list of principles and action steps.
- Ask God to bless your understanding of what you have learned in order to be more effective in your service to Him.
- Finally, listen to the Lord as you begin taking the action steps that He will use to make these principles part of your life.

Do this for your personal spiritual life and for your ministry.

If you are involved in a formal group devoted to ministry—a local church, a denomination, a missionary organization, or other type of Christian organization:

- Ask God how these principles might be adapted and applied in your organization.
- Encourage others from your group to read the book.
- Discuss how the various principles presented here might be applied through your particular group.
- Finally, consider formulating appropriate *action steps* for your organization.

Our prayer is that as we acknowledge with honor the life and ministry of Dr. Bill Bright, God will be praised and glorified in and through your life and ministry.

PART ONE

Personal Principles

CHAPTER 2

Faith

JOON GON KIM
On Staff since 1958
Director, Korean Campus Crusade for Christ

Serious misunderstandings about faith exist within the community of Christians. Many people who claim to be Christians believe faith should be based on their subjective feelings or mystical experiences: dreams, visions, and prophecies. Others believe only what can be rationally explained. Then there are those who say, "If you strongly and positively believe something, it will happen according to your faith." They believe a person's mental image determines his success. Such positive thinking can be a great motivator psychologically, but it is not faith.

What is true biblical faith? Doctrinally, I believe the Apostles' Creed is the most acceptable standard of all creeds. It begins with the words, "I believe." The early Church identified Christians by the fish symbol, an abbreviated form of "Jesus Christ the Son of God and Savior."

The Gospel of John is the gospel of believing. The verb form of "believe" is recorded 98 times. Concerning the purpose of his Gospel, John says, "These are written that you may believe that Jesus is the Christ, the Son of God, and that by believing you may have life in his name" (John 20:31). There are three elements in faith:

First, faith has an *intellectual* element. We must know who God is and that the Bible is God's Word. We also must know who Jesus is and what He has done for us. But knowing is not enough. Even the demons have great knowledge of God, yet they have no faith in God.

Second, faith has an *emotional* element. The apostle Thomas confessed his faith in Jesus as "my Lord and my God." His was not just an intellectual recognition of Jesus as Christ, but an emotional element was included. Emotions can vary and can at best be merely expressions of true faith.

In the New Testament, we have a great chapter of faith, Hebrews 11, in which the Old Testament heroes of faith are listed. In this chapter alone, the words "by faith" are recorded twenty times. These were the people who trusted in and obeyed God's Word. Foremost among all these is Abraham. He believed in God, and God credited it to him as righteousness (Genesis 15:6). Abraham's confession of faith included sincerity of the heart, that is, an emotional element of faith.

Third, faith has a *volitional* element, the personal application—accepting Jesus Christ as our Savior and the Lord. John 1:12 says, "Yet to all who received him, to those who believed in his name, he gave the right to become children of God." This verse clearly indicates that the decision of receiving Him is up to each person's will.

Dr. Bright's train diagram in *The Four Spiritual Laws* booklet, a distilled presentation of the gospel, explains these three elements. The booklet says that we must know the "fact" (God and His Word) and have "faith" (our trust in God and in His Word) as well as "feeling" (the result of our faith and obedience). Salvation by faith alone is the biblical teaching.

No area of the Christian life is divorced from faith. Faith is the source of all graces that we receive. We are saved by faith. We live by faith. We pray by faith. We walk by faith. We appropriate the filling of the Holy Spirit by faith. By faith we overcome the world. All these blessings and virtues of the Christian life are rooted in faith. The more we trust, obey, and faithfully serve God, the more we grow in our faith.

MY LIFE AND MY FAITH

Three important events have contributed in a major way to my life and to my faith:

The first event, which I will never forget, was forced enlistment by the Japanese army (1944–45). Life in the Japanese army was like a hell to me. On the first day of the camp's training orientation, I was informed that I should not think of myself as a human being any longer. Shinto and emperor worship were compulsory as a daily practice. As a Christian, I felt compelled to refuse the officers' commands. Brutal torments and assault were the rewards for my refusal to participate in these practices.

The pressure to conform in the camp was so great that I put my life at risk to escape from the army. I ran away toward Russia through China. However, to avoid the Japanese border guards, I escaped through the snowy mountain areas and lost my direction. Yet Jehovah, my Provider, took me to a pastor who had escaped from the Japanese conscription and had been living in a mountain village.

I hid in the village for about a year. I spent the time reading the Bible and praying. I had one meal per day. Every day, I prayed that Japan would be utterly defeated. I also prayed with an oath to God that I would commit my whole life to the evangelization of my nation if God would save my life. The vision for the national evangelization of Korea was placed in my heart during that time.

The second event was the Korean War. In 1950, North Korea invaded South Korea. The North Koreans swept through the whole peninsula in just three months so that all the South Korean people except those in Pusan came under communist reign. My wife and I and our four-year-old daughter fled to a remote island of the southwestern Korean peninsula where my father was living.

Again, we fell into the hell of the devil. It was like the "killing fields" in Cambodia. Communist soldiers came to that island. After putting the village people on trial, the communists dragged our family to the mountain to be killed because my father had been outspoken against communism and my wife and I were Christians. The communists, who used bamboo spears and clubs for weapons, killed my father and my wife. I was beaten and left for dead, yet by God's grace I survived. As I became conscious, I heard my daughter crying; together we crawled off into the hills to hide.

Later, something strange happened in my heart. I began to have a desire to forgive and love all the enemies who had tormented and killed my family. I even saw a vision of Jesus Christ shedding His blood on the cross for these people.

I visited the head of the communist groups of my village and shared the gospel of Jesus with him. He received Jesus as his Savior. I was set free from the fear of death and the chain of hatred. About thirty communists expressed a desire to become Christians. That was my starting point of personal evangelism.

There had been only one prayer site on the island, but now there are thirty-six churches. The once communist island is now a Christian island.

Through those moments of life and death, suffering and affliction, I learned to pray for my nation as John Knox had done for Scotland, and to envision the restoration and salvation of my nation and people like the reunion of Judah and Israel portrayed in Ezekiel 37:15–23. God has faithfully answered all my prayers.

The third event that dramatically impacted my life was meeting Dr. Bill Bright. In 1957, Fuller Theological Seminary gave me a full scholarship to study in the U.S. My fellowship with Dr. Bright began there. He and those he was discipling seemed the special kind of men who were portrayed in the Book of Acts. Their Christian lifestyle was a vivid lesson to me. I learned firsthand and experienced for myself the life of being filled with the Holy Spirit by faith.

Dr. Bright asked me to begin the Campus Crusade for Christ (CCC) ministry in Korea as the first overseas ministry of CCC International. I initiated the ministry of Korea Campus Crusade for Christ on my return to Korea in October 1958. I coined a phrase, "Win the Korea campus today, win the Korean nation and the world tomorrow." I just took Dr. Bright's vision, "Come Help Change the World," and transferred it to Korea.

Arnold Toynbee once said, "The ship that apostle Paul was aboard was the ship that carried the torch of the gospel to all of Europe." In the same way, it is difficult to measure how much Korea's Campus Crusade for Christ, which has been carrying the seed of Campus Crusade for Christ initiated by Dr. Bright, has influenced the spiritual destiny of the Korean people and the nation.

Dr. Bright is such a man of humility. I am unworthy to untie his shoelaces. If my Lord Jesus gives me a small crown of life when I meet Him, I will humbly offer it at the feet of my Lord and I will credit it to Dr. Bright.

FOUR SPIRITUAL LAWS BOOKLET

The crystallized form of the "by faith" concept taught in *The Four Spiritual Laws* booklet was a great discovery for the Korean church. It might be compared to the truth discovered by the apostle Paul in Romans 1:17, the truth that "the just shall live by faith," which was later discovered by Martin Luther. This had been an unrecognized concept in the Korean church. To become a Christian, they felt that the new believer needed to be edified or enlightened. At that time, the new believer had to go through two years of preparation to be baptized in the Korean church: one year as a student of Christian doctrines and another year of preparation for baptism. But *The Four Spiritual Laws* booklet taught such a simple concept of salvation "by faith" that it brought a revolution in the Korean church.

The training of Korean Christians by Korea Campus Crusade for Christ began in rural areas during the 1960s, usually as a packaged training program in sessions lasting from ten hours to a conference of four nights and five days. Due to that training, some churches experienced a growth of up to ten times as many people.

We selected 300 churches throughout the nation and trained them as model churches. All these churches were aflame like the Church after Pentecost. The Leadership Training Institute, four days and four nights in length, grew in attendance to 1,000 attendees, to 8,000, and then to 10,000 as time went by.

In the midst of such expansion of Christianity in Korea, I happened to participate in Explo '72 in the United States. There I was strongly inspired by the Holy Spirit to train two-thirds of all the Korean Christians at one site, Yoido Plaza in Seoul.

When I returned from the States, I immediately started making plans to host Explo '74 in Korea. The logistics for such a conference were an absolute impossibility for Korea Campus Crusade for Christ to accomplish. Our Korean staff listed 74 barriers or reasons why such a conference could not be done. They included such things as:

- How do we get 300,000 people from all over Korea to come to such a conference for a week of training?
- How do we house all these people for a week?
- How do we feed all these people for a week?
- How do we register them and get them to the appropriate training locations?
- How do we train them in smaller groups of forty or so?
- How do we prepare all the teachers needed?
- How do we prepare all the printed materials needed for the training?
- How do we get all the people to and from Yoido Island for the mass rally once a day?
- How do we provide simultaneous translation for the 3,000 foreign delegates?
- How do we pay for all this when most Koreans who come will not have the money to pay?
- How do we back all of this in prayer?

We realized that it was an impossible task for us, but we believed that God wanted us to hold the conference. So we simply moved ahead in faith and saw God remove the barriers one by one. The staff who had problems trusting God to remove the barriers were willing to move ahead based on my faith.

We knew that God wanted us to do this because of what it would mean in fulfilling Christ's Great Commission (Matthew 20:18–20) in Korea. We also believed that God wanted to use what happened in Korea as an example of what could happen in nations all over the world. We felt that God would raise up many Koreans to go to the other nations as missionaries.

The result was beyond our wildest imagination! Barriers toppled one by one. On August 13–18, over 323,000 believers participated in Explo '74.

One of the massive logistical challenges that organizers faced was feeding people. It was a job that kept a staff of 380 men and women working from 5 a.m. until late in the evening. Beginning early in the morning, rice was washed, placed in stainless steel pans, and inserted into steamers. Each steamer held 64 pans of rice, enough to serve meals for 5,000 to 7,000 people. (The steamers had to cook two loads of rice to provide enough for one meal for the delegates.) After the rice was steamed, it was scooped into plastic buckets, placed on one of eighty trucks, and delivered to the different sites where the delegates were staying.

In addition to rice, the delegates were given *duk kwang*, a yellow radish-type vegetable, and *saewoo*, a type of fish. The delegates themselves provided additional side dishes as well as their own bowls and eating utensils. They ate rice for breakfast and dinner and bread for lunch. A total of 600 tons of rice, 150 tons of *duk kwang* and *saewoo*, and 3.6 million pieces of bread was served to the delegates during Explo '74.

A strong emphasis on prayer undergirded Explo '74. For a year prior to August 1974, Christians all over the republic prayed for the conference. At least thirty fasted and prayed for forty days and nights. On August 13, a spontaneous, unscheduled prayer meeting brought together nearly 300,000, many of whom stayed all night to pray. Each night during the conference, thousands prayed until daybreak for an explosion of the Holy Spirit's power, the evangelization of Korea, a peaceful reunion of our country, and a worldwide spiritual awakening.

Those were just two of the barriers that we saw toppled as we were preparing for Explo '74.

In the advance publicity, we stressed that the real purpose of the conference was to provide intensive discipleship training for Christians. In other words, we proposed to teach delegates how they could, as a way of life, appropriate the ministry of the Holy Spirit by faith, and we wanted to teach them how to share the claims of Christ more effectively. We selected these two main emphases as the most powerful concepts to accelerate the fulfillment of the Great Commission in Korea and around the world.

For hundreds of years, many vital truths—such as electricity and atomic energy—were hidden to the mind of man. The same was true in the spiritual realm. Until the Reformation led by Martin Luther, salvation by faith was a truth that for many years was hidden from the average layman.

Likewise, I believe that the clear understanding of the ministry of the

Holy Spirit, *whose presence and power we appropriate by faith*, has been a hidden truth for most Christians. At Explo '74, this great truth was presented clearly to several hundred thousand Christians, most of whom responded to the challenge to allow the Holy Spirit to control and empower their lives by faith, thus setting the stage for a powerful spiritual awakening.

A number of firsts in Christian history were set during Explo week, including the largest number of decisions for Christ at one time (an estimated 70 percent of the first-night audience of 1.3 million people indicated that they had received assurance of salvation by faith). This was a result of the message, which explained how they could receive Christ and be assured that He was in their lives. Afterwards, pastors Kyung Chik Han and Cho Choon Park of the famous Young Nak Presbyterian Church in Seoul explained this unusually large response. "Many of them were receiving Christ for the first time," said Rev. Park, "while many others, although they had received Christ before, were, *for the first time*, based on the authority of God's Word, by faith completely assured of their salvation."

On average, more than one million people gathered to hear the gospel message every night. Dr. Bright and I were the main speakers at Explo '74, and both of us spoke only about Jesus Christ. Every major newspaper of Korea expressed wonder that so many people were gathered at one place.

Dr. Bright's faith and vision for Explo '72 in Dallas, Texas, was the spark that ignited my faith and vision for Explo '74 in Seoul, Korea. Dr. Bright wrote concerning Explo '74: "As I review the almost unbelievable events of Explo '74, my mind is staggered with the magnitude of it all. I felt as if I were on holy ground all week. Every meeting was a demonstration of the power of God."

After Explo '74 was over, I did a survey to determine the influence of the event on the growth of Korean churches. In 1974, Korea Campus Crusade selected at random 1,000 churches and collected their weekly bulletins, which recorded their attendance and amount of offerings. One year later, July 1975, we did the same survey and compared the statistics. The attendance had increased by 33 percent (about 1.1 million people) and the offerings by 64 percent. During the 1970s, Korean churches continued to experience a great revival and growth—growing by 400 percent over the next 10 years.

Another historical gathering of spiritual revival for Korean churches was "Here's Life, Korea," held in August 1980. The number of people attending this gathering was nearly double that of Explo '74. The statistics determined by the newspapers and the police count indicated that about 2 to 2.7 million people gathered. It was the largest gathering recorded in Korean history, including both political and other religious gatherings. It became a legend among Korean Christians and resulted in increasing the spiritual explosion of Christianity in Korea.

KOREA CAMPUS CRUSADE FOR CHRIST

The prayers and ministries of Korea Campus Crusade for Christ are aimed at the evangelizing of our nation and the reunification of South and North. We continue to pray that the day will come when all the resources of Korean churches—prayers, finances, and manpower—will be used for world missions.

For this purpose, we organized The Volunteer College Students Service Corp for Reunification with 100,000 college students and dedicated them to our Lord Jesus in 1995. Every year since 1990 during the summer and winter vacations, Korea Campus Crusade for Christ has sent short-term mission teams, an average of 3,000 members, to more than 28 countries.

For the 42 years of the Korea Campus Crusade ministry, approximately 300,000 students have been introduced to the Lord and trained, and are now serving the Lord in various segments of Korean society. We estimate that about 3 million lay Christians have gone through our Leadership Training Class (held on a campus or in a church) and Leadership Training Institute (usually held in a retreat setting).

Korea Campus Crusade is planning to send our college students for at least one year to 8,000 colleges and universities around the world for the purpose of spreading the gospel. And when North Korea is opened, we will send about 100,000 college students as the seeds of mission into North Korea.

Last summer as a part of aid to North Korea, Korea Campus Crusade sent 10,700 milking goats (300,000 Won per goat), supplying at least one milking goat to every North Korean farming family. We believe this small activity will serve as a spark to kindle the Korean churches to cooperate together in aid to North Korea.

DR. BRIGHT'S VISION AND FAITH

If my Lord Jesus were to ask me to choose only one whom I honor and love most in this world besides Him, I'd select Dr. Bill Bright without any hesitation. In all the letters and books that he has sent to me, he always writes Acts 1:8 and 1 Corinthians 13. He also never fails to write, "Come help change the world." He still signs every letter, "Yours for fulfilling the Great

Commission in this generation." He often prays, "Make me not commit any sin and always be honest. I would rather that God would take my life than I commit any sin." I've often heard him weeping with compassion for lost souls when we pray together. When someone speaks ill of him, he says, "Just love him."

Bill Bright is always humble and simple, whether he is in personal conversation or speaking in front of a gathering of millions. He often saves money when he is fasting and sometimes gives me $50 or $100 and asks me to give it to the poor around me. He has on quite a few occasions observed a forty-day fast for the revival and evangelization of America and the world. I have often heard him cry for his nation and the world like Jeremiah wept for his people. It is widely known that he and his wife, Vonette, made a contract with the Lord, a commitment to surrender all their life and possessions to Him.

Dr. Bright is a man of God, a holy man, a man of the Word, a soul winner, a praying man, a visionary, a Spirit-filled man, a great man of faith, a faithful servant. He wants to be a slave of the Lord. He presents Jesus wherever he is, whether he is in a hotel or on a plane. The emphasis on being filled with the Holy Spirit by faith is his trademark.

The exposure of 4.5 billion people to the gospel through the ministry of Campus Crusade's 17,000 full-time staff, 200,000 volunteers, and the JESUS Film Project would not be a reality without his vision and faith. Certainly, God has honored his faith, vision, and prayer. Under Dr. Bright's leadership, more people have been introduced to the Lord than through any person throughout 2,000 years of church history. Literally, "the gospel for every person" will be realized in his lifetime by means of the Internet evangelism plan that is now underway.

He is a man of four absolutes: absolute faith, absolute commitment, absolute training, and absolute action.

CHAPTER 3

The Basics of the Christian Life

THOMAS ABRAHAM
On Staff since 1967
Vice President for Asia, Oceania, and Latin America

Throughout the fifty years of the Campus Crusade for Christ ministry, Bill and Vonette Bright and the rest of the staff have consistently preached, professed, and practiced certain basic principles of the Christian life without any substantial change. I personally attribute the ministry's unwavering commitment to these principles to Dr. Bright, our founder and president. He not only preached them to others, but also practiced them without apology. Bill and Vonette taught all those associated with the Campus Crusade ministry around the globe that the simplicity and transferability of our message are critical to producing change in people's lives.

Bill has always modeled the basic principles of Christian living and has sought to show us how to practice them. He has constantly talked about such things as maintaining our first love for the Lord, exercising our faith, walking in the power of the Holy Spirit, and being faithful in prayer and praise to God.

At least seven basic principles of the Christian life that Bill has taught repeatedly have made a deep impact on my personal life and ministry. Let me list these principles and illustrate how they have made a difference in my own life as well as in the lives of others around the world.

PRINCIPLE ONE: ALLOW CHRIST TO BE THE LORD OF YOUR LIFE

This basic principle of allowing Christ to be the Lord of your life has revolutionized my own life. As a former follower of Karl Marx and communist ideologies, I had to surrender my life totally to make Christ the Lord of all. Colossians 1:27 speaks of "Christ in you, the hope of glory." Colossians 2:9,10 says, "In Christ all the fullness of the Deity lives in bodily form, and you have been given fullness in Christ, who is the head over every power and authority." I knew I had to totally surrender all that I had previously stood for and crusaded for to turn completely to my new Lord.

As I allowed Him to be the Lord of my life, I began to realize more fully who He really is. This Jesus is the King of kings, Lord of lords, the First and the Last, the Creator of the universe, the Lily of the Valley, the Bright and Morning Star. He is the One who feeds the hungry, clothes the naked, heals the sick, and raises the dead. He is certainly worthy to be first in my life.

We can express it this way: He is the only way to heaven, the freeway to freedom, the highway to holiness, the broadway to beauty, the sideway to sanctification. He is also the Bread of heaven, the Light of the world, the Door of the sheep, the Good Shepherd, the resurrection, and the life. Christ is the way, the truth, and the life, and He is the vine for us as branches. How aptly our need for Him is described in John 15:5: "I am the vine, you are the branches. He who abides in Me and I in him, bears much fruit; for without Me you can do nothing" (NKJ).

Realizing this basic principle helped me journey toward living the life Paul described in Galatians 2:20: "I have been crucified with Christ, it is no longer I who live, but Christ lives in me" (NKJ). Bill and Vonette have demonstrated this crucified life, always thinking of themselves as the slaves of Jesus. Just as dead men have no rights, they never demand any rights for themselves. They continually place Christ first in their lives and ministry.

The best example of making Christ the Lord of our lives and keeping Him as the President of our lives is seen in the way many Christian wedding ceremonies were conducted in Nepal in the late 1970s. In 1976, there were fewer than 500 Christians in the whole country. After that time, the number of Christians began growing rapidly. They had no idea how Christian marriage ceremonies should be conducted. They were familiar with *The Four Spiritual Laws* booklet because many of them received Christ through someone sharing it with them. So they decided to use those principles in the ceremony. After the first prayer, the one who conducted the ceremony read through *The Four Spiritual Laws* booklet. When he came to the fourth law, he asked both the prospective husband and wife where Christ was in relationship to their lives. If both agreed that Christ was in the center of their lives, they were admonished to keep Him there continually. If both had Christ in the center of their lives and were willing to live together under the presidency of Jesus Christ, they were pronounced husband and wife. Christians were seeing the great importance of allowing Christ to be Lord of their lives, not only individually, but also as marriage partners.

Nepal, a Hindu kingdom, now has more than 3.5 million Christians. I attribute the great growth of Christianity there to believers making Christ the center of their lives, allowing Him to be the Author and Finisher of their faith.

PRINCIPLE TWO: DEVOTE YOURSELF TO BIBLE STUDY AND PRAYER

From the inception of Campus Crusade, great importance was given to the study of God's Word and prayer. This became our firm foundation as we expanded the ministry. Everyone everywhere was admonished to study the Word, listen to God for His instruction, and pray. Throughout the Bible, we see God encouraging man to listen to His Words and to talk to Him through prayer. Both of these are non-negotiable, basic principles for a victorious walk with Christ.

The foundation for studying the Word of God is found in 2 Timothy 3:16,17: "All Scripture is inspired by God and profitable for teaching, for reproof, for correction, for training in righteousness; so that the man of God may be adequate, equipped for every good work" (NASB). Studying His Word keeps the line of communication open for God to speak to man. In places like India where religious rituals take precedence over a relationship with Christ, the emphasis on the study of the Word became the bread and butter in our lives.

As we sought to understand how to develop a heart of prayer, we used this acrostic:

P—Personal Preparation
R—Recognize the sovereignty of God
A—Acknowledge our shortcomings
Y—Yield to the will and the way of God
E—Expect results whatever they may be
R—Rejoice in the Lord whatever the result is

When we trust God in prayer, He promises wonderful results. Matthew 7:7,8 says, "Ask, and it will be given to you; seek, and you will find; knock, and it will be opened to you. For everyone who asks receives, and he who seeks finds, and to him who knocks it will be opened" (NASB). We can cite many illustrations from our ministry of how God answered prayer.

One example occurred in India. When my wife, Molly, and I were starting the Campus Crusade ministry in India, church denominations and their leaders were not very happy about it. Some of them openly criticized us and tried to discourage those who were willing to join our movement. These denominational leaders tried to close doors for our ministry. As we and our friends prayed, God changed the environment and brought about better communication. He opened doors beyond our imagination.

One amazing development took place. A prominent bishop of a major denomination joined India Campus Crusade for Christ as a full-time staff member. He was used by the Lord significantly in the overall development of our ministry and in the building of bridges with various denominations. Today, more than 500 major partners, including various denominations and Christian organizations, are in vital partnership with us. This doesn't mean we are without problems or opposition, but we have learned that if we pray and trust God in difficult situations, He makes a way of escape.

God receives glory when we pray and trust Him at all times. God's glory is the overwhelming drive behind the emphasis on prayer. The number of people who make decisions for Christ, all the funds that Christians give, and the millions of Christians trained for evangelism are worth nothing unless God's greatness and power are clearly reflected by staff members who depend on the Lord to live and work through them.

We have felt the power of prayer so many times in our ministry. One example was when Jameson and Usha, a staff couple in India, and the participating churches and students organized 96 hours of continuous prayer for a conference. Five people prayed every hour for the duration of the conference. The gathering was held outdoors under a tent so when it began to rain, the prayer warriors prayed specifically about that obstacle. The downpour ended and the local Muslims who were watching commented, "How could you pray and stop the rain?" God received glory when His people prayed.

What better way to demonstrate dependence on God than through specific prayer? Because we know how important prayer is to the heart of God, we increasingly emphasize prayer throughout our ministry.

PRINCIPLE THREE: LEAD A SPIRIT-FILLED LIFE

After I came to know the Lord, I was encouraged by many leading Christians to experience the filling of the Holy Spirit. As a result, I was looking for an ecstatic experience and even spent a number of days praying and fasting for that. Nothing seemed to happen.

When I learned about the "Spirit-filled life," it was a liberating moment for me. That liberating knowledge—that the Spirit-filled life is one in which Christ lives His life in me in the power of the Holy Spirit and I am just a vessel for His walk, talk, compassion, etc. to be seen—took me to greater heights in my walk with Christ. I realized that the Spirit-filled life means a Christ-controlled life, letting Christ be in the center of my life as my President. The result of being filled with the Holy Spirit is obedience and sensitivity to the presence of the Lord in our lives. It was a great day when I discovered that I could be filled by the Holy Spirit, not through trying, but by trusting in God's promises.

Being filled with the Spirit and walking in the Spirit are two inseparable principles Bill and Vonette have taught. Galatians 5:25 reads, "If we live by the Spirit, let us also walk by the Spirit" (NASB). *The Living Bible* says, "If we are living now by the Holy Spirit's power, let us follow the Holy Spirit's leading in every part of our lives." Millions of people have had their walk with the Lord revolutionized after applying these principles in their lives.

Bill and Vonette also continually demonstrate the principle of leading a Spirit-filled life. At all times, the fruit of the Spirit, as mentioned in Galatians 5:22,23, is evident in their lives. Their heart's desire is to do the will of God in spite of what others may say or think. Matthew 5:6 declares, "Blessed are those who hunger and thirst for righteousness, for they will be filled." I can confidently say that this is true of their lives.

As I teach and share with others how to live a Spirit-filled life, many lives are transformed. Many think this life is a complicated phenomenon and needs a lot of time to accomplish. But once they understand that the Triune God—the Father, Son, and Holy Spirit—comes to live in them the moment they receive Christ by faith, and that all they need to do is allow the Holy Spirit to continually be the President of their life, they are set free.

The "spiritual breathing" principle that Dr. Bright uses in relationship to the Spirit-filled life is easy for people to understand. He compares physical breathing with spiritual breathing. As breath is to physical life, so the Spirit is to a healthy spiritual life.

Physical breathing is a process of breathing out the bad air and breathing in the clear air. In the same way, when Christians sin they need to "breath out" their sin by agreeing with God concerning their sin and confessing it to Him, according to 1 John 1:9. Their sin is then forgiven and blotted out. When we sin, we take control of our lives, so we need to surrender our lives back to His control. This second part of the spiritual breathing process can be compared to "breathing in the good air," acknowledging God's forgiveness of sin. Just as in physical breathing, spiritual breathing needs to be a continual, moment-by-moment process.

Many people around the world have expressed how this simple process of spiritual breathing has transformed their lives. One prominent church leader in India expressed his experience this way after he prayed to be filled with the Holy Spirit: "I was always asking the Lord and pleading with Him all these years to fill me with His Spirit, but now I realize the Spirit-filled life is mine and I need only to claim it by faith." Again, this wonderful life can be experienced, not by trying in our own strength, but by trusting in the promise that God has already given.

PRINCIPLE FOUR: LIVE BY FAITH

My experience in working with Bill over the last 33 years has proven, without a doubt, that he lives by faith in the faithfulness of God. Regardless of circumstances, he believes that by faith we can overcome any obstacle. We read in the Book of Nehemiah that Nehemiah trusted God when he faced the overwhelming problem of the walls of the holy city being broken and the gates being burned to ashes. It was an absolutely pathetic situation. But Nehemiah believed God for the impossible to become possible. Bill follows the same process of living by faith in the God of the impossible.

I find that I often try to solve problems through my own efforts. When this proves unsuccessful, then I trust God to bring about a solution. Bill operates in the opposite way. He turns to God for direction first and places his trust and faith in the power of God.

I have heard Bill cite Psalm 23 many times. Because of this, I have looked very closely at this psalm. What a wonderful picture of the Great Shepherd's promise to provide, protect, and prepare us for the future. If we follow our Shepherd in faith, we shall not want for righteousness, relief, food, recognition, joy, or resources. My times are in His hands, and whatever happens, I can put my faith and trust in Him. Bill demonstrates with his life, words, and actions that victory is not always easy, but by faith, victory is sure and certain.

Bill practices uncompromising, unwavering, and unprecedented faith. The underlying principle he holds on to is highlighted in Hebrews 11:1: "Faith is the assurance of things hoped for, the conviction of things not seen" (NASB). Over all these years, Bill has been obedient to the call of a life of faith. That call of God in Bill's life can be compared to the call of God in Abraham's life. Without knowing what was ahead, Bill was willing to step out from his business and surrender all that he owned to God. He and Vonette signed a contract with God. As Abraham did, so Bill decided to follow God with no thought of turning back. He had great confidence in God, knowing that God alone is sufficient and that He had promised to provide everything he and Vonette would need for the rest of their lives.

Bill believes and puts his faith in God first, above everything and everyone else. All that we see now in the Campus Crusade ministry is the by-product of his faith. He takes the promise of God at face value and demonstrates his faith in these promises without seeing tangible evidence of the outcome. His demonstration of faith has deeply influenced the lives of staff around the world, as well as the Christian community at large. I can personally testify that my life is continually transformed as I witness Bill exercising his faith in our great and mighty God.

I still recall the courage and faith it took for Molly and me to say yes to Bill when he asked us to return to India from the States to start the Campus Crusade ministry there. His challenge was to help reach India for Christ in his generation. We thought that meant 40 years, as we count a generation. But on arriving in India in August 1968, Bill wrote a letter challenging us to reach India by 1980. I thought, *That's just 11 years!* I cried out to God, "That's impossible. What can we do as only one couple?" Then all of a sudden, being reminded of how Bill and Vonette exercised their faith, we too put our faith to the test.

We prayed and developed a target of 5,000 people to pray to invite Christ into their lives through our personal ministry in 1969. We never stopped to realize that 5,000 is a lot of souls to help usher into the kingdom! We can only say, "To God be the glory" because by the end of 1969 we had seen 5,067 people make decisions for the Lord. How true it is, "'Not by might nor by power, but by My Spirit,' says the Lord" (Zechariah 4:6, NASB).

From that experience, our faith grew tremendously. Now I don't have a problem believing God for the supernatural explosion of the gospel throughout the world. Recently, while reading statistics on the number of presentations of the gospel in India, I was not surprised at the number. We have only a billion people in India, but presentations have been made to an aggregate number of 1.2 billion since the beginning of the ministry. This doesn't mean that each person has heard the gospel (some have heard it more than once), but we praise God for all that He has done in that land.

The Christian life is a life of faith. Bill and Vonette have championed that principle throughout their lives, and we praise God for their wonderful example.

PRINCIPLE FIVE: LOVE BY FAITH

Love is both an old and a new commandment. In the Old Testament, God says to love Him with all your heart, with all your soul, and with your entire mind. Jesus acknowledges that first great commandment and gives a second one: "You shall love your neighbor as yourself" (Matthew 22:39, NASB). Earlier, he had said, "Love your enemies and pray for those who persecute you" (Matthew 5:44, NASB).

God not only commanded us to love one another, but He demonstrated true love to the world by giving His only Son to die on the cross so He could reconcile the world to Himself. While we were enemies, Christ died for us. God's love for us is completely unconditional.

First Corinthians 13 is not only the greatest description of God's love, but also the kind of love He wants us to have for others. I memorized the thirteen verses of that chapter, but still I had people in my life I was not able to love in that way. One day, I was listening to Bill explain the concept of loving by faith. "The Word of the Lord is very clear: 'If you love Me, you will keep My commandments'" (John 14:15, NASB). It suddenly dawned on me that I couldn't keep from loving any person because it is a command from Him. Since there were people for whom I felt no love, I realized I was not keeping God's commandment and thus not loving Him. Coming to grips with the principle of loving others by faith truly revolutionized my life and helped me practice it in my daily life.

I still clearly remember one of the leaders of a Christian organization accusing me of being an agent of the USA and seeking to destroy God's work in India. Although I felt hurt, I politely apologized to him for the misunderstanding I caused in his life and thanked him for being candid with me. Even so, he still was mad and stormed out of my room. Although I tried to stop him to pray with him, he refused. Because of the "love by faith" principle I learned from Bill, I was able to pray for that individual and thank the Lord for the situation. In less than a year, the same person came to my home and apologized for his behavior. God reconciled us through His love, and we have worked closely together for the last 25 years. What a revolutionary concept!

Once I was giving a talk on the "love by faith" principle. As I concluded my talk, I encouraged my listeners to write down the people they didn't love and ask the Lord to give them faith to love them. After that meeting, many came to me one by one and thanked me for explaining that principle. As they accepted the need to "love one another" as a command and claimed God's promise from 1 John 5:14,15, many experienced peace in their lives.

The next morning, one man returned rejoicing and said, "I was angry with my neighbor who at one time was my close friend. We have not been on speaking terms for seven years. Last night, I called him to ask his forgiveness and told him that I would like to be his friend. The man was shocked and put the phone down. After a few minutes, he came to my home and hugged me and apologized for being cruel. We became friends in a few moments as I practiced the 'love by faith' principle."

Bill and Vonette have modeled this great truth in many challenging situations. Recently, a theologian criticized him publicly on his stand with another Christian group. Later, the same person asked Bill to write a foreword for his new book. Bill might naturally have had a feeling of anger toward that man. Instead, Bill said, "I don't have anything against him. If he has something against me, that is his problem. I am just a slave and a slave has no personal rights. I am commanded to love, and I have no choice except to obey." Loving by faith is a practicable principle for experiencing a victorious Christian life.

PRINCIPLE SIX: LIVE A HOLY LIFE

Another principle that Bill and Vonette have demonstrated in their lives is the need to live a holy and pure life before God. Bill continually reminds the staff of the need to choose to live their lives in a way that will bring honor and glory to God. We can appear loving and gracious on the outside, but if our inner thoughts are not aligned with the Word of God, we will not be pleasing to God.

One way that Bill lives a holy life before God is by filling his life with praise. He gets out of bed each morning and drops to his knees in praise and adoration of his God. Before he goes to bed each night, he again gets on his knees and worships God for who He is and the ways He has worked in Bill's life that day.

Throughout each day, he meditates on God's Word so that his inner thoughts as well as outward actions follow biblical principles. He lets Scripture govern his walk and talk, thus keeping him on God's path. With all that Bill experiences day by day—the overwhelming responsibilities of leading this worldwide ministry, the call for decisions from every corner of the world, the conflicts that need to be resolved—he could be tempted to think a variety of thoughts about different people and situations. However, because he begins his day with God in his inner spirit and aligns himself with God's Word throughout the day, his thought-life is transformed and his mind is renewed.

Romans 12:1,2 helps us understand God's directive to us. In verse 1, He urges us to "present your bodies a living and holy sacrifice . . . which is your spiritual service of worship" (NASB). He wants my life to be alive and vital, but also holy and pure. Then He gives the "how to" of doing this in verse 2: "Do not be conformed to this world, but be transformed by the renewing of your mind" (NASB). The decision to lead a holy life or to ignore God's directives begins with the mind. If we are willing to let God transform our mind rather than allowing the world to dictate choices in our life, we will experience the power to be different from the world. We will experience the power to be increasingly aligned with the image of God and to lead a life that is holy and acceptable to Him.

Bill continually demonstrates the vital importance of keeping our minds filled with how awesome God is. Writing the book *God: Discover His Character* fulfilled a desire of Bill's heart to help Christians around the world realize the awesome character of God. Sometimes when we make impure or unholy choices, we subtly think we can cover up the results. But when we stand in awe of who God really is—especially compared to our humanness—we cannot but humble ourselves before Him and submit to His authority. As we worship and praise Him continually throughout our day as our Commander, our Lord, and our King, and as we let His Word fill our minds and hearts, we experience the power to lead holy lives that will bring honor and glory to our God.

Following Bill and Vonette's example, Molly and I practiced beginning the day praying together and ending the day with thanksgiving and praises to our great God. Because of our decision to follow their pattern, Molly and I never could go to God in prayer if we were not first reconciled with one another or with God. The thrill of my life is that I have no regrets as I look back on our last night together. At 10 p.m. that evening, we prayed together, thanking the Lord for everything and asking for His grace to live holy lives despite all the hardships we were experiencing with Molly's terminal cancer. I was able to rejoice in how Molly was promoted to glory. God in His mercy took her home fifty minutes after our prayer time together. Holy living brings peace and joy!

PRINCIPLE SEVEN: WITNESS IN THE SPIRIT AS A WAY OF LIFE

The Great Commission has always played an important role in Campus Crusade. At the beginning of the ministry, Bill began signing his letters, "Yours for the fulfillment of the Great Commission in this generation." This declaration sparked a fire in the hearts of Christians around the world. If anyone asks about the overall goals of Campus Crusade, without reservation the answer will be to give everyone a chance to hear about Jesus.

More than just talking about it, Bill has demonstrated this commitment throughout his life. It doesn't matter whether he is in a taxi, in the supermarket, or walking down the street, he always tries to pass the message of the gospel to everyone, everywhere. Without reservation, we can say that Bill has helped bring the Great Commission into focus and helped champion the cause of fulfilling it in the world.

Bill gave a fresh outlook to the message of Matthew 28:18–20 and 2 Timothy 2:2 because he is passionately involved in helping to reach the world with the claims of Christ. "Win, build, and send" has been our motto over the years, and both personal and mass evangelism has been our foundation.

In relationship to the Great Commission, we explain two concepts: addition and multiplication. From the inception of this ministry, we have been admonished to practice spiritual multiplication rather than addition. Addition is simply reaching one person at a time and adding them to your discipleship group. However, multiplication has a very different meaning.

The best illustration I have found of multiplication is the atomic bomb. Fast-moving neutrons are used to cause friction to occur within the bomb. As the neutron strikes the nucleus of a radioactive substance such as uranium, it causes it to split, forming two new, different nuclei. In so doing, it releases three more neutrons, each of which may strike a new nucleus and repeat the process. As each nucleus splits, energy is released. A chain reaction occurs, and the energy released takes the form of an explosion.

In the process of spiritual addition, person A reaches B, C, D, and so on. In the process of multiplication, however, A reaches B; B reaches C; C reaches D; and D reaches E. During this time, A, B, C, D, and E all continue to reach others, and the process expands.

Bill uses the concept of "witnessing in the Spirit" to clarify the simplicity of reaching others. This principle has impacted millions around the world, encouraging them to simply share the message of Christ and trust God for the results. Especially in our evangelism training seminars, we emphasize, "Success in witnessing is simply taking the initiative to share Christ in the power of the Holy Spirit and leaving the results to God." Acts 1:8 explains that ordinary Christians around the world who are filled with the power of the Spirit can become successful witnesses for God.

I still remember that in my early days of ministry, many people had a hard time witnessing due to fear and lack of self-confidence. But when they learned that Christ gave the command for us to follow Him and He promised to make us "fishers of men," they were liberated to witness in the Spirit. They began to trust Christ to bring about the results rather than trying to bring others to Him through their own efforts.

One day I led a high school boy to the Lord and gave him *The Four Spiritual Laws* after he prayed to receive Christ. I challenged him to share this message with others and trust the Holy Spirit to reach others for Christ through Him. Within six weeks, he used that booklet to share the message of the gospel to all 38 of his classmates, plus his teacher. After hearing that message, 25 students and the teacher prayed to invite Christ into their lives.

In conclusion, one of the guiding philosophies of Bill is to "stick with the basics." He always sought to develop methods and materials based on simple and transferable principles. Even though he is the author of *The Four Spiritual Laws* and has shared it with thousands around the world, he still goes through the booklet page by page when he has a chance to share it with someone. Bill is one of greatest Christian statesman of the century. He could very well develop hundreds of other great principles, but he has voluntarily chosen to emphasize a few basic principles. He encourages everyone not only to study them, but also to put them into practice in their own lives and then share them with others.

Bill is like a basketball coach who wants to make sure that all the members of his team master the fundamentals of the game: passing, dribbling, guarding, rebounding, and shooting. Someone can play the game well only after he has mastered the fundamentals. Bill tries to teach others by modeling these fundamental principles of the Christian life and ministry.

This emphasis on the fundamentals has helped make and keep Campus Crusade effective over the years. As a movement, we continue to uphold these principles and seek to present them in a simple and transferable way for the generations to come. These seven principles are ones that every believer needs to follow so that the Master will one day say, "Well done, good and faithful servant."

As a member of Campus Crusade for Christ, I can truly say that Bill and Vonette have preached, professed, practiced, and propagated these principles in a way that has helped to revolutionize the Christian world, particularly mine. I will always be thankful for the impact their personal example has had on my life.

Whoever you are and whatever your ministry, determine what the basics of the Christian life are, seek to master them in your own life, and share these with others when you minister. Train them to do the same. The seven principles of this chapter are a good place to begin. Master these basics in your personal life and ministry—and watch God use you!

CHAPTER 4

Intimacy with God

GORDON KLENCK

On Staff since 1952

Professor of Leadership Development and Church Planting, International School of Theology

What is the secret of the phenomenal worldwide ministry of Campus Crusade for Christ and the influence of Bill Bright? There are many contributing factors, but doubtless the central, foundational key is God and His sovereign plan to bring multitudes into a vital, personal relationship with Himself. However, on a human level, I am convinced another key is Bill Bright's personal intimacy with God—the infinite, loving God for whom this man has such an obvious personal passion. God has marvelously used Bill as he has walked with his Lord for more than fifty years.

For 48 years, it has been my great privilege to know Bill Bright personally. I was among the first six to join Campus Crusade staff in 1952. To me, Bill and Vonette were like a slightly older brother and sister. But they were far more than that. They were models and mentors, instilling in each of us first staff (and all subsequent staff) an incredible vision to give our lives fully to Jesus Christ and to fulfilling His Great Commission to "make disciples of all nations."

During those early years we saw and shared in their lives up close. Many of us have been in their home scores of times. And over the intervening years, Bill and Vonette have remained warm, personal, welcoming, and loving in their availability and personal relationship.

Among the thousands of brothers and sisters in Christ whom I have known in my seventy years of life and in ministry, none has exemplified greater personal intimacy and love of Jesus Christ than Bill Bright.

I admire many Christlike qualities in Bill's life. These include his incredible vision for fulfilling Jesus' Great Commission, his leadership giftedness, his ability to attract thousands of people at all levels of society to the

Crusade movement, and his allowing God to use him to build the amazing worldwide staff and ministry of Campus Crusade.

In our time, few people, if any, have influenced more people directly and personally, as well as indirectly through the multiple ministries of Campus Crusade and through his writings, than Bill Bright. According to George Gallup, Jr., "He has reached people in a depth and in numbers matched by few others in history."[1]

Over all the years I have known Bill, no one has more consistently manifested the fruit of the Spirit (nine qualities listed in Galatians 5:22,23). I attribute all the above to one thing—his daily, moment-by-moment intimacy with Jesus Christ. I believe this personal relationship with God is the foundation to everything else. Church historian John Hannah, who teaches at Westminster Seminary, says, "Most assuredly, Dr. Bill Bright will go down in history as one of the great Christian men who has ever lived."[2]

From my first days of being around Bill, his personal excitement, admiration, and love of Jesus Christ fascinated and drew me. At first I wondered if his attitude was just nice talk. I had known and observed a number of Christian leaders and noted the zeal of many and their commitment and dedication to Christ and ministry. But in a different way, I sensed in Bill Bright a deep personal fascination, admiration, and love for the Savior that I had not seen in others in quite the same way.

I am not attempting to glorify Bill Bright. He is as human as any of us and has weaknesses. But I know of no other person who over the years has so consistently manifested the quality of intimacy with God that Bill has.

Because I cannot get into his mind and heart, I cannot say unequivocally that he walks intimately with God *every moment*, but based on Jesus' criteria ("by their fruits you shall know them") and my long-time observation of Bill's life, I believe he does so as much as or more than others I have met. This is the central, remarkable feature I sense about him.

His vision, discipline, and passion for fulfilling the Great Commission all seem to come back to his personal relationship to his Savior, and being captivated by the love and reality of Jesus Christ in his life and the vision God has given him. Both his life and his words convey this.

In the mid-nineties, Bill spoke to a Campus Crusade All-Asian Staff Conference. An American staff member, Ken Kremer, was present. Ken was so impressed by what Bill said that he obtained a copy of his remarks. Read what Bill Bright said and see his heart.

> For fifty years, I have had the joy and privilege of knowing God, the mighty, all-powerful Creator of the universe and His visible Presence on earth, our Lord Jesus Christ. I have known the unspeakable wonder

> and adventure of walking and talking with Him. He is my dearest friend. He is my closest companion. He is the source of my strength (Isaiah 4). He is the source of my wisdom. He is my delight in living.
>
> I humble and bow myself before Him in reverence and awe, for He is a holy and righteous God—a God of justice and wrath. I embrace Him with delight and enthusiasm and smother Him with my love, for He is my loving, holy, heavenly Father. He is my Savior; He is my Lord; He is my master; He is my King. I long after Him with all my heart. I desire to please Him, to honor Him, to glorify Him more than I desire to live.
>
> I am a son of God. I am an heir of God. I am a joint heir with Christ; I have been crucified with Christ. I have been buried with Christ. I have been raised with Christ. I am seated with Christ in the heavenlies at the right hand of God the Father at the place of authority and power with Him. He has liberated me out of the dark and gloom of Satan's kingdom and brought me into the Kingdom of His dear Son, who bought my freedom with His blood and forgave all my sins. He has filled me with His Holy Spirit. He directs my steps daily. He fights the demonic powers of darkness for me. Daily, He meets my every need.
>
> Oh, dear brothers and sisters in Christ, to know our great Creator God and heavenly Father and His only begotten Son, our Savior, is to love Him. To love our Savior is to obey Him; to obey Him is to serve Him; to serve Him is to dedicate all that we are and have to Him.

Do you sense the heartbeat of this man for God? There is no greater relationship than intimacy with God, and no higher calling. May God make this increasingly true in each of our lives.

A major purpose in writing this chapter is to acknowledge my personal debt to Bill Bright for his modeling the reality and benefit of living life in intimate relationship with Jesus Christ. His example has had a profound impact on my own personal walk with our Savior.

A second motivation for this chapter is to explore and encourage each of us to deepen our intimacy with God and to suggest several guidelines on how to cultivate our own relationship with our wonderful Creator. How has Bill Bright cultivated this intimacy with God and how can each of us do the same? And what results will follow in our lives?

WHAT IS INTIMACY WITH GOD?

So that this chapter is not simply a description of Bill Bright but will also stimulate us to evaluate and develop our relationship to God, I suggest the following preliminary questions for each of us to ask ourselves:

- How close and intimate am I with God?
- How real is God in my life at this time?
- At this moment how aware am I of His presence, guidance, and care for me today and every day?
- Am I aware of His indwelling at this very moment?
- Am I responsive to His prompting and obedient to His will each moment?
- Do I set aside unhurried time to be alone with Him, listening for what He wants to communicate to me through His love letter to me (the Bible) and expressing my gratitude and love and worship of Him?

The greatest need of every human being is to know God personally. And for all who have opened their lives to Christ, the most important and central need is a growing awareness of and response to His indwelling presence. A deepening understanding of Him and our relationship to Him impacts all aspects of our lives.

Intimacy is a relationship in which another person is really "with" you in your mind and heart and knows your deepest feelings. It is being heard by that person and sensing that the other really cares about you and your concerns, enters into them, accepts you, and helps you experience those dreams. Intimacy is the togetherness of two persons. Intimacy with God is similarly an awareness and deepening experience of the love of the infinite, eternal Creator of the universe and an increasing response to Him.

In the Gospel of John, Jesus clearly and categorically makes claims about Himself and about the benefits of intimacy with Him. When we respond to Him, He promises to wonderfully meet the deepest hungers of our hearts and to enable us to live life "to the full." Jesus invites each of us into this kind of abundant living. How can we really know this for ourselves? Are these not the results of genuine, ever-deepening intimacy with our Savior—the kind of life and relationship He offers us? I long to continually experience this in an ongoing way. And I suspect you do also. Could it be that the reason many believers are not consistently experiencing these is our lack of a deep ongoing personal relationship with Jesus?

The kind of relationship that Christ offers every human being is twofold: first, that we will enter His presence forever when physical life as we know it on earth ends; and second, that in every day of our present lives on earth we can experience a deep personal relationship with Him. He says, "This is life eternal: that they might *know* you, the only true God, and Jesus Christ whom you have sent" (John 17:3). The unending life Jesus describes is knowing God experientially and existentially right now in our daily, earthly lives and forever.

The Greek word for "know" used in John 17:3 is *ginōskō*. It implies a "relationship between the person knowing and the object known [in this case the object is a person, God Almighty] . . . Nor is such knowledge marked by finality but suggests . . . progress in [that] knowledge."[3] Knowing God requires an ever-deepening experiential love relationship with Him, the One who lives within us. Ephesians 3:17–19 makes clear that as we increasingly, experientially "know the love of Christ," we will "be filled with all the fullness of God."

How full are you and I with the fullness of God? The answer to this question doubtless manifests the degree of our intimacy with Jesus and the Father.

The New Testament word for intimacy is *koinōnia*. The Scriptures speak of fellowship with the Father, with the Son, and with the Holy Spirit (1 John 1:3; 1 Corinthians 1:9; 2 Corinthians 13:14). It is a new relationship with God based on forgiveness of sins and on the work of His Holy Spirit living in us.[4]

Intimacy with our infinite, eternal, omnipresent Father God was the central reality of Jesus' life. It was also the reality that the disciples experienced following the resurrection and coming of the Holy Spirit. Certainly, many of the most effective saints down through church history testify to this. The apostle Paul verbalized it this way: "For me to live is Christ" (Philippians 1:21). Can we honestly say that about our relationship with God? This has been the passion of Bill Bright's life. And this can be increasingly the focus of each of our lives.

HOW TO DEEPEN INTIMACY WITH GOD

What are some specific practices we see from God's Word that have been modeled by Bill Bright and that will enable each of us to cultivate and deepen our own relationship to our triune God? A number could be mentioned. However, three stand out in my mind.

The first is clearly understanding from Scripture the amazing truth that the Lord Jesus in the person of the Holy Spirit in all His divine power has come to indwell every believer from the moment of conversion. The second is understanding how to be filled with the Holy Spirit and how to continually "walk in the Spirit." And the third is investing daily time alone with God. These are all part of one great truth: God lives in us and will live out His life in power through each of us human beings if we will allow Him to do so.

Since a colleague, Wayne Johnson, is writing a chapter in this *Festschrift* on the ministry of the Holy Spirit, I will treat the first two of these only briefly and elaborate more on the third.

First: Recognize the Indwelling of the Holy Spirit

Scripture teaches that when we open our lives to Jesus and receive Him into our hearts, we are regenerated (John 1:12,13; 3:3). In that moment, we become children of God, receive new life, and enter into a relationship with God as our Father, with Jesus as our Savior and Lord, and with the Holy Spirit as our indwelling life-giver and guide.

When Jesus left the earth and returned to the Father in heaven, He promised to come and live in our lives through the Holy Spirit whom He would send. We are in Christ and He is in us (John 14:16–20). In John 15, Jesus describes the marvelous relationship we can experience with Him personally. He teaches us that He literally will live in us and we in Him, and thereby we can experience a new quality of life that results in fruitfulness. The key is what He calls abiding, remaining, dwelling in Him.

> Remain in me, and I will remain in you. No branch can bear fruit by itself; it must remain in the vine. Neither can you bear fruit unless you remain in me... If a man remains in me and I in him, he will bear much fruit; apart from me you can do nothing... If you remain in me and my words remain in you, ask whatever you wish, and it will be given you... Now remain in my love. If you obey my commands, you will remain in my love, just as I have obeyed my Father's commands and remain in his love (verses 4–10).

This is another way of saying that we can live in continuous intimate relationship with our indwelling Savior and triune God. It is apparent that Jesus and the Father reside in us in the person of the Holy Spirit. In God's economy, the Father and Son sent the Holy Spirit to take the place of Jesus' physical presence by His spiritual presence in every believer wherever they may be on earth. Jesus said the Holy Spirit, the Counselor (*paraclete*), "will be *in* you" (John 14:16–18; 15:26; 16:7; see also John 16; Romans 8; 1 Corinthians 3:16; 6:15,19,20). The Spirit's purpose is to indwell, teach, comfort, convict, lead, empower, and fill us, and to reveal Christ to us.

Bill Bright's conscious awareness of the indwelling Spirit has impacted all of his attitudes, words, ministry, and ways of relating to others. This has been evident in his marriage and with his sons and extended family. We on the staff of Campus Crusade have also seen this in his relationships with us and with the entire Body of Christ, and in his attitudes toward nonbelievers and his desire to introduce them to the Savior. Finally, his realization of the Holy Spirit's indwelling and control of his life has resulted in his vision for the entire world—and even his attitude toward material things.

Isn't this the greatest need of every Christian—to continually maintain, cultivate, and deepen intimacy with the wonderful God who indwells us in the person of the Holy Spirit?

Having considered the fact that the infinite God in the person of the Counselor, the Holy Spirit, now lives in every believer, including you and me, the next questions are: Are you living in constant response to Him? Have you come to experience what it means to live moment by moment under the direction and leading of the infinite God who lives in you? Is this kind of intimacy a reality in your life? Do you know what it means to be controlled and empowered by Him? Do you know how to be filled with the Spirit as Paul commands in Ephesians 5:18? Is it your experience? Paul says, "Since we live by the Spirit, let us keep in step with the Spirit" (Galatians 5:25). What does the Scripture teach about this?

Second: Experience the Filling of the Holy Spirit

This second great truth, which has been modeled and taught extensively by Bill Bright, is that we need to learn both how to be filled with the Holy Spirit and how to live each day increasingly controlled and empowered by Him. This will profoundly deepen our intimacy with our triune God.

Ephesians 5:18 is a key Scripture. Paul gives here a very straightforward command. He contrasts two ways of living: drunkenness versus being full of the Spirit of God. In the way they affect our attitudes and conduct, the contrast between them is striking.

Paul says, "Be not drunk on wine which leads to debauchery. Instead be filled with the Spirit. Speak to one another with psalms, hymns and spiritual songs. Sing and make music in your heart to the Lord, always giving thanks to God the Father for everything, in the name of our Lord Jesus Christ. Submit to one another out of reverence for Christ" (Ephesians 5:18–21). Being full of wine leads to degradation. But experiencing God's fullness in our lives leads to what all of us need and want: joy (making music in your heart to the Lord), thanksgiving (always giving thanks to God the Father for everything), reverence for Christ, and humble submission to one another. Is this not the abundant life that Jesus promised us (John 10:10)?

Why is it, then, that many, if not most, Christians do not experience this life "to the full" that Jesus promised? The obvious answer is that either we do not understand how or we are not living "filled with the Spirit" moment by moment.

We need to recognize two aspects of what it means to be "filled with the Spirit."

The first is how to be filled. The second is how to "walk in the Spirit." As we have seen, every true believer in Jesus is *already* indwelt by the Holy Spirit. At the moment an individual receives Jesus Christ (John 1:12,13), the Holy Spirit of God comes to indwell him or her. The Spirit of God does not enter our lives in a partial sense. He brings with Him all of His omnipotence and power (Titus 3:6; Acts 1:8; Ephesians 1:19; 3:20; 6:10; 2 Peter 1:4).

For years, I understood from Scripture that the Holy Spirit indwells me. However, I did not grasp the fact that He lives in me *in all His power* and will live out His life through me if I will allow Him to. My failure to recognize His power in me meant that when temptations came, as they always did, I often gave in and reverted to my old, former way of living. The same is true of many Christians.

In 1 Corinthians 3:1–3, Paul writes to believers, "Brothers, I could not address you as spiritual but as worldly—mere infants in Christ... You are still worldly. For since there is jealousy and quarreling among you, are you not worldly? Are you not acting like mere men?"

Notice that in these three verses, Paul refers to three categories of people: 1) "spiritual," 2) "worldly—mere infants in Christ," and 3) "mere men" (humans who are unregenerate and do not have the Holy Spirit living in them).

The difference between the "worldly" believers and the "spiritual" is that although the Spirit lives in both, the worldly are living "like mere men," like unregenerate humans who do not have the Spirit of God (1 Corinthians 2:14).

The implication is that although these Corinthians were believers in Christ ("brothers") and therefore indwelt by the Holy Spirit (as Paul declares later in 1 Corinthians 3:16; 6:19), they obviously were not manifesting the fruit of the indwelling Spirit (Galatians 5:22,23) in their attitudes and conduct. They were acting like "mere men." They were not living in an intimate relationship with Jesus.

So the critical issue centers on the recognition and response of the believer to the indwelling Holy Spirit. In Galatians 5:16–18, Paul writes, "So I say, live by the Spirit, and you will not gratify the desires of the sinful nature. For the sinful nature desires what is contrary to the Spirit, and the Spirit desires what is contrary to the sinful nature. They are in conflict with each other, so that you do not do what you want. But if you are led by the

Spirit, you are not under law." The believer has the choice of either living in an intimate relationship with God, responding to the promptings of the Spirit, or responding to the desires of his old sinful nature.

Dr. Bright suggests several specific steps to enable us to live under the control of the Holy Spirit. The first step is a sincere desire (Matthew 5:6). In John 7:37,38, Jesus says, "If anyone is thirsty, let him come to Me and drink. Whoever believes in Me, as the Scripture has said, streams of living water will flow from within him." Then John adds, "By this He meant the Spirit."

The second step is to confess our sins, and to acknowledge that we have been controlling our own life. We must recognize that Christ died for *all* of our sins (Colossians 1:14,22; 2:13; Ephesians 1:7) and that He will forgive us the moment we turn to Him in repentance for our sin (1 John 1:8–10). The third step is to honestly turn from all known sins and present every area of our life to Him (Romans 12:1,2). Fourth, we invite the Holy Spirit to "fill" us, counting on Him to do just that.

This last phrase, "counting on Him to do just that," is where many believers stumble. Some people seek an emotional experience before they can believe that Christ has actually come into their lives when they invite Him in. In the same way, many believers seek an emotional experience to confirm that the Holy Spirit has truly "filled" them after they meet the conditions and invite Him to take control in their life. However, an emotional experience is not a condition. Even as salvation and spiritual birth are by faith in what God has promised (John 1:12,13), so the filling of the Spirit is by faith in what Jesus said in John 7:37,38. The Spirit of God fills our life when we meet God's conditions, not on the basis of our feelings.

Bill suggests that we pray according to the promise in 1 John 5:14,15. On the basis of this promise, we can "know that we have the requests which we have asked from him" and thank God that the Holy Spirit is now in control of our lives.

But being "filled with the Spirit" is not a once-for-all experience. The command to "be filled with the Spirit" in Ephesians 5:18 is a present tense imperative, and therefore implies that we are to be filled constantly and repeatedly. The idea of "filled" implies that every part of our life is permeated and controlled by Him. In light of this, the *New English Bible* uses the translation "let the Holy Spirit fill you."[5]

This brings us to the second aspect of the Spirit-filled life: "walking in the Spirit." Galatians 5:25 says, "Since we live by the Spirit, let us keep in step with the Spirit." This is what it means to live intimately related to God.

Because Scripture teaches that the work of the Holy Spirit is an ongoing way of life, we must understand not only how to initially be filled, but also how to continue to live under His control. Bill has written and spoken extensively on both of these aspects of the Spirit-filled life. (See his Transferable Concepts titled *How You Can Be Filled with the Holy Spirit* and *How You Can Walk in the Spirit.*)

Bill explains that walking in the power of the Spirit includes four truths to practice.

The *first* is to be sure the Holy Spirit is controlling and empowering you. The moment you realize you have sinned in any way, acknowledge it to God, accept the fact that Christ has died for that sin (and all sin), repent (turn) from it in attitude and conduct, then invite the Holy Spirit to again fill and control you. Bill likens this to physical breathing: exhaling (by confession of sin) and inhaling (by appropriating the fullness of God's Spirit by faith).

The *second* truth to practice is to be prepared for spiritual conflict. Satan will throw at us all kinds of temptations, distractions, and direct spiritual attacks.

We need to realize and be prepared for them and confront them by a *third* truth to practice: to know and draw upon our resources as a child of God. These resources are prayer and biblical truths and promises.

Finally, the *fourth* truth to practice is to choose to live by faith in God and His Scriptures, relying upon on Him and what He says in His Word.

The biblical teachings of the filling of the Spirit and walking moment by moment under His control have revolutionized the lives of thousands of Christians—including my own. I came to realize that as a believer I no longer needed to respond as I often had in the past, either by living in ongoing guilt over some sin I had committed or by feeling that I could not live the Christian life. I have come to recognize that a whole new dynamic is at work within me—the indwelling Holy Spirit of God. And I must continually be alert to and practice the four truths of living and walking in loving response to Him and His power in me. I need to continually allow the Holy Spirit to live out through my life moment by moment; therefore, I need immediate and continuous obedience to the Spirit's direction and promptings as He empowers me. This is living in His fullness.

Deepening intimacy with God involves learning to be sensitive and obedient to the Spirit's scriptural direction in our lives. Increasingly, I have found that this has fostered a new closeness with God. God longs to live in and through each of our lives in loving attitudes, activities, and words. He has commanded us to share with everyone about who He is and what He has done for each of us and to tell others of the new relationship and eternal life He offers every human being. As our intimacy with God deepens, our sharing becomes more spontaneous and natural. As Paul writes, "Everywhere we go we talk about Christ to all who will listen" (Colossians 1:28, TLB).

Third: Invest Personal Time with God

The third specific practice that will deepen our intimacy with our wonderful triune God is to invest unhurried personal time alone with Him each day listening to Him, conversing with Him, and worshiping Him.

To develop an ongoing awareness of God's presence, we need to get to know Him better. Two individuals can become initial friends in a crowd, but an intimate relationship develops only when these two invest quality time together genuinely sharing their lives. The more we open up to one another and really listen, the deeper our acquaintance becomes. Do you really listen for God's prompting and directions, daily and throughout the day? And do you talk with God about everything? He invites us to (Philippians 4:6; 1 Peter 5:7; Hebrews 4:15,16).

Isn't our tendency to turn to God only when we are deeply concerned or in trouble? However, our greater need is to be powerfully aware of His constant presence, to have an intimate listening relationship, and to recognize that He is always with us, watching and caring about everything in our lives (1 Peter 5:7).

Consider Jesus' relationship with His Father (and ours). By looking at how Jesus cultivated this intimacy, we too can deepen our experience of closeness with God. With the Holy Spirit's power, we can follow His example. Let's look at what are, without a doubt, two keys.

First, in Luke 5:16 we read, "Jesus *often* withdrew to lonely places and prayed." The context of this statement is found in the previous verse. Jesus was extremely busy! Isn't that typical of our lives much of the time?

At this time in Jesus' life, He was having a very full, effective ministry. Great crowds were flocking to Him, continually pressing about Him, many seeking physical healing, others wanting to be near Him and hear His teaching. In the midst of a "very successful ministry," Jesus clearly sensed His need to spend more time alone in God's presence to seek His perspective and direction. So Scripture says that He "often withdrew" to be alone with His Father. Notice it does not say *occasionally*, but *often*.

Do you and I "often" withdraw to be alone with God? When was the last time?

Mark records another occasion of Jesus' time with the Father: "Very early in the morning, while it was still dark, Jesus got up, left the house, and went off to a solitary place, where he prayed" (1:35). The day before had been packed with many things: teaching in the synagogue, healing "many who had various diseases," and driving "out many demons." But "very early" the next morning, He went out to "*a solitary place*" to be alone with His Father. Most of us would have slept in. And on some occasions that may have been proper, but not for Jesus in this instance. Why not?

Jesus wanted and needed to be alone in His Father's presence. Perhaps He sought direction about what to do next. In verse 38, after His disciples searched for Him and found Him, they exclaimed, "Everyone is looking for you!" But what did Jesus tell them that the Father had evidently revealed to Him? They were to go to other villages so He could preach there also.

In addition to frequent withdrawal to be alone with His Father, Jesus lived continually in a loving relationship and responsive obedience. Is this not the same as "walking in the Spirit"? He was always aware of His Father's presence and did His Father's bidding. In John 8:29 our Savior said, "The one who sent me is with me; he has not left me alone, for *I always do what pleases him*." At Lazarus's tomb, Jesus prayed, "Father, I thank you that you have heard me. I knew that *you always hear me*" (John 11:41,42). For Jesus, intimacy with the Father was a moment-by-moment way of life. Unbroken awareness of the Father's presence and continual response to Him characterized our Savior's life. He truly lived a Spirit-controlled life.

These are but two examples out of Jesus' life, but from these and the rest of Scripture, we recognize that we too may live in constant awareness of God's indwelling and grow in responsiveness—pleasing our indwelling Counselor, the ever-present Spirit of the Father and Son. Is this not what it means to "walk in the Spirit"?

Bill Bright has often shared how for years his daily practice upon arising in the morning is to kneel beside his bed. There with his Bible open, he reads, meditates, worships, listens to, and talks with his Lord. He gives himself afresh to Jesus to live through him throughout the day. In the words of his biographer, this is:

> ...his physical and mental preparation for the day. This is his best time. "The most precious hours of my day," he has said, "are when I'm alone with Jesus; He is with me all day, of course, but when just the two of us are there, I can say: *Now* I can be with Him *alone*." It's during these moments that he prays, "Lord, I'm just Your slave; You are the Master. Here is my body. Wear me like a suit of clothes today. Move around in my life however You want to move. Help me to be sensitive to Your leading. May I not say or do anything that would bring discredit to

Your dear name. Lead me only to bring worship, glory, and praise to You."[6]

The last thing in the evening, Bill concludes each day by kneeling before his Savior and reading from the Scriptures.

Do we experience this ongoing direction from our heavenly Father on a day-to-day basis? If not, could it be that we are not *frequently* (even daily) going off to a solitary place to meet with our Father? The solitary place need not be a desert or mountainside. It can be in your bedroom, study, office, a park, or even in your car in a parking lot. Henri Nouwen suggests: "When we have met our Lord in the silent intimacy of our prayer, then we will also meet him... in the market and in the town square. But when we have not met him in the center of our own hearts, we cannot expect to meet him in the busyness of our daily lives."[7] If we invest little time with God, how can we expect much intimacy with Him?

MY OWN EXPERIENCE

About a dozen years ago, I was making my daily thirty-minute drive down the mountain from Lake Arrowhead, California, to the International School of Theology at Arrowhead Springs, where I was teaching. I was listening to an audiocassette tape of selections from the Psalms. When it came to Psalm 1, suddenly the power and promise of that Scripture profoundly gripped me. "Blessed is the man who does not walk in the counsel of the wicked... but His delight is in the law of the Lord and in his law he meditates day and night. He is like a tree planted by the streams of water, which yields its fruit in season and whose leaf does not wither. Whatever he does prospers" (verses 1–3).

I locked onto the promise "whatever he does prospers." Then I asked myself, "If that is true, why don't I make this a sustained, ongoing habit of my life—to continually meditate and delight in God's Scripture?" That day I determined that henceforth before I read anything else each morning, and the last thing before sleep at night, and at frequent intervals throughout the day, I would turn to the Scriptures and listen to what God might want to say to me. In a new way, I began to memorize and meditate on key passages in God's Word.

In addition, I determined that regardless of anything else (with rare exceptions), I would schedule unhurried time with God the first thing every morning. Also, to realistically do this, I would go to bed earlier each evening.

This time with God has had a profound impact on my outlook and perspective and on my growing awareness of God's presence in these ensuing years. The promises and commands of Joshua 1:5–9 have come alive in a new way and become an integral part of my life. One of the central conditions and promises for me has been in verse 8 where God says to Joshua, "Do not let this Book of the Law depart from your mouth; meditate on it day and night so that you may be careful to do everything written in it. Then you will be prosperous and successful." The condition for prosperity and success is meditating on and being careful to do what God's Word says. Of course, I realize the prosperity and success God promises here are something far greater than materialism. They refer to ultimate success in God's eyes.

HOW DOES INTIMACY TAKE PLACE?

A personal relationship and friendship with God begins at conversion. However, as in any relationship, for our intimacy with God to grow, we must spend ongoing time with Him—both planned and unplanned.

Unplanned, spontaneous times in a relationship are not usually a major issue. Scheduling planned time together is the crucial issue. In a relationship between a single man and a single woman, calling and scheduling dates is foundational to seeing that relationship develop. Likewise in a marriage, if a couple does not plan times alone, the press of daily living will crowd out times of deepening intimacy. So, if we do not plan time alone with God, intimacy with Him will not likely develop.

We are all familiar with the phrase, "If you fail to plan, you plan to fail." Yet many times we fail to plan times to "withdraw to a solitary place" and listen to our Lord.

A first step in investing time with God is planning when we will meet with Him. We need to prayerfully look at our schedules and decide the best time to meet regularly with our loving Father. To do so, we each need to ask several questions of ourselves.

How often do I need to be alone with God: Monthly? Weekly? Daily?

The famous concert pianist Paderewski once said, "If I miss practicing three days in a row, my audience will notice it. If I miss practice two days in a row, my teacher will notice it. If I miss practice for one day, I will notice it."

I need time alone with God every day. Without it, the press of each day's responsibilities and the pull of this immediate temporary world through my five senses dulls my awareness of God and His clear direction and priorities in my life.

How much time should I schedule in meeting with God? This depends on our unique needs and circumstances. We each need to ask God to impress on our heart and mind the amount of time we need.

I need all the time with God that I can carve out of each day. Generally, it takes me 15 to 30 minutes just to settle down mentally and physically, to focus on God's presence, and begin to genuinely sense God speaking to me. As a result, I try to schedule at least an hour, and preferably longer, alone with God daily. In wanting to hear God speak to me through Scripture, I need to meditate on what I read and how it applies practically to my life. In addition, I need to talk to God about the immediate concerns and activities that are most on my mind, including the needs of people who are near and dear to me. Scripture also exhorts us to pray for pressing local and world conditions, including our national leaders and others in authority.

Since time alone with God is the foundation for everything else we do, I find it inconceivable that I would invest only a few moments alone with Him each day. I need adequate time! What about you? He longs for time with you and me to hear Him speaking to us and to assure us of His love and presence (John 14:21).

I suggest beginning by taking whatever brief time with God you presently feel you must have. Then as this becomes a daily practice, the desire to increase the amount of time with your Lord may increase.

What are my priorities? The time crunch is obviously a major issue in all our lives. I never seem to have the time to do all the things I would like to do each day. Only as I daily come before God, walk intimately with Him, and seek to follow His priorities moment by moment are my mind and heart kept at rest.

Each of us needs to get our individual direction from God regarding His priorities for our lives. Every human being has exactly the same number of hours and minutes in each day, and God is the One who knows how He wants each of us to invest that time. He reminds us in Ephesians 5:15, "Be careful, then, how you live—not as unwise but as wise, making the most of every opportunity, because the days are evil."

Shouldn't we put our daily time alone with God as the very top priority of our "to do" list? Is anything more important?

Have you noticed that when you do not have regular time with your spouse or children, the quality of your relationship begins to suffer? It is no different in our intimacy with God. If we do not regularly converse with Him and continually listen for His direction, we cannot possibly discern what He is trying to communicate to us. Consequently, we cannot daily experience His guidance and be certain of His will.

When is the best time? Morning? Evening? Midday? The answer to this question depends on the most effective time for each individual. This may vary at different times in our lives or on different days.

I find that generally I am freshest in the morning. This is also when I have fewer, if any, interruptions. But to be fresh in the early morning, most of us need adequate sleep. The battle for me in getting up in the morning is usually won or lost the night before. Getting to bed at night is dependent on scheduling other things in the evening, especially TV. If TV is hindering our daily time with God, we would do well to evaluate which is more important: an hour or more in front of the television or equal time with our infinite, loving Father. In the words of Ann Ortland, "eliminate and concentrate."[8]

Some have found it helpful to turn off or turn down the phone. We may need to inform friends that we are not available after a certain hour—except in emergencies or for very important matters.

Quantity or quality? The question of whether to spend quantity or quality of time with God is not a matter of either/or but both/and. I read a good rule of thumb by Peter Wagner, one of my former professors and a very influential Christian leader. He wisely recommends, "It is more advisable to start with quantity than quality in daily quiet time. First, program time. The quality will usually follow."[9]

I have found that to be very true in my own experience. I cannot rush my time with God. As in other relationships, intimacy with Him requires unhurried time for listening and speaking to one another—quality communion.

Dallas Willard agrees. "Quiet time . . . doesn't work for many people because being in Jesus' presence takes time. Six ten-minute quiet times are not as effective as one sixty-minute time with God. If you want a shower, one drop every five minutes for two years is not enough . . . Take time to be undistracted, to enjoy the presence of Jesus . . . Plan your week to include longer times when you can be alone with God."[10]

Where is the best place? To deepen our intimacy with God, is one place better than another? This is like asking, "Where are the best places to cultivate friendship with another human being?" A logical answer is: "Anywhere mutually convenient for the two persons and that will be conducive to quality interaction."

Since God is omnipresent and indwelling every believer, we can and should turn to Him and seek His guidance at all times in all circumstances. These include times of trial and testing, times of danger, times of uncertainty and indecision, times of tragedy and darkness, and in times of blessing, joy, victory, and fruitfulness.

Many godly people down through history have suggested having a specific place to meet with God daily. When Jesus was in the vicinity of Jerusalem, Scripture indicates His practice was to go to the Mount of Olives. When in Galilee, He often went "up into the mountains" to seek His Father's face. Scriptures I mentioned earlier spoke of Jesus going to "a solitary place" and "lonely places." These imply that He went away from others so He could be alone with His Father.

The main point for each of us is to *find a place where we will be undisturbed and alone* in our Father's presence.

PROBLEMS WITH INTIMACY

Satan does not want you and me to deepen our intimacy with God. He will do everything possible to hinder us. Scripture warns us, "Be self-controlled and alert. Your enemy the devil prowls around like a roaring lion looking for someone to devour. Resist him, standing firm in the faith" (1 Peter 5:8,9). Therefore, anticipate, prepare, and watch out for all kind of strategies he will use to keep you from investing time privately with God. Satan will attempt to distract, interrupt, and neutralize time you plan alone with God. Satan also uses work, busyness, drowsiness, wandering thoughts, temptation to read literature other than the Bible, telephone calls, TV, family needs, and other hindrances too numerous to mention.

For example, while praying recently, I thought of something I needed to do later that week. I didn't want to forget it, so I shifted my computer from one program to my "task list." I discovered I wanted to delete some "to do" items on my list, then quickly got sidetracked in trying to learn some new things on my computer. Suddenly, I realized that I had invested almost thirty minutes in doing so. I had to acknowledge my digression to God, confess my failure to seek His direction, ask His forgiveness, and again ask to hear His voice and experience His leading. Satan repeatedly uses similar tactics in times I schedule to be alone with the Lord.

Having acknowledged this, I also want to be quick to state that we must never allow our planned times alone with God to become legalistic. Satan and our old nature will always try to push us to one extreme or the other: either to legalism or to laxity/license.

Dallas Willard says, "The popular image of a quiet time is probably not workable for more than 5 or 10 percent of the people . . . One reason is that it's often done as if it were medicine instead of a joyous meeting with God."[11]

Bill Bright stated, "In my own life, as I have come to know God better and to live more fully in the power and control of the Holy Spirit, my daily devotional reading and study is not a duty or a chore, but a blessing; not an imposition on my time, but an invitation to fellowship in the closest of all ways with our heavenly Father and our wonderful Savior and Lord. Remember, God delights to have fellowship with you."[12]

We must never see our relationship and times alone with our glorious Father, Savior, and Holy Spirit as a duty but rather as an incredible privilege. With this perspective we must also recognize that Satan will try to use everything possible to hinder us from our planned time with God.

For this reason, I have made it a practice to plan all other activities and appointments (each day's schedule) around my time with God. But like anything else worthwhile in life, being consistent in meeting with God takes discipline yet flexibility. Periodically I have to remind myself that having a quiet time is not my 'lord,' but God Himself is Lord in my life. Because of a variety of changes in my schedule I frequently have to change the time of day in which I get alone with God. As a result of making sure I do get daily quiet time with Him, I often have to postpone items on my "to do" list until another day.

SEEK AFTER GOD

Increasing intimacy between two persons, including intimacy with God, is *always a process that requires time*. We must recognize this and continue to seek hard after our God. We must not get discouraged but continually pursue an ever-deepening awareness and response to our living, loving God. Our response to God must be ongoing. Relationships are never stagnant (2 Peter 1:5–11). The three practices outlined in this chapter will keep our relationship with God vital and flourishing.

A. W. Tozer captures this idea of deepening intimacy:

> The modern scientist has lost God amid the wonders of His world; we Christians are in real danger of losing God amid the wonders of His Word. We have almost forgotten that God is a person and, as such can be cultivated as any person can. It is inherent in personality to be able to know other personalities, but full knowledge of one personality by another *cannot be achieved in one encounter*. It is only after long and loving mental intercourse that the full possibilities of both can be explored[13] (emphasis added).

So let us make it our lifelong pursuit to continually deepen our acquaintance and love relationship with our incomparable, indwelling Lord. Everything else will flow from this: all the nine elements of the fruit of the

Spirit in each of our lives (Galatians 5:22,23), the realization of the Great Commandment in and through believers everywhere (Matthew 22:37–40), and finally the worldwide fulfillment of the Great Commission of our magnificent Savior (Matthew 28:18–20).

Jesus promised, "I am the vine; you are the branches. If a man remains in me and I in him, he will bear much fruit; apart from me you can do nothing... This is to my Father's glory, that you bear much fruit, showing yourselves to be my disciples" (John 15:5,8).

God has wonderfully used Bill Bright's life, example, and ministry over the years to encourage me to this end. I pray the same for each person who reads this article. Few things would please Bill Bright more. And more importantly, God desires this for each of us. Review the principles of this chapter and prayerfully determine what God would have you do, then follow through. Develop an increasingly intimate relationship with God.

NOTES

1. Michael Richardson, *Amazing Faith* (Colorado Springs: WaterBrook Press, 2000), 238.
2. Ibid.
3. W. E. Vine, *An Expository Dictionary of New Testament Words* (Westwood, NJ: Fleming H. Revell, 1962), 286.
4. J. Schattenmann, *New International Dictionary of New Testament Theology*, Colin Brown, ed. (Grand Rapids: Zondervan Publishing House, 1986), 1:643.
5. Francis Foulkes, "The Epistle of Paul to the Ephesians," *Tyndale New Testament Commentaries* (Grand Rapids: Wm B. Eerdmans Publishing Company, 1976), 152.
6. Richardson, 231,32.
7. Henri Nouwen, "Gracias!" *Christianity Today*, November 13, 2000, 102.
8. Ann Ortland, *Decision Magazine*, Vol. 41, No. 6, June 2000, back cover.
9. C. Peter Wagner, *Prayer Shield* (Ventura, CA: Regal Books, 1992), 86.
10. Dallas Willard, "Wide Awake," *Leadership Journal*, Vol. XV, no. 4 (Fall 1994), 24.
11. Ibid., 23,24.
12. Richardson, 264.
13. A. W. Tozer, *The Pursuit of God* (Camp Hill, PA: Christian Publications, Inc., 1982), 13.

CHAPTER 5

Commitment to the Great Commission

TED MARTIN

On Staff since 1960

Dean Emeritus and Professor of Theology,

International School of Theology

"A great commitment to the Great Commission and the Great Commandment makes a great Christian."[1] To me, this slogan epitomizes the life and ministry of Bill Bright. What is more important than being committed to loving God with all our heart, soul, and mind? These two things have been the passion of Bill Bright and the commitment of the organization he founded. Bill's first priority is to keep alive his "first love" for God as a slave of Jesus Christ. Then, in his devotion to Christ, he spends every waking hour—and probably most of his dreaming hours—working to help fulfill the Great Commission.

The first letter I ever received from Bill Bright was signed, "Yours for fulfilling the Great Commission in this generation." This was the way he signed all his letters. As I joined the staff of Campus Crusade for Christ, I quickly learned that Bill Bright was really serious about fulfilling the Great Commission in his generation. It wasn't that Bill believed that he or Campus Crusade for Christ would accomplish this alone. Bill has often said that Campus Crusade is only a leaf on a twig, on a branch, of the vine, which is the Church, the Body of Christ. But he firmly believes that Campus Crusade is to be a catalyst to the rest of the Body of Christ, encouraging all believers everywhere, all denominations, all Christian ministries to be involved in the task of fulfilling the Great Commission.

WHAT IS THE GREAT COMMISSION?

Exactly what is the Great Commission? Because several Bible passages are referred to as the Great Commission, I think it might be best to explain it this way: The Great Commission is the personal marching orders that Jesus Christ gave to His Church through His apostles during the time between His resurrection from the dead and His ascension. He tells His Church what she is to be doing until He comes back to earth again.

The Great Commission was given on at least three different occasions and locations: first, on the evening following His resurrection in a room where His disciples were gathered in Jerusalem; second, on a mountain in Galilee where Jesus had instructed His disciples to meet Him; and third, on the Mount of Olives outside Jerusalem just before His ascension to heaven. The Commission is stated in different ways in five different places in the New Testament: at the end of each of the four Gospels and at the beginning of the Book of Acts. These passages are each essentially saying the same thing, yet in different ways, with different emphases.

Before we discuss the Great Commission, may I suggest that you read all five of these passages in your Bible in their various contexts so that you will have them in your mind as we discuss them. They are found in the last chapters of Matthew (28:15–20), Mark (16:14–20),[2] and Luke (24:44–53), in the next to the last chapter of John (20:19–23),[3] and in the first chapter of Acts (1:1–11). These all involve post-resurrection appearances of Jesus.

THE PRINCIPLES OF THE GREAT COMMISSION

Putting the five passages together, let me suggest that there are seven major principles involved in the Great Commission. We will list them, and then see how Bill Bright and the ministry of Campus Crusade for Christ have sought to be faithful to each of these. These principles are not just for the original apostles, although Jesus originally gave these to them. We know these principles are for us today because Jesus told the apostles that they were to make disciples and teach them to obey all the commands He had given them, which certainly included the command of the commission He was giving them (Matthew 28:19,20). Then to make it crystal clear that it is for us, He adds, "I am with you always, even to the end of the age" (NASB), that is, until Jesus comes again. For this reason, in the following points I will state the principles of the Great Commission in terms of "us"—all the followers of Christ today.

1. As the Father sent Jesus into the world, now Jesus is sending us to all

the world (Matthew 28:19; Mark 16:15; Luke 24:47; John 20:21; Acts 1:8).

2. We are to go in the authority of Christ (Matthew 28:18,19; Mark 16:20; John 20:21).
3. We are to proclaim the gospel of Christ to every person in the entire world (Mark 16:15; Luke 24:47; Acts 1:8).
4. We are to be personal witnesses concerning Christ (Luke 24:48; Acts 1:8).
5. We are to make disciples of those who respond to the gospel (Matthew 28:19,20).
6. We are to go in the power of the indwelling Holy Spirit (Luke 24:49; John 20:22; Acts 1:8).
7. We are to continue to do this until Jesus comes again (Matthew 28:20).

Now let us look at each of these.

1. We Are Sent by Christ to the World

Jesus was sent by the Father into the world to live, to die for the sins of the world, and to begin the process of taking the message of salvation to the world. With His limitations as one man, He could not physically go to all the world, so He trained others to go. When He left, He sent them and now us to take the gospel to the rest of the world. He left us to fulfill the Great Commission.

Before I joined Campus Crusade, I attended six full weeks of missionary conferences as a student at Dallas Seminary where I listened to some of the top missionary speakers of the world. I heard much about the Great Commission. But as I met Bill Bright, I noticed something different about him. He wasn't just interested in some jungle tribe here or there, or some overlooked people group, or even some neglected country. He felt the responsibility for the entire world: every nation, every tribe, every person. He could say with John Wesley, "The world is my parish," but he could mean it in an even fuller sense than Wesley. He was also the first person I had ever met who was really optimistic about the possibility of the fulfillment of the Great Commission in his generation.

The vision that God had given Bill was never simply for the college campus. The campus was to be the primary source of manpower for getting to the world. When I joined the staff of Campus Crusade in 1960, all Crusade had was a campus ministry, but the motto on the wall in the front of the chapel where Staff Training was held said, "Win the Campus for Christ Today. Win the World for Christ Tomorrow."

At that time, there were about 100 people on staff on about 25 campuses in the United States. We were just starting in two countries overseas: Korea and Pakistan. A couple of years later, we had grown to about 400 staff. I remember a meeting of directors. We divided the United States into twelve areas with area directors to develop the campus ministry. We divided the world into six regions where we would send directors to recruit national leadership to begin the ministry in every nation possible. We were implementing a strategy for getting to the world.

When the staff numbered 100, Bill was talking about 1,000 staff. By the time we reached 400, he was talking 10,000; later 100,000; now 1,000,000 full-time and volunteers. At present, we have staff in 191 countries. But again, we are not trying to do the task by ourselves. We are seeking to help encourage the entire Body of Christ in fulfilling the Great Commission. We have partnered with hundreds of other Christian organizations and thousands of churches to work together in this great task. Our target is every person in every nation.

2. We Are to Go in Christ's Authority

Who are we as Christians to presume that we have the right to tell people that they are to completely change their thinking and the way they live their lives and start following what we tell them? What presumption! This isn't politically correct. But we are under divine authority. We are ambassadors of Christ (2 Corinthians 5:20). Either Jesus was and is who He claimed to be, the Son of God sent in the name of the Father, or He was a mad man. If He is who He claimed—and He proved this through His resurrection from the dead—we are obligated to obey Him.

All authority was delegated to Jesus Christ. In this authority, He sends us. Bill Bright senses that authority. He goes as a humble servant, but in the authority of God. When he speaks, those who hear him sense that delegated authority. He speaks of Christ freely to people with authority, whether they are scholars or leaders in business, government, or the military. To become president of the United States to Bill would be a demotion. He realizes that he is under much higher orders than that.

All Christians go in this same authority of Christ.

3. We Are to Proclaim the Gospel to Every Person

The best known element of the Great Commission is the command to take the message of Christ to people throughout the earth. "Go into all the world and preach the gospel to all creation" (Mark 16:15, NASB). But what is the "gospel"? The Greek word simply means "good news." It is the message that God loves us in spite of our sinfulness. In His love and in fulfillment of many prophesies of the Old Testament, God sent His Son Jesus to earth to live and then die as a sacrifice for the sins of the world. Jesus then rose from the dead, giving proof of who He is and of His victory over death. As people believe this message and turn in repentance and faith to Jesus as their Lord and Savior, God grants them forgiveness of sin, spiritual rebirth, eternal life, and a righteous standing before God. (See Isaiah 53:4–11; Luke 24:46–48; 1 Corinthians 15:1–8; John 3:16; 20:31; and many other passages.)

This was the message of the apostles and the early Church. It was the message of the reformers, who called the Church back to the teachings of the Bible. It is the message of the spiritual awakenings that have impacted the world with such great blessings. It transforms lives as it is preached and believed today. It is still good news.

One of the things Bill Bright has consistently emphasized throughout his ministry is the proclamation of the gospel. He has made it a personal practice that whenever he is alone with a person for more than a few moments, he will seek to share the gospel with that person. He has shared the gospel with people on skid row, with sorority and fraternity members, with athletes, with militant radicals, with educators, with the wealthy, with governmental leaders, with taxi drivers, with hotel maids, with the people seated next to him on airplanes. He shares lovingly and sensitively. The message is always basically the same. If a person has questions, Bill simply shares the uniqueness of Jesus: "There has never been another person like Him, and He loves you and died for your sins and rose again. He wants to live in and through you as your Lord and Savior. He can give you pardon, peace, purpose, and power for your life. Wouldn't you like to receive Him?"

Bill has insisted that all Campus Crusade staff be able to share the gospel and introduce others to Jesus Christ. I know that even after I had received a doctoral degree in theology, I was still not very effective in presenting the gospel to groups or even to individuals. Then I came on Campus Crusade staff and received training. As I went into sororities, fraternities, and college dormitories to present Christ, I began to see many people respond in faith to the gospel.

Bill doesn't believe that just because a person is a member of a church, he has a personal relationship with Christ. As Bill has spoken in many wonderful churches, he has discovered that often even a majority of the church members do not have a personal assurance of their relationship with God. The pastors often simply assume that everyone knows and understands the gospel. Bill's burden is that, whether in churches or in secular groups, whether one-on-one, in small meetings, or in large meetings of even a million or more,[4] people will hear, understand, and be given an opportunity to respond to Christ and the gospel.

Bill believes that every Christian should be trained in how to share the gospel with others. This led him to write *The Four Spiritual Laws* booklet, which people can use to explain the gospel to others to help them put their faith in Jesus Christ as their Lord and Savior. This booklet has been translated into hundreds of languages, and more than 2 billion copies have been printed and used all over the world.

For us as believers to be convinced that we need to proclaim the good news all over the world, we need to be convinced that people without Christ are lost and are in need of salvation. Many professing believers reject this teaching. But it is clearly the teaching of Scripture (Mark 16:16; Romans 6:23; etc.). Every believer needs to see it as his or her responsibility to share the gospel with others. To our shame, after 2,000 years, we the Church still have not reached the entire world with the message of the gospel. Part of the problem is that the average Christian does not see the spreading of the gospel as his own responsibility; we think it is the job of the "clergy."

Campus Crusade staff use the phrase "initiative evangelism" for the concept of taking the gospel to others. As Crusade staff, we have taken the gospel on campus to sororities and fraternities, to the dorms, to athletic teams, to student unions, to free-speech platforms, to faculty, to international students, to student leaders—wherever we can get a hearing. Through other ministries of Crusade, we have taken the gospel to prisons, the military, inner cities, high schools, business and professional people, and diplomats. In various countries of the world, we have taken the gospel from the college campuses to the remotest villages.

But most believers do not take the initiative in sharing the message of Christ with others. Churches need to realize that we are to take the message to the entire community. We are not simply to wait for people to come to us in our church meetings. We are each to go to our neighbors, our relatives, our friends, our fellow workers, our acquaintances, to the people we meet. We are to go to them prayerfully, with love and good works, but also with the gospel.

4. We Are Witnesses for Christ

In Jesus' Commission to the apostles, He told them that they would be His witnesses (Acts 1:8). In one sense, they were unique: they lived and ministered with Jesus; they witnessed His miracles and heard His teachings; and in a special sense they were witnesses to His death, burial, and resurrection from the dead, and later to His ascension. We have not personally witnessed these things; we can only repeat the apostles' testimony in these matters. However, in another sense we can personally bear witness of Christ. We can testify to our own personal relationship with Him: what life was like before we met Christ; how we put our faith in Him and came to know Him personally; and how He has changed our life since. This witness can have a powerful impact on others. It is a witness to the fact that Jesus is alive and at work in the world and in our lives today.

Bill Bright is always bearing testimony to the fact that Christ is alive and at work in his own life. Almost every time he speaks, he talks of the significance and work of Christ in his life.

All the Campus Crusade staff and their disciples are trained to share their personal testimonies. They are asked to write and memorize a three-minute version of their testimonies. In many meetings where I have presented the gospel, I have had others share how they came to know Christ. This really gets people's attention and prepares them for hearing the gospel and for realizing that they too can know God in a personal way.

People are made in such a way that they seek peace, meaning, and purpose in life, and they are attracted when they see someone who has found these in Christ. As witnesses who testify that Jesus Christ has brought these things into our lives, we can influence others. People whose lives are not consistent with their profession of faith are negative witnesses for Christ. Many people have stumbled over the hypocrisy or lack of love in a professing Christian's life. On the other hand, it is hard to resist a life marked by love, joy, peace, patience, kindness, goodness, faithfulness, gentleness, and self-control.

5. We Are to Make Disciples

The emphasis of Jesus' Commission in Matthew's Gospel is *making disciples:*

> Go therefore and *make disciples* of all the nations, baptizing them in the name of the Father and the Son and the Holy Spirit, teaching them to observe all that I commanded you; and lo, I am with you always, even to the end of the age (28:19,20, emphasis added).

The Greek word used by Matthew for "make disciples" in its root significance means "to make learners."[5] In the Greek world, the term "disciple" was used to designate a follower of some teacher and that person's teachings (perhaps of a philosopher such as Socrates or Plato or of a religious person such as John the Baptist).

The Matthew passage itself instructs us how we are to make disciples. In the Greek text, the passage has one main verb and three participles related to it. The main verb is the command "make disciples." The three participles are "going," "baptizing," and "teaching."[6] These basically explain phases that are involved in "making disciples": a proclamation phase, an enlistment phase, and a training or instruction phase.

First, the proclamation phase: We are to go proclaiming the gospel. This we have already discussed.

Next comes the enlistment phase: The new believer needs to identify himself as one of the followers of Christ. In the Great Commission, belief in the gospel is to be signified by the step of baptism. This is the outward sign that the baptized person has repented and responded in faith to Christ, but it is also a first step in discipleship. In baptism, the person becomes identified with Christ as His disciple. The person also becomes identified with other followers of Christ and becomes a part of the visible Church. It is in the context of other believers that the ongoing process of discipleship is to take place.

Finally, there is the training phase: "teaching them to observe all that I have commanded you." Teaching people obedience to all of the commands of Christ is an ongoing task that is never fully accomplished. But it is a necessary task. We are blessed when we obey Christ's commands from the heart. The proclamation and enlistment phases of the Great Commission would never be fulfilled without this training phase. Who will take the gospel message to the world except those who have become obedient followers of Christ?

Within Campus Crusade for Christ, how has this emphasis on making disciples been accomplished? We have already discussed the proclamation phase where we take the gospel to people wherever they are. But what do we do in the enlistment phase? As we go, we always seek to have people indicate their response to the message. We use such things as comment cards so that people can indicate a decision or an interest, giving us their name, address, and telephone number. We then contact them, meet with them, go over the gospel with them individually, help them with faith and assurance.

Because Campus Crusade for Christ is not a local church, wherever we have worked independently of local churches, such as on college campuses, we have considered it best for our ministry not to baptize the new believers but to leave this to local churches. We encourage new believers to be baptized and join churches where Christ is honored and the Word of God is preached. We encourage students who are in strong churches to invite other students to join them. But we do help the new believers make sure of their personal relationship with Christ and help them begin to grow in their Christian faith.

Then in the training phase, we get new believers involved in one-on-one follow-up, where they learn to study the Bible and pray under the leadership of more mature believers. Here they learn the principles of Christian living: how to deal with sin in their lives and how to walk by faith in dependence on the Holy Spirit. In small groups with other believers, they learn from one another and encourage each other in the Christian life. We also get them into beginning, intermediate, and advanced leadership training classes. Here they learn to share their faith with others: how to give their testimony in a winsome way, how to share the gospel and lead others to faith in Christ, and how to follow-up other new believers. These disciples become actively involved in beginning to help fulfill the Great Commission.

So often in churches, members function as if the goal is to get people to make a salvation decision for Christ or perhaps be baptized and join the church. These should be only the beginning goals. Believers must become mature disciples, obedient to all that Christ has commanded.

Dr. Bright teaches that much more time will be spent in disciple building than in evangelism. But he has been equally insistent that a person isn't really an obedient disciple until he or she is introducing others to Christ. It is only through training disciples that we can hope to build up the army that we need to evangelize the world. We must have both the evangelism and the "teaching to obey" aspects of the Great Commission.

6. We Go in the Power of the Holy Spirit

Jesus told the disciples that they were to remain in Jerusalem until the Holy Spirit came and clothed them with the power they would need to be His witnesses (Luke 24:49; Acts 1:8). Jesus knew that it would be better for His disciples if He went back to heaven and sent the Holy Spirit, for then His Spirit would dwell in each person who put trust in Him. This sending of the Holy Spirit originally occurred on the Jewish feast day of Pentecost. But since then, this "sending" occurs when a person puts faith in Jesus Christ as Lord and Savior.

As we go in Christ's power, He powerfully works through us to convict people of sin and of their need for Christ. He convinces them of who Christ is and brings them to faith in Christ. But where is this power in the average believer today? The church often limps along as if it were powerless and defeated. It doesn't seem to realize the power it has. It doesn't seem to know how to appropriate and use its power.

If there is any message that Bill Bright preaches or teaches more often than the gospel of salvation in Christ, it is the message of how to be filled (directed and empowered) by the Holy Spirit through faith. He reasons that if he can teach others how to appropriate the power of the Holy Spirit in their lives, they in turn can lead others to Christ, and this will result in the multiplication of evangelism.

Again, I remember my first Campus Crusade staff training conference. Bill Bright spoke on how to be filled with the Holy Spirit. I had been to seminary. I had even taken an entire course on the doctrine of the Holy Spirit. But I saw other people around me at the conference who were younger and had less training than I had, yet they were more on fire and effective in ministry than I was. I didn't hear anything radically different from what I had studied in school, but I clearly sensed that I did not really understand in a practical way the power of the Holy Spirit as Bill was explaining it. I had on a number of occasions before sought to surrender my life completely to God, to yield, to dedicate, to rededicate my life totally to Him. I remember that after Bill's message, I went out under the stars in Mound, Minnesota, and prayed, "Lord, what is wrong?"

I didn't hear a voice, but the answer couldn't have been clearer if I had. God was saying, "Martin, the trouble with you is, you are seeking to qualify by your own efforts, by your yielding, by your dedication. You are looking at the quality of your surrender, but you're not expecting Me to do it." I was not by faith appropriating God's power to work in and through me, so I prayed, "I thank You, Father, for what You are going to do." In a new way, I expected God by His Spirit to work in my life, to overcome sin in my life, and He did. I simply expected Him to work through me by His Spirit to introduce others to Christ, and He did. Expectancy—faith—changed my Christian life and ministry. I began to experience the power of the Holy Spirit working in and through me in a new way.[7]

7. We Are to Continue to Fulfill the Great Commission Until Christ Returns

The Great Commission itself was the same for Peter and for Paul, but their specific roles in it were different (Galatians 2:7–9). Jesus gave them each a specific part of the task that He wanted them to fulfill (John 21:15–19; Acts 9:15,16). This is still true today. The Commission for all believers is the same, but the specific role Jesus wants each of us to play varies from person to person. Each of us needs to wait before God and ask Him for His specific instructions for our particular role in helping to fulfill it. He will give us the instructions we need if we ask Him. It may come directly from the Lord, or it may come through other believers, or through God's Word, but He will lead us by His Spirit as we look to Him.

I think of God's special commission to Bill Bright. Bill cautiously tells the story of one night when he was in his senior year of seminary. Not long before that night, he and Vonette, in an act of commitment, had surrendered their lives, their ambitions, and their wills to God, signing the title deeds of their lives over to God. Then on this particular night, Bill and a seminary classmate were seated at a desk in the Brights' living room studying for a Greek exam when suddenly, Bill sensed the presence of God in a way he had never known before. In a brief moment, Bill had the overwhelming impression that the Lord in a supernatural way was unfolding before him a scroll of what he was to do with his life. Bill describes it this way: "At this time and in a very definite way, God commanded me to invest my life in helping to fulfill the Great Commission in this generation, specifically through winning and discipling students of the world for Christ. How to do this was not spelled out in detail; that came later as the Lord gave additional insights for the implementation of the original vision."[8]

I think of Paul's words before King Agrippa concerning the vision God had given him on the road to Damascus, "I did not prove disobedient to the heavenly vision..." (Acts 26:19). Bill Bright has not proved disobedient to his vision. Bill would be the first to admit that he is not perfect and that he makes mistakes of various kinds. But those of us who have worked closely with him must admit that in everything he does he seeks to do it in light of his vision of helping to fulfill the Great Commission in this generation.

One of the reasons Bill does not say much about this experience is that he knows it may cause others to seek experiences. We have enough teaching from the Bible to know that we should be involved in seeking to fulfill the Great Commission—with or without a vision. We also can get enough detail from Scripture and the leading of the Holy Spirit in our hearts to know what part God would have each of us play. A good New Testament example would be Timothy. As far as we know, he never had a vision from God, but he played a vital part in Paul's ministry. He had Paul's example, but he also had the Scriptures and he had the Holy Spirit (2 Timothy 3:10–17). But God had a special role for Timothy to play in the fulfillment of the Great Commission (Philippians 2:19–22).

God has a special role for you to play in the Great Commission. It may be reaching your family, friends, and neighbors for Christ. It may involve helping your church reach your community for Christ. God may want you to become a missionary to some other land, or perhaps help send missionaries to other lands. God may give you a special vision, but more likely He will give you a special burden of heart in one direction or another to use the gifts and abilities He has given you to serve Him to help reach and disciple others. God has a special place for you in the Great Commission. As you are available to Him and are obedient to His directions, He will show you what else He wants you to do in helping fulfill the Great Commission.

WHAT IS "FULFILLING" THE GREAT COMMISSION?

What exactly is meant by the "fulfillment" of the Great Commission? Is it when every person clearly hears the gospel and is given an opportunity to respond? Or is it when everyone who responds to the gospel becomes fully obedient to all of the commands of Jesus Christ? Those who speak of the "fulfillment of the Great Commission" use the idea of fulfillment only in the first sense. I know that is the way Bill uses it. It would be impossible to measure fulfillment in the second sense, but we must emphasize the second part of teaching disciples to become obedient to the commands of Christ or we will never fulfill the Commission in the first sense. But Jesus told the disciples, "This gospel of the kingdom will be preached in the whole world for a testimony to all the nations, and then the end will come" (Matthew 24:14).

I don't suppose that the disciples ever imagined that it would take 2,000 years or more to complete the task. They probably did not dream of the size of the earth nor of the number of ethnic groups or languages in the world. But wrong teachings and practices, ignorance of the teachings of the Word of God, pride, prejudice, materialism, preoccupation with secondary issues, unbelief, and other sins have certainly slowed the Church down much more than the size of the task has.

In the apostolic and post-apostolic ages, Christianity spread around the Mediterranean world and even as far as India. Then it spread north into what is now France, the British Isles, Northern Europe, and later Scandinavia. But with the militant rise of Islam in the 7th century and following, the Church all but disappeared from much of North Africa. The Middle East Nestorian Christianity (the 6th through the 14th centuries) was missionary minded and took the faith to India, Arabia, Turkestan, and for a short time even as far east as China, but for various reasons Christianity did not remain. In the 9th century, Cyril and Methodius took Christianity to the Slavic people. In 988, the Orthodox faith became the official religion of Russia. Following the discovery of America by Columbus, Roman Catholicism spread to Mexico, Central and South America, and part of Canada. The United States and much of Canada were influenced by Protestant Christianity.

But modern Protestant Christianity has emphasized the Great Commission and missionary effort for less than 300 years. As a result of a spiritual awakening, the Moravians in Germany began to study the Bible and see the need to reach the lost. They sent out perhaps the first Protestant missionaries to the Virgin Islands, North America, South America, South Africa, and other places (1732–1760). In the wake of the Great Awakening in the American colonies and the Evangelical Awakening in the British Isles (1735–1760), there was an increased concern for taking the gospel to the world. William Carey, widely known as the "father of modern missions," went to India in 1793. Not only did he see the necessity of translating the Bible into the languages of the various people, but he inspired others to think in terms of missions. With continued waves of spiritual awakenings in the United States, Britain, and Protestant Europe, many more missionaries went out. From 1888 until about 1925, a great missionary effort crescendoed under the Student Volunteers, lead by John R. Mott. With their motto of "the evangelization of the world in this generation," they saw more than 20,000 of their members become foreign missionaries.

Since World War II, evangelical missionary activity has increased. The Wycliffe Bible Translators have set a goal of seeing the Bible translated into all of the languages of the world. Many missionary organizations recently have been meeting and working together in cooperative efforts to reach all the unreached people groups of the world—to pray and reach out to the unreached, especially to resistant areas: countries that are predominantly Muslim, Hindu, Buddhist, Communist, or formerly Communist.

Special efforts were made by various missionary groups, including Campus Crusade for Christ, to meet certain outreach goals toward fulfillment of the Great Commission by the end of the year 2000. Was the Great Commission fulfilled by then? Not fully. Not everyone has heard the good news, but much more progress was made than would have been without this extra concerted effort to do what we could by the close of the millennium. There is still much more to accomplish in this new millennium, but praise God for what has been accomplished in these recent years.

A TIME FOR OPTIMISM

Fifty years ago when Bill Bright began to sign his letters, "Yours for fulfilling the Great Commission in this generation," one did not hear a lot of optimism about the possibility of doing this. But slowly the atmosphere has been changing. A pastor friend shared with me how his whole outlook was changed when a group of Crusade students from a local university, who were new believers, began attending his church because he preached the Bible. He saw their enthusiasm and attitude of expecting God to work.

This revolutionized his own attitude to one of expecting God to work and to fulfill the Great Commission. This story has been repeated hundreds of times. In the past thirty-five years, the whole climate among evangelicals has changed. There is a greater expectancy of seeing God work.

It is exciting to see a single large church in Baker, Louisiana, under the leadership of pastor Larry Stockstill, doing an intensive study of all the unreached people groups of the world. They say that their church will adopt 52 of these groups and will be responsible before God to see that these people are reached for Christ and that a multiplying group of churches is planted among each of those groups. The church will also encourage additional churches and groups to adopt the other unreached people groups.

It is encouraging to see a local pastor like Rick Warren, who is promoting the concept of the "purpose-driven" church, teaching other pastors in the United States and all over the world that the primary purpose of the local church should be "a great commitment to the Great Commandment and the Great Commission."

What a thrill to see the Lighthouse Movement, where millions of church members are being recruited to a "prayer, care, share" strategy to reach their neighbors for Christ! Evangelism is no longer being seen as the job of the so-called "clergy."

In many places, missionaries are starting church-planting movements, which are driven by lay evangelism and where the leaders of the house churches or cell groups are primarily laypeople. These movements increase exponentially as the new churches start other new churches through people from within that people group rather than through professional church planters or missionaries. The Church spreads like wildfire, even in the face of persecution. It sounds like Paul's church-planting ministry in the New Testament times.

People are beginning to go from all sorts of "third-world" countries to the unreached world. It is exciting to see a nation like Korea sending out more missionaries than any Western nation. An increasing number of local churches are sending out both short-term and long-term missionaries.

No one—with the possible exception of Bill Bright and Campus Crusade ministry director Paul Eshleman—could have dreamed of the impact the *JESUS* film has had and is continuing to have. It has been translated into hundreds of languages and is being used by countless missionary organizations around the world. Many people have received Christ; many others have become receptive to the gospel; and many churches have been planted as this tool has been used.

The Bible has been translated and is being translated, printed, and distributed into many new languages. Radio and television have been used by God to open many hearts to the gospel as the gospel is beamed even behind closed doors. The Internet will be used increasingly as a tool for both evangelism and discipleship training in all parts of the globe. What exciting days in which to live! It is "harvest time"!

It is my opinion that through his influence Bill Bright has done more to promote the cause of the fulfillment of the Great Commission than any other person in the second half of the twentieth century. Factors that have contributed to this have been several: his constant emphasis on the Great Commission, his emphasis on the ministry of the Holy Spirit, his emphasis on lay evangelism and on training people for evangelism, his recruiting of leadership and especially the recruiting of national leadership in many countries of the world, his emphasis on fasting and prayer for revival and the fulfillment of the Great Commission, and his vision for projects that impact many, not the least of these being the *JESUS* film. Other chapters of this book explain many of the factors that relate to Dr. Bright's impact.

Other names that might be mentioned in relation to the fulfillment of the Great Commission are Billy Graham and Donald McGavran. Billy Graham is the most visible and doubtless one of the best known people of the twentieth century. Because of his visibility, he has had great influence. Not only is he an evangelist, but he has sponsored a number of conferences that have had a worldwide influence on evangelism. I like to compare Billy Graham and Bill Bright to George Whitefield and John Wesley. Whitefield was the evangelist, the silver-tongued orator who could draw and influence large crowds on both sides of the Atlantic. Wesley was the methodical planner and organizer. He organized and harnessed the energy of the Awakening, and as a result probably had the greater lasting impact on the Church and the world.

Donald McGavran is known as "the father of the church growth movement." I met him through Bud Hinkson, former Crusade director of Eastern Europe, in 1966 when we were training a large Crusade team who would launch the ministry of Campus Crusade in England and then help in Europe. I remember remarking after the meeting, "This is the first person I have ever met who, without being influenced by Bill Bright, is optimistic about the fulfillment of the Great Commission." In the sixties, he was asked to head up the School of World Mission and Institute of Church Growth at Fuller Seminary. He trained many missionaries and nationals from all over the world and imparted to them "church growth eyes" and has left a great impact on world missions. He also influenced such mission leaders as Ralph Winter, the founder of the U.S. Center for World Mission, and Peter Wagner, who in turn have greatly influenced many others.

Even with the accomplishments of these men and many others far too numerous to mention, I still believe that when the final books of history are written, Bill Bright will go down as having had the greatest influence for the fulfillment of the Great Commission of any person in the last half of the twentieth century.

Because of Bill Bright's emphasis on fulfilling the Great Commission and a similar emphasis by others, an ever-widening circle of people are involved in the task of the Great Commission, with a growing optimism about the prospect of its fulfillment in this generation. Increasingly, the proclamation and recruiting phases are being emphasized, along with the teaching-obedience phase. There is also a greater emphasis on the necessity of dependence by faith on the power of the Holy Spirit to enable us to accomplish the task Jesus Christ commissioned us to do. Let me encourage you to ask God, "What do you want *me* to do?" and to keep the vision before your mind by adopting Bill Bright's slogan, "Yours for fulfilling the Great Commission in this generation."

In his faith, Bill Bright seems ever to be out in front of us. A group of us had a meeting with Bill in the closing days of the year 2000. Statistics document that, through Campus Crusade for Christ and the many organizations partnering with us, especially in showing the *JESUS* film in more than 600 languages, in the year 2000 alone more than 20 percent of the world's population had heard the gospel in presentations where the people could be counted and were given a personal opportunity to respond. This does not include others who had seen the *JESUS* film shown over special millennial television showings. It did not include countless other presentations of the gospel by individuals, churches, and Christian organizations that did not make reports through the Campus Crusade network. Bill had just received this information from the vice president of Campus Crusade who was overseeing its international operations. We were rejoicing in the information he shared. Then Bill said to us, "I have recently changed the way I sign my letters. I now write, 'Yours for fulfilling the Great Commission every year until our Lord returns.'"

NOTES

1. In his conferences on the "Purpose-Driven Church," Pastor Rick Warren has coined the phrase, "A great commitment to the Great Commandment and the Great Commission makes a great church." He is right. I have given a twist to his slogan.

2. There is a debate, even between theologically conservative scholars, about whether Mark 16:9–20 was the original, genuine ending of Mark's Gospel. This portion is not found in the two oldest manuscripts of Mark that exist. In these, Mark strangely ends with verse 8. Nor is this portion found in some other very early translations of Mark into other languages, nor in quotations by early Church Fathers. Most later manuscripts include it, but some later manuscripts contain a brief alternate ending that comes after verse 8. This is not the place to debate the issue. Its inclusion or exclusion does not dramatically change the basic elements of the Great Commission. So for our discussion, I will include the Mark passage as genuine. The principles found in it are supported from the rest of the New Testament.
3. John 14–17, often called the "upper-room discourse," is closely related to the Great Commission and gives what Jesus told His disciples the night before His crucifixion, to prepare them for the events that followed that are related to the Great Commission. Actually, much of the New Testament plus a number of Old Testament passages are closely related to the Great Commission.
4. In 1974 in Seoul, Korea, a crowd of approximately one million heard Bill explain the gospel. At the invitation, people were asked to stand indicating that they were either receiving Christ or were making sure of their relationship with Christ. (The field where people were seated was so packed that there was not room for them to come forward.) It appeared that most of the crowd stood. Later, I read a report of evaluations of the conference, in which we had trained more than 300,000 church people for an entire week. Ninety percent indicated that they had trusted Christ or had received personal assurance of salvation during the conference.
5. Some interpreters have suggested that this passage simply means "enlist disciples." They argue that the word "disciple" in the Book of Acts is used as a synonym for Christian or believer. They are correct that the word is used this way in Acts. (See 11:26; 14:20–22,28.) Even so, they overlook the fact that the early Christians were by definition learners.
6. The Greek of Matthew 28:19,20 consists of one *aorist* participle, "going," indicating that this is logically prior to the main verb "make disciples." As implied from the other Great Commission passages, the "going" includes the proclaiming of the gospel as we go. The main verb is an aorist imperative, "make disciples" of all nations, which is the main thing He is commanding them to do. It is followed by two *present* participles, "baptizing" and "teaching." The present tense here implies that these actions are part of how the main verb is to be accomplished. These explain how they are to make disciples. The first is "baptizing," which is the climactic event of the recruiting phase, and is by nature a one-time event for each believer, an initial step in becoming a disciple. The final participle is "teaching," an ongoing phase that takes time. This is followed by the Greek infinitive "to observe," which is a *present* infinitive. This implies an ongoing obedience to the commands of Christ.
7. Bill Bright is convinced that the Holy Spirit is essential to the power needed for the fulfillment of the Great Commission. By the time I first heard him, Bill had written a pamphlet called *Ye Shall Receive Power* explaining the filling of the Holy Spirit by faith. Since then he has written a booklet, similar in style to *The Four Spiritual Laws*, to help Christians explain to others how they too can appropriate the power of the Holy Spirit. The title is *Have You Made the Wonderful Discovery of the Spirit-filled*

Life? He has written Transferable Concepts on *How to be Filled with the Holy Spirit* and *How to Walk in the Spirit*, as well as a book on the Holy Spirit.

8. As Bill sought out the wisdom of mature Christians, he shared his experience with one of his favorite seminary professors, Dr. Wilbur Smith, who in response affirmed repeatedly, "This is of God. This is of God." A day later, Dr. Smith called Bill aside and gave him a piece of paper with the letters CCC written on it, explaining that God had provided the name for Bill's vision, "Campus Crusade for Christ." Bill does not often share much of his vision, except that it became like a tidal wave that involved the entire world.

CHAPTER 6

The Filling of the Holy Spirit

WAYNE JOHNSON
On Staff since 1976
Associate Professor of Theology, International School of Theology

Dr. Bright has frequently commented that he needs just two booklets to start a conversation with anyone: *The Four Spiritual Laws* and the Holy Spirit booklet. Either a person needs to know Christ, or the person knows Christ but may not understand the spiritual abundance and power available to the believer through the Holy Spirit, or the person should be encouraged to share the content of these booklets with others.

This simple paradigm, while in no way exhausting the faith and ministry of Dr. Bright, does indicate the focus and the distinctive commitments that have characterized him since the beginning of his ministry. It is no accident that God has richly blessed the ministry of Campus Crusade for Christ throughout the world. Its commitment to the Great Commission has been accompanied by a corresponding emphasis on the need for continual filling of the Holy Spirit in the lives of believers.

The topic of the Holy Spirit remains a vital and controversial one today. Most theological libraries have shelves full of books on the Holy Spirit. Paradoxically, despite all these books, many of them will begin with the observation that this is one of the most neglected doctrines in the life of the Church.[1] Furthermore, when teaching on the Holy Spirit is not neglected, it is often promoted in an unbalanced way. In *Keep in Step with the Spirit*, J. I. Packer highlights this imbalance while offering his own perspective.[2] Unfortunately, he omits any discussion of one of the central roles, if not *the* central role, of the Holy Spirit: the empowering of believers for the fulfilling of the mission of the church.[3]

In light of the importance of the Holy Spirit in the ministry of Dr. Bright and Campus Crusade for Christ, and because the Spirit's role in the mission of the Church is given little attention, the purpose of this article is twofold. First, I hope to demonstrate the central importance of the Holy Spirit for the fulfillment of the Great Commission. The Great Commission is at the heart of God's activities in the world. It is also inextricably linked to the identity of the Church (what the Church *is*). Second, I intend to explore what it means to be filled with the Spirit in the context of the Church's Great Commission mandate. There is a good deal of ambiguity, confusion, and disagreement about what it means to be filled with the Spirit. By looking at instances of filling in both Testaments as well as other teaching on the Holy Spirit, it is hoped that a more balanced perspective will render some practical help in understanding what it means to be filled with the Spirit.

THE HOLY SPIRIT, THE CHURCH, AND THE GREAT COMMISSION

An often-neglected dimension of the Holy Spirit's work is His role in carrying out the Great Commission. African missionary John Taylor writes:

> The chief actor in the historic mission of the Christian church is the Holy Spirit. He is the director of the whole enterprise... This fact, so potent to Christians in the first century, is largely forgotten in our own ... "It all depends on me" is an attitude bedeviling both the practice and the theology of missions these days.[4]

Undoubtedly, such an attitude is not intentional. Many mission endeavors may function simply from obedience to Christ's command to go into the world. The underlying presumption is that Christ is leading and empowering behind the scenes. The strength of Dr. Bright's emphasis is that the need for and dependence upon the Holy Spirit for missions is elevated to the conscious level. The work of the Great Commission is the work of the Holy Spirit. The work of the Great Commission is fundamentally a work of the Trinity and is central to the identity (calling and purpose) of the Church.

The Missionary Heart of God

Well-known writer and pastor A. W. Tozer notes that what we think about God is the most important thing about us. He contends that "we tend by a secret law of the soul to move toward our mental image of God."[5] Who we understand God to be and what we believe to be His purposes, activities, and expectations will largely determine our character and activities. One aspect of God's character and work that deserves more attention is His *missionary heart.*

From the very beginning of humanity's fall into sin, God's love, concern, and intention to bring salvation to sinful humanity have been evident. The fundamental story of the Bible is the story of God's actions in the world to redeem from judgment a people of His own. The promise of a Redeemer was made at the Fall (Genesis 3:15). Implicit in God's promise to Noah not to again destroy sinful humanity by flood (Genesis 6–9) is the anticipation of salvation. Through Abraham, God raised up a people for Himself who were intended to be a blessing to the world (Genesis 12:3). That Israel had at least some consciousness of its mandate to be a witness to the world is evidenced in such incidents as Solomon's prayer of dedication for the temple (cf. 1 Kings 8:41–43), by David's prayer in Psalm 67:1,2, and by Isaiah's anticipation of a Messiah who would bring a salvation that would include the whole world (Isaiah 49:6).

The birth of the Messiah, Jesus, was the focal point of God's plan to bring salvation to the world. The angels announced to the shepherds that a Savior for all people had been born in Bethlehem (Luke 2:10,11). By the Spirit, Simeon recognized that this Child was a Savior for the Gentiles as well as the Jews (Luke 2:29–32). Alongside His coming as a ransom for our sin (Mark 10:45), Jesus' own stated purpose was that He came to "seek and save the lost" (Luke 19:10; cf. Mark 1:38; Matthew 9:35–38). His purpose was not only to be an atonement for our sin, but also to inaugurate a mission to the world that would continue until He personally returned. Thus, when Jesus gave the command to the disciples (and through them to the whole Church throughout history) to make disciples in every nation (Matthew 28:18–20), He was expressing God's missionary heart and purpose, which have been evident from the beginning. Jesus even stated that God would not bring history to a close until the gospel has gone out to the entire world (Matthew 24:14).

We cannot accurately think about God without including this awareness of His missionary heart. John 3:16 is more than a verse on salvation. It is actually programmatic for God's activities in the world. "God so loved the world that he gave his one and only son, that whoever believes in him shall not perish but have eternal life." Since sin entered into the world, God's activity in human history has centered on delivering us from the effects and guilt of our sin and restoring us to fellowship with Him (2 Corinthians 5:19). The sending of His Son is the center of the Father's actions of love and redemption in human history. God has made Himself known as a God who has a heart of concern, mercy, and love for a world lost in sin, separated from Him, and facing divine judgment. To know and follow this God is to know and follow His missionary heart.

Jesus as God's Missionary

Jesus' primary mission was to seek and save the lost and to give His life as a ransom for many. He came not only as God's provision for salvation, but as God's missionary. The English word *missionary* comes from the Latin *mittō*, which means "to send." The missionary is "one sent" by God and the church to proclaim salvation and to build the Church in the world.

The Gospel of John especially establishes Jesus' *missionary consciousness*. Thirty-eight times in this Gospel, Jesus refers to Himself as having been sent by the Father.[6] Every chapter of the Gospel of John between chapters 3 and 17 contains at least one reference to His status as having been sent by the Father. "For God did not send his Son into the world to condemn the world, but to save the world through him" (John 3:17). "I seek not to please myself but him who sent me" (John 5:30). "Yes, you know me, and you know where I am from. I am not here on my own, but he who sent me is true. You do not know him, but I know him because I am from him and he sent me" (John 7:28,29). Jesus was very conscious of His "missionary" status.

All that Jesus did and said related to the mission on which the Father had sent Him. There was no division between His fundamental identity as the divine atonement and the divine mandate of the Great Commission. Jesus oriented His entire life to prepare Himself for the atonement and to prepare leaders who would continue the Father's mission to the world once He was gone. Jesus knew Himself to be God's missionary and God's mission to the world. Everything He did related to this mission.

The Holy Spirit of God's Mission

Roland Allen, Anglican missionary to China and Africa and a pioneer thinker in the area of the indigenous church, writes:

> Our conception of the work of the Holy Spirit has been almost confined to the revelation of truth, of holiness, of church government and order. Missionary work as an expression of the Holy Spirit has received such slight and casual attention that it might almost escape the notice of the casual reader.[7]

To the degree that Allen's observation is correct, we not only skew our understanding of the work of the Holy Spirit, but the Church also handicaps its God-given mission and purpose of witness. The Church runs the risk of attempting to do in the flesh what can only be accomplished in and through the Holy Spirit.

The Book of Acts has sometimes been called the "Acts of the Holy

Spirit." This is because the real story of Acts is the promise and giving of the Holy Spirit, which resulted in the expansion of the Church. Allen points out that to really appreciate the story of Acts, we need to recognize that this books starts out with a promise, not a command.[8] The disciples were instructed to sit tight until the Holy Spirit was given (Acts 1:4; cf. Luke 24:49). The promise was then given that when the gift of the Holy Spirit did come, they would be empowered to be witnesses to the world (Acts 1:8). Virtually every subsequent mention of the Holy Spirit in Acts involves some mission-oriented activity.

When the Holy Spirit was poured out at Pentecost, the immediate result was proclamation and evangelism (Acts 2). The tongues, which were a tangible evidence of the outpouring of the Holy Spirit, enabled the recipients to declare "the wonders of God in [human] tongues" (Acts 2:11). The Holy Spirit was subsequently given to all who believed (Acts 2:38), and thousands were coming to Christ (Acts 2:41,47). This dramatic harvest was not simply due to the proclamation of the gospel; it was the result of the work of the Holy Spirit through the proclamation of the gospel. This is a fundamental, not a subtle, difference.

Throughout the rest of the book, the Holy Spirit is effecting the mission activity of the early believers.[9] Allen rightfully points out that the story of Acts is not that of early believers witnessing in dedication to Christ or obedience to His commands (though they certainly were). It is really the story of "men who, receiving a Spirit, were driven by that Spirit to act in accordance with the nature of that Spirit."[10] The expansion and successes of the early Church were due to one thing: the work of the Holy Spirit through believers.

Just as our conception of God is skewed if we focus on His attributes to the exclusion of the outworking of His missionary heart, so we will handicap our understanding of the Holy Spirit if we focus on His regenerative and sanctifying work without giving full recognition that the Holy Spirit has come to equip the Church for its mission to the world. God gave the Holy Spirit specifically to carry out His missionary designs by enabling the Church to "seek and to save" a world languishing in need of God's love and forgiveness. A church or believer that is truly *filled with the Spirit* will be active in reaching out to others in need of Christ.

The Church as Mission

It has been argued that missionary concern describes the heart of God, the coming of Christ, and the activities of the Holy Spirit. It naturally follows that God's mission is central to the identity and purpose of the Church.

While the Great Commission (Matthew 28:18–20) is an important passage for the Church's understanding of its calling, I believe John 17:15–18 is an even more important and fundamental passage for understanding the basic identity of the Church. Here Jesus prays,

> "My prayer is not that you take them out of the world but that you protect them from the evil one. They are not of the world, even as I am not of it. Sanctify them by the truth; your word is truth. *As you sent me into the world, I have sent them into the world*" (emphasis added).

The significance of this is heightened in light of Jesus' awareness of being God's missionary to the world. All along Jesus was preparing His disciples to continue the mission He began. Just "as you sent me into the world, I have sent them into the world." These words do more than tell the Church (and individual Christians who compose the Church) what we are to *do:* go into the world. More fundamentally, they tell us what we *are:* God's mission to the world.

The Church's fundamental identity as God's means of fulfilling His mission to the world comes out clearly in the Book of Acts. The pouring out of God's Spirit upon believers in Jerusalem in Acts 2 was the inauguration of a new era in the historical outworking of God's plan of salvation for the world. It marked the beginning of the Church as we now know it and of a time when the Holy Spirit would uniquely indwell all believers to accomplish the work God intended on earth in and through believers. In contrast to the occasional filling or giving of the Spirit in the Old Testament for specific works of service, at Pentecost the Spirit was given specifically (though not exclusively) for the purpose of equipping the Church and all its members for service in the mission and purposes of God.[11] The remainder of the Book of Acts records the expansion and mission activities of a Church filled with the Spirit. Just as Jesus exemplified in His own life, these believers did not view missions simply as something they *did*. God's mission was fundamental to their identity and purpose. Missionary describes what they *were.* They were God's means for fulfilling His mission.

Our lives and the life of the Church will be radically affected when we truly understand the distinction between doing and being. *Missions* will not just be one of the many programs we are involved in or simply another budget category. Rather, it will shape our very identity so that everything we do relates to that *mission*. The reality is that most of us don't see ourselves in these terms, and the Church sees itself more in terms of a fellowship of believers than as God's redemptive mission to the world. The strongest indicator that this is true is that missions and evangelism play a relatively minor role in the activities and budget of most churches, and few believers are involved in evangelism and mission activities (however broadly defined). There may be many reasons for this state of affairs. In part, it relates to how we think about ourselves. However, most fundamentally it comes down to the Church as a whole not being characterized as "full of the Spirit."[12]

The Holy Spirit—who is the Spirit of creation, of regeneration, and of sanctification, who renews our hearts and empowers the believer to live the Christian life—is also the Spirit of mission, accomplishing in the world the redemptive heart and purposes of God. At Pentecost, the Church was filled with the Spirit to empower and enable it to fulfill its mission mandate. This is basic to accurate reflection on the nature and activities of the Trinity as well as on our own identity and conduct in the world.

Being Filled with the Spirit of Mission

Ephesians 5:18 has been a cornerstone in the ministry and teaching of Campus Crusade for Christ. "Do not get drunk on wine, which leads to debauchery. Instead, be filled with the Spirit." This passage has received differing interpretations. On the one hand, most writers agree that "filled" means that the Holy Spirit is in control, having His way in the life of the individual or church. But this is where the agreement ends. When we go further and explore what "filling of the Spirit" means in terms of its outcome in our lives or what one does to be filled, the views begin to diverge between emphasis on manifestations of the Spirit at one extreme and on a more implicit, covert operation of the Spirit in the Christian's life at the other end.

Nowhere does the Bible explain what is meant by being filled with the Holy Spirit. The task of explaining what is meant is further complicated by the fact that the term is not used frequently in the New Testament. The phrase "filled with the Spirit" is used ten times (Luke 1:15,41,67; Acts 2:4; 4:8,31; 9:17; 19:9,52; Ephesians 5:18). All these instances, except one, describe what occurred or the people who were filled. In addition, the description *full of the Spirit* occurs only six times, once in Luke and the rest in Acts (Luke 4:1; Act 6:3,5,8; 7:55; 11:24). Only in Ephesians 5:18 are we commanded to be filled, and this is the only time Paul uses the phrase *filled with the Spirit.*

When considered in the context of the entire New Testament, sixteen occurrences of being filled with the Spirit may not seem all that significant. However, when the concept occurs fifteen times in the two books by the same author, it ought to get our attention. Luke's use of the term *fill* with respect to the Spirit does not define Paul's use in Ephesians 5:18, but it does inform it. Paul knew what *filled with the Spirit* was in the Lucan sense (Acts 9:17). The significance of the mention of Paul being *filled with the Spirit* in Acts 9:17 probably has more to do with his calling to the Gentiles than with his conversion.[13] In what follows, I will explore the meaning of being filled with the Spirit in light of similar terminology in the Old Testament and Lucan writings as well as in the context of Pauline theology.

THE FILLING OF THE SPIRIT AS THE ENABLING FOR THE ACCOMPLISHMENT OF GOD'S MISSION

To understand the filling of the Spirit in the Books of Luke and Acts, we must begin with the Spirit's explicit ministry in the Old Testament. This concerns either the Spirit's work in equipping individuals for specific service to God or the future eschatological work of the Holy Spirit.[14] Luke's particular emphasis on the ministry of the Holy Spirit is mostly continuous with the work of the Spirit in the Old Testament.

The Holy Spirit in the Old Testament

First, in the Old Testament, the Holy Spirit came upon individuals for the purpose of accomplishing a specific work of God. In some cases, for some prophets and kings, the Spirit appears to have stayed with them for the duration of their ministry on behalf of God (cf. Numbers 11:17; 1 Samuel 16:13; 2 Kings 2:9; Zechariah 7:2). In most cases, however, the Holy Spirit's working was limited to a specific task. In all cases, though, the purpose was to accomplish some task for God.

The Bible uses a variety of metaphors in describing the Holy Spirit's influence upon individuals. Often the Spirit is simply said to have *come upon* (or *was on*) the individual (cf. Numbers 24:2, Judges 3:10; 2 Chronicles 15:1; 20:14; 24:20). But the individuals are also said to be *filled* (Hebrew *mālē'*) with the Spirit (Exodus 28:3; 31:3; Deuteronomy 34:9; Micah 3:8), or *clothed with/by* the Holy Spirit (Judges 6:34; 1 Chronicles. 12:18; Hebrew *lābēsh*), or the Holy Spirit *rested upon* or *perched on* (Numbers 11:16,17,25–29; Hebrew *nûach*), or that the Spirit *rushed upon* (Judges 14:6,9; 15:14; 1 Samuel 10:6,10; 1:13; NIV renders it "come upon with power"; Hebrew *tsālach*). Regardless of the terminology, the result is always the same. The individual is enabled by the Holy Spirit to accomplish God's specific work.

The anticipated work of the Holy Spirit with respect to the eschatological kingdom of God is the second aspect of the Holy Spirit's ministry in the

Old Testament. God would put His Spirit upon the Messiah, who would bring in the eschatological kingdom of God (cf. Isaiah 11:2; 42:1; 61:1ff). In addition, the prophets anticipated a general outpouring of God's Spirit when the eschatological kingdom comes (Isaiah 32:15; 44:3). Ezekiel promised a new work of God's Spirit within the individual who would enable one to walk in God's ways (Ezekiel 36:26,27).[15] Joel likewise announces a general outpouring of God's Spirit in the time of the Messiah in which all of God's people would receive gifts and workings of the Spirit that have previously been limited to select servants of God (Joel 2:28,29).

The Old Testament's emphasis is on the work of the Spirit in the equipping for and executing of God's work and purposes through individuals. Being *filled* is but one of several metaphors used to describe the Spirit's work (and the one repeated in the New Testament). Through the Holy Spirit, God's work is accomplished and the individual is equipped and enabled to do that work. From the Old Testament, the Holy Spirit can be regarded as the "Effecter" of God's work and purposes.[16] It was anticipated that this work of the Spirit, which was limited to selected individuals in the Old Testament, would happen to the fullest possible measure in the coming eschatological kingdom.

The Holy Spirit in the Books of Luke and Acts

Now let's look at the references to the Holy Spirit in the books authored by Luke—the Gospel of Luke and the Book of Acts.

In Luke's Gospel, all but one of the references to the Holy Spirit specifically refer to the preparation for and ministry of the Messiah. (The exception is Luke 11:13.) It was announced that John the Baptist would be *filled with* the Spirit in order to carry out his prophetic ministry of preparation for the Messiah (Luke 1:15–17). Elizabeth and Zechariah were *filled with* the Spirit, resulting in their speaking words from God (Luke 1:41; 1:67). Then Simeon came by/in the Spirit (NIV: moved by the Spirit) when Jesus was presented in the temple, resulting again in a prophetic word from God.

The remainder of the instances refer to Jesus. The Spirit descended upon Him when He was baptized, fulfilling the Old Testament promise that God's Spirit would be on the Messiah (Luke 3:21). Being *full of the Spirit*, Jesus was led into the desert to face Satan head on (Luke 4:1ff). It was by the power of the Spirit that Jesus returned to Galilee (Luke 4:14). Finally, Jesus applied Isaiah 61:1 to Himself in the synagogue, "The Spirit of the Lord is on me..." (Luke 4:18ff). That the Spirit was on Jesus not only identified Him as the Messiah but also signified that the Spirit was empowering His life and ministry as the Messiah.

Luke links the presence of the Holy Spirit with the arrival of the Messiah. Each reference to the Spirit explicitly involves the enabling for a work being done by God through human agency. The main difference between the work of the Spirit in the Gospel of Luke and in Acts hinges on what happened at Pentecost. Prior to Pentecost, Luke limits his references to individuals specifically related to the coming of the Messiah. After Pentecost, the Holy Spirit becomes the leading figure in the creation and expansion of the church.

In the Book of Acts, we observe three different senses in which the phrases *filled with* and *full of* the Spirit are used. These three senses are not limited to historical description. They describe how the Spirit works now and will help us understand the notion of *filling with the Spirit* when we turn to Ephesians 5:18.

First, all the believers present in Jerusalem on the Day of Pentecost were *filled with the Holy Spirit* (Acts 2:4). In this particular case, the Spirit's presence was dramatically demonstrated in the speaking of other languages (tongues) and in the praise and proclamation that resulted. Peter explicitly affirmed that this outpouring of the Spirit was in fulfillment of Joel 2:28,29 (Acts 2:14–36). In other words, the promised eschatological age has begun because the promised outpouring of the Spirit had occurred. We are in the anticipated time of the Messiah! The Samaritan believers subsequently *received* the Holy Spirit (Acts 8:17) while the Holy Spirit *came on* those at Cornelius' household and John the Baptist's disciples (Acts 10:44; 19:6). The significance of the reception of the Holy Spirit by the Samaritan believers, by Cornelius' household (that is, Gentiles), and by John's disciples was to show the inclusion of all these in the promise of the Holy Spirit and the eschatological kingdom (that is, in God's work of salvation).[17]

In fulfillment of God's promise, the fullness of the Holy Spirit was being poured out or given to believers. Peter promised that this same gift will be received by every believer upon conversion (Acts 2:38). This is what Paul means when he says in 1 Corinthians 12:13 that we have all been baptized in/by one Spirit into one body.[18] We have not only been united into the body of Christ by the Holy Spirit, but believers have also been given the Holy Spirit in all His fullness. This means that in and through the Spirit, God has given us every resource needed to live and serve as God's purposes for us.

There is a second way in which Luke describes someone as being *filled with* the Spirit. On four occasions, Luke uses the term to describe specific workings of the Spirit. Peter spoke before the Sanhedrin as a result of being *filled with* the Spirit (Acts 4:8).[19] In Acts 4:31, all who were gathered to pray in light of threats against them were "all *filled with* the Holy Spirit and spoke the word of God boldly." In Acts 13:9, Paul, *filled with* the Holy Spirit, spoke a specific word of judgment against the sorcerer Elymas. Probably the incident in which Stephen is described as *full of* the Holy Spirit fits here as well (Acts 7:55). It was at that moment that he had a vision of God's glory and reported his vision. All four of these are instances of a special working of the Spirit through the lives of people who had already received the fullness of the Spirit. In one respect, these occasions parallel the work of the Spirit as described in the Old Testament. In these instances, *filling with the Spirit* describes the fact that the Spirit works in and through individuals to produce the specific works that God desires. These instances describe occasional occurrences, not a continuous state of affairs.

Third, Luke occasionally describes believers as being *full of* the Spirit, a characteristic way of being for the persons to which this applies. In Jerusalem, the Christians were directed to choose seven men who would see to the needs of the widows among them (Acts 6:1–6). They were directed by the apostles specifically to choose men *full of* the Spirit as well as of wisdom. That is, they were to choose men in whom the continuous presence and working of the Holy Spirit was evident. Unfortunately, we are not told more about these men that would help understand what being *full of* the Spirit looked like. But there must have been a difference between men so characterized and other believers who did not quite fit this description. In Acts 11:24, Barnabas is described as *full of* the Spirit and faith. The fullness of the Spirit characterized Barnabas, which appears to be tied into his effectiveness in evangelism.

The programmatic theme of the Book of Acts is Acts 1:4–8: "Do not leave Jerusalem, but wait for the gift my Father promised... In a few days you will be baptized with the Holy Spirit... You will receive power when the Holy Spirit comes on you; and you will be my witnesses... to the ends of the earth." God called the Church to go to the world. God gave His Spirit to empower, or enable, the Church to do just that. The rest of Acts describes how this in fact began to happen during the first generation of believers. The Church went to the world—not *because* they were obedient to Christ's earlier commands or *because* they were inspired by Jesus' life or by what Jesus had done in their lives (which of course they were). The Church was going to the world *because* they were *filled* with the Spirit. The Church had received the fullness of the Spirit, and the Spirit was equipping, empowering, and impelling believers to this end.

EPHESIANS 5:18

The Spirit's work of mission is one of two general ways in which the Spirit works in believers. The other is His work of sanctification. The Spirit not only enables us to authentically serve Christ, but He also enables Christlikeness to characterize us. In other words, the Holy Spirit enables us to live the Christian life in all its dimensions. To be *full of the Spirit* is to be evidencing a growing Christlikeness in our total being (mind, affections, behavior, and so on).

The Meaning of Being Filled with the Spirit

Two questions arise with respect to Ephesians 5:18. Is Paul using the term *filled with/by the Spirit* in the same way Luke does in Acts? If so, which of the three senses discussed above fits Ephesians 5:18?[20] Three considerations will help clarify what Paul is saying and what he is instructing the believer to do.[21]

The first consideration is what I would call the "contrasting analogy." In Ephesians 5:18, Paul contrasts being filled with the Spirit to being drunk with wine.[22] On the one hand, Paul establishes an analogy. Just as drunkenness on wine results in a life or behavior typical of the darkness out of which the Ephesian believers came, so being filled with the Spirit results in behaviors consistent with the Spirit and the light to which they now have been called. However, there is a contrast in behavior and conduct as well. As New Testament scholar Gordon Fee explains, the significance of this contrast along with the word *filled* is that it depicts "a person—and in this case a community!—whose life is so totally given over to the Spirit that the life and deeds of the Spirit are as obvious in their case as the effects of too much wine are obvious in the other."[23] Thus, this analogy implies both behavior and cause of behavior.[24]

The second consideration in understanding the command to be filled by the Spirit is Paul's underlying theology of the Holy Spirit in relation to the Christian life. Again, Fee's insight is helpful about Paul's command to be filled by the Spirit:

> . . . it is merely another way, a more powerfully metaphorical way to be sure, of repeating Paul's basic imperative found in Gal. 5:16: "Walk in/by the Spirit." All truly Christian behavior is the result of being Spirit people, people filled with the Spirit of God, who live by the Spirit and walk by the Spirit.[25]

A brief look at this "basic imperative" in Galatians 5:16–25 will be helpful as it summarizes the foundation of the Christian life. This passage instructs us that the life of a Christian is life in the Holy Spirit (Galatians 5:25, "Since we live by the Spirit . . ."). The believer's spiritual life is both the ongoing work of the Holy Spirit and the realm in which he lives. Romans 8:5–17 teaches that the Christian no longer belongs in the realm of the present world, which is lived according to the flesh. Rather, he belongs to a heavenly realm which is the product and ongoing work of the Holy Spirit. The realm of the Spirit is typified by such fruit of the Spirit as listed in Galatians 5:22,23. This is in stark contrast to the works of the flesh, listed in verses 19–21.

Galatians 5:25 continues to exhort us Christians that, because we live by (and in) the Spirit, we ought to keep step with the Spirit. In other words, our lives ought to conform to the values, practices, and behaviors in keeping with the Holy Spirit. A proper understanding of verse 16 is important here. Because we belong to this realm, keeping in step with the Spirit is essentially a matter of doing Christian activities and behaviors. Throughout the Church's history, this has probably been the most common conception, as practiced, of what it means to be a Christian. Because we belong to Christ, our primary task is to obey: do the things Christ has instructed us to do and follow the instruction and example given us by the Spirit and by Christ. It is assumed that the Holy Spirit makes obedience possible.

Galatians 5:16, however, says far more than this: "Live by the Spirit, and you will not gratify the desires of the sinful nature." The NIV rendering here is actually very unfortunate. The word here is *peripateō*, which has the basic meaning *to walk*.[26] Unfortunately, many miss the real impact of this command by taking the dative case of Spirit in a locative sense, missing the agency or instrumentality of the Spirit. When taken only in a locative sense, walking in the Spirit is too easily reduced to an ethical mandate. That is, conduct your life according to the realm of the Spirit. The caution of Galatians 3:3 applies to any of us who reduce the Christian life to conformity to Christian conduct. "After beginning with the Spirit, are you now trying to attain your goal by human effort?" The danger is not so much that our theology or theories of sanctification and the Christian will advocate self-effort. The danger is that because we take for granted, or are unaware of, the work of the Spirit, we in practice reduce the Christian life to personal efforts of obedience and conformity, however well-intentioned.

Therefore, it is important not just to recognize the instrumentality of the Spirit in Galatians 5:16, but also to emphasize the immediate and ongoing agency of the Spirit. Just as in Ephesians 5:18, Fee contends that in Galatians 5:16 the instrumental sense is primary, though we should not dismiss the locative sense.

> Thus the combination of the imperative "walk" joined by the dative "by the Spirit," puts the two basic matters together. Ethical life is still a matter of "walking in the ways of God," but for Paul this is empowered for God's new covenant people by God's empowering presence in the person of the Holy Spirit.[27]

The ethical life of the believer (that is, genuine Christlikeness) is possible only when the Spirit produces this in our lives. This is the basis for freedom and victory over the flesh. Galatians 5:16 does not mean "don't gratify the flesh and then you'll be living or walking in the Spirit." Nor does it mean "walk according to the ways of Christ and then there'll be no room for gratification of the flesh." Rather, it means that when the Holy Spirit is producing His effects in our life, the flesh will not have its ways. Success over the flesh does not come from obedience. It is the result of the Holy Spirit producing Christlikeness in our lives.

The third consideration in understanding what it means to be filled by the Spirit is the way this term and similar terms are used in Scripture. We have already noted that when the term *filled* (and similar metaphors) is used in the Old Testament and in Luke and Acts, the emphasis is always on what the Holy Spirit is accomplishing at that moment. We are not told how the Spirit fills or exactly what happens in us. But we are told the results. The result is always the accomplishment of what God wants to do at that moment. The Holy Spirit is unhindered in accomplishing what He desires.

Is Paul using the term *filled* in the same way as it is used in Acts, and if so, which particular usage applies? Paul's understanding of the work of the Holy Spirit and usage of the term *filled* is in full agreement with Luke in the Book of Acts. However, Paul's usage in Ephesians 5:18 is most likely in line with Acts when *filled* is used to describe a believer characterized by the life of the Spirit. Since we have depended on Fee's exegetical and theological study so much, it seems fitting to conclude this section by quoting him once again.

> Here, then, is the ultimate imperative in the Pauline corpus: God's people so filled by/with the Spirit's own presence that they come to know God in all his fullness and reflect such in the way they live in relationship to one another and to God himself.[28]

To be filled with the Spirit means that the Holy Spirit is accomplishing in an unhindered way what He wants to accomplish at that moment. Since the command to be filled is in the present tense, the exhortation is to let this continually be the case so that the Spirit is continually producing His desired effects in and through our lives.

How to be Filled with the Spirit

What is the appropriate response of the Christian to Ephesians 5:18? The fact that Paul commands us to be filled clearly implies that *filling of the Spirit*, as Paul speaks of it here, is not a reality to be assumed in our lives. It is possible not to be *filled* by the Spirit. Otherwise, the command would not make sense. The unfortunate reality is that many of us are not filled by the Spirit or spend considerable periods of our lives not filled. First, let us summarize what we understand by filling of the Spirit in this context, then consider what is the implied response to Paul's command to be filled.

All Christians have received the Spirit in all His fullness at conversion (the first sense in Acts as discussed earlier). Every Christian always has all the Spirit, who was poured out for the Church at Pentecost, and each of us has been given all of God's Spirit that God intends to give. But this is not what Paul is addressing here. Therefore, the command does not imply that we are to receive the Spirit anew or that we expect to receive more of the Spirit than we already have.

When a believer is *full* of the Spirit, he is seeing the evidence of the Spirit's work in and through his life, and others are seeing the Spirit's work manifested in his life. The Spirit's work in his life is unhindered and is being more fully expressed. Being *filled* with the Spirit in this sense is not an issue of maturity. It is a matter of the Spirit being able to fully express Himself and work in a believer's life. As in all cases in which the Spirit is said to *fill* or *come upon* or similar expressions, the issue is not what the individual does, but on what the Spirit does. Thus, in the command of Ephesians 5:18, the issue is not what we do or are to do. The focus is on the Spirit's *filling*, that is, working out His purposes and effects in our lives.

If this is the case, then Paul is not implying that we *do* something when we are commanded to be *filled by the Spirit* in Ephesians 5:18. The implied command is to let the Holy Spirit *do* something in our lives. The desired outcome in the immediate context that follows Ephesians 5:18 is worship, mutual encouragement, and submission. The outcome of the principle generally applied is that the Spirit will be able to work freely in and through our lives according to the Spirit's desire and the needs of the situation. This is not to suggest that our response is to be utterly passive. The implied response to the command is first volitional (reflected in our attitude and will) and second reflected in our action. An active response is expected.

Faith is the first implied response to the command. Faith is the foundational element to every aspect of the Christian life. Paul says, "Just as you received Christ Jesus as Lord, continue to live in him" (Colossians 2:6). Faith is how Christ is received. Faith is how we continue to live in Christ. It is no more possible to live a godly life on our own as a Christian than it was to become a Christian without faith. Both conversion and sanctification are wholly a work of God. There are several dimensions to faith, but in essence faith involves two basic aspects. First, it involves belief, or accepting as true what God says. Second, it involves trust. We personally embrace what God says as true by depending upon God to do what He said He would do. Faith involves acting upon what we accept as true.

A second response follows from both the import of the command itself and from the meaning of being filled. This is a response of *yieldedness.* I suppose the Holy Spirit could forcibly take control and produce His desired effects. This may have been the case when Baalam's donkey spoke (Numbers 22:28) or when Caiaphas spoke prophetically (John 11:49–52). But this is not the normal way in which the Holy Spirit works. Nor does the Holy Spirit force the process of sanctification upon us. We must be yielded to the Holy Spirit in both sanctification and service. True faith is always accompanied by yieldedness to what God wants to do in your life.

A third response to the command is to *confess* any known sin to God. Sin grieves the Holy Spirit and hinders both fellowship and the Spirit's working. Sin keeps us from experiencing all that God has for us through His Spirit. Because of this, there can be no real yieldedness unless there is also confession of known sin. Sin has many roots—rebellion, desire for things of the world, lust of the flesh, fear, disappointment with God, even emotional scars and baggage, to name a few. In each case, though, a believer closes himself off from what God's Spirit wants to do. There will always be sin in our lives in the sense of falling short of God's standards and expectations. The Spirit addresses this in His timing as we walk in the Spirit. When the Spirit makes these things known, the Spirit is working. We confess the sinfulness, thank God for making these things known to us, and continue walking in the Spirit. It is the deliberate (though not always conscious to us) sinning that grieves the Spirit and must be confessed if we are to be yielded to what God wants us to do.

A fourth implied response is *obedience*—both generally to what God says in Scripture and specifically to what God may be saying at the moment. Obedience is a response that flows out of the responses of faith, yielding, and confession. Faith and yieldedness that do not result in obedience are meaningless. Obedience that does not issue from faith and yieldedness is vain self-effort at best.

Finally, in Campus Crusade for Christ literature, we speak of the need to *desire* to be filled by the Spirit almost as a condition of filling. This is simply a matter of making explicit what is implicit in the response to the command to be filled. For if we don't want the Spirit's fullness in our experience, we won't seek it, nor is it profitable to go through the motions. On the other hand, if it is our desire to know the Spirit's presence in all His fullness, we can be assured that this is God's desire as well. "Blessed are those who hunger and thirst for righteousness, for they will be filled" (Matthew 5:6; NASB says "satisfied"). Jesus promises that those who sincerely and deeply desire to experience righteousness in relation to God will experience satisfaction within themselves and within their relationships with others. Those who elevate other desires will not enjoy the full blessings of righteousness. The same is true for experiencing the fullness of the Holy Spirit's work of sanctification and equipping for service. The sad reality is that out of fear, ignorance, and other sins, many Christians don't know this fullness and are not serving God as He intends. For those whose heart is to know God in all His fullness, to walk with God, and to serve God, they will be satisfied through God's Spirit. In the meantime, the Spirit seeks to lead us to the point of desiring this fullness.

The specific manner in which a believer appropriates the fullness of the Holy Spirit is not given to us. It is not so important whether a person prays a specific prayer, or quietly expresses this desire in his heart, or simply lives out his faith in yieldedness. In fact, it is probably not even necessary that he is conscious that he is responding specifically to the Spirit. However, it is to the believer's advantage to be knowledgeable of the gift of the Spirit which we all have and of the fact that no genuine aspect of Christian life and service is possible apart from the Spirit. The Bible inevitably encourages us to continually and consciously seek the will and mind of Christ, thereby avoiding the prospect of the Christian life becoming simply routine and habitual. To know this increases the likelihood of experiencing the power of Christ's presence through the Holy Spirit. Being led in a specific prayer to be filled with the Spirit does not, of course, in itself bring about this filling. It can, however, serve to concretely help us understand and begin to embrace the truth of the Spirit-filled life.

The real genius (if I may put it this way) of the ministry of Bill Bright and Campus Crusade for Christ is not its commitment to the Great Commission, nor its tools (*The Four Spiritual Laws*, the Holy Spirit booklet, Transferable Concepts, etc.), nor in its strategies (win-build-send, evangelism, follow-up, discipleship). These are all important and have been valuable parts and contributions of this ministry. The real genius has been the emphasis on the ministry of the Holy Spirit. As shown, the Holy Spirit is the One who is carrying out God's purposes of mission. God's mission reflects the very being and activity of the triune God. For Scripture reveals from Genesis to Revelation that the Father's purpose and heart is to reverse the effect of sin in the world and to redeem a people of His own who will know Him, love Him, and serve Him. Christ the Son came as God's missionary to make God known, but especially to make salvation possible through His life and atonement. The Holy Spirit has been the One carrying out the triune God's purposes in history from the beginning, and "in these last days" has been poured out upon the Church specifically to fulfill God's purposes in history. The Great Commission is the work of the Holy Spirit. To be *filled with the Spirit* is not just victory over sin, holiness, and Christlikeness. It will also be shown in living out our identity as God's missionaries to the world. May we as individuals and as the Church keep in step with the Spirit.

I encourage you to consider how the ministry of the Holy Spirit and God's mission of reaching others for Christ and helping them become obedient disciples of Christ are reflected in your life and ministry. Ensure that both of these are vitally linked.

NOTES

1. For example, see Michael Green's observation in *I Believe in the Holy Spirit* (Grand Rapids, MI: Wm. B. Eerdmans Publishing Company, 1975), 11.
2. J. I. Packer, *Keep in Step with the Spirit* (Grand Rapids, MI: Fleming H. Revell, 1984), 17–54.
3. In fairness, Packer may not be presenting a full theology of the Holy Spirit in *Keep in Step with the Spiri*t. A primary concern of the book is to interact with characteristic issues related to the Charismatic perspectives on the Holy Spirit.
4. John V. Taylor, *The Go-Between God* (New York: Oxford University Press, 1979), 3.
5. A. W. Tozer, *The Knowledge of the Holy* (New York: Harper and Row Publishers, 1961), 9.
6. See John 3:34; 4:34; 5:23,24,30,36–38; 6:29,38,39,44,57; 7:16,28,29,33; 8:16,18,26,29,42; 9:4; 10:36; 11:42; 12:44,45,49; 13:20; 14:24; 15:21; 16:5; 17:3,8,18,21,23,25; 20:21.
7. David M. Paton, ed., *The Ministry of the Holy Spirit: Selected Writings of Roland Allen* (Grand Rapids, MI: Wm. B. Eerdmans Publishing Company, 1960), 21.
8. Ibid., 4.
9. For specific examples, see Acts 4:23–32; 5:29–32; 6:8,10; 7:53; 8:26,39; 10:19; 11:12,15–18,22–24; 15:8,27. For the occasions on which Paul was being led by the Spirit in his ministry, see Acts 9:17–20; 13:4,9; 16:6; 20:22–24; 21:11.
10. Ibid., 5.

11. For an excellent discussion of the role of the Holy Spirit in the Old Testament and a perspective that the most unique aspect of the general outpouring of the Holy Spirit at Pentecost was to equip and enable all believers to serve God's purposes, see Gary Fredricks, "Rethinking the Role of the Holy Spirit in the Lives of Old Testament Believers," in *Trinity Journal* 9NS (1988), 81–104.

12. This is not to suggest that the Church and believers do not have the Spirit, or even that the Spirit is not working in other dimensions of our lives. However, I am suggesting that biblically speaking a church or individual that can be characterized as "full of the Spirit" will be fruitfully involved in the mission activities that are at the heart of God's intentions and purposes.

13. In fact, that may be the main reason Luke includes mention of the filling with the Spirit here. In Acts 9:15,16, Ananias is told of Paul's calling to the Gentiles. Given both the Old Testament emphasis on the Spirit's work in equipping for service and Luke's similar focus in the Gospel and Acts, this may be the real significance here. Paul has been uniquely called out by God to take the gospel to the Gentiles. The Spirit has been given to equip him for this task. Of course, Paul's conversion is part of this. But only a brief mention is made of his being baptized (Acts 9:18).

14. I say "explicit" ministry because some maintain that salvation and sanctification are no more likely apart from the working of the Spirit in the Old Testament than they are in the New Testament. While this aspect of the Spirit's work is not discussed in the Old Testament, this in itself would not rule this out. However, the Spirit is spoken of explicitly as working in specific individuals from time to time to accomplish God's purposes.

15. Ezekiel uses the Hebrew *`āsāh*, meaning "to do or make." Keil & Delitzsch indicate that the syntax is difficult but conclude that it means "to make or effect your walking." C. F. Keil and F. Delitzsch, *Commentary on the Old Testament* (Grand Rapids: Wm. B. Eerdmans Publishing Co., reprinted 1983), vol. 9, p. 111. It would be the Spirit of God within who would effect inner transformation resulting in adherence to God's law and ways.

16. Boyd Hunt gives the Holy Spirit this title. He summarizes the general work of the Holy Spirit as being "the effecter of God's comprehensive kingdom purpose as revealed through the crucified yet risen Christ." Boyd Hunt, *Redeemed! Eschatological Redemption and the Kingdom of God* (Nashville: Broadman and Holman Publishers, 1993), 15. Even before the coming of Christ, the Holy Spirit is effecting God's mission purpose (historical salvation actions of God).

17. This is clearly brought out in the case of Cornelius. See Acts 11:15–17; 15:8,9.

18. This is supported by the fact that Luke cites Jesus, who described the impending event of Pentecost as being "baptized with the Holy Spirit" (Acts 1:5).

19. F. F. Bruce says, "We should distinguish between this use of the aorist passive, denoting a special moment of inspiration, and the use of the adjective [full] to denote the abiding character of a Spirit-filled person." In "The Book of Acts," revised edition, *The New International Commentary on the New Testament* (Grand Rapids: Wm. B. Eerdmans Publishing Co., 1988), 92, footnote 18.

20. I pose these questions because some writers contend that Paul's use of the term *filled* is different than Luke's. I am hoping to demonstrate that all three ways in which Luke uses the term are but different aspects of the working of the Holy Spirit. Although Paul's emphasis may be different, his teaching of the work of the Holy Spirit provides a fuller understanding of the phenomenon described in Acts rather than a competing or different understanding.
21. I should mention an assumption I am making here. Paul is using the term *filled with/by the Spirit* in a specific context, and the contextual outcomes of filling are manifested in community worship and in submission. I will not be dealing with the specific context and outcomes so much as what I understand to be the general principle. I am following Gordon Fee, who contends this is but a particular, perhaps dramatic, way for Paul to talk about or apply the concept of *walking in/by the Spirit* which reflects his fundamental understanding of the Christian life.
22. Scholars tend to see the reference to being drunk with wine as either an analogy or a contrast. If viewed analogically, the emphasis is usually on the Holy Spirit as the source of God's power, just as wine is the source of drunkenness. If this is to be seen as a contrast, then the emphasis might be on behavior stemming from the Spirit that is polar opposite to the behavior of our pre-Christian days. I suggested the phrase "contrasting analogy" because there seems to be both an analogy and a contrast involved here.
23. Gordon D. Fee, *God's Empowering Presence: The Holy Spirit in the Letters of Paul* (Peabody, MA: Hendrickson Publishers, 1994), 721.

24. There is some debate over whether the phrase *filled with the Spirit* should be understood as filled *by* the Spirit or *with/in* the Spirit. In the first case, the emphasis is on the Spirit as the instrument or source of filling. When taken this way, many emphasize the empowering or actions of the Holy Spirit over the substance or content with which one is filled (though the context of Ephesians 5:18–21 tells us the specific outcomes Paul had in mind in this particular situation). The other way of understanding it emphasizes the content or substance with which one is filled, i.e., the Holy Spirit Himself. Or sometimes, the emphasis is put on the *sphere* into which the Christian is placed. Because we are baptized by the Holy Spirit into the Body of Christ we have been placed into the realm of life in the Spirit and we are to live accordingly (cf. Rom. 6:5–14).

    These are subtle nuances of meaning, but they have important implications. The situation is made more difficult because the Greek language permits both ways of understanding this phrase and this is the only time *filled with/by the Spirit* includes the preposition *en*. And because Paul does not use the term *fill* in relation to the Spirit anywhere else in his epistles, we cannot draw conclusions from other Pauline usages. Gordon Fee is probably right in asserting that in light of Paul's overall theology of the Holy Spirit (which we'll look at next), it is unnecessary and artificial to separate the two emphases in this case. He contends the instrumental sense is most likely Paul's intention, i.e., be filled *by* the Spirit. But it naturally follows that the Spirit is also the substance of filling. The Spirit fills the believer with His own fullness, which is also the fullness of Christ and the fullness of God. Fee argues that being filled by the Spirit is essentially analogous to what Paul is saying in Ephesians 3:14–19. In this case, Paul's prayer is that the Ephesians "be empowered by the Spirit so that as Christ thus dwells in them by the Spirit they come to be 'filled unto the fullness of God' himself." (See Fee, p. 721, footnotes 196 and 722.)

25. Fee, 721.
26. The word translated *live* in verse 25 is *zaō*, which basically means to live.
27. Fee, 430.
28. Fee, 722.

CHAPTER 7

Prayer

M. EVERETT DAVIS
On Staff since 1963
National Prayer Coordinator, JESUS Video Project

Author and speaker S. D. Gordon writes, "The greatest thing anyone can do for God and man is pray." He goes on to say, "It is not the only thing. But it is the chief thing."[1]

This quote is certainly true of Dr. Bright's approach to life and ministry. Many disciplines characterize his life, but the one that seems to impact and support all others is *prayer*. This was true from the very inception of Campus Crusade for Christ, as the movement was actually birthed through prayer. He says, "Vonette and I and our friends undergirded the ministry in constant prayer. We often found ourselves praying, 'Lord, where do you want us to launch this ministry?'"

In *Come Help Change the World*, Dr. Bright recalls that the ministry was launched at UCLA with the aid of a 24-hour prayer chain that was organized by "dividing each day into 96 fifteen-minute segments. Church friends, advisory board members, and other caring Christians were invited to sign up for one or more of the segments each week." Very positive results soon transpired at the Kappa Alpha Theta Sorority. Bill and Vonette prayed for one or two students to trust Jesus as their Savior that evening. "At least 30 of the women indicated they wanted to know Jesus Christ personally."

Dr. Bright gives his reason for this success, and ultimately the successes for years to come: "I am convinced that the positive results we witnessed were due to two things: First, we were simply being obedient to God's obvious direction in our lives, and second, through the 24-hour prayer chain and many hours of fervent prayer, we surrounded everything we did with constant prayer for God's guidance and blessing." He felt that "this unprecedented demonstration of God's blessing was no accident because during the next few months more than 250 students committed their lives to Jesus Christ." Prayer made the difference and is still a key emphasis today.

A COMMITMENT TO PRAYER

Shortly before that first meeting at UCLA, Bill and Vonette had been on their knees surrendering themselves and all they possessed through a signed contract to God, their heavenly Father and Master. They were simply acting out God's promise to guide and use them. They belonged to Him.

Dr. Bright took God's promises very seriously. Jeremiah 33:3 says, "Call to Me and I will answer you, and I will tell you great and mighty things, which you do not know" (NASB). In Ephesians 3:20, Paul indicates there is more to asking than we could imagine, "Now to Him who is able to do far more abundantly beyond all that we ask or think, according to the power that works within us" (NASB).

Dr. Bright believed that God's power was at work in him. Over the years, he asked God and asked big. Some people questioned his grand prayer requests and plans, yet in simple faith he continued to believe God for "great and mighty things." Dr. Bright proved, by faith, God's original vision for Campus Crusade for Christ. Dr. Bright has always dreamed big and prayed big because he believes in and serves the Almighty God. He says, "Think of it: the omnipresent Creator God, who created the heavens and earth and the vastness of billions of galaxies, has come to die on the cross for our sins and to take up residence within us. There is nothing too big for us to attempt for the glory of God."

From the time Dr. Bright committed his life to Christ, he made evangelism and discipleship a priority. These are still the hallmarks of Campus Crusade. Evangelism coupled with prayer is critical in reaching people for Christ. Dr. Bright says in the *Ten Basic Steps Toward Christian Maturity*, "The divine order is first to talk to God about men, and then talk to men about God." He goes on to say, "Prayer is really the place where people are won to Christ; service is just gathering in the results of our prayer."

A few years ago, Dr. Bright made a list of lessons he had learned about evangelism and follow-up. Among the thirty lessons listed was prayer. He said, "Prayer is one of the most important factors in successful evangelism and follow-up. The Scripture gives our basis for prayer: We have not because we ask not (James 4:2). God is 'not willing that any should perish' (2 Peter 3:9). God wants all of His children to be more and more like Christ in every way. Therefore, according to 1 John 5:14,15, we know God will hear and answer if we pray for multitudes to become Christians and for many to become disciples, because we know that we pray according to God's will."[2]

The privilege of prayer and the promises of God encouraged Dr. Bright from the moment he accepted Jesus Christ as his Savior and Lord. One of his early prayer requests was for his childhood friend, Vonette, to commit her life to Jesus Christ. She received Jesus three years after he started praying, before they were married. As a couple, they have practiced praying together before they go to bed at night, the first thing as they get out of bed in the morning, and many times during the day as suggested in 1 Thessalonians 5:17 ("Pray without ceasing," NASB). These daily times of prayer when they are together are part of what helps sustain the ministry and also forms the basis of deep communication and intimacy in their marriage. Bill states in *Managing Stress in Marriage*, "No matter how much public ministry we have or how many individuals we introduce to Christ, that's only part of our lives. The success or failure of our marriage and our service to the Lord stems from the private sanctuary of our hearts. A consistent prayer life keeps us in touch with the Source of our success."

PRAYER AND THE GROWTH OF THE MINISTRY

Another example of a mighty answer to prayer was the bold prayer request in 1969 for finances to purchase Arrowhead Springs in California as the headquarters and training center for Campus Crusade for Christ. (Accounts of the purchase can be read in *Amazing Faith* and *Come Help Change The World.*) Much prayer, planning, and some contracts ultimately brought in $2 million. There were many challenges to the process, but Dr. Bright says, "Every financial move was a prayerful one." Prayer was not only Dr. Bright's avenue, but also that of the board, staff, students, and friends of the ministry. Dr. Bright has dedicated his life to following God, no matter what, even when there were no extra dollars. The purchase of Arrowhead Springs prompted Bill and Vonette to pray "that everything God would do through Campus Crusade for Christ and through their own lives would be characterized by the supernatural and the miraculous," so that onlookers would realize God was responsible, bringing glory to God instead of to man.[3] After all, God is the all-powerful, sovereign King of the universe.

Dr. Bright has often said that the ministry has no money left over at the end of each day. God always supplies what is needed, when needed, but not enough to put away for a rainy day. From an urgent need of $485 to $10,000, and now several million dollars, God continues to supply, and to a large extent, supply through prayer.

To help expand the needed prayer requested by people all over the nation, a prayer chapel was built at Arrowhead Springs in 1969. It housed the telephones, notebooks of requests and answers, and a prayer room for intercessors who were part of the 24-hour prayer ministry. Dr. Bright participated in the prayer chain, and he encouraged the headquarters' staff to do the same—sign up and pray for a segment of time every week. Bill was and is so committed to the prayer chain that he says, "If any staff does not want to be on the prayer chain, maybe they should consider if this is the right place for them."

As the staff and ministry of Campus Crusade for Christ grew, Vonette felt that she was making less of a contribution. In 1971, three outstanding Christian women leaders shared with her how women had been organized into prayer groups to pray for the Billy Graham Crusade in London. Vonette was concerned about the moral condition of our country and felt that prayer was the way she could make a significant impact for our country. After reading Acts 4:24, she said, "This is it! Prayer mobilization can unite Christians against the forces of evil in our land. With prayer, we can draw God's power into all the affairs of our nation."

Vonette took her idea to Bill, and he exclaimed, "I like it. Do it."

Soon after, the Great Commission Prayer Crusade was launched with the first large prayer focus for Explo '72, a gathering of more than 80,000 students and leaders to be trained in evangelism and discipleship in Dallas, Texas. The Great Commission Prayer Crusade conducted prayer workshops, organized prayer rallies, developed prayer resources, published a monthly prayer newsletter, and mobilized people all over the United States to pray. When the Great Commission Prayer Crusade was started, it was one of a handful of prayer ministries that developed prayer resources and organized prayer groups.

Vonette says, "Involvement in a prayer ministry has added to our entrepreneurial responsibilities." With Bill's encouragement and support, Vonette has been instrumental in helping to start the National Prayer Committee. She also gave leadership to the International Prayer Assembly of the Lausanne Committee for World Evangelization and served on its Executive Committee. She helped steer a bill through Congress for the National Day of Prayer to be set each year on the first Thursday of May.

Today, Earl Pickard directs the Campus Crusade U.S. Prayer Ministry, which is called Prayerworks. The Campus Crusade International Prayer Ministry, which is still called the Great Commission Prayer Crusade, is directed by Dr. Ben Jennings. These prayer ministries develop resources that are continually being brought before people by way of materials, seminars, and strategy ideas.

In 1981, Bill and Vonette asked me to give leadership to the Great Commission Prayer Crusade because they felt it best for Vonette to travel more with Bill and to expand her speaking opportunities. In January 1983, my family and I moved to Arrowhead Springs, California, to begin giving leadership to the U.S. part of the Great Commission Prayer Crusade. Shortly thereafter, Dr. Ben Jennings came to lead the International part. I had the opportunity to have many meetings with Dr. Bright, and no matter what the subject, we always prayed, whether it was an issue of the 24-hour prayer chain, ministry finances, or involving more people in prayer. Dr. Bright always wanted to know how I personally was doing. One day, I shared that I recently found my staff account in deficit. Bill prayed for my family and me, and then said that he and Vonette would like to help meet some of that shortfall.

PRAYER AS A LIFESTYLE

I remember a time when I was traveling with Dr. Bright while he visited several countries in West Africa. We would pray in the morning, during the day, before personal appointments, and before speaking engagements. One day, we were in an airplane going down the runway for a takeoff when we heard a loud explosion. One of the two jet engines blew just before we lifted off the ground. The airline had to call another country for a replacement aircraft, meaning that we would stay overnight, missing our engagements. As we were giving thanks to God for our safety and the missed engagements, he said, "These people are probably very open to spiritual matters right now. Why don't we share the gospel with anyone who is open?" So we did!

Ken Kremer, a fellow Campus Crusade staff member, related that when he traveled with Dr. Bright in Asia, Bill was always up in the morning before everyone else—praying. On one of those early mornings, Dr. Bright finished his prayer time and began polishing the shoes of the national staff.

Brad Bright, Bill's son, said of his father, "Whenever things came into his life that I regarded as problems, his first response was always to go to his knees and say, 'Father, what do you want me to do?' It really was just another opportunity to see God work, whether it was big or small."

Another testimony to Dr. Bright's commitment to prayer is from Dr. Earl Radmacher, past president of Western Baptist Theological Seminary in

Portland, Oregon. After speaking to a conference of students hosted by Campus Crusade for Christ, he said, "We met together for prayer before we left. We prayed on the way to the meeting in the car. We prayed when we got to the assignment before we got out of the car. All of us continued in a spirit of prayer before the meeting, and on the way home we prayed, thanking the Lord for what He had done, asking Him to continue to work in the hearts of the students. Never before had I seen such a great volume of prayer surrounding any other Christian activity. I concluded that these people associated with Campus Crusade for Christ must be truly dependent upon the Lord, or they wouldn't pray so much."[4]

In staff leadership meetings, Dr. Bright not only encouraged prayer at the meetings, but also ensured that prayer would be organized for the various decisions and events that flowed out of those meetings. At one small meeting of staff leadership, a fairly new staff member was making a presentation for the leaders to consider. He was anxious to get started and began as soon as everyone sat down. Dr. Bright stopped him and asked that the meeting be committed to God in prayer. The staff member was a little embarrassed, but caught the importance of prayer.

Howard Ball, a long-time Campus Crusade member, says that Dr. Bright "simply takes God at His Word." The study of God's Word, His character, and His promises are foundational to Dr. Bright's prayer life. In claiming God's promises, he says we are to: "1) Ask expectantly; 2) Ask believing; 3) Ask according to God's will; and 4) Ask in Jesus' name." No matter what the request, large or small, for people or for finances, he quickly says, "To God be the glory."

POWER IN PRAYER

One may ask, "What makes a person like Dr. Bright powerful in prayer?" Dr. Bright practices what he gives as the ingredients for a powerful prayer life. These ingredients, as listed in the *Ten Basic Steps to Christian Maturity Teacher's Manual*, are as follows:

- Faith—Hebrews 11:1,6
- Yieldedness—Romans 12:1,2
- Steadfastness and abounding in God's work—1 Corinthians 15:58
- Righteousness—James 5:16
- The filling of the Holy Spirit—Ephesians 5:18
- Abiding in Christ and letting His Word control us—John 15:7

- Thanksgiving in all things—Ephesians 5:20 and 1 Thessalonians 5:18
- Praying according to God's will as revealed in His word—1 John 5:14,15

Dr. Bright's commitment to prayer is so important that he has encouraged the staff in various locations to set aside a half-day per week for prayer. For many, the half-day is spread over the week, giving some time each day for prayer. Also, twice a year, in October and April, a full day called Worldwide Day of Prayer is devoted to prayer. It is "worldwide" because it involves every ministry of Campus Crusade for Christ in every location in the world. All staff pray for all facets of the ministry using a common handbook of requests from each Campus Crusade ministry branch.

One may also ask, "Why does a movement like Campus Crusade for Christ have or need an emphasis on prayer?" Dr. Bright explains, "We are engaged in a spiritual ministry, a ministry of changing people's lives, a supernatural ministry... We must depend upon the supernatural resources to accomplish supernatural objectives."[5] Another reason is that we have the awesome privilege of personal conversation with Almighty God, but the most basic reason is that God commands us to pray. The commands are for all individual Christians, the local church, and Christian movements like Campus Crusade for Christ. In his Transferable Concept *How You Can Pray With Confidence*, Dr. Bright offers a few of those commands:

- Pray continually—1 Thessalonians 5:17
- Watch and pray—Luke 21:36
- Pray with thanksgiving—Philippians 4:6; Colossians 4:2
- Pray in the Spirit—1 Corinthians 14:15
- Always pray and do not give up—Luke 18:1
- Pray for those in authority—1 Timothy 2:2
- Pray for boldness—Acts 4:29

Dr. Bright goes on to give other reasons why we need to pray:

- Because of our Lord's example
- Because of the examples of the disciples and others
- To have fellowship with God
- To communicate with God
- To receive spiritual nurture
- To obtain results
- To become a fruitful witness for Christ

What attitude should we have when we pray? According to Dr. Bright, "Because the one to whom you pray is the King of kings and Lord of lords, the Creator of heaven and earth, you come into His presence with reverence." Dr. Bright senses that reverence and awe as he simply communicates with God. He believes that "prayer is the greatest privilege of the Christian life and the most revolutionary source of power known to man." He challenges all believers, "If you were to take seriously the promises of God and begin to claim by faith in prayer all that you have been promised, you would experience miracles in your life and ministry, multitudes would be introduced to our Lord Jesus Christ, the whole course of history would be changed, and you would help fulfill the Great Commission during your lifetime."

PRAYER AND THE GREAT COMMISSION

Two recent decisions have been made by Dr. Bright to accelerate prayer for the purpose of fulfilling the Great Commission. The first was the establishment of a World Prayer Center at the Campus Crusade International Headquarters in Orlando, Florida. The emphasis on prayer is being expanded so that intercessors, using up-to-date computer technology, can have at their fingertips the latest prayer requests and answers to prayer involving the worldwide movement of Campus Crusade for Christ. People are able to call by telephone or pray on-site using the personal prayer spaces. Recruitment and training in prayer are also being provided for every country in the world.

The second decision toward fulfilling the Great Commission was to start and help promote the Fasting and Prayer Movement. In *The Coming Revival*, Dr. Bright says, "In the providence of God, I believe the power of fasting as it relates to prayer is the spiritual atomic bomb of our moment in history to bring down the stronghold of evil, bring a great revival and spiritual awakening to America, and accelerate the fulfillment of the Great Commission."

Dr. Bright undertook a forty-day fast in the summer of 1994, then in December 1994 he called Christian leaders from across the nation together to fast and pray for revival in our country. Since that time, there has been a yearly gathering of thousands to fast and pray. The conference is also broadcast via satellite to churches so that thousands of people may participate in fasting and praying for our nation. "Revival is a sovereign work of God—in answer to sincere, prevailing prayer," says Dr. Bright. He combines fasting with prayer according to 2 Chronicles 7:14. He states that "when one fasts, he humbles himself, he has more time to pray, more time to seek God's face, and certainly he would turn from all known sin." Dr. Bright is praying for two million North Americans to fast and pray for forty days for an awakening in America and the fulfillment of the Great Commission.

It is easy to conclude that Dr. Bright is committed to the value and practice of prayer. His life, ministry, writings, and speaking point to this vital discipline as it relates to all of his other character qualities. Dr. Bright feels so strongly about the priority and necessity of prayer that he has said that someday he wants to give himself completely to prayer because it is the answer to everything—funding, administration, results. He believes, "Absolutely, beyond any shadow of doubt... the most important thing we as staff can do individually and corporately is to pray."

OUR CALL TO PRAYER

Let us strive to emulate Dr. Bright's emphasis on a life of prayer. It would thrill Dr. Bright if all Christians would make prayer a daily part of their lives, just as he and Vonette have done.

Start by talking with God the first thing in the morning, committing the day to Him. At the end of the day, thank Him for all He has done. Bring to God all your needs according to Philippians 4:4–8 and cast all your cares on Jesus as instructed in 1 Peter 5:7. Begin asking God for big things according to His promises in His Word. If you find it helpful, use the ACTS model of prayer as you communicate with your heavenly Father:

- Adoration
- Confession
- Thanksgiving
- Supplication

Another possible model prayer to consider is the prayer of Jabez found in 1 Chronicles 4:10.

Keep a record of your requests and answers, and see how your faith will grow. Pray with your spouse if married, and join a prayer group in your church or neighborhood. Pray for your neighbors to come to know Jesus Christ and for revival in our nation. Pray that your life will be a lighthouse of praying, caring, and sharing. And pray for the worldwide fulfillment of the Great Commission. To God be the glory!

NOTES

1. S. D. Gordon, *Quiet Talks on Prayer* (London: Fleming H. Revell Company, 1859), 12.
2. Michael Richardson, *Amazing Faith* (Colorado Springs, CO: Waterbrook Press, 2000), 138.
3. Ibid., 99.
4. Ibid., 107.
5. Ibid., 107, 108.

CHAPTER 8

Servant Leadership

CARL COMBS
On Staff since 1973
Director, International Leadership Academies

Bold faith, a large vision, enlistment of thousands of staff to join together in helping to fulfill the Great Commission are images that come to mind when portraying Dr. Bill Bright's concept of leadership. Yet he gives profound respect and encouragement to others as he seeks, not so much to direct or command them, as to come alongside to serve the Campus Crusade for Christ staff that he has led since the early 1950s. He lives as a servant of his Savior, following his Father's commands. The following event illustrates a moment that is not at all unique in his leadership style.

A SERVANT LEADER

In the early 1960s, the Chongbuk National University in South Korea awarded Dr. Bright an honorary doctorate. While Bill was in Korea to receive the degree, he met with the thirty Korean staff of Campus Crusade at a Christian conference center near Seoul. The staff were housed for the conference in a dormitory, and the Koreans, by cultural tradition, left their shoes in the hallway outside the dorm rooms when they entered their rooms for the night.

Early one morning, an international representative of Campus Crusade who was attending the conference went downstairs. He found Dr. Bright polishing the shoes that were in the hallway. The staff member watched for some time. Finally he approached Dr. Bright and quietly asked, "May I ask what you are doing?"

The scene remained etched in the staff member's mind, and he never forgot Bill's response: "I was hoping that no one would see me, except for perhaps the Lord. But I am so overwhelmed with the quality and dedication of these Korean staff friends that I just wanted to do something to express my appreciation."[1]

When Bill Bright thinks of servant leadership, he thinks of the Lord Jesus as his example and says:

> Though He was God, He humbled Himself and even went to the cross. A servant leader is one who knows where he is going, and encourages others to join him with the spirit of a servant, not as a dictator saying, "This is the way it's going to be," and "This is what I want you to do." It's someone who knows where he is going and is able to motivate others by his gracious, humble, servant spirit.[2]

Bill Bright seeks to follow Jesus' example of servant leadership. It has been a privilege to follow Dr. Bright's faith-stretching servant leadership over the years and observe the many people he has mentored to a similar mindset and style. As a former engineer, my best form of learning is by observing success and analyzing failure. One classroom I have had the privilege of attending has been observing and interacting with Bill Bright for thirty years. For much of my life, my father, who led as many as four thousand men, would often walk me through the huge projects he was building where I observed the dignity and kindness with which he led others. Most recently, Stacy Rinehart, a leader in the Navigators and author of the excellent book *Upside Down, The Paradox of Servant Leadership,* has had a great impact on me by putting a clear definition on the biblical role that I had been observing in Bill and Dad.[3] I want to deeply thank the three of them and commit to each that my passion will be to pass on what I have learned from them. God's way is *the* way.

The two men on staff that have been able to observe Bill's leadership the longest are Gordon Klenck and Roe Brooks, who were the first and second to join the staff. Forty-nine years later, these two are still part of the Crusade organization. Both have had leadership roles and have the same character of bold risk-taking. Both leave a legacy of ministry impact around the world. The following are comments from these men concerning Bill and servant leadership.

Dr. Gordon Klenck serves as Professor of Church Growth at the International School of Theology. He says:

> It was in the spring of 1952. Two fellow university students and I were conducting a weekend youth ministry in a city several hours from my East Coast university. Friday evening I received a long-distance phone call from Bill Bright. He was visiting my campus seeking young men who would join him in an exciting new ministry to university students. He

asked me if I could return to the campus to meet with him. Saturday after our interview, he invited me to apply to the staff of this new Campus Crusade for Christ movement which God had used him to begin at UCLA.

In our first meeting, he impressed me as a successful young businessman with a tremendous love and devotion to Christ and with a great vision to win and disciple university students.

In August of that year, I traveled to California to attend the first Campus Crusade for Christ staff training. It was an exciting challenge as Bill began to prepare us for ministry to university students. He came across as a slightly older peer with a real servant's heart. He never talked down to any of us. We were a team with him to launch a movement that would eventually encircle the globe.

Bill exuded a love for Christ and a tremendous vision for reaching the student world. His motto captured our hearts: "Win the campus today and you will win the world tomorrow."

In the ensuing years, Bill has consistently manifested servant leadership—as a glad, devoted "slave of Jesus Christ" himself and a fellow servant of all on the staff of this worldwide movement. He is always caring, encouraging, humble, thoughtful, concerned, loving, and yet by his example, always challenging each of us to be fellow "slaves" with him of our Master, the Lord Jesus Christ. He has never been pompous. He's down to earth, always ready to talk with any of us staff about our concerns. He is without guile, never promoting himself, always promoting Jesus.

From those first days almost fifty years ago, I have always sensed in Bill his servant heart first toward God and then toward all of us in this movement. He is a true servant leader.

Roe Brooks, who joined Campus Crusade for Christ as the second staff member, serves as a full-time staff member with the International Leadership Academies, a ministry of Crusade, at its headquarters in Scottsdale, Arizona. Roe says:

In the fall of 1952, Bill Bright was speaking in seminary chapel. Seminary chapel does not normally have a student standing on a mountaintop thrilled with the speaker's outlook. However, here was a speaker, without a seminary degree, a businessman, telling what God was doing and asking for help.

Students and faculty on the UCLA campus, known as "the little red schoolhouse," were responding to the message of Christ. Two hundred and fifty athletes and fraternity/sorority members had received Christ. The noontime carillon chimes were playing hymns heard across the campus. Bill said, "I am looking for fifty men who will spread this awakening to campuses across America."

My heart demanded that I ask to be one of the fifty.

Being involved in ministry with Bill is inspiring because he is a servant leader. I have seen Bill moved to tears when he realized he had offended certain staff members. At times, he senses we are struggling to believe what he feels God is going to do. He comfortingly says, "Faith is a muscle. It grows with use. Don't worry. Go along with my faith that God is going to do this."

In 1951, Bill began signing his letters, "Yours for fulfilling the Great Commission in this generation." Where did he get that idea? How did he expect to be a part of such a program? "Small plans cannot enflame the minds of men," he says.

After serving with Bill Bright for forty-eight years, I would describe him with these words: "He cares enough to cry, and he cares enough to try."

In this chapter, I will focus on Dr. Bright's character and ministry as it portrays his view and style of leadership—servant leadership. Those close to him recognize and appreciate his visionary mindset, but equally important is his humble encouraging manner as a servant leader.

WHAT IS SERVANT LEADERSHIP?

The primary source for understanding leadership is the Bible. To set the course for our study, let us define and clarify some terms and see how they relate to Bill Bright. Harvard Business School Professor John P. Kotter, in his book *A Force for Change*, defines how the function of *leadership* differs from that of *management*. Leadership is essential in giving vision that determines what the outcome should be. Good management is extremely important to assure quality and quantity outcomes.[4]

Leadership primarily establishes direction, aligns people in a focused effort, and then motivates and inspires them toward completion. Management involves planning and budgeting, organizing and staffing, controlling and problem solving. Without capable management, goals are often unmet, costs exceed expectation, personnel are frustrated, and problem solving and accountability are often neglected.

When limited leadership is available, a task can become merely the development of a fine product, the result of a well-tuned and efficient system that has focused on the product but may have missed the movement of the marketplace. History is paved with stories of missed opportunities because of failure to have or to follow bold, innovative leadership. One such example illustrates this difference between leadership and management.

The event took place in the early 1900s in the manufacturing plant of the James H. Birch Carriage Company in Burlington, New Jersey. Birch's success with vehicle manufacturing attracted the attention of young, not yet well-known Henry Ford. Ford was fascinated with Birch's use of assembly-line procedures. During a meeting, Ford approached Birch with an offer to partner in a new endeavor to build automobiles with an assembly-line approach using Birch's plants.[5]

Birch and his company were renowned in producing a fine vehicle—maybe the world's leader in its production. After discussing and reviewing Henry Ford's idea and offer, Birch stated that he was already producing a vehicle that was experiencing great success and had a proven customer base. But he was impressed with the axle and hub assembly that Ford had developed.

The outcome was simply that Birch continued his carriage production using the Ford hub and axle components, passing up the offer to join in building the assembly line for the "tin lizzy." The owner's son, Mr. James H. Birch Jr., a progressive merchandiser, wanted to convert to automobiles. His father took an adamant stand. The 1907 Birch catalogue carried a full-page picture showing a horse gaily trotting past two automobiles stranded in ditches. The caption read, "The Passing of the Horse."[6]

Today, Mr. James H. Birch of Burlington, New Jersey, stands out in the memories of people who file through the Burlington Corson-Poley Center to view possibly the only remaining evidence of a well-managed company which lacked visionary, market-tracking leadership: a human-drawn *rickshaw* with Ford hubs!

History records the destinies of these two men. One company looked for good management to meet a visionary need; the other ignored the vision of a leader who recognized a changing transportation market and continued to improve the management systems of his present product.

The function of leadership is to track the market and determine the products that fill ever-changing needs. The function of management is to develop the staff to produce the finest and most effective form of the products. Leadership defines the product. Management determines the process.

Confusion also surrounds the terms *leadership* and *leader*. *Webster's New World Dictionary* devotes seventy-two lines to defining *lead* and *leader* and only three lines to *leadership*. Definitions vary all the way from the physical pulling of a dog by a leash to guiding and inspiring others to follow.

Leadership is a role or function. Leader is a position. Management personnel who are in charge of marketing, accounting, manufacturing, and so on, are all considered leaders. Some have leadership skills, but many don't. Many in leadership have excellent leadership skills and limited management ability. Yet in both leadership and management, the primary persons may be called leaders. Leader is a position nomenclature. Leadership is a function, usually focused on continually evaluating the organizational direction and its response to changing needs and opportunities.

How do these definitions of leadership and management relate to Dr. Bright and his role in developing Campus Crusade for Christ? For half a century, he has looked over the horizon and established direction, aligned people, and continued to motivate and inspire those joining him in "helping to fulfill the Great Commission in this generation." People attracted to his vision and determination are motivated to join the Campus Crusade movement. They are drawn by his humble spirit, his close walk with the Lord, and his bold faith.

People find him credible when they review the growth and accomplishments of Campus Crusade. The organization, initially only he and his wife, Vonette, has grown to more than 24,000 full-time staff based in approximately two hundred countries. This growth is the result of his ability to attract a very capable management team that has aligned with his vision and has been attuned to his sense of ever-changing and expanding horizons of ministry. The relationship is not a contest of differences but a blending of complementary functions, leadership and management.

Dr. Bright's style has been to continue to expand Campus Crusade's activities and influence. Highly focused toward the fulfillment of the Great Commission he is. Highly controlling of his staff he is not. His style is to equip, empower, encourage, embolden, and release staff to succeed within their assigned area of responsibility. He fully understands that high control stifles creativity and limits results.

The Campus Crusade staff ministry is very similar the world over. The methods vary based on culture or assigned target, but the task is always the same—evangelism, follow-up, discipleship, involvement, training, and multiplication—which leads to ongoing movements. The fulfillment of the Great Commission—through thousands of *JESUS* film showings, large gatherings, small discipleship groups, athletes, television, an illusionist, satellites, printed materials, every culture, executives, tribes, rich, poor—*is* Campus Crusade's great commission!

His leadership vision is not merely to build an organization. His vision is to expand a kingdom, the kingdom of Christ, and he is only one of the workers. He has assumed the role of leadership; "may his tribe increase" within the entire community of Christ. We must pray for capable Christian leaders to take on the role of leadership in reaching every community in the world with the good news of the gospel.

Now let us look at the term *servant. Webster's New World Dictionary* defines *servant* as: "1) a person employed to perform services, esp. household duties, for another; 2) a person employed by a government; 3) a person devoted to another or to a cause, creed, etc."

If the first and third definitions are combined into an application of *servant leadership*, the definition might read: a person devoted to performing services for another, a person devoted to helping others succeed in their efforts or cause. This is the essence of servant leadership. As a servant leader selects and directs an individual in a task, the leader is obliged to serve that person in such a way as to help him accomplish his task. The leader becomes the enabler. Succeeding in moving the task or cause forward is the prime consideration. If there is credit to be given, a servant leader sees that the individual worker receives the credit and not the leader.

One staff member remarked that when he sees Dr. Bright, the conversation opener invariably will be, "What can I do to help you?" With the mindset of the servant leader, everyone profits: the leader, the task worker, and those who benefit from a task well done. Who gets the praise? They all do.

The leader succeeds when he chooses to build a team of next-generation servant leaders. They will be the leader's finest products, men and women nurtured into capable leadership.

A relevant example of Dr. Bright's role of mentoring others is the recent appointment of Steve Douglass as Campus Crusade for Christ's president. Steve has been closely associated with Dr. Bright since he graduated from MIT and Harvard in the late 1960s. His outstanding educational credentials, decades of service in the Crusade ministry, and his proven abilities have prepared him for this new role. Possibly the prime consideration in his stepping into this position is his continuation of the bold servant leadership that has been the masthead of this ministry.

Passing the baton of leadership is a decision that makes or breaks the continuing impact of any organization. Even above the skills of good management, the senior executive must possess and exhibit the ability to sense new direction, align people toward the vision, and continually motivate and inspire the staff. Dr. Bright and the Board of Campus Crusade have made a good decision.

From the very beginning of their relationship, Bill mentored Steve into a servant leadership mindset. Steve relates an incident from the early days of his thirty-plus years of association with Dr. Bright.

Perhaps the best way Dr. Bright mentored in the area of servant leadership was by modeling it. For example, the first trip I took with him was to Japan in 1969. Four of us were to stay at a guesthouse in Tokyo before driving on to the conference. Dr. Bright went into the sleeping room first. He didn't take the obvious best bed in the room but instead took the worst one, which was the top bunk. He put the needs of others above his own and continues to do so after all these years.

That is servant leadership in a mentoring role.

BIBLICAL LEADERSHIP

Let us now look at leadership in the Bible. Through the years, some people in leadership roles have claimed to follow the Old Testament style in which the man of God spoke or wrote words as told to him by God, carrying the authority of God to the nation of Israel. They have forgotten that, with the exception of John the Baptist, the ministry of such prophets ended about 400 B.C. with the close of the Old Testament.

By God's standards a man was not a true prophet just because he claimed to be a prophet. People of the Old Testament times were given tests by which they could tell a true prophet from a false prophet (Deuteronomy 13:1–5; 18:15–22). If a prophet did not meet the test, that is, if he did not prophesy in the name of the Lord, or if he prophesied saying, "Let us go after other gods," he was a false prophet. Or if what he prophesied did not come to pass, he was a false prophet and the people were not to listen to him.

Some modern-day leaders who claim the authority of God are given to displays of arrogance toward their followers. In a spirit of arrogance, they demand strict adherence to their edicts. However, when we look in the Old Testament, we see humility as a characteristic of leadership. Scripture says that Moses was the most humble man who ever lived (Numbers 12:3).

In the New Testament, Jesus became an example and a teacher of servant leadership. Philippians 2:5–11 holds Him up as an example of humility. He became a servant, literally a slave, for our benefit.

Jesus gave a mandate to His disciples, and thus to us, to grow in maturity and to become change agents: to know His voice, to listen to and obey His Word, and to lead others to new life in Him. He wanted His followers to be great, but within a different definition for greatness.

Jesus was a revolutionary. From the beginning of His life and ministry, most of the things He said and the manner in which He led His life on earth were in contradiction to the culture of the day. The religious and political leaders of the time were so infuriated with the influence of His life and teachings that they wanted to kill Him. Whether He was healing someone on the Sabbath or setting the sinner free, Jesus caused a great stir throughout His ministry.

Perhaps one of the most teachable moments Jesus had with His disciples was when they were on their way to Jerusalem. Jesus took the twelve aside to tell them about His imminent death (Mark 10). For nearly three years, the disciples had observed Jesus' miracles and listened as He taught them. But they couldn't appreciate the validity of Jesus' words foretelling the end of His life on earth.

It is at this point that we come to that teachable moment. James and John came to Jesus with the request to sit at Jesus' right and left in His kingdom. As the other disciples began to show contempt toward James and John for their self-serving request, Jesus used the moment to teach about true greatness. He spoke about the rulers of the Gentiles who exercised a "lording over" in their leadership and contrasted this with their type of behavior if they were to be the greatest. "Whoever wants to become great among you must be your servant" (Mark 10:42).

The disciples knew very well that Jesus was proposing something radically different from what they would gravitate toward in their humanness. In one instance, after Jesus had served His disciples by washing their feet, He said, "I have set you an example that you should do as I have done for you" (John 13:15). A servant in their culture was a person of low prestige and honor.

Even today in our human nature, we aspire for success that comes from an exalted position. By contrast, a servant leader is one who influences others within the context of relationships by imitating Jesus' example in thought, word, and deed. The goal is to spur each person to maximize his God-given potential.

Stacy Rinehart outlines leadership in Jesus' style:

1) Jesus publicly confronted the power-oriented, legalistic system and its leaders.
2) His leadership style was that of a servant, even though He truly had all the power and authority of heaven.
3) He did not speak of an organization, institution, or any specific structure through which the apostles were to facilitate the spread of the gospel.
4) When the religious establishment sought His death, He submitted.[7]

Up to the day of Pentecost, God sent His Spirit to rest upon a select few who were supernaturally appointed and anointed to speak on behalf of God. Jesus told the disciples in the upper room, "But you know Him [the Spirit], for He lives with you and will be in you" (John 14:17). The indwelling Spirit would lead through believers who served.

Peter, who was taught servant leadership by the example of Jesus, in turn passed on the teaching to New Testament leaders, the elders (1 Peter 5:1–5). Leaders were not to lord it over the flock, but were to be examples. Timothy, a reserved young man who found himself in the role of a church leader, received instruction from the apostle Paul (1 Timothy 1 and 2). Paul held before the readers of his epistles the requirements for leadership that evidence humility: not quarrelsome, not pugnacious or quick-tempered, but gentle, peaceable, and self-controlled (1 Timothy 3; Titus 1).

Bill Bright shares something of the lasting influence of Paul's teaching and modeling of servant leadership:

> God will always honor you as you operate on a biblical basis. There is no place in the Christian world for ego-driven leaders. Paul writes, and he was one of the greatest leaders of the centuries, "I am crucified with Christ, and I no longer live, but Christ lives in me. The life I live in the body, I live by faith in the Son of God who loved me and gave himself for me." I've never known anyone to be of real significance for the kingdom who has not had an experience of Galatians 2:20.
>
> Let me share a story with you. I was in Rome on one of my first trips. I was told to go to a place that is a big hole in the ground, which now has become a tourist attraction. But then it was just a big, dirty hole where the apostle Paul once was incarcerated before his martyrdom. I was alone because it was not a popular place. I got down on my knees there, remembering that Paul, though he was a great influence in my life, really was according to his words, a slave—a slave of Jesus.
>
> Paul had played a major role in Vonette and me signing our contract in 1951 that we would be slaves of Jesus. So there I was, having my deeply meaningful spiritual time in that hole.
>
> Later that night across the street in the Roman Forum, I was enthralled as I sat listening to a dramatic presentation of light and sound telling about the days of early Rome. Suddenly, it occurred to me that into this Forum would come the great generals who'd won countries for the empire, who'd accomplished great feats. Here the senators met to determine the laws that governed the Roman Empire. Here Julius Caesar was assassinated.
>
> It was a marvelous experience until it occurred to me: You know, I don't remember any names of the generals, and much of what happened

in the Forum has long since been forgotten. But the apostle Paul, who was taken to martyrdom from that hole in the ground, has had an impact on the lives of billions of people through the centuries. Still he is one of the greatest influences in history, because he discovered what it means to be a servant. He was a slave of Jesus and a model for us.

Today as God's children, we have His Spirit living in each of us, and we possess an understanding and capability to carry out His will. We are not *the* voice speaking for God, but we are one of millions of voices uniting as the voice of hope with arms to hug and feet to serve in His name.

SOME BARRIERS TO GROWTH IN SERVANT LEADERSHIP

In the Christian community, people filling positions such as pastor, group leader, president, director, and professor are usually designated leaders. While some may have been born with a bent toward leadership and naturally gravitate to it, other individuals can be mentored to fill the function of leadership. Then there are those who sincerely desire to serve in leadership to do the Lord's work but are inadequately prepared or misunderstand this function.

At times in the Christian community, individuals are appointed to leadership roles based on their academic or theological credentials alone. They can be individuals with a pure heart who sense a clear call from God, but have limited leadership experience or natural inclination in leadership. Often they are asked to lead older individuals who have more experience in life and who may have seen significant success in secular leadership positions.

These followers have a desperate need for good teaching and discipling from a quality leader. Christian organizations have a desperate need for persons to provide the overall leadership function of determining change and giving a reason and direction for that change.

Often in secular industry when a candidate enters the organization with the academic credentials to do the job but is lacking in leadership skills, the individual is placed on a mentoring path toward growth in leadership. Unfortunately, the Christian system has usually not given its leaders the opportunity to be mentored in leadership. These individuals may have to obtain their leadership growth through bruising experiences and many transfers. This can lead to frustration for all concerned.

Some Christian leaders simply surrender leadership responsibility, thereby allowing others to determine the organizational focus and direction. The rationale for their decision may be that the gifts of the abdicating leader are better used if applied to just one component of ministry, such as teaching, preaching, organizational management, or even building programs. This lets someone else (often a committee) determine organizational direction. Occasionally, this works in unique situations.

SERVANT LEADERSHIP IN THE SECULAR VOCATIONS

The question arises: Is servant leadership equally appropriate in business as it is Christian ministry? Concerning this Dr. Bright says:

> The need for servant leadership is especially true in ministry but is also true in business—every facet of society. It's the law of God: God honors the humble and disciplines the proud. Truly, truly effective leaders are always people who care for their people, care for their associates. I've known some of the great leaders of the business world whose spirit is one of true humility. They've accomplished what they've accomplished because, in most cases, they do it as unto the Lord. They're not on a big ego trip.

Bill shares his own experience in business:

> In the business world as a pagan, I was just a happy pagan, and I was determined to be a success. The bottom line was my goal. I had been taught to be honest, but I had not known how to control my ambition. So if a door didn't open, I'd knock it open in my old nature, the old Bill Bright.
>
> As I became a believer, things began to change; I realized my life was not dependent on me. The Christian life is a supernatural life, and the only one who can live it is Jesus. If I try to live the Christian life in the energy of the flesh, I'm going to foul it up. So increasingly, as I have grown more and more to understand God's ways, I have developed a great sense of reverence and fear of God, in a good sense.
>
> Scripture says the fear of the Lord is the beginning of wisdom, and God honors those who reverence Him. He reveals to them His best secrets (Psalm 25:14). The more I've walked with the Lord and understood His Word and seen Him work His miracles, the more I have recognized the need to be a servant instead of a dictator. It's been a growing process. I still haven't achieved; I haven't yet arrived.

Concerning the importance of serving others, Albert Einstein put it well when he said, "The highest destiny of the individual is to serve rather than to rule."[8] Paul Moody put it this way, "The measure of a man is not the number of his servants, but is the number of people whom he serves."[9]

Let me share a couple of examples of effective use of servant leadership in secular vocations. Dr. Ewen Holmes, pastor of Fountain Hills Presbyterian Church in Arizona, relates the story of Dean Smith, former head basketball coach of the University of North Carolina:

> Coach Smith believed the best seat in the house for a basketball game was the coach's seat—because it put him in charge of the game—it gave him control. He could determine the outcome of the game, but he never handled the ball for a score. Most of us think, "If I could just sit in some star's seat for one day, then . . ." But in reality the coach's seat was the best seat in the house for Smith, because it was there that he had the opportunity *to make other people* into star players. The better he did his job the more attention was paid to the players he developed.
>
> The coach's seat allowed him to develop such players as Michael Jordan and countless others who have played and continue to play in the National Basketball Association. Coach Smith understood the role of servant in building others into success.

The character quality of servant leadership is applicable to every culture and environment. It is not a style reserved for only those in vocational Christian ministry. It is, rather, a character quality that followers of Christ should seek to apply in the marketplace as well.

Another example of servant leadership in the marketplace is Ray Bellefeuille, the owner and president of Phoenix Logistics. His education is in the field of electrical engineering, and he credits his "can do" mindset to his French-Canadian father who taught him how to make "anything." One of his maxims is: "Give me four weeks and I'll ship it to you."

He started his company in 1991 with little more than a shoestring as collateral. Not only has the company been quite successful financially, but his impact in leadership is profoundly innovative. He titles himself simply an "associate," since he has yielded the control of the business to his Savior.

It was easy for him to make use of his leadership skills in setting up the company. Then he assumed the role of leader in management for the next seven years to build an efficient and effective organization.

Ray took about three years to boil down his mission statement and subsequently the mission statement of his company: "to grow moral and ethical leaders." Just about everything he does in the company pertains to growing moral and ethical leaders. For example, as a part of fulfilling this mission, he matches younger employees with older mentors to teach them about the business. Life lessons are learned in the interaction in the workplace between seasoned employees and newcomers.

Employees have business cards with their picture but no titles. The cards are similar from president to janitor. This has had a profound effect on the employees because all employees are encouraged to consider themselves "associates" of Phoenix Logistics.

Employees are encouraged to begin their own product lines with a vision toward personal majority ownership of the line. Ray mentors these talented employees over an extended period. His desire is to equip his employees to succeed.

Ray acknowledges the confusion that arises at the mention of "servant leadership." It is considered by many to be an oxymoron. People question the concept of being both a leader and a servant and often have not seen it demonstrated. Yet it is central in the latter teachings of Jesus.

GOD USES CIRCUMSTANCES TO SHAPE HIS INTENDED LEADERS

God often uses the various situations of life to shape a person's style of leadership. In the Old Testament, this was certainly true in the experiences of Joseph and Moses. In the New Testament, this is clearly seen in the life of Paul. It is true of leaders today as well. Bill Bright shares his own experience:

> The Lord orchestrates times of testing and trial to develop us into individuals who can be used. In my case, I went through a period of about five years of tremendous testing when I wasn't aware that anybody but Jesus really cared about Bill Bright or believed in Bill Bright. That was in the '40s, early '50s. I'm sure that if I had not gone through that adversity, God would have never chosen me to be the one who would give leadership to this movement.
>
> When you take iron ore out of the mountain, it's worth a few dollars a ton. You put it through the furnace under tremendous heat and pressure, and you develop a fine grade of surgical steel. I've never known anyone to amount to anything to the kingdom who has not gone through difficulties. None of us enjoy them, but we always look back on them and say, "Even though it was with tears and a broken heart, I'm grateful I went through it."

Bill lists other experiences in the course of his ministry that have further shaped his leadership style:

> I would say one of these was the original vision, which was a vision to help take the gospel to the whole world, not just to the campus (but we had to start somewhere). Also, there was the faith to move to the campus at UCLA in the fall of '51, to see God do such incredible things from the very beginning, and to see how others were inspired to want

to be a part of it. Then there was the purchase of Arrowhead Springs without any money. We gave $2 million for property that was appraised for $6.7 million, but we had no money. We borrowed $15,000 as a deposit, and it was a cliffhanger every day. We never were sure we were going to be able to raise the money. We were hanging over the cliff like the proverbial elephant with his tail wrapped around a blade of grass. That is faith-stretching. And God always met our need.

There are dramatic examples of when we needed $485, and when we needed $10,000, and when we needed a million, and then when God gave the vision for a billion. It's a growth factor. Faith is like a muscle; it grows with exercise. The move to Orlando was another major faith step. And Explo '72, Explo '74, and Explo '85, all these were dramatic.

INTERNATIONAL LEADERSHIP

How does servant leadership relate to different cultures? Some people maintain that servant leadership works well in the freedom-loving West, but it doesn't work in other cultures. Bill's answer is this:

> It's a biblical concept. And biblical concepts relate to all cultures, just like the Ten Commandments: "I am the Lord thy God. Thou shalt have no other gods before me. Thou shalt not make unto thee any graven image," and so forth. Those are truths that apply to every culture.

When Jesus taught His disciples about servant leadership, He made it clear that this principle was contrary to the concept of leadership in the culture of that day. It might be contrary to the culture, but it is to be the norm for Christian leadership in every culture.

Bill Bright has a hope and prayer for Campus Crusade for Christ and for the Body of Christ around the world with regard to the application of servant leadership. He says:

> We're starting what we call, for lack of a better term right now, our academy—our West Point, our Annapolis of Crusade where we train our world leaders. And they in turn train people including the newest recruits. I've wanted to establish an academy for the last 25 years. The goal would be to train millions of leaders, not just for the Christian ministry, but for business and government, for the judicial systems of the world. People who would be true, biblical servant leaders who know how to make things happen, but do it in God's way instead of the ways of the world and the ways of the flesh. So that's a part of our world strategy.
>
> I would like to think that 25 years from now, many, many millions of Christians will be in positions of leadership in every facet of society in

every culture and country of the world. And of course, the International Leadership Academies of Campus Crusade are involved in the same concept of training true servant leaders.

It has been my privilege to work with and give leadership to a ministry of Campus Crusade for Christ that Dr. Bright commissioned in 1992 called the International Leadership Academies. The purpose of these academies is to provide leadership for the church in areas of the world where such leadership is lacking. In the beginning, Dr. Bright requested that we develop a ministry that would:

- Produce a new kind of leader
- Use a new form of training
- Partner Campus Crusade with friendly churches receptive to new believers
- Produce churches, but not Campus Crusade churches

Later, he added the element of desiring that this new ministry would:

- Have a strong movement mentality

Dr. Bright's directive required rethinking Christian leadership preparation to produce this "new kind of leader." The result is more than in-depth biblical, theological, and field ministry training. It has required the added elements of character growth, leadership understanding, modeling, and demonstration, in addition to understanding how to integrate the typical para-church-ministry disciple into a receptive, nurturing fellowship. The local fellowship needs to have the leadership mindset of discipling and equipping this new believer to immediately be ministering in his community or area of influence as part of his own spiritual maturing process.

This has required developing a systems approach to preparing this "new kind of leader." It has involved leadership system-thinking that focuses on selecting and preparing available local believers to initiate movements of evangelism, discipleship, outreach, and permanent fellowships for spiritual growth. Outside help and training is used only to initiate the process. It must be maintainable and sustainable within the context of the local area and culture.

One of the biggest elements of this preparation process became retooling the heart toward being a servant rather than an autocratic director. For the majority of the developing world as well as many other countries, this leadership style is seldom observed. Yet servant leadership is the mandated approach of our Savior. Dr. Bright's servant leadership example is absolutely captivating to others.

The function of leadership is more caught than taught. Intrinsic within this function is risk, adventure, failures, repeated efforts, and the inherent loneliness of leadership. Yet when a person is inspired and encouraged to think of bringing about needed change rather than just improvements, he often begins to see the role of leadership as the route to the fulfillment of his goals. As the concept of servant-leadership academies spreads from continent to continent and as more is understood about the preparation of servant leaders, many agencies will see movements of Christian growth that require little assistance from other countries.

EXAMPLES FROM INTERNATIONAL LEADERSHIP ACADEMIES

Let me share with you some stories of how students in our academies have been affected by training with a servant leadership emphasis.

From Russia

Sanjik Kukeev, who comes from the unreached people group known as the Kalmyk, stands out among this year's graduates. Sanjik is from the Kalmyk Republic in southern Russia. When the Kalmyk people migrated west from Mongolia in the 16th century, they crossed the Volga River and established the town of Tsagan-Ama. Living nomadic lives on the steppe, they were absorbed into the Russian Empire and served the Tsar as border guards and in elite military units. They were allowed to retain their practice of Tibetan Buddhism and were thus the only Buddhist people group in Europe. Only one of their temples survived communism—the one in Tsagan-Ama.

At age 15, Sanjik caught the eye of the Lama of this temple. There was something spiritual about this young man, and he was invited to become an apprentice, to train to become a spiritual leader for his people. But God had other plans for him.

In 1995, he heard the gospel through the ministry of Campus Crusade's Athletes in Action. In 1997, he entrusted his life to the Lord, and in 1998, he was challenged to come to the International Leadership Academies' New Life Bible College in Moscow. As a new student, Sanjik did not believe you could share the gospel one-on-one. After observing other students do it and seeing people come to faith, Sanjik came alive to evangelism. He won many of Moscow's non-ethnic Russian population to Christ. Two years later, Sanjik is truly ready to be a spiritual leader for his people, and he has a plan.

For the last two years, he has introduced people to Christ every time he visited home, and these people meet regularly for fellowship and prayer. When he returns after graduation from the academy, they all will participate in an evangelistic campaign, and then a church will start to meet formally. Sanjik's priority is to train one of them to become their pastor so that he can begin evangelizing the surrounding villages. Within three years, he expects to evangelize the 9,000 or so in the Tsagan-Ama district. There are four more tribes and thirteen districts after that, and 150,000 of his people in the Kalmyk Republic (a province of Russia).

There are another 200,000 Russian, Ukrainian, and Kazakh people living there as well, and he doesn't intend to ignore them. Sanjik believes, with a well-reasoned faith, that the entire republic can be evangelized and churches planted in every town over the course of seventeen years. His well-developed plan reflects every step and detail.

From Nicaragua

Jimmy Hassan, a former Nicaraguan judge who is presently the director of the Nicaraguan International Leadership Academy, says:

> Training servant leaders is not like producing hamburgers. Rather than telling students what kind of vision they should have, we want to put them in the path that God has for them. It would have been a tragedy for Paul to produce another Paul instead of helping Timothy become a Timothy.

From Costa Rica

Eric Cordero, a professional who loves God and his country, is representative of the students at the Costa Rican International Leadership Academy. Each month, students write reflections on what they are learning. Here are some of Eric's thoughts:

> The leadership classes have shown me my worth as a servant of God and have confirmed my calling. I have recognized my positive attitudes and, with the help of the Holy Spirit, the negative ones as well. Truly, I feel that God is working in me! I have reassessed my priorities, giving an importance I didn't before to my family. Now I'm not so occupied with the Lord's work as with the Lord.
>
> Students have experienced the godly love and affection that each visiting professor has shown us. It's been a foreign experience, but we know in our hearts that their leadership is biblical, and that through the academy, God is raising up a generation of leaders whose style will be biblical.

> Pastors from North America teaching two-week modules have served as visiting faculty for all the International Leadership Academies. Dr. Steve Mason, first American faculty member at the Costa Rican academy, taught, "The first task of a leader is to be the kind of Christian you are asking your followers to be."

These are simply the thoughts of a few of the many we are seeking to help train to be servant leaders in the Body of Christ.

In this chapter, we have looked at the concept of servant leadership; we have sought to define the concept; we have looked at the biblical teaching on the matter; we have discussed its use both in Christian ministry and the secular marketplace; and we have visited the life and practices of Dr. Bill Bright and others as they walk the path of servant leadership. Most of all, though, this chapter and this book resonate with the example of Dr. Bill Bright, a significant Christian world leader who leads by serving. One cannot be close to him without sensing his humble spirit, incredible vision, amazing faith, and his contagious desire to let God do the impossible through him and others. His great faith in his great God has allowed him to lead in and experience accomplishments for his Savior that few have equaled. Thank you, Bill.

On a personal note, writing this chapter has generated in me considerable personal reflection and an increased desire to be more consistently a servant leader. Through the adventure of examining Scripture as well as the pragmatic role of leadership, my personal viewpoint has been dramatically strengthened to allow God to be God in providing His leadership where and when He desires and to be willing to allow Him to use me.

I invite you to reflect on your own servant leadership. Every believer is a leader in some way. You may be a parent. You may be a leader of others in your job or among your friends. You may simply be an example to others in some area of life, perhaps as a good neighbor. You may be a leader in your church: a teacher, a small group leader, a board member, or even a pastor. You may be a leader in an organization, secular or Christian. Think of your various roles of leadership. Then think through the principles of servant leadership in this chapter. Prayerfully consider what God would have you do to be a more effective servant leader. How can you help others? How can you encourage servant leadership among others?

May God bless you as you seek to serve others and help them succeed.

NOTES

1. Personal notes from Ken Kremer, a Campus Crusade staff who recently passed away, shortly after submitting the account of this experience with Dr. Bright.
2. Personal remarks by Bill Bright and others quoted in this chapter have been taken from various interviews.
3. Stacy Rinehart, *Upside Down, The Paradox of Servant Leadership* (Colorado Springs: NavPress Publishing Group, 1998), 72.
4. John P. Kotter, *A Force for Change* (New York: Simon and Schuster, The Free Press, 1990), Chapter 1.
5. *Burlington County Times*, Dec. 30, 1980, Burlington, NJ.
6. John T. Cunningham, "The Round the World Lines," *The Royle Forum*, No. 124, September 16, 1968.
7. Rinehart, 72.
8. Albert Einstein, quoted on www.cybernation.com.
9. Paul D. Moody, *Praxis* (Scottsdale, AZ: International Leadership Academies), Fall 1999, 4.

PART TWO

Ministry Principles

CHAPTER 9

Excellence Before God and Men

STEVE DOUGLASS

On Staff since 1969

President-elect, Campus Crusade for Christ

I have had the immense privilege of working beside Bill Bright for more than thirty years. I know him to be a man of unquestionable integrity. He has truly hidden the Word of God in his heart that he might not sin against Him. He is committed to doing everything with excellence—to the glory of God.

SOME INSIGHT INTO THE MAN

The very first time I saw Bill, his appearance, his speech, everything about him spoke of excellence. I was impressed! Since then, I have often heard him say, "You only have one chance to make a good first impression," and, "It doesn't cost that much more to do it right."

He believes in doing things right. As Colossians 3:23 says, "Whatsoever you do, do it heartily, as to the Lord" (NKJ). Bill does that and he expects that.

For example, years ago Bill called me to his office and beckoned me to the window overlooking the front lawn at Arrowhead Springs. "Do you see those brown spots?" he asked.

I asked, "What brown spots?"

He pointed out some places nearly out of sight that the sprinkler had not reached. Since care of the grounds was under my supervision, he said, "We've got to do something about that. If we're going to have a lawn, we need to have a good lawn."

It is not difficult to imagine how in every area, under the leadership of

Bill Bright, Campus Crusade for Christ has had a penchant for excellence. Since the very beginning of the ministry, Bill has been willing to examine every aspect and continually seek better ways to accomplish its goals and bring glory to God.

EXPERT OUTSIDE COUNSEL

Bill always wanted to surround himself with the best advisors he could find. He knew that successful business leaders could help him keep the many administrative aspects of Campus Crusade on course. He also knew that expert consultants could help in finding and implementing the best practices to help ensure the best results in ministry. He wanted this kind of expertise to be woven into the fabric of the movement.

The Board of Directors was reorganized during the early years to include many highly successful businessmen. This strategic makeup of the board has provided Campus Crusade with excellent oversight. Today, the board is composed of eight outstanding business leaders and three staff members. All are strong Christians, committed to biblical ethical standards and willing to give of their time and talent to give direction.

I actually joined the staff of Campus Crusade in 1969 in a role very much like a consultant—to help implement the findings of a study. During my final term as a master's degree candidate at Harvard Business School, I had to do a research project. My roommates and I were already interested in Campus Crusade, so we decided to do a study of the organization of the ministry. Of course, we needed the blessing of Bill Bright.

While meeting with Bill to discuss the plan for our study and ask his permission, I learned about some recent turnover in the leadership. As a result, he was highly motivated to look for ways to improve. He accepted our project enthusiastically.

It didn't seem a coincidence at all that God had provided us with a great project mentor, Dr. C. Roland Christensen, one of the most highly respected teachers at Harvard Business School. This was just the kind of expertise Bill Bright prayed for God to provide.

When we presented the findings of our study to Bill, he asked, "Who will help us implement this?"

The four of us said, " We will." Two of us even joined full-time staff at that time.

Another example of seeking outside expertise occurred shortly before we began our study. Bill had asked Dr. Henry Brandt, a renowned consultant, to explore ways for Campus Crusade to become more efficient in managing its many ministries, to make better use of its time and resources, and, in turn, to become more effective at reaching the world with the gospel.

Effectiveness is actually a written "value" of Campus Crusade for Christ. It is a value because Bill Bright has made it so. For fifty years, Bill has been in the process of finding what works best.

A good working definition of effectiveness is: that which brings the best result for the effort and funds expended. Campus Crusade is always searching for faster, better, less expensive ways to get the good news of Jesus Christ to those who have not heard.

SEEKING AND DEVELOPING STRONG LEADERS

Reaching and recruiting leaders has also been a goal of the ministry from the beginning. The first outreach Bill and Vonette made on the UCLA campus was to student leaders. Today, Campus Crusade for Christ has several ministries that seek to reach leaders in society, not because their souls are any more valuable, but because they have a larger sphere of influence and can expose even more people to the gospel as their lives change. Also, they can provide leadership within the ministry and, as a result, be instrumental in bringing about greater excellence.

Many staff members came to Campus Crusade from leadership positions in the secular world. They brought leadership expertise to help many of the ministries achieve a greater level of effectiveness. Many have actually begun new ministries. These leaders often have a quality about them which draws others to work with them as well as to emulate them. They tend to bring out the best in others as they strive for excellence.

Campus Crusade has also expended great effort over the years to train and develop its own leaders. This also has been a significant contribution to excellence. For example, in the 1970s, "The Ministry of Management" was developed to train our leaders in the basic principles of management. Later, "The Leadership Track" was developed to enhance leadership training. Currently, there is a major task force examining our overall leadership development plan worldwide, and in the spring of 2001, the first President's Academy for leadership training was launched. A few years ago, the ministry formed the International Leadership University.

SEEKING EFFECTIVENESS IN MINISTRY

God gave Bill Bright a vision, a vision that showed him the direction and purpose for his life and for the ministry that came to be known as Campus

Crusade for Christ. That mission: to do all possible to help fulfill the Great Commission in this generation. In the pursuit of that vision, he has encouraged individual ministries to be formed to help reach and disciple people in the best possible way.

In Bill's search for effectiveness, he has been willing to try new, untested, even unconventional ministries and methods that seemed to have the promise of success.

For example, in 1963 Bill accepted a young man on staff who wanted to form a ministry of Campus Crusade for Christ. The young man was an illusionist. This was not exactly the mainstream Christian approach for reaching the lost, yet André Kole through his ministry has now exposed millions of people to the message of Christ—as a Christian magician!

Also, Josh McDowell joined Campus Crusade's team as a speaker, although he is not a traditional evangelist. Through his lectures and books, he has brought Jesus Christ to millions. His ministry has spanned the globe, and his compelling writings have confounded even staunch skeptics. He has spoken live to more students than any person in history!

Bill Bright wants to be sure everyone is given an excellent chance to know the truth of the gospel. It is his passion to help fulfill the Great Commission in this generation. Jesus said in Matthew 28:19,20, "Go therefore and make disciples of all the nations, baptizing them in the name of the Father and of the Son and of the Holy Spirit, teaching them to observe all things that I have commanded you" (NKJ).

Therefore, Bill has been relentless in his search for even greater methods of evangelism. In the early 1960s, he wrote *The Four Spiritual Laws* as a tool his staff could use to present the gospel consistently. Using this booklet, a believer can share the message of Christ with confidence. That message is clear, "God loves you and offers a wonderful plan for your life." This simple method of sharing Jesus has been used for more than thirty-five years. To date, more than 2.5 billion copies of the booklet have been printed, and it has been translated into more than 100 languages.

The relentless search for better ways to share the gospel is what eventually brought about the JESUS Film Project. One-to-one ministry had been the main method used by Campus Crusade, but Bill envisioned more expansive methods. For years, he even thought of a film about the life of Christ. Then, in 1979, the *JESUS* film came along. The potential seemed unlimited.

The dream of translating the film into other languages, more than 600 to date, has come to pass. That effort alone has exposed more people to the gospel of Jesus Christ than any other tool in history.

Today, people are also being reached with the *JESUS* video, audiocassette, radio program, DVD, CD, and Internet site. The videos are being distributed to homes all over the United States.

At colleges and universities, the Campus Ministry is distributing the "Freshman Survival Kit." These are packets that contain a Bible and a variety of other items that a student can use and enjoy. They're easy to give away. The students like to receive them; donors love to give them. The kits have been very effective in presenting the gospel on the college campus. They even contain information about a website the students can visit to learn more about Christ. More than 201,300 kits were given away to students during the fall of 2000 alone.

Campus Crusade for Christ is working to greatly expand its presence on the Internet. Over the next few years, we should have many more websites with opportunities for people to learn about a large variety of topics, in addition to leading them into questions about their spiritual condition and their relationship to Jesus Christ. Already, Christian Leadership Ministry has a site for college students with more than 7,000 topics for use in preparing research papers. The site averages more than 4.75 million hits per month.

SETTING A STANDARD OF FINANCIAL INTEGRITY

Financial integrity is a very key element to the reputation of any organization. Bill has always been concerned that there be no cause to question Campus Crusade's financial integrity. Therefore, from early in the ministry's existence, an outside annual audit has been conducted. In the mid-1970s, Campus Crusade contracted with one of the largest accounting firms in the world, Arthur Young, to do its audit and publish an annual report.

A young reporter came to my office just a few months after that first annual report was printed. He commented that most Christian organizations did not have an annual report and that he supposed that we did not have one either. Much to his surprise, I got out the report and slid it across the table. Campus Crusade did not receive any negative press from him.

Over the years, *Money* magazine has repeatedly ranked Campus Crusade among the top charities of its type in the percent of contributions spent on programs versus administration and fund raising.

Dr. John T. Zietlow, Professor of Finance at Indiana State University, did a study of non-profit organizations and ranked Campus Crusade one of the best run of those he examined.

Campus Crusade for Christ was one of the ministries instrumental in bringing into existence the Evangelical Council for Financial Accountability (ECFA), an independent organization to which Christian organizations can subscribe. Members open their finances to inspection and their entire operations become subject to the high ethical standards of the ECFA. Member organizations benefit from the reputation of the ECFA as an effective watchdog for the non-profit sector.

This is another example of how Bill Bright helped lead the way in excellence and effectiveness in the handling of finances.

EXCELLENCE IN FACILITIES

Throughout the history of this movement, Bill has believed that excellent facilities are conducive to excellent training. The first real training facility Campus Crusade had was a small property in Minnesota. By 1960, the ministry had outgrown the facility, and the need existed for a year-round training location, one that would exude excellence. Bill began to search for something in Southern California, a place people would love to visit.

The first time he saw Arrowhead Springs and walked alone into the lobby of the hotel, it was as if God told him, "I've been saving this place for you and Campus Crusade." From that moment on, Bill believed it would be the new headquarters and training center, and he knew that only God could bring it to pass.

Arrowhead Springs is a lovely resort in the San Bernardino Mountains outside Los Angeles. Since the 1920s, it had lured the elite of the Los Angeles social scene. During its heyday, movie stars visited in abundance, and some movies had even been filmed there. The wonderful natural hot springs had beckoned people year-round from all over the world. It was a premier property—just the kind of place that would attract people to the training seminars. And attract it did! From the very first year Campus Crusade opened its headquarters there in 1962, hundreds of people came for training each week. Arrowhead Springs remained the headquarters and training center for more than thirty years.

In 1991, after an extensive search for God's location, Campus Crusade moved its headquarters to Orlando, Florida. The original facility we occupied was adequate for our needs at that time, but it did not offer the expansion possibilities that Bill envisioned. In April 1999, we moved into our brand-new headquarters, also located in Orlando. This beautiful campus is not only lovely, but also a highly functional administrative facility. Visitors coming to learn more about the ministry are often in awe as they get their first glimpse of the buildings and grounds. Only God could have selected and provided such a wonderful location and facility. It's a place with plenty of room for expansion. It is an excellent facility.

For fifty years Bill Bright has been setting a high standard of excellence in all areas of his life. He is a faithful, loving husband. He is a caring, considerate father. He is an honest, upright citizen. He is a leader of integrity in the Christian world. He consistently demonstrates the kind of life Jesus commands us to live.

Bill Bright is a man of excellence because God has called him to be just that, to become conformed to the image of Jesus Christ.

He is not an exception. All Christians have that same calling on their lives. All have different levels of visibility, but the world is reading our lives to see if Jesus and the Bible make a difference. We can make an incredible impression on those people and our world by being people of excellence—just like Bill Bright.

CHAPTER 10

Teaching by Example

CURT MACKEY
On Staff since 1957
International Ministries

My conviction is that Christians learn most of what they know about spiritual leadership from the Word of God and from godly examples they see around them. Unfortunately, they have all too few examples. Many important lessons that I have learned about spiritual leadership are a result of my association with Campus Crusade for Christ, and especially my close involvement with Bill Bright through the years.

I first met Bill while I was a student in graduate school in 1956. He shared his calling and vision from God for Campus Crusade for Christ and invited me to prayerfully consider joining the growing staff team of about thirty. After examining my own vision and calling, I took him up on his challenge. My wife, Lois, and I have been staff members since 1957.

During the early years of Campus Crusade, we worked closely with Bill and Vonette, first at UCLA, and later (1969–1974) as his personal assistant at Arrowhead Springs, where the international headquarters was then located. While working with him, not only did we discuss leadership, but I had years in which to observe his approach to leadership—his own leadership style.

Perhaps the most valuable lessons on leadership learned through those years were the ones that were "caught rather than taught." We are encouraged in Scripture to follow the godly examples set by others. Paul said in 1 Corinthians 11:1, "Follow my example, as I follow the example of Christ." Bill, like Paul, has been very aware that he is teaching by example. I want to highlight some lessons learned from watching Bill.

AN EXAMPLE OF PASSIONATE VISION

One of the first things that attracted me to Bill and Campus Crusade was his vision. I remember well his visit to my campus. He spoke in chapel of his call to help fulfill the Great Commission and how God led him to initiate a ministry of evangelism and discipleship among university students. He passionately shared that through reaching students today, we could help reach the world with the gospel in the future. He invited any who wanted to know more to meet with him.

In an appointment later that day, he talked about how he shared his then-unnamed vision a few years earlier with one of his professors at Fuller Seminary, Dr. Wilbur Smith. As Dr. Smith listened, he paced back and forth, contemplating Bill's calling and vision. Then he said, "This is of God! This is of God!" The next time Dr. Smith saw Bill he handed him a piece of paper. On it were written the letters *CCC* and the words *Campus Crusade for Christ.* He said, "I believe God has given me the name for your vision." God used Dr. Smith and others like Dr. Henrietta Mears to confirm that those marching orders were from Him.

Over the years, I have observed that because the call and vision were so strong and clearly from God, when times of testing, difficulty, and disappointment came, Bill never looked back or questioned the leading of God. He pressed on.

Apart from a calling and vision from God, you cannot effectively lead a movement of God. The Bible is replete with dynamic stories of this principle being worked out in the lives of men of faith. Nehemiah is an Old Testament example of a man who bonded to God's vision for his life. He was an ordinary man that God used in an extraordinary way, a man to whom God spoke, as expressed in the Book of Nehemiah.

> I set out during the night with a few men. I had not told anyone what my God had put in my heart to do for Jerusalem (2:12).
>
> Now the city was large and spacious, but there were few people in it, and the houses had not yet been rebuilt. So my God put it into my heart to assemble the nobles, the officials and the common people for registration (7:4,5).

God similarly spoke to Bill and put CCC on his heart. People will follow a person who has been entrusted with a vision from God, one who knows where he is going. Others will catch the vision from his vision.

AN EXAMPLE OF BALANCING LIFE

One of the challenges of leading a spiritual movement is balancing a personal walk with God with the work over which He has given you stewardship. Clearly, Bill's priority has been to keep his focus on God. How often I have heard him say to staff, "Your walk and life before God are most important. Who you are is of utmost importance, and what you do is secondary."

His days at Arrowhead Springs, the first international headquarters, were often long and filled with appointments. As his assistant, it was always a real challenge to maintain a schedule. Meetings always started with prayer, and usually Bill would follow that with questions about how we were doing, or he would share something that he had gotten that day from the Word.

Toward the end of the day, Mrs. Griswold, his personal secretary, would gently remind me that Bill promised her time to go over his correspondence and do some dictation. She was a dear saint, well into her seventies at the time. Either he would get to the work she had for him during the day, or he would come back in the evening or call her and do what was needed over the phone. While on the road, he would call her nearly every day to take care of any urgent correspondence.

In the midst of a flurry of phone calls, correspondence, appointments, and other administrative obligations, he would acknowledge his dependence upon the Lord by taking time out to pray or by opening his Bible to seek wisdom from God. He believed Psalm 32:8: "I will instruct you and teach you in the way you should go; I will counsel you and watch over you." He recognized his dependence upon God and would say to anyone within the sound of his voice, "I'm just a leaf on a twig on a branch, on a limb on the trunk of a tree."

I believe Bill was successful in balancing his life because he practiced Matthew 6:33,34: "Seek first his kingdom and his righteousness, and all these things will be given to you as well. Therefore do not worry about tomorrow, for tomorrow will worry about itself. Each day has enough trouble of its own." Personally, I appreciate greatly his commitment to priorities both in his spiritual life and in "the business" of all the responsibilities involved in leading the ministry.

AN EXAMPLE OF DEPENDENCE ON THE HOLY SPIRIT

One of the "open secrets" of the incredible blessing of God upon the worldwide ministry of Campus Crusade has been our belief and continual emphasis on the presence and power of the Holy Spirit in the life of every believer. Many of us got our first insight into the work of the Holy Spirit through Bill's life and ministry.

Although Bill continually talked about the dynamic of the Holy Spirit, in 1957, I remember him going away for several days to a cabin at the Forest Home Conference Center in the San Bernardino Mountains of California. At the time, we were in the process of developing discipleship materials for our staff to use on U.S. college campuses.

Several days later, he returned to the little office on Westwood Boulevard off the UCLA campus. He came with a collection of cardboard he had saved from laundry along with various notepads. (In those days, a small sheet of cardboard was used with each shirt to hold the press.)

On the various and sundry cardboard sheets was the initial draft of an article on the Holy Spirit entitled "Ye Shall Receive Power." From that day forward, the emphasis on the Holy Spirit has been a centerpiece in Bill's personal ministry and that of Campus Crusade worldwide.

He would remind us that the Holy Spirit came so that Jesus could be everywhere. "I tell you the truth: It is for your good that I am going away. Unless I go away, the Counselor will not come to you; but if I go, I will send him to you" (John 16:7).

In his mind and heart, Bill believed that the more Spirit-filled staff and volunteers involved in ministry, the greater the potential for more love, more evangelism, more discipleship, more equipping and helping to fulfill the Great Commission. What a difference!

He would say, "To truly be a leader in kingdom work, one must be continually dependent upon and filled with the Holy Spirit." He lived his life to the full with the Spirit. His continual emphasis on the Spirit-filled life, through his preaching and the discipleship materials developed earlier on the ministry of the Holy Spirit, is still vital to the message of Campus Crusade today. It has not been kept a secret.

Bill emphasizes the importance of this message by saying, "If I could give only one message, it would be 'Ye Shall Receive Power' because every time a Christian learns how to be filled with the Holy Spirit, he has the potential to reach countless others with the gospel."

Bill never just talked about the Holy Spirit, he demonstrated what it means to be filled and to walk in the power of God in season and out. He taught by example.

AN EXAMPLE OF EVANGELISM

From his earliest days as a believer, Bill has been totally committed to the

Great Commission. Evangelism was never far from his thinking, and he taught that, whenever possible, we should seek to follow-up (disciple and train) those we had the privilege of leading to Christ.

Bill interviewed me for joining staff while I was a graduate student. He must have asked me a lot of questions that day, but the one that stands out in my memory is, "Have you ever led anyone to Christ?" It was obvious then and now that evangelism is very important to Bill.

Over the next few years, he demonstrated repeatedly just how important evangelism was to him. For years he has championed three words: Win, Build, Send. Early on, he developed three basic messages; the first was How to Experience God's Love and Forgiveness.

A story well-known in the Crusade family underlines the importance of evangelism to him. At staff training one year, we had a speaker who was a salesman in the business world. He trained others how to sell. He spoke to us about the importance of training our staff. He said he thought that when Bill witnessed to someone, he said pretty much the same thing to each person. Initially, Bill objected to such a notion, but later as he thought more and prayed about it, he realized it was true. Out of that experience, Bill developed *The Four Spiritual Laws*. At first, we wrote the words on paper napkins in campus cafeterias and student unions, but later we had them in booklet form. Through this little booklet, which has been translated into many languages, multiplied millions have heard the gospel message.

Soon we had training on how to use the booklet to lead someone to Christ. In the training, Bill was careful to say, "In using this tool, we must remember that the secret to effective witnessing is to take the initiative to share Christ in the power of the Holy Spirit and leave the results to God."

For five years I traveled the world with Bill, and I saw firsthand that he practiced what he preached. We would get into a taxi after a speaking engagement, and almost before the driver could be told our destination, Bill would hand him a copy of *The Four Spiritual Laws*. His question would be something like, "Have you ever seen this booklet before?"

If the driver said, "No," Bill would say, "You drive and I'll read it to you." More often than not, when Bill asked if the contents of the booklet made sense and invited him to receive Christ, he would say, "Yes." Then Bill would say, "I'll pray the prayer a phrase at a time, and you repeat it after me." Afterwards, Bill would encourage the driver in his newfound faith and tell him of the importance of church for his spiritual growth.

Of course, once we got on the plane, Bill would often pass out several booklets and invite anyone who wanted to talk about what they read to come over to where he was sitting. Sometimes, he would tell me that he considered the people assigned to sit next to him as divine appointments.

We would arrive in another city and be picked up by a staff member. While the person was driving us to our hotel, Bill would ask how the ministry was going. "Are students coming to Christ?" was often the first question.

At the hotel, he would give the booklet to the bellboy, the housekeeper, and anyone else he encountered and tell them how important the truth in the booklet is. He would then tell them that he would like to talk about this message, which had changed his life.

Anyone who knows Bill is aware that he doesn't just talk about sharing the good news, he does it as a way of life. I know of no one who has more consistently taken the initiative to share Christ with others.

Those who have traveled with him have learned through his example what he means by taking the initiative. Those who have heard him speak have heard him share some recent story of leading someone to Christ. He sets the pace for the staff.

AN EXAMPLE OF DISCIPLESHIP TRAINING

Bill's vision is to help fulfill the Great Commission according to Matthew 28:18–20 and Mark 16:15:

> Then Jesus came to them and said, "All authority in heaven and on earth has been given to me. Therefore go and make disciples of all nations, baptizing them in the name of the Father and of the Son and of the Holy Spirit, and teaching them to obey everything I have commanded you. And surely I am with you always, to the very end of the age."

He said to them, "Go into all the world and preach the good news to all creation."

As believers we have been given what is needed to accomplish this task.

> It was he who gave some to be apostles, some to be prophets, some to be evangelists, and some to be pastors and teachers, to prepare God's people for works of service, so that the body of Christ may be built up until we all reach unity in the faith and in the knowledge of the Son of God and become mature, attaining to the whole measure of the fullness of Christ.
>
> Then we will no longer be infants, tossed back and forth by the waves, and blown here and there by every wind of teaching and by the cunning and craftiness of men in their deceitful scheming. Instead, speaking the truth in love, we will in all things grow up into him who is the Head, that is, Christ. From him the whole body, joined and held together by every supporting ligament, grows and builds itself up in love, as each

part does its work (Ephesians 4:11–14).

> You will receive power when the Holy Spirit comes on you: and you will be my witnesses in Jerusalem, and in all Judea and Samaria, and to the ends of the earth (Acts 1:8).

We face the same challenges as those encountered by Jesus and the first-century Christians. "'What a huge harvest!' he said to his disciples. 'How few workers! On your knees and pray for harvest hands!'" (Matthew 9:37, 38, *The Message*). God gives His people gifts to do the work to which He calls them.

From the earliest days, Bill's mindset on deploying "harvest hands" has been that training makes the difference. He has strongly led in developing the best training possible for our staff. This training is for all new staff and continues throughout their careers with the ministry. He also clearly believes that the Great Commission calling is for the whole Body of Christ and that as an organization we must make available to others everything that God gives us. This is accomplished through relevant materials and training.

According to 2 Timothy 2:2, "win, build, train, and send" is a key to the fulfillment of the Great Commission: "The things you have heard me say in the presence of many witnesses entrust to reliable men who will also be qualified to teach others." We often refer to this as "spiritual multiplication." Bill's philosophy in this area is expressed through a series of basic messages he developed in the early days of Campus Crusade. Accompanying how-to seminars provide a package that has given us the ability to pass this philosophy on to a new generation of staff and others "without dilution," as Bill would say.

This training is now available for our staff throughout the world through the Great Commission Training Centers and New Life Training Centers.

Bill's dream for the future includes making discipleship and other training available through the use of technology. To do this effectively will mean a lot of creative work. What we want to pass on will require that the content be put into an interactive format. Distance learning and discipleship through satellite technology could help to disciple the masses of new believers in developed as well as developing countries.

Bill again is a model—a model in discipleship training that will result in training still other disciples who will train others.

AN EXAMPLE IN BREAKTHROUGH THINKING

Another aspect of Bill's leadership style is what I like to call breakthrough or cutting-edge thinking that keeps us blazing new trails. Throughout our ministry's history, we have often encountered challenges or hurdles that must be overcome. When faced with them, Bill will often respond by saying something like, "Man's problems are God's opportunities." Or, "Whatever the problem, give it to God; it's an opportunity for Him to show His power."

One of these hurdles occurred the year I joined staff. Until that time, Bill had been responsible for raising all the funds for ministry and staff support. I was at home in Norfolk, Virginia, preparing to leave for California and my first staff assignment at UCLA. The day before I was to leave, he called and announced a change that was to affect all staff from that time to the present. "Curt, the Lord has shown me that I can no longer be responsible for all the funds necessary to run Campus Crusade. From now on, every staff member will have the privilege of trusting God for his own personal support needs. You need to trust God for $100 a month [this was before inflation], and you need to find it before coming to California."

As it turned out, that proved to be a real test of the strength of my call. We had not been trained to raise finances, and we had no tools to help. But God proved His faithfulness in this area, and He has continued to do so for 45 years.

Staff raising their own salaries was not a common practice among organizations such as ours. Some thought this requirement would be a death knell for CCC, but God used it to bless our ministry, and instead of losing staff, we grew dramatically. Forty-five years later, we are still growing.

Another challenge faced early on was the need for a staff-training facility. In March 1958, my temporary staff assignment was in Arizona. A call came from California informing us that Crusade had just been given property in Mound, Minnesota. The grounds had formerly been a Keswick Conference Center. The property included a nice home on the lake and two older houses that needed refurbishing. We immediately needed to assemble a team of staff to go and build a chapel to accommodate the training needs for that summer.

Two weeks later, about fifteen of us arrived in Mound. Over the next three months, we experienced some remarkable miracles. None of us knew very much about building, but we worked day and night. On the day that staff training was to begin, we all gathered on the grounds. Bill joined us, and together we laid sod and had a great time of rejoicing. The impossible had been accomplished.

These two illustrations—having the staff raise their own support and this unusual building project undertaken with a handful of novice builders—were great risks. They could have failed, but God used both to test our faith and build it in preparation for what He wanted to do through us. Bill has always been a "risk taker" for God, willing to make difficult and sometimes unpopular decisions. More often than not, his decisions have proven correct.

By his example, Bill taught us to move out in faith and trust God. We may not keep up with Bill, but almost all of our staff have learned to break through barriers by faith.

AN EXAMPLE IN THE AREA OF FAMILY

My family and I were the Bright's neighbors for five years at Arrowhead Springs. As Bill's neighbors and his personal assistant, I had a lot of time and opportunity to observe him and his relationship with Vonette as well as their sons, Zachary and Bradley.

There has never been any question for me concerning the priority that he placed on his family. Even though he was the founder and president, for fifty years he has kept his priorities in their proper order: God, family, then ministry. Matthew 6:33 is the key: "Seek first his kingdom and his righteousness, and all these things will be given to you as well."

How was this demonstrated? For as long as my memory serves, Bill has always referred to Vonette as cofounder of Campus Crusade. When the boys were young, she did not travel with him much, but when events like staff training, lay conferences, and the like were held at Arrowhead Springs, she was very much involved. She was a wonderful model for our staff women. Campus Crusade has always underscored that both husband and wife must be called to staff and involved in ministry while maintaining a standard of God first, then family, then ministry. No couple demonstrated this commitment more beautifully than Bill and Vonette.

We would be in the office in a strategy meeting or handling the myriad situations facing a burgeoning young world ministry when the phone would ring. If it was Zachary or Bradley, Bill would call a time-out to talk with him and then return to his work. His sons knew that they had a direct line to their father. He wanted them to know how important they were to him.

I remember the day Bill said, "We need to do something special for our boys." He was referring to his younger son, Bradley, and my son, Shaun. "Let's build a tree house for them," he said.

We chose a eucalyptus tree halfway between his house and mine. He did what he did best: he envisioned what it should look like, and I asked my friend, a carpenter, if he would help us build it. I don't remember how many nails Bill drove, but between us and the boys, we got it done. The boys' eyes lit up with pride when it was completed. I had the privilege of spending the first sleepover in it with the guys.

Bill and Vonette demonstrated their love and appreciation for the staff family in many ways. At Christmas, they would have a series of parties for those who worked at headquarters. We would go to their home in small groups for singing, celebration of the Lord's birth, and delicious food. They were great at showing hospitality.

Staff members are very important to them. When a staff member faced some difficulty or sorrow in the family, Bill and Vonette would be quick to call, offer comfort, or ask what they could do to help. They would say, "When our staff rejoice, we rejoice with them. When they hurt, we hurt." Many times, I saw Bill's heart for the staff family as he wept with someone who had suffered a loss.

The time came when Bill felt impressed to do something special for staff to mark and celebrate their years serving God through Campus Crusade for Christ. He decided that he personally would raise the money and give appropriate gifts to mark certain milestones in their careers. He wanted the staff to know how important that are to him.

Here's a humorous aside. People who know Bill at close range know that he has a "weakness." We would be coming home to Arrowhead from the airport. Our schedule had been busy; he had spoken several times and had met with many staff. When we got in the car, it would be only a few minutes before he was catching a catnap. Suddenly, his eyes would open and he would say, "Was that a Baskin Robbins we just passed?"

I would kid him by saying, "This car will pass any place on the road except an ice cream shop."

On occasion, I would go to his bungalow in the evening to do some work. He would take me into the kitchen where he had been trying out a recipe someone had sent him for sugar-free, fat-free ice cream. He loved ice cream and was always on the lookout for just the right formula with great taste. We fought that battle together.

When it comes to family—either personal family or our staff family—Bill and Vonette have set a wonderful, godly example for us to follow.

AN EXAMPLE IN PRAYER

Prayer has always been an important part of the Campus Crusade ministry and emphasis. The ministry was begun and established at UCLA in the midst of a 24-hour prayer chain. That pattern has continued for the last fifty years. One of the "secrets" of God's blessing throughout the years has been our commitment to prayer, starting with Bill's leadership in this area.

I'm reminded of the story of Daniel of old. Those jealous of his position as manager of one of the most significant nations in his era spied on him to discover his secret. What they learned was that he was more loyal to his God than he was to the king. He prayed even when prayer was forbidden. God vindicated his devotion and commitment, expressed through his prayer life.

The incredible blessing of God on the ministry of Crusade and the Brights is the result of a personal life of prayer lived out in the sovereignty of God's plan. Their secret life with God has etched itself in their faces, as well as brought wonderful blessings that God has showered upon them and the ministry they have faithfully shepherded.

Prayer and praise go together. At UCLA, we met often as a staff team to pray for our ministry. When Bill was in town, he would join us. After one such time together, he asked me to lead our next gathering. Because of how he modeled dependence upon God in prayer and was so quick to offer praise, I was inspired to spend time in the Word. So I put together a collection of promises related to prayer as well as passages on praise.

The next week when we met, I had several typewritten pages with passages on prayer and praise. He and Vonette were so excited that we often used them as a guide for our staff times of prayer and praise.

During the years at Arrowhead as his assistant and director of the headquarters ministry, I remember his first response to difficulties and problems. "Let's thank God!" We would pray, thanking God for whatever it was, and then give the burden to Him and ask for His solution. First Thessalonians 5:16–18 gave the pattern: "Be joyful always; pray continually; give thanks in all circumstances, for this is God's will for you in Christ Jesus."

Often, Bill would combine prayer and action. When faced with a ministry need, he would pray and ask God for the solution, then pick up the phone and talk to someone about that need. But sometimes he would close his door and ask not to be disturbed. I remember while at UCLA that the ministry was faced with a critical financial need. He talked to God about the need. It was a Saturday and Bill was at home when he felt impressed to go to the office. Bill was the only one there when a knock came on the door. It was the mailman with a registered letter. When Bill opened the letter, it contained a check for exactly the amount needed sent by a man who had no knowledge of the need. The man had responded to the Lord's impression to send it.

Through the years, those kinds of answers to prayer have encouraged us to keep on praying, to keep on trusting, and to keep on pushing out the boundaries. Jesus gave us His instructions:

> When you pray, do not be like the hypocrites, for they love to pray standing in the synagogues and on the street corners to be seen by men. I tell you the truth, they have received their reward in full. When you pray, go into your room, close the door and pray to your Father, who is unseen. Then your Father, who sees what is done in secret, will reward you. And when you pray, do not keep on babbling like pagans, for they think they will be heard because of their many words. Do not be like them, for your Father knows what you need before you ask Him.
>
> This is how you should pray: Our Father in heaven, hallowed be your name, your kingdom come, your will be done on earth as it is in heaven. Give us today our daily bread. Forgive us our debts, as we also have forgiven our debtors. And lead us not into temptation, but deliver us from the evil one.
>
> For if you forgive men when they sin against you, your heavenly Father will also forgive you. But if you do not forgive men their sins, your Father will not forgive your sins.
>
> When you fast, do not look somber as the hypocrites do, for they disfigure their faces to show men they are fasting. I tell you the truth, they have received their reward in full. But when you fast, put oil on your head and wash your face, so that it will not be obvious to men that you are fasting, but only to your Father, who is unseen; and your Father, who sees what is done in secret, will reward you (Matthew 6:5–18).

One of Bill's dreams has just been fulfilled at our new headquarters in Orlando, Florida. A prayer center was recently dedicated which uses the latest technology to provide up-to-date prayer requests and answers to prayer.

Bill Bright has been not only the founder and president of Campus Crusade, but also the leader of our movement, leading by example. His godly leadership has been observed and respected. The Body of Christ worldwide has been greatly benefited and the cause of the Great Commission extended to multiplied millions because of his commitment to following the Lord.

He has successfully utilized various forms of leadership styles validated by leaders in both the Old and New Testaments. Like Nehemiah, his leadership style provides a great example for our day: an organizer and pragmatist with a passion for God and devotion to prayer. There is also the model provided by Jesus Himself in Philippians 2:5–11:

> Your attitude should be the same as that of Christ Jesus: Who, being in very nature God, did not consider equality with God something to be grasped, but made himself nothing, taking the very nature of a servant, being made in human likeness. And being found in appearance as

> a man, he humbled himself and became obedient to death—even death on a cross! Therefore God exalted him to the highest place and gave him the name that is above every name, that at the name of Jesus every knee should bow, in heaven and on earth and under the earth, and every tongue confess that Jesus Christ is Lord, to the glory of God the Father.

Jesus was imbued with great authority, yet He exhibited an attitude of a servant. Bill has sought to lead according to Jesus' model. Although Bill has had authority, he has sought to exercise it in a humble, Spirit-filled manner.

As a servant of Christ, he has been careful, from the earliest days until now, to maintain and exhibit the character expected in a Christian leader by the power of the Holy Spirit. Much of what I value on the subject of leadership and have sought to apply in my life and ministry has been these lessons learned from observing him. Thank you, Bill, for your walk with God and the example you have set for others.

We each need to realize that we teach at least as much by example as by what we say—probably more. Paul knew that he had set the example for Timothy and that Timothy followed his teaching, his conduct, his purpose, his faith, his patience, his love, his perseverance, and even his persecutions and sufferings (2 Timothy 3:10,11). I think Bill knows we staff members and many of those we have ministered to seek to follow his vision, his determination to make God the first priority, his dependence on the Holy Spirit, his focus on evangelism, his training of disciples, his breaking through barriers by faith, his example of making his family and his staff family a priority, his prayer life, even his teaching others by example. He has set the pace in these and in many other ways.

If God has called you in some way to be a leader of other Christians, seriously consider your responsibility to lead by example. Your life speaks so loudly, people can't hear what you say. Be a conscious example for them.

CHAPTER 11

Every Believer an Evangelist

ROE BROOKS

On Staff since 1952

Associate Director, The International Leadership Academies

Gulliver, the hero in *Gulliver's Travels*, wakes up tied by cords and stakes to the ground by little people—Lilliputians. His dilemma is that to free himself, he must thrash about and harm these little people. Which should he do: stay bound or hurt someone?

Perhaps you and I are not too far removed from a similar dilemma. What ties your feet and hands and stops your movement of following Christ and sharing His message with others? Do you wake up with restraints on presenting Christ? Do you worry, "How can I start? How can I avoid offending my friends, or sounding unintellectual, or being too personal, or forcing my beliefs on others?"

Our rules of effective relationships may include "never talk about religion or politics." We may face some kind of persecution if we speak up. Or we may feel that it is only the clergy who should be witnesses. We think we face a choice: either we stay bound by the rules society puts on us about not sharing our faith or we can venture out and risk offending others and perhaps even hurting ourselves.

Individuals composing the sleeping giant of the church in America and around the world have for years awakened to God's call to witness only to find themselves tied down by various social cords and stakes. Has God made a way for us to be free of society's restrictions?

THE NEW TESTAMENT PICTURE OF LIBERATED LAY WITNESS

Reading the New Testament examples of a liberated lay witness should be a great encouragement to us. It is a snapshot of what actually has happened throughout church history, as the witness of evangelical laypeople led to various Christian movements. This is still happening today. Our question as we discover our history should be, "Lord, what do You want to teach me about my witness and a spiritual movement in my city?"

We may begin with an encouraging prayer like this: "Lord, thank You that You made me with a desire and ability to speak about what I have seen and heard." Be positive. Realize that men and women are created to share their deepest joys with others. Why is it that shy children are enthusiastic and winsome in "show and tell" times? They are created that way. You are created that way.

In John 12:17–19, ordinary men and women created a movement by relating the story of Jesus raising Lazarus. They were not actual disciples yet, nor had they been recipients of the Holy Spirit and His gifts. However, their witness created a movement, which was totally discouraging to the enemy's power structure:

> So the multitude who were with Him when He called Lazarus out of the tomb, and raised him from the dead, were bearing Him witness. For this cause also the multitude went and met Him [as He was entering Jerusalem on Palm Sunday], because they heard that He performed this sign. The Pharisees therefore said to one another, "You see that you are not doing any good; look, the world has gone after Him" (John 12:17–19, NASB).

Those who testified about this miracle helped cause the elation of Palm Sunday!

Another example of the inherent power of verbal witness—combined this time with the deep power of God's Word—occurred when disciples of John the Baptist approached Jesus with John's question about whether He was the Messiah or not. John was in prison, brushing death's door. He needed affirmation that the signs of the descending dove and voice from heaven at Jesus' baptism really meant He was the Messiah.

Jesus told John's disciples to encourage him by telling him what they had seen and heard—in other words, to relate their "story." Because John and his disciples were familiar with the prophecies in Isaiah 35:5 (about opening blind eyes and deaf ears) and Isaiah 61:1 (about preaching good news, binding the brokenhearted, and proclaiming liberty to the captives), Jesus said, "Go and report to John what you have seen and heard: the blind receive sight, the lame walk, the lepers are cleansed, and the deaf hear, the dead are raised up, the poor have the gospel preached to them" (Luke 7:22, NASB). Their ability to tell what they saw and experienced is the built-in, divinely created, "sow and tell" mechanism with which they served Jesus Christ. They sowed the gospel seed by telling others what they had seen and heard. We also have this ability to "sow and tell" today.

A friend and former dean of Eastern Nazarene College, a wonderful Christian, illustrates this trait. When she traveled, Ann would ask the person next to her on the plane if he wanted to hear her "story." Even though some were busy or angry-looking, they said yes! She had amazing results. She also had a little song to sing about Jesus working in her life. It was her unique "sow and tell" time. Why was she constantly asked to travel and speak? It was because people wanted to hear her "story." People were profoundly encouraged to hear how businessmen and women, grieving mothers, counterculture types, and young married people responded to her. Her approach was so strange that listeners concluded that God was anxious to help them, also, to "sow and tell"—which is why she spoke.

Jesus' Example

The "sow and tell" mandate started when Jesus trained His disciples to do outreach through His teaching and by His own example. He then sent them out two by two: "He summoned the twelve and began to send them out in pairs; and He was giving them authority over the unclean spirits" (Mark 6:7; see also Matthew 10:1ff and Luke 9:1ff).

Not only did Jesus work with His disciples in field-training, but He creatively trained them on four occasions as they traveled to other areas: 1) beyond the Sea of Galilee (Matthew 10; Mark 6; Luke 9; John 6); 2) in Tyre and Sidon (Matthew 15; Mark 7); 3) at Phoenicia, Mt. Hermon, and the Decapolis (Matthew 15; Mark 7–8); and 4) in Bethsaida and Caesaria Philippi (Matthew 16; Mark 8; Luke 9). These were times when He equipped the disciples for their future ministry.

Eventually, scores of disciples were trained and sent out with spiritual power over Satan: "Now after this the Lord appointed seventy others, and sent them two and two ahead of Him to every city and place where He Himself was going to come... The seventy returned with joy, saying, 'Lord, even the demons are subject to us in Your name'" (Luke 10:1,17, NASB).

New Testament Greek scholar A. T. Robertson points out that Jesus and His disciples saturated the Jewish villages with personal witness while intensely evangelizing Galilee.[1] Robertson is certain that Jesus made two, possibly three, tours throughout Galilee. Jesus also sent out the seventy (or seventy-two) two-by-two (Luke 10:1–24). Jesus spent three years in indefatigable witness, then added the witness of His disciples so that every open heart could respond to Him as the Messiah.

The Example of the Early Church

After Pentecost, the disciples fully experienced Christ's promise (divine assistance) in Acts 1:8: "You shall receive power when the Holy Spirit has come upon you; and you shall be My witnesses both in Jerusalem, and in all Judea and Samaria, and even to the remotest part of the earth."

To fulfill this promise, a marvelous ministry began in Jerusalem, the city where it was impossible for Jesus to minister. Ministry then spread to Samaria through Philip (Acts 8:4–8), and through Philip to the Ethiopian government (Acts 8:26–39), and then to Caesar's household through Paul —to the uttermost parts of the earth.

The powerful witness of the happy, giving Jerusalem church fellowship pictures what has occurred at different times in church history. Changed, godly, unselfish, rejoicing lives promote people-movements. Here is a passage describing the phenomena in the early church.

> So then, those who had received [Peter's] word were baptized; and there were added that day about three thousand souls . . . Everyone kept feeling a sense of awe; and many wonders and signs were taking place through the apostles. And all those who had believed were together and had all things in common; and they began selling their property and possessions, and were sharing them with all, as anyone might have need . . . [They were] praising God, and having favor with all the people. And the Lord was adding to their number day by day those who were being saved (Acts 2:41–47, NASB).

Spiritual gifts—in the case of Jerusalem, sign gifts—developed the church immensely. Acts goes on to tell of other dramatic experiences.

> Peter said, "I do not posses silver and gold, but what I do have I give to you: In the name of Jesus Christ the Nazarene—walk!" And seizing him by the right hand, he raised him up; and immediately his feet and his ankles were strengthened. And with a leap, he stood upright and began to walk; and he entered the temple with them, walking and leaping and praising God . . . While he was clinging to Peter and John, all the people ran together to them at the so-called portico of Solomon, full of amazement. But when Peter saw this, he replied to the people, "Men of Israel, why do you marvel at this, or why do you gaze at us, as if by our own power or piety we had made him walk? The God of Abraham, Isaac, and Jacob, the God of our fathers, has glorified His servant Jesus" (Acts 3:6–13, NASB).

> And at the hands of the apostles many signs and wonders were taking place among the people; and they were all with one accord in Solo-

> mon's portico...And all the more believers in the Lord, multitudes of men and women, were constantly added to their number; to such an extent that they even carried the sick out into the streets, and laid them on cots and pallets, so that when Peter came by, at least his shadow might fall on any one of them. And also the people from the cities in the vicinity of Jerusalem were coming together, bringing people who were sick or afflicted with unclean spirits; and they were all being healed (Acts 5:12–16, NASB).

But these experiences are not confined to the early church. This last biblical account also depicts what happened at a recent *JESUS* film showing. Jesus' power to heal blindness occurred as a blind woman asked Jesus to heal her during the film. Many came to Christ as a result of her healing.

The lives of Christians, the apostolic words, and spiritual gifts overwhelmingly created a people-movement in Jerusalem. But God even had another force at work to maintain a verbal witness—an angel!

> The high priest rose up, along with all his associates (that is the sect of the Sadducees), and they were filled with jealousy; and they laid hands on the apostles, and put them in a public jail. But an angel of the Lord during the night opened the gates of the prison, and taking them out he said, "Go your way, stand and speak to the people in the temple the whole message of this Life" (Acts 5:17–20, NASB; note also Peter's experience in Acts 12:7–11).

Once again, this seems to depict what a *JESUS* film team experienced—angelic protection from men who were creeping into position at night to assassinate the sleeping team. But God intervened.

The way in which a person comes to Christ, along with the experiences leading up to that decision, provides a unique testimony of God's power that can be used to "sow and tell." Note how Ananias told Paul that God had been working in his life so that he could be a witness: "The God of our fathers has appointed you to know His will, and to see the Righteous One, and to hear an utterance from His mouth. For you will be a witness for Him to all men of what you have seen and heard" (Acts 22:14,15, NASB). Each of us can be encouraged that God has shaped our lives to give us a platform for ministry. God gives each of us our "story" to tell. That story, freely told by laymen and women, is the liberated lay witness that will change the world.

REFORMATION HISTORY OF THE LIBERATED LAY WITNESS

In the twelfth century, a wealthy merchant of Lyon, businessman Peter Waldo, who wanted to know the way to heaven, was told by a theologian to sell all he had and give to the poor if he wished to be perfect. In 1176 he did just that. He was inspired by Christ's teachings in a French translation of the New Testament, so he started his own lay movement! Dressed like Christ, he preached in towns and cities. Taking no purse, he emulated the disciples on their missions. The moral appeal of his example, in sharp contrast to the corrupt churchmen of southern France, made Christianity very attractive.

Waldo soon attracted followers who called themselves "the Poor Men of Lyons." They went about two by two and lived on what was given them by their audiences. The movement spread rapidly and was soon planted in Spain, Italy, Germany, and Bohemia. Converts memorized large portions of the New Testament in their native languages and followed its teachings. In this movement, laypeople preached, conducted the Lord's Supper (Eucharist), and heard confession. The movement had its own leaders—bishops, priests, deacons. Because of persecution by the Roman Catholic church, they fled to the alpine valleys of Switzerland, and the movement continued into the time of the Reformation in the sixteenth century.

As the Reformation reintroduced many biblical truths to the common man, a dynamic lay witness arose. However, this movement did not mean that all the branches of the Reformation were active in promoting lay witness.

Of the Lutheran, Calvinist, Anglican, and Anabaptist churches involved in the Reformation, only the Anabaptist movement in Switzerland, Germany, Austria, Hungary, Bohemia, Moravia, and Holland promoted a lay witness. The other Reformation churches tended to confine witness to the clergy.

Lutherans and Reformed churches were founded on the Constantine concept that a state must be united in religious belief. Luther and Calvin were convinced that cultural chaos would result if common men interpreted Scripture, created theology, and formed churches of different sorts. The state therefore had to have only one theological belief, handed down by approved scholars, to which all citizens must subscribe. All must belong to one state-church structure.

The Anabaptist lay movement was cruelly persecuted by Lutherans, Calvinists, and Romanists. Thousands of Anabaptists were hunted by churchmen and soldiers, and were burned at the stake, beheaded, or drowned. Roman Catholics were more merciful, though. They burned Anabaptists with a bag of gunpowder around their necks![2]

As a result of a belief in state churches, German citizens became Lutheran because the prince was Lutheran. The Swiss were Reformed because the Swiss cantons (and city government of Geneva or Zurich) were Reformed. The English became Anglican because Henry VIII formed the Anglo-Catholic church. (It has been said that the Anglican church was the only denomination founded by divorce. Later, the Thirty-Nine Articles gave it a more biblical basis.) Since Reformation churches practiced infant baptism, a German, Swiss, or English citizen became a church member through citizenship and infant baptism.

Unlike the Anabaptists, the other movements did not insist upon an inner transformation by faith. Anabaptists, however, required personal regeneration and believer's baptism for church membership. For them, baptism was the point at which a believer committed himself to Christian ethical conduct and to assistance from the church to live the Christian life. At the Lord's Supper, the believer recommitted himself to the same conduct. This meant that the believer committed himself to church discipline, as reflected in Matthew 18:15–18. If, after attempted correction for sin, a church member was unwilling to repent, he was to be treated as a heathen.

Therefore, the life of an Anabaptist was much different than others in the Reformation. For instance, any man who did not drink excessively, curse, or abuse his workers or family could be suspected of being Anabaptist. And this meant persecution!

Anabaptists stood in contrast to a majority of Lutheran laymen, who mistakenly felt that works included moral behavior, and since the Christian is not to live by the works of the Law, Lutheran Protestantism often removed moral restraints. Among the Lutherans, there was almost a complete separation between clergy and laity, with nothing for the laity to do. As Ralph Winter observes:

> The Lutheran movement did not in a comparable sense (as Roman Catholicism had done) readopt the sodalities, the Catholic orders, that had been so prominent in the Roman tradition. This omission, in my evaluation, represents the greatest error of the Reformation and the greatest weakness of the resulting Protestant tradition. Had it not been for the so-called Pietist movement, the Protestants would have been totally devoid of any organized renewing structures within their tradition.[3]

Luther reportedly was depressed because the Lutheran church held multitudes who had not experienced the liberation and love for God that he experienced through justification by faith. This lack of freedom (cords and stakes) robbed many of their "story."

Dirck Willems is an example of singular Anabaptist Christian character. He was fleeing for his life across a frozen lake when his pursuer broke through the ice. With the man in mortal danger, Willems turned back and rescued his pursuer—knowing he would die for doing so. As a result, Willems was imprisoned and burned at the stake in 1569. This was the kind of lay witness that ignited the spread of the gospel.

Anabaptists were largely an underground movement, populating over 2,000 towns and villages of Germany, Switzerland, and Austria. Their movement knew no political boundaries and was spread through the testimonies of ordinary people. In the first two years, they lost virtually all their leaders. Despite persecution, the movement spread rapidly into nearly all European countries, but mainly among the lower classes. This was accomplished through direct evangelism—sending people out to proclaim the gospel.

Today's descendents of Anabaptists are represented by such groups as the Mennonites, Amish, Mennonite Brethren, Hutterites, and Brethren in Christ. They have had a great impact on all of Christianity. The following descriptions will give you an idea of the power of lay witness.

> All over Austria, there was a great spread of the Gospel and numerous churches were founded, which after long and heroic suffering were scattered and crushed by persecution. In Tyrol and Gorz a thousand persons were burnt, beheaded, or drowned... So, in place after place, the Lord's witnesses were raised up by the preaching of Jesus Christ and Him crucified, and in the most literal way followed in His footsteps. Troops of soldiers were sent through these countries to search out and kill those called "heretics" without trial.
>
> In the Tyrol, [Hans Mandl] baptized over 400 persons. He was repeatedly imprisoned... Shortly after one of these escapes [from prison], he addressed a meeting of a thousand brethren and sisters in a wood, but was captured again the same year (1560).[4]

Stories of individuals who were committed to lay witness are inspiring. Hans Hut, who died in prison in 1527, was a book peddler who made more converts in southern Europe than all Anabaptist leaders combined. He had a three-year ministry goal. Since he was convinced that the Lord would return in three years, he wanted to raise up 144,000 Christians.

Hans Hutter (1500?–1536) was another who rose from the ranks of the common man. He was "a scantily educated hatter; Hutter served only two years as leader (of the Anabaptists) in Tyrol and Moravia, yet he managed to unify this group according to the apostolic model of community of goods in Acts 2–5. Consequently, this group became known as the Hutterites and 450 years later are still thriving as Christians living communally against the backdrop of an opposing worldly reality."[5] Hutter was hunted down, tortured, whipped, immersed in freezing water, doused with brandy, and publicly burned at the insistence of the Austrian king, a Roman Catholic.

Luther's Bible of 1534 has a caricature of an Anabaptist preacher before a small village group on the title page of Hosea. These lay preachers were itinerant missionaries who moved on to other towns and villages after only a few days of instructing converts. In the spirit of the times, they sometimes remained silent about their identities. In short, the Anabaptist movement provided testimony by life and lip of the layman.

The eras of greatest evangelism in America were not primarily lay-witness movements. The Great Awakenings in America were wonderful times in which laymen were brought to Christ in clergy-led evangelistic meetings and in churches. Later, the "altar call" was developed. But this too was clergy evangelism, where the preacher was expected to evangelize through meetings at the church building. This is a reversal of lay evangelism in which the "church scattered."[6] The work of evangelists like Dwight L. Moody and Billy Sunday promoted mass evangelism and follow-up, which Dr. Graham has further perfected. But as those who were converted wanted to serve Christ, laypeople found opportunities to serve through a new concept: the Sunday school. The American Sunday school movement led to much outreach among children and then among their parents. This, too, was largely within church buildings or under church auspices; however, laypeople did much of the work.

RECENT HISTORY OF THE LIBERATED LAY WITNESS

Lay witness, then, has been shackled over the centuries by the rules which discouraged the common man from "sowing and telling." But in the 1960s, it became obvious that laymen wanted and needed training to share Christ with others. That was just the kind of liberated lay witness that Bill Bright envisioned.

By 1963, so many college students had responded to a challenge to witness that many Campus Crusade banquets for laypeople were sponsored by Bill Jones of Los Angeles. At these banquets, a new Christian student usually gave a testimony, which was followed by a testimony by a disciple whom that student had led to Christ. Students would tell of personally reaching and developing disciples on their campus. They would share their vision of intensely evangelizing their campus by going out witnessing two-by-two. They aspired to reach other parts of the world by becoming Campus Crusade staff members.

It was not unusual to have laymen and women come to the head table and say, "I have been a Christian for thirty years, but these students are more mature and capable than I am. What do you teach them?" Bill Bright, who would speak at our banquets, heard this many times in his travels and had begun several years before to minister to adults in day-long Christian Living seminars in churches.

The Campus Crusade staff were encouraged not to wait for Bill to come and speak, but to minister to these friends and supporters by taking a Saturday to share what we taught students. As campus staff, we all felt reticent about inviting successful professionals and men and women old enough to be our parents to hear us speak about effective Christian living and witness. However, I was inspired by a report from Ted Martin at the University of Minnesota. His experience in successfully training laypeople had been heartwarming.

In 1963, I invited interested adults to a Saturday training event in Boston's historic Park Street Church. We shared the truths of confession of sin, of cleansing, and of appropriating the power of the Holy Spirit by faith. Furthermore, we had those who attended practice sharing *The Four Spiritual Laws*, two by two. By noon, they were sufficiently prepared to share Christ through *The Four Spiritual Laws* in the adjoining Park Street Common.

Because I informed them of this phase of outreach only minutes before it was to happen, it seemed half of the audience was about to suffer a heart attack. But they bravely ventured forth. Returning for our bag lunches an hour later, their faces registered an inner change from fear to joy, faith, and love. Each pair had seen a decision for Christ. After eating our lunches and sharing, we finished the day with instruction on walking in the Spirit and witnessing in the Spirit. They left different people than when they came. The difference was that now the Holy Spirit was using them in the lives of others as they yielded to His control.

To return to our Lilliputian dilemma: As Bill had seen in his seminars, the cords of social uneasiness and fear of witnessing were severed by confession of sin and appropriation of the Holy Spirit by faith. Great joy followed as a believer trusted the Lord in outreach. The cord of not knowing how to begin or close the conversation was severed by knowing how to introduce and use *The Four Spiritual Laws* effectively. Training and effective tools were two of the keys to a liberated lay witness. And the great joy was that as these cords were severed, lay witness was accomplished without causing undue harm to anyone.

RESTORING FREEDOM TO THE CHURCH

In 1964, I was asked to transfer from Boston to the Arrowhead Springs headquarters to develop weeklong Lay Institutes of Evangelism in cities throughout America. This would be more effective training than a day-long seminar.

Howard Ball and Kenneth Berven, two effective businessmen from Illinois and Washington (a Methodist and a Lutheran), left their businesses to join Campus Crusade to help teach these Lay Institutes. Their lives had been changed. God gripped their hearts through Bill's messages. They wanted to invest their lives in changing Americans as they had been changed. They wanted to raise up a lay movement. Business and money no longer compared to the anticipation of seeing lives changed by Christ. They planned to arrive early in 1965 at Arrowhead Springs, as soon as they could disengage from their business ventures. I was challenged to train them in citywide, weeklong Lay Institutes, *which had yet to be developed!*

Bill found a friend, Pastor Joseph Hemphill of the San Gabriel Union Church, who was willing to donate his church on the eastern edge of Los Angeles as a site for the training. My responsibility was to invest several months in devising an area-wide Lay Institute for the San Gabriel Valley. The second step would be to create a manual of procedures and lesson plans to share with Howard and Ken, as well as other committees, so that Lay Institutes might be developed across America.

The anticipation of seeing thousands of lives changed in city after city was energizing. Because of that vision, the effort and long hours were a joy. My wife and family unselfishly invested in that vision by allowing me to travel and work with committees in large cities.

As a result, Lay Institutes were held in Oklahoma City, Kansas City, Atlanta, Dallas, Portland, Minneapolis, San Diego, and Los Angeles. Some approached four or five thousand in attendance.

The citywide Lay Institute was designed to unite as many denominations and churches as wished to participate in training. Young and old could participate in training fitted to their age and circumstances. The audience came together amazed at the army of believers in their city. Lay witness had become a movement!

Throughout the week, excitement increased, starting with the evening messages of "Cleansing by Confession," then "Appropriating the Filling of the Holy Spirit by Faith," "Walking in the Spirit," and "Witnessing in the

Spirit." Evening by evening, we could see the people change in friendliness and love. Besides the message in the main auditorium, there were seminars on effectively presenting *The Four Spiritual Laws*, developing a testimony, giving initial follow-up, and incorporating new believers into the church fellowship.

On the last day, Saturday, thousands of Christians were assigned sections of the city for door-to-door evangelism. As a result, after one week of training Christians how to share their "story," hundreds of people were introduced to Christ. Laymen, not professionals, were reaching men and women for Christ. This was the exciting beginning of the lay division of Campus Crusade for Christ.

After the Saturday outreach, the participants returned to the auditorium to share their witnessing experiences—thrilling stories of people coming to Christ. For most, God had used them for the first time in their lives to bring another person to Christ. They had new freedom in presenting Christ. They told moving stories of new Christians' gratefulness for their witness. They shared how being controlled by the Spirit of God had revolutionized their lives. The Institute always seemed to end with an atmosphere of great joy and love. Families who attended became more united in Christ. It was such a revival experience that it was usually difficult to go to sleep after the Institute.

These men and women felt what the disciples felt upon their return from sharing the kingdom message two by two—"Lord, even the demons submit to us in Your name" (Luke 10:17, NASB). It appeared that we had captured the essentials of training that Jesus used when He trained and sent out the disciples in two-by-two outreach to evangelize a city. The joy and the freedom of the early church had been duplicated. Bond after bond had been severed. It was truly a solution to the Lilliputian dilemma of the church.

There can be many approaches to evangelism, but the elements of training and involvement in personal evangelism, when coupled, create a first-century experience.

RECENT EXAMPLES OF LAY WITNESS

Freeing laypeople to witness reaped a bountiful harvest! For example, in 1980, Tom Saab, a real estate agent from Salem, New Hampshire, attended a free showing of the *JESUS* film in Burlington, Massachusetts. I was in charge of the showing. He helped counsel those who made decisions. After the event, he returned to his city to personally follow-up those who made decisions. This was all so exciting to him. He had learned that he could have a personal *and* a mass ministry in his small city. Then he trained laymen in his church and established a free Salem Christian Film Festival. He trained laymen in more churches. By 1993, the Salem festival attracted 14,000 and registered 400 decisions. Other cities learned of this and began seeking his assistance.

In 1996, a group of Christians from various churches in Salinas, California, asked for Tom's help. In their fourth year (2000), 13,000 attended, registering 800 decisions.

In 1997, Tom incorporated the idea as The Christian Film Festivals of America, Inc. He has created attractive publicity. More cities are responding.

In October 2000, San Clemente, California, secured his assistance for their first Film Festival. The *JESUS* film was one of the films shown. The personnel from The JESUS Film Project office have enthusiastically worked with Tom. As the festival was in progress, he reported that 6,000 attended and 225 made commitments to Christ. Tom rejoiced that in the twelve Christian Film Festivals he has developed, 8,000 persons have made decisions for Christ. Theatres in Orlando, Florida, have contacted him, granting free use if he would develop an Orlando Christian Film Festival for 2001. He is in the process of developing a group of laymen who will hold the festival.

Tom is still a businessman. He leaves his agency in the hands of his employees as he travels to train laymen and churches to establish their own citywide Christian Film Festivals. He loves to lead people to Christ personally, but he has also established this means of helping many other men and women become involved in this dual version of personal outreach and mass evangelism. The use of films, particularly the *JESUS* film, has opened communities to Christ. Tom Saab's personal strategy is not far from what has been found to be effective around the world. When lay believers are trained and encouraged to "sow and tell," movements are created.

Campus Crusade for Christ began as an American college student movement. However, with the expansion of Campus Crusade to other countries, the movement has turned to community evangelism and discipleship, not merely student evangelism. In many countries, the students live at home and commute to the university. In Mexico City, Christian students would ride the buses and give evangelistic messages to the commuting students. Many times, universities would be closed down by Communist agitation so the students would be at home. Utilizing this opportunity, Campus Crusade staff in these countries have combined the vision of community and student outreach. As with Tom Saab, the *JESUS* film became a tool to reach a community. Some youth who were reached by these showings were formed into film teams to reach the greater community.

In Hoogli, West Bengal, Rajat shows the *JESUS* film. Rajat came to Christ four years ago when the *JESUS* film was shown during Hindu festivals. Through film showings, he has begun three New Life training groups to whom he ministers.

In one village, he faced serious persecution. A Hindu put a pistol to his chest and said, "We won't allow you to preach this message here. Promise us that you will not work here, because if you don't, next time we will kill you."

Rajat answered, "As God wills. God has called me to preach the gospel here and I am here with His message. As I live, I will live for God. If I die, I will die for God. I do not fear man." The Lord allowed Rajat to continue ministering for three months even as the men continued to threaten his life.

The *JESUS* film showings create commitments, follow-up opportunities, and New Life groups. Pastor V., who started as a lay witness, began with a film team in Jammu, India. He wanted to reach his area because so few Christians lived there. Many responded to the film. He followed them up and began a small fellowship in his home. Finally, he became the full-time pastor of the church that he had started in his home. Today, he partners with the film ministry. "By keeping the *JESUS* film team in partnership, I can cover more villages than I could ever cover alone. The teams bring new seekers to the church every week. This makes my work with India Campus Crusade a blessing. I am planning to add more partnership teams in the future."

The *JESUS* video has given laymen additional strategies. An Alabama doctor purchased enough for distribution to every household in the state; other individuals distribute it in their community. In Muslim areas, the video provides a strategy for outreach as well.

Liberated lay witness is a great force to reach neighborhoods. For example, the Lighthouse Movement has provided Americans with the challenge to pray for ten households on their street, to care for the families and seek to meet needs of these households as much as possible, and to share Christ, possibly through the Christmas gift of a *JESUS* video or through Christian literature. Perhaps your church could train people how to be a part of this lay witness movement.

THE CHALLENGE

Whether it is the men and women in first-century Jerusalem, or later among the Waldensians, Anabaptists, or Wesleyans, a believer's life has to be attractive to be an effective testimony. This means that Christians must allow the Holy Spirit to give their lives holiness and the power to share Christ effectively. The Lay Institutes emphasize appropriation of the Holy Spirit by confession and faith. This is an essential first step in witnessing.

Second, effective personal witness needs a strategy through which to share the gospel with others so that they can respond to Christ as Lord and Savior. We must not merely share the facts. Many want to respond, but do not know how. We need to explain how with a winsome invitation to prayerfully receive Christ as Lord and Savior. I encourage you to view the close of the *JESUS* film where the explanation of *The Four Spiritual Laws* shows how you might invite another to receive Christ. Or you could use *The Four Spiritual Laws* booklet.

Third, if our winsome invitation leads to prayerful commitment, we then need to provide immediate and long-range follow-up. We must be committed to sacrificing ourselves and our time to follow-up. Immediate follow-up may be provided by using the material in the back of *The Four Spiritual Laws* booklet or other relevant follow-up material. Then do further personal follow-up or, if that is impossible, follow-up by mail or phone.

The history of Christian movements illustrates that God begins by raising up lay leaders who are committed to sharing Christ and His Word. These leaders provide inspiration, example, training, and tools.

God then uses these equipped laypeople to spread the message of Jesus Christ. God also gives to the church the Holy Spirit's desire to share Christ with every person on earth. Through His power, we are freed from our restraining bonds to "sow and tell." This liberated lay witness will result in a movement.

God is such a gracious Father to His children. May we seek His face to give leadership and desire to the Body of Christ to keep fulfilling the Great Commission. Our goal must be for every believer to become an effective evangelist.

NOTES

1. A. T. Robertson, *Harmony of the Gospels* (New York: Harper & Brothers, 1922), Matthew 9:35 footnote.
2. John S. Oyer, "Sticks and Stones Broke Their Bones and Vicious Names Did Hurt Them!," *Christian History*, Issue 5, 18.
3. R. D. Winter, "The Two Structures of God's Redemptive Mission," address to All-Asia Missionary Consultation, Korea, 1973.
4. F. H. Broadbent, *The Pilgrim Church* (Pickering & Inglis, Ltd., 1950), 170,171,176.

5. "A Gallery of Factions, Friends & Foes," *Christian History*, Issue 5, 15.
6. Bee Robert Coleman, "The Origin of the Altar Call in American Worship," *Asbury Seminarian*, Winter 1958, 19.

CHAPTER 12

Transferable Training

LOIS MACKEY
On Staff since 1957
International Ministries

Second Timothy 2:2 reverberates throughout the Campus Crusade for Christ materials, philosophy, strategies, and ministry training. It always has. We began using the old *King James Version* of the verse back in the fifties: "The things that thou hast heard of me among many witnesses, the same commit thou to faithful men, who shall be able to teach others also." Now we might include a paraphrase, "Pass on what you heard from me—the whole congregation saying Amen!—to reliable leaders who are competent to teach others" (*The Message*).

As then—so now.

THE SOURCE OF TRAINING

Historically, in Campus Crusade for Christ, we always go first to Scripture to investigate the biblical basis for all of the transferable materials, methods, and training that we develop. The apostle Paul was one of the most effective ministers of New Testament times. Some of the principles we have learned from his life and ministry have guided us on our journey of developing transferable training. Paul labored tirelessly for Christ, expressing his efforts this way:

> I am the least of the apostles and do not even deserve to be called an apostle, because I persecuted the church of God. But by the grace of God I am what I am, and his grace to me was not without effect. No, I worked harder than all of them—yet not I, but the grace of God that was with me (1 Corinthians 15:9,10).

He sought to reach the Gentiles for Christ and bring them to God. In describing his labors, he wrote to the church in Rome:

> So from Jerusalem all the way around to Illyricum, I have fully proclaimed the gospel of Christ. It has always been my ambition to preach the gospel where Christ was not known, so that I would not be building on someone else's foundation... But now that there is no more place for me to work in these regions, and since I have been longing for many years to see you, I plan to do so when I go to Spain (Romans 15:19–24).

Not only did Paul minister hard and effectively, he also successfully trained others to minister. The Book of Acts explains his work in Ephesus:

> He took the disciples with him and had discussions daily in the lecture hall of Tyrannus. This went on for two years, so that all the Jews and Greeks who lived in the province of Asia heard the word of the Lord (Acts 19:9,10).

Paul remained in Ephesus, but those he trained took the gospel to the entire province. One way that Paul trained others was by his example. He could say:

> Follow my example, as I follow the example of Christ. I praise you for remembering me in everything and for holding to the teachings, just as I passed them on to you (1 Corinthians 11:1,2).

The Greek word for "holding to," *katecho*, has the sense of "being bound to, possessing, and keeping the teachings throughout." That reduces dilution as the teachings are being passed from one generation to the next as disciples multiply. Paul reminds Timothy that he has followed his example in many ways: his teaching, conduct, purpose, faith, patience, love, perseverance, even persecutions and sufferings (2 Timothy 3:10,11). Paul trained others by teaching them, but he expected them to teach others the same things. He says to Timothy: "The things you have heard me say in the presence of many witnesses entrust to reliable men who will also be qualified to teach others" (2 Timothy 2:2). He wanted his teaching to be transferable from one generation of disciples to the next. Not only did Paul minister, but he successfully trained others to minister.

Perhaps most enduring of all, Paul trained by his written materials, his epistles, that were copied and circulated to the early churches, just as they are printed and circulated for us today. This was his most transferable training. Paul intended that these letters would be passed to others. He said in the Colossian epistle: "After this letter has been read to you, see that it is also read in the church of the Laodiceans and that you in turn read the letter from Laodicea" (Colossians 4:16). To the Thessalonians he wrote: "I charge you before the Lord to have this letter read to all the brothers" (1 Thessalonians 5:27).

Peter also admonishes his disciples to read what Paul had written in his letters:

> So then, dear friends, since you are looking forward to this, make every effort to be found spotless, blameless and at peace with him. Bear in mind that our Lord's patience means salvation, just as our dear brother Paul also wrote you with the wisdom that God gave him. He writes the same way in all his letters, speaking in them of these matters. His letters contain some things that are hard to understand, which ignorant and unstable people distort, as they do the other Scriptures, to their own destruction (2 Peter 3:14–16).

Paul is a model for us today in transferable training and how we are to view each other in ministry.

Training crosses gender lines. As a woman and a wife in ministry, it is refreshing to see how Paul viewed the ladies who labored beside him, along with their husbands. Scripture gives the example of Priscilla and Aquila and their ministry of multiplication in their house church in Ephesus:

> Meanwhile a Jew named Apollos, a native of Alexandria, came to Ephesus. He was a learned man, with a thorough knowledge of the Scriptures. He had been instructed in the way of the Lord, and he spoke with great fervor and taught about Jesus accurately, though he knew only the baptism of John. He began to speak boldly in the synagogue. When Priscilla and Aquila heard him, they invited him to their home and explained to him the way of God more adequately. When Apollos wanted to go to Achaia, the brothers encouraged him and wrote to the disciples there to welcome him. On arriving, he was a great help to those who by grace had believed. For he vigorously refuted the Jews in public debate, proving from the Scriptures that Jesus was the Christ (Acts 18:24–28).

It is significant that Paul recognized the equality of women in ministry. Women often view themselves as inadequate, but women and men are seen as equal in Paul's and the Lord's sight. Bill Bright has always included Vonette in the ministry and urged her to find her fullest ministry potential in the Lord. They have dynamically modeled this through the years for the rest of us.

It is exciting in these Scriptures to understand that the Greek word for "apostles" and "messenger" is *apóstolos*. Paul recognized others in ministry with the same word that he used regarding himself.

> Greet Andronicus and Junias, my relatives who have been in prison with me. They are outstanding among the *apostles* [*apóstolos*], and they were in Christ before I was (Romans 16:7).

> But I think it is necessary to send back to you Epaphroditus, my brother, fellow worker and fellow soldier, who is also your *messenger* [*apóstolos*], whom you sent to take care of my needs. For he longs for all of you and is distressed because you heard he was ill (Philippians 2:25,26).

Therefore, we are to treat the believers we train with the same regard Paul had for those he trained.

TRANSFERABILITY

In our movement in the past and at present, the greatest challenge in developing materials for winning, building, training, and sending others is transferability of scriptural principles. The principles need to be in a form that will be readily grasped, retained, and communicated again to another generation of seekers—with as little dilution as possible. This is at the heart of helping believers, staff, or other teams of people grow into multiplying disciples. Transferability has been the most important component in what we develop and share with others as mentors, evangelists, teachers, and trainers.

The part my husband, Curt, and I have played in the creation and development of materials has been in making them user-friendly to the greatest number of people. Then they can be used, absorbed, and passed on in the power, tutelage, and vitality of the Holy Spirit to another generation of seekers.

We are presently involved in a very exciting new project of Campus Crusade with the International Leadership University. The task is to help make our training more interactive and let millions worldwide be involved via cyberspace, whether as individuals in a classroom, church, or small group. The question is always asked, "What do students and others today need to know to become multipliers and movement builders who will bring about change that honors Christ in their societies?"

We must be prepared to present a timeless Christian message to a country and world that are constantly changing. Here's what an article in *EXPLORER Lite* had to say about the new urban geography:

> What began in a garden will find its ultimate conclusion in a city. A massive migration of people to the world's cities is underway, and here in the U.S., our cities are decentralizing and urban areas are being reshaped and redefined.
>
> "In 1900, about 8 percent of the world's population lived in sizeable cities. A century later, over 50 percent or more than 3 billion people live

in cities," according to urban missiologist Ray Bakke. "What this means from a ministry perspective is that more than two billion of the world's non-churched people are no longer geographically distant from the church; they are still culturally distant, but they live in the largest cities of the world."

"Fifteen of the largest 25 U.S. cities have lost 4 million people since 1965, while the nation's total population has risen by 60 million. At the same time the large 'vertical cities' have lost population, mid-sized horizontal cities, better able to offer a quality of life comparable to the suburbs, have grown rapidly," according to Fred Siegel, professor of history at the Cooper Union. For example, in the age of horizontal high-tech cities, Austin, TX, now has more population than Boston.[1]

Our materials for winning, building, training, and sending worldwide have always reflected the mission statement and goals of Campus Crusade for Christ. After forty-four years of being vitally involved with implementing all these principles, Curt and I have a real sense of being at the end of the beginning as we enter this new millennium. Our mission statements today vary little from those of the earliest days, except that they believe God for even more now.

For example, the International Leadership University mission statement differs only in visionary expansion: "The mission of the International Leadership University is clear. The goal is to educate and equip millions of Christians from America and around the world who will reach their countries with the gospel and effectively lead and influence their key national institutions: the media, the courts, business, government, the schools, and the church."

Today, materials for winning, building, training, and sending are tailored to specific situations. The materials, along with the *JESUS* films and videos, address the diverse flavor and high-tech communication on campuses and in communities worldwide. All our diverse ministries, from embassy/executive, family, children, ethnic, and cultural to inner-city emphases, require materials. The ministries to the military, prisons, churches, theological schools, the marketplace, professionals, New Life Training Centers, and Great Commission Training Centers, as well as the ministries of André Kole and Josh McDowell, utilize up-to-date tools. The International Leadership University will integrate satellite communications in its educational and training programs.

From the beginning, Bill Bright has always placed great importance on communication with staff, donors, and prayer partners, keeping them informed about the many facets of ministry. Campus Crusade started on U.S.

campuses in the early fifties. Next, it was launched by Dr. Joon Gon Kim in Korea, and soon after by Kundan Massey in Pakistan. Then it expanded to the rest of the world. The first periodical was called the *Communique*, then the name changed to *Challenger*, then to the *Collegiate Challenge*, and today we have *Worldwide Challenge*, along with our various websites and e-mail. The monthly *Brightside* is always anticipated by staff and others. The Brights include a message to all of us, as well as other challenging and insightful articles about happenings in Campus Crusade for Christ International.

We learned early to communicate that the remedy for sin is God's active abundant grace, and its dynamic is instant as we turn from our sin and surrender the authority of our lives to Christ. We are born broken, and grace is God's glue that puts us together. This response to grace carries through in our materials and training. One of Bill's core values is excellence. Excellence is an attribute of God, and Jesus Christ is our source and model for all aspects of life. Discerning, high-quality content, prepared in some high-tech expression, is therefore vitally important to us.

Bill has always encouraged creatively upgrading our materials without muddying our distinctives. He is very particular about what goes into print. He often says, "Remember, once something is in print you can't take it back. Campus Crusade for Christ's literature determines the movement."

MODELING THE VISION

Over the years, we have learned greatly from the Brights' visionary lifestyle regarding training. We caught this vision from them and the Lord. They helped us define what it means to first seek the Lord in everything we pass along to others. They have modeled hungering and thirsting for righteousness, spending time with our Lord, looking for His vision and direction, even though there is a desk piled high with priority training items to accomplish that day. As with the Brights, this all fleshes out by being obedient enough to pray and yield to the Holy Spirit's direction, keeping our hearts focused on Christ, His Word, and His standards. God's standard is the training game-plan that offers satisfaction and completion in Him, not just accomplishing goals. It keeps us fresh and open to seeking God's ideas instead of manipulating in frustration to gain some financial bottom line. Also, working closely with likeminded people enables us to have accountability in pulling the vision and materials together. Keeping a sense of humor in the midst of intensity is always important too.

In 1957, the opportunity to participate in all this began for me as a young, New York commercial artist on my first airplane trip out to wild and wondrous Hollywood. I had no idea that events there would change the course of my life. The visit was a holiday to visit my kindergarten mate and sister by bond, Ingrid Steensland. She had gone to California two years previously and was eager for me to meet her new friends and colleagues (the Crusade staff was about sixty folks then), as well as share in what she was learning and experiencing in her growing walk with the Lord.

We spent one portion of our holiday (five days) in the lovely San Bernardino Mountains at Forest Home Christian Conference Center, venue for the College Briefing Conference. This was part of Campus Crusade's staff training in those days. Along with hundreds of other collegians and young professionals, we were unabashedly challenged and called to serve Christ totally.

One afternoon in front of the cabin where Bill and Vonette stayed, Bill shared with me the ministry of the Holy Spirit as Ingrid sat quietly beside us praying. And quite unequivocally I had my mountaintop experience. I was from a very legalistic background. The refreshing breath of the Holy Spirit urged me to accept the moment-by-moment abundant life in Christ, to understand the cleansed life, and to receive the Spirit's power to share Christ's claims with others, which I longed for.

Earlier that day, Major Ian Thomas, founder of Torchbearers, had urged us to drop the tools of our careers and with our whole lives follow Christ to the world. We were encouraged to claim a country for Christ through prayer. Bill and Vonette placed their names on Russia, Ingrid on Norway, and I put mine on Australia. My artist's brush was dropped a couple of days later. Bill was the old man at about 35, and we were in our mid-twenties. We would tag along on his coattails on our great adventure, out on the edge with the Lord and Campus Crusade for Christ.

My employer was less appreciative of my request to help train a replacement and terminate by October. They acquiesced, but not before they sent a stinging letter to Bill about his proselytizing activities. Then came my folks—that was another story.

DEVELOPING MATERIALS

These were formative years for all of our basic materials. *The Four Spiritual Laws* was being written on paper napkins in Student Unions around the country. "God's Plan" was an evangelistic presentation for individuals and groups. The *Ten Basic Steps Toward Christian Maturity*, a series of follow-up Bible studies, were being cranked out on the mimeograph machine. (You young readers don't even know what that wondrous machine is, with its big, drippy drum.) Our favorite item (and probably Bill's) was the Praise and Promise Scripture sheets that were the bedrock of our vision and prayer lives.

Dottie Hauser Graham, Bill's first office manager, reminded me recently that this was Bill's "red period," in which we mimeographed red-letter editions. (During the years in his candy business, his signature colors were deep red and gray.) The first booklet we printed was in early 1958 on the ministry of the Holy Spirit in the life of the believer. It was entitled *Ye Shall Receive Power*. It went from Bill's notes on varied pieces of paper and assorted laundered shirt cardboards to mimeograph and then to print.

You can imagine that the booklet on the Holy Spirit's ministry in our lives was high on my list, and, of course, it has always been special to Bill. He has often said, "I would rather have a believer understand the ministry of the Holy Spirit than share *The Four Spiritual Laws* with someone." He feels that many more will come to Christ as believers are filled and empowered with the Holy Spirit. Although we agree with him, we don't know that we fully believe him—he loves to share with anybody and everybody about how they can know Christ personally and begin the great adventure for which Christ created them.

To our delight, a former staff member and outstanding department head at Columbia International University recently told the board at International Partnerships[2] that a must for all our young Ukrainian staff is a solid understanding of assurance of their salvation, the cleansed life, and the ministry of the Holy Spirit. He explained how vital these issues were to him as a growing young leader years ago, as well as today. These are the basic issues of all our training.

Next, we printed *The Uniqueness of Jesus* in a separate booklet. "God's Plan for Your Life" in article form was mimeographed, and we all memorized it for use in varied team meetings, dorms, and athletic groups—any place there were seekers. Bill's encounter with a businessman resulted in a letter based on "God's Plan" which he called "The Van Dusen Letter"—our first "leaving piece" (mimeographed on our letterhead) to give to a person after an evangelistic appointment. During our appointments, we drew our diagrams, which were later printed in *The Four Spiritual Laws* booklet in early 1965. The model and much of the theological basis for *The Four Spiritual Laws* is found in our Lord's encounter with the Samaritan woman at the well, recorded in John 4. A Toledo businessman persuaded Bill to consider printing the booklet because he felt that laypeople had trouble memorizing something that lengthy.

One time at a staff training gathering, it was great fun to see Bill process what a marketing guru said about Bill's witnessing style. It stuck in Bill's craw a little at first. But it was through this encounter that the "transferability" principle of training materials really took root. The marketing guru said something like, "Bill thinks he's so original when he talks to people about spiritual issues. But I bet he tells everybody virtually the same thing, from skid row to embassy row." He was right. And Bill realized that too.

Vonette got us started in putting all these great principles into a workable, communicative, training format. A few years earlier, while working on her Masters at USC, she took a curriculum writing course under a distant relative, C. C. Crawford. In light of her training, she would arrange us in groups with a major subject for each group. Then we asked and answered "how to" questions that would exhaust each subject: how to conduct fraternity and sorority meetings, how to present *The Four Spiritual Laws*, how to dress and practice proper etiquette. We wrote the answers on slips of paper, then collected and edited the information from the slips. A very user-friendly manual resulted to help young, eager, but often uninformed, staff start and run an effective ministry on a distant campus.

The Training Manual was effective and well-used by all our staff. During a Christian Educators Conference at Arrowhead Springs, Dr. Kenneth Kantzer, the Dean at Trinity Evangelical Divinity School in Illinois, asked Dr. Ted Martin if he could borrow a Staff Manual to read overnight. When he returned it the next day after reading most of the night, he said, "Now I know why Campus Crusade has been so successful in its ministry."

The "how to" concept is still relevant. We recently put the young team in Kherson, Ukraine, through the same "how to" slip-writing exercise. They wanted to have clear instructions on how to plant and develop a new church in their city, one that would be related to International Partnerships. We categorized and prioritized the main subjects regarding church planting, from philosophy, church purpose, and doctrinal position to pastor selection, music, and children's ministry. We then asked "how to" questions about the subjects one at a time and answered them as exhaustively as we could. After evaluating and editing all the information gathered, we arrived at our "how to" instructions on starting a church.

As then—so now.

A PARTNER IN MINISTRY

In the late fifties, our wonderful mates were only a distant, prayerful hope for Ingrid and me. The little Crusade office was a floor shared with World Tennis Associates in Westwood, just off the UCLA campus. With remarkable activities and events in the College and Professional Department at Hollywood Presbyterian Church, we never lacked for opportunities to learn. We enjoyed gifted teaching of the Word by Bill, Dr. Henrietta Mears, Dr. Bill Thomas (pastor of First Baptist, West Los Angeles), and others. Our burgeoning little group of staff and peers provided all the social life that two vital, hardworking young women could handle.

But in August 1958 at our training grounds on the shores of Lake Minnetonka in Mound, Minnesota, in the chapel he helped build that summer, Curt asked me to marry him. In June 1959, we were married in Miss Mears' lovely living room at Stone Canyon in Bel Air, where Bill, Vonette, and their sons, Zach and Brad, lived at the time. Ingrid was maid of honor; Miss Mears was the stand-in for Curt's mother; Zach was ring bearer; and Bill escorted me through the beautiful anterooms where Dr. Thomas conducted the ceremony. Vonette pulled off the high-tea reception of the summer with her usual flair and graciousness. Ingrid and Bruce Bunner met and married three years later. Bruce has been a member of the Campus Crusade for Christ board of directors for many years.

Visions of diagrams danced in my head and heart for several years from the late fifties to the mid sixties as the *Ten Basic Steps Toward Christian Maturity* were revised three times. In about 1964–65, the various booklets were put in one volume, and a *Teacher's Manual* soon followed.

A few months ago, a personal supporter, who helped us at the Expo '67 world exposition in Canada, wrote to say how meaningful the *Ten Basic Steps Toward Christian Maturity* had been in establishing his walk with the Lord in his young years. He emphasized how valuable they still are to him today.

LEADERSHIP DEVELOPMENT

The importance of leadership development is not a new think-tank buzz word to us. Follow-up and grounding in the Word have always been primary with Bill. In a 1965 introduction to the *Ten Basic Steps Toward Christian Maturity Teacher's Manual*, Bill wrote:

> The *Ten Basic Steps Toward Christian Maturity*, together with this *Teacher's Manual*, are a product of necessity. As the ministry of Campus Crusade for Christ expanded rapidly to scores of campuses across America, thousands of students committed their lives to Christ. Individual follow-up of all new converts soon became an impossibility. Who was to help them grow in their newfound faith?
>
> In 1955, several members of our staff were assigned to assist me in

the preparation of materials which we hoped would stimulate both Christian growth and evangelism on the part of the new believer. The contribution by campus staff members was especially significant because of their constant contact with students, introducing them to Christ and meeting regularly with them to assist them in their Christian growth.

Thus, the *Ten Basic Steps Toward Christian Maturity*—a study in "Follow-up Evangelism"—was the fruit of our combined labor. After several revisions and many printings, this Bible study series is used by hundreds of churches and other Christian groups across America, in many countries and in several languages.

This *Teacher's Manual* and the *Ten Basic Steps Toward Christian Maturity* have been prepared with the prayer that this study will encourage multiplied thousands of students and adults around the world to become true disciples of the Lord Jesus Christ.

The first Leadership Training Classes based on the *Ten Basic Steps Toward Christian Maturity* and classic writings of authors like Andrew Murray, E. M. Bounds, and Oswald Chambers began in late 1958 at UCLA. Gordon Klenck, while attending Fuller Seminary and leading the ministry at USC, was the leader. It is great fun to look at my first assignment sheets and see how interactive the emphasis was. I was creatively involved, then as now, in becoming a person God can use to communicate through effectively by His Spirit. It took hard work—then as now. This was my first foray into leading groups. I was scared silly! But I was learning who is my Source and Resource.

The Lay Ministry sprang from the campus ministry in late 1959. Bill and other trusted leaders prepared what were called the "Basic Messages." These are the principles deemed essential for people to understand in order to make their initial commitment to Christ and begin the great adventure of living for Him. We later put the messages through a stringent editing process and added diagrams. They were first printed as separate booklets called the *Transferable Concepts*. Later, they were put in one volume entitled *Transferable Concepts for Powerful Living*.

In the mid-seventies, Curt and I joined our colleagues Bailey and Elizabeth Marks in Asia, where God's Spirit was moving across that great continent. We had previously taken part in the first Agape Intensive Training program—a prerequisite for all staff going to overseas assignments. Tom and Betty Sue Brewster, language development specialists involved in the program, began adapting *The Four Spiritual Laws* for different cultures and languages. They also developed communicable gospel presentations in picture form for illiterate societies. The gospel message never changes, but it must be made relevant for all audiences.

The initial development of International Training for Asian leaders was taking place under Bailey with Kent and Diane Hutcheson's effective leadership. At the Great Commission Training Center in Manila, thousands of staff received yearlong acculturated, advanced ministry and theological training in the morning, and practical field experience in the afternoon. The *Agape Discipleship Series* was developed, as well as some fine beginning media training. Most people who attended the Great Commission Training Center did so at significant personal sacrifice, but the impact to this day can't be measured. Many thousands began new life in Christ through the availability of Spirit-filled, trained staff and volunteers worldwide.

RECENT DEVELOPMENT IN TRAINING

With the explosive presence of the *JESUS* film overseas, the need again arose in the early eighties for laypeople to have the same quality training and materials as staff enjoyed. We began in the form of month-long training at what were first called Here's Life Training Centers, and later called New Life Training Centers. As the New Life 2000 strategy took form, we hastened to prepare appropriate materials along with our extremely capable colleagues in the Central Asia and Pacific Office.

As the Soviet walls crumbled in the nineties, Curt and I went another notch up in International training as we forged strong partnerships with others in the Body of Christ. As a result of the *JESUS* film premiering in 1991 in the former Soviet Union, the fine curriculum used in schools, entitled *Christian Morals and Ethics: A Foundation for Society*, was developed under the leadership of Dr. Blair Cook and some professors of the International School of Theology. In the shadow of the Kremlin by invitation of the Russian Ministry of Education, the first World View Conference for educators/administrators was conducted. This was a way to make the film as well as the curriculum, Bibles, and other vital materials available to educators and their students.

In late 1991, the CoMission was birthed through our joint effort with Walk Thru the Bible and the Association of Christian Schools International. The three formed the foundation of an evangelism and discipleship movement for the purpose of sending lay teams for one year to the cities where conferences had been held. More than 80 groups joined together. Many still work together. As a result, in 1997 Curt and I had the pleasure of helping birth International Partnerships. During one International Partnership conference, God called a Ukrainian couple, Nick and Maia Mikhaluk, into ministry, and three years later there are more than forty university-educated young men and women in nine cities. Their focus is on educators and others of influence in their society in 26 regions of the country.

During the late eighties and the nineties, vibrant children's materials were developed by Vernie Schorr and made available worldwide. Today, there is also an outstanding children's version of the *JESUS* film. In the mid-nineties, Bailey Marks, Jr., and his team developed a timely new curriculum directed toward teachers and students, addressing the severe AIDS epidemic in our world. That curriculum is being used in many countries of Africa, Latin America, and Europe.

JOYFUL POSSIBILITIES

Walking by faith in the power of the Holy Spirit in our often dark, chaotic, challenging world is what winning, building, training, and sending is all about to us. When we choose not to walk by faith, we lose our joy, and that is always an indication that we aren't filled with the Spirit. It's a wakeup call from God to depend on His Spirit. How gracious. At this time in our lives, Curt and I really don't want to go very long without our joy. You too?

Darkness passes away when we delight, praise, pray, and meditate in God's Word. It passes away when we choose to be cleansed and walk by faith in the vitality of the Holy Spirit. Then life is always filled with good possibilities, no matter what the circumstances are. The results of the faith-filled life are not always positive from our point of view. But they are always worth it when we realize what God has for us and for those we have had the opportunity of introducing to Him.

Character building is a very popular talking point around the world today. In 1999, Bill made available his excellent study on the attributes of God titled *GOD: Discover His Character*. There is a pocket card that is helpful in showing doubters how they can come to faith by examining God's character, as well as a three-volume video series.

Curt and I kid each other that the older we get, the more Presbyterian we become. Maybe we have to get older and experience some tough things to get a better handle on the total realization of who God is. His sovereign, awesome, gracious, loving, merciful, compassionate presence is right here with us through the good, the bad, and the ugly. He isn't some fearsome, bearded tyrant calling down from heaven, "I love you. Try to find Me." His awesome presence is here with us in the midst of life. Bill has said to us several times in recent years, "Everything about our lives is determined and influenced by our view of God."

So these humble materials have been sought from God to empower others through the Holy Spirit to build worldwide movements of spiritual multiplication that are surrendered to Christ. Utilizing the latest high-tech, culturally relevant, excellently prepared materials and methods for winning, building, training, and sending others is a must. As we go filled with the Holy Spirit, armed with our Bibles and transferable training materials, we can go anywhere and begin a viable ministry of evangelism and multiplying discipleship.

Any church, Christian organization, or movement needs to have transferable materials if it wants to be effective and multiply its ministry through others. This might include training materials on how to lead others to Christ, lesson plans for a new members' class, procedures on how to lead a small home group—whatever you need, from the very simple to the most complex. You may invent these from scratch, borrow them from others who are more experienced, or adapt the materials of others to fit your situation. But you need transferable training materials.

Bill often exhorts us, "Never lose your first love for God!" Therefore, we exhort you with *The Message* paraphrase from Hebrews 10 and Philippians 1:

> Remember those early days after you first saw the light? Those were the hard times! Kicked around in public, targets of every kind of abuse —some days it was you, other days your friends. If some friends went to prison, you stuck by them. If some enemies broke in and seized your goods, you let them go with a smile, knowing they couldn't touch your real treasure. Nothing they did bothered you, nothing set you back. So don't throw it all away now. You were sure of yourselves then. It's still a sure thing! But you need to stick it out, staying with God's plan so you'll be there for the promised completion.
>
> "It won't be long now, he's on the way;
> he'll show up most any minute.
> But anyone who is right with me thrives on loyal trust;
> if he cuts and runs, I won't be very happy."
>
> But we're not quitters who lose out. Oh, no! We'll stay with it and survive, trusting all the way (Hebrews 10).
>
> So I plan to be around awhile, companion to you as your growth and joy in this life of trusting God continues. You can start looking forward to a great reunion when I come visit you again. We'll be praising Christ, enjoying each other.
>
> Meanwhile, live in such a way that you are a credit to the Message of Christ (Philippians 1).

As then—so now!

NOTES

1. *EXPLORER Lite*, an e-publication of Leadership Network, August 14, 2000.
2. International Partnerships is an organization formed in the Ukraine as an outgrowth of CoMission. Its members seek to evangelize and disciple influencers in the Ukraine. Several new churches have been planted.

CHAPTER 13

Spiritual Multiplication

DARREL HEIDE
On staff since 1971
Dean of Field Ministry and Associate Professor of Evangelism and Discipleship, International School of Theology

Bill Bright may not be the first Christian leader to emphasize the priority of spiritual multiplication, but he was the person who first introduced the idea to me. In the 1960s, Dr. Bright led all of us to believe that we could fulfill the Great Commission in our generation. What made this credible to us as enthusiastic college students was that he proposed a way that it could be done. He urged us to pursue spiritual multiplication as opposed to spiritual addition. This approach is outlined by Dr. Bright in his Transferable Concept, *How to Help Fulfill the Great Commission.* He writes, "Suppose you led five people to Christ and began to work with them, teaching them to feed themselves from the Word of God and to share their faith with others. Suppose that within one year those five began to train five others. Now there are 25. In another year, as each of those 25 introduces five others to Christ and begins to build them, the number grows to 125. At this rate, the entire population of our world, theoretically, could be reached in just 14 years!" Frequently, Bill would point out that because not everyone we talked to would respond to Christ, the world could be exposed to the gospel in less than 14 years if we were faithfully looking for multiplying disciples. In the process of "teaching others who could teach others," every individual in the world could hear the gospel in this generation.

After returning from Explo '72 in Dallas, our staff team was planning a follow-up conference in our local area. My responsibility was to present a talk on "Spiritual Multiplication." That assignment began a process for me of studying the Scriptures to determine if Jesus had a plan for how He wanted the Church to pursue the fulfillment of the Great Commission. The following discussion will argue that spiritual multiplication was Jesus' intent for His disciples and that this principle was modeled and taught in the early Church.

JESUS' PRIMARY CONCERN

Have you ever wondered what was the primary concern on the heart and mind of Jesus as He walked on this earth, teaching the multitudes and building into the lives of His disciples? Jesus answers this question in His comments to His disciples in Matthew 9. As Jesus moves among the multitudes, He describes them as "sheep without a shepherd." Matthew, one of Jesus' disciples, notes that Jesus "had compassion" for the multitude. In His deep concern for the "lostness" of the multitudes, He turns to the disciples and helps them begin to understand what is of primary importance. He implores His disciples to "ask the Lord of the harvest to send out workers into his harvest field" (verse 38). A natural response in this situation could have been to ask the Lord of the harvest to remove the spiritual blindness of the multitude so they could know their Creator. But Jesus makes it clear that His request of the Father is to raise up laborers for the harvest. Subsequently, in chapter 10 He begins training and preparing His disciples for the role they will eventually play in the spiritual harvest.

Was Jesus' statement concerning the need for laborers a priority concern for Him? If it was of primary importance, we would expect to see it emphasized in the teaching Jesus gave to His disciples as He prepared to go to the cross. Jesus' discourse in John chapters 14 to 16 is precisely such a time of instruction, and it is climaxed with Jesus' prayer for His disciples in John 17. This section of Scripture shows Jesus' commitment to fulfilling the Great Commission through the teaching and equipping of disciples who could teach and train others.

In John 17:1, Jesus "looked toward heaven" in prayer and begins to rehearse all that He has accomplished in His earthly ministry. In verse 4, He states, "I have brought you glory on earth by completing the work you gave me to do." In verse 6–8, Jesus further describes the work that He has completed, "I have revealed you to those whom you gave me out of the world... They knew with certainty that I came from you, and they believed that you sent me."

In verse 9, Jesus finally arrives at the focus of His prayer. He says, "I pray for them." "Them" clearly refers to the disciples who were the focus of His finished work in verses 6–8. Jesus then makes a disclaimer that seems to be tremendously significant in revealing the strategy He has chosen to make His kingdom a reality on this earth. He said, "I am not praying for the world." Is it not incredible that as Jesus ends His ministry and prepares to be reunited with the Father, He makes it very clear that He is choosing to depend on His disciples for the ultimate success of His time on this earth? This is the Son of God who could have called on the rocks to cry out on His behalf. Instead, He chose to depend on disciples or laborers who would be faithful and obedient. With this, He confirms the approach that He first unveiled in Matthew 9.

As He is about to leave them, Jesus goes on to express several concerns He has for His disciples. These concerns seem to be very much related. He is concerned that the Father will keep the disciples secure from the attacks of the evil one (verse 15). This is especially necessary because He is also praying that His disciples would be sent into the world (verses 15,18). He wants the disciples to be fully engaged in a world that hates them, all the while drawing on the power of the name of the Father (verse 11). Jesus prays that the result of this dependence will be unity among the disciples (verses 11,21). He prays that this will happen as they are set apart by the truth of God's Word (verse 17).

In John 17:20, we are introduced to a second group of people for whom Jesus prays: "My prayer is not for them alone. I pray also for those who will believe in me through their message." The amazing thing about this prayer is what is not included. Nowhere does Jesus pray that His disciples will take His word to others or that they would multiply themselves in the lives of others. Rather, He assumes that His disciples will be fruitful and reproduce other disciples. His concern is that there be unity between these generations of disciples.

FROM JESUS TO THE EARLY CHURCH

How is it that Jesus can assume that the disciples will reproduce when so many disciples through the ages have not reproduced themselves in the lives of others? A possible answer can be seen in the discourse Jesus had with His disciples leading up to His prayer. In John 17:21, Jesus prays "that all of them may be one, Father, just as you are in me and I am in you. May they also be in us so that the world may believe that you have sent me." Again in verse 23, He repeats, "I in them and you in me. May they be brought to complete unity to let the world know that you sent me."

The meaning of these two passages is not obvious to the casual reader.

What was to be the basis of the unity between the disciples and those who believed through their words? To fully understand the meaning of Jesus' words, it is helpful to look at them in the context of the earlier conversation He had with His disciples. The language of these passages seems strangely familiar when you refer back to John 14:20. It reads, "On that day you will realize that I am in my Father, and you are in me, and I am in you."

What is Jesus referring to when He says "on that day"? In the preceding verses, you see that Jesus is referring to the coming of the Holy Spirit. When the Holy Spirit is given, the unity that exists between the Father and the Son will also exist among the generations of disciples. In both verses 21 and 23 of chapter 17, Jesus prays that this unity, made possible by the Holy Spirit, will cause the world to know "that you [the Father] have sent me."

Jesus' use of the analogy of the vine and the branches in John 15 might also have been on the minds of the disciples as they heard Jesus pray. Jesus knew that if after He was gone, the disciples would abide in Him through the power of the Holy Spirit as a branch abides in the vine, fruit would be the result. He makes it clear in John 15 that the purpose of abiding in the vine is to bear fruit. In fact, He states that branches that do not bear fruit will be cut down and destroyed (verse 2). Jesus' main concern was that His disciples would be set apart by God's Word to be a unified body of believers through the presence of the Holy Spirit. It appears Jesus was confident that if this happened, fruit would be the inevitable result and the Great Commission could be accomplished in any generation.

If Jesus' intent was to use laborers or multiplying disciples as the means to fulfill the Great Commission, the big question remains: Did the early Church implement Jesus' intended strategy? The rest of this discussion will seek to propose that spiritual multiplication was very much a part of the teaching and ministry strategy of the early Church.

THE EXAMPLE OF COLOSSE

Our search for evidence of spiritual multiplication in the New Testament Church will begin in the Book of Colossians. Five verses, which at first seem obscure, tell us a lot about how the Colossian church came to be:

- "Because we have heard of your faith in Christ Jesus and of the love you have for all the saints" (Colossians 1:4).
- "I want you to know how much I am struggling for you and for those at Laodicea, and for all who have not met me personally" (Colossians 2:1).
- "You learned [the gospel] from Epaphras, our dear fellow servant, who

is a faithful minister of Christ on our behalf, and who also told us of your love in the Spirit" (Colossians 1:7,8).

- "Epaphras, who is one of you and a servant of Christ Jesus, sends greetings. He is always wrestling in prayer for you, that you may stand firm in all the will of God, mature and fully assured" (Colossians 4:12).

Although the epistle gives us limited knowledge about the beginning of the Colossian church, some very important facts are included. First, we learn that Paul never met the Colossians or the Laodiceans in person and that there were other churches in this category for whom Paul had concern. The knowledge that Paul has of the Colossian church he heard from others. The likely link is Epaphras, who evidently was originally one of the Colossians. How he first came in touch with Paul, we are not told. However, it does seem that he is with Paul at the writing of the Colossian letter and is very much in prayer for the Colossians. Do we have any biblical references that might explain how Colosse, Laodicea, and other churches, which Paul had not visited, came into being? Luke gives us some clues in the Book of Acts:

> Paul entered the synagogue and spoke boldly there [Ephesus] for three months, arguing persuasively about the kingdom of God. But some of them became obstinate; they refused to believe and publicly maligned the Way. So Paul left them. He took the disciples with him and had discussions daily in the lecture hall of Tyrannus. This went on for two years, so that all the Jews and Greeks who lived in the province of Asia heard the word of the Lord (Acts 19:8–10).

In this passage, we learn that Paul spent two years ministering daily to a group of disciples in Ephesus. The text says the result was that "all the Jews and Greeks who lived in the province of Asia heard the word of the Lord."

To what extent was Asia reached? Were any churches planted? Do we have any other reference in the Scripture that might shed further light on what was accomplished in Asia?

For those who are familiar with the Bible, Revelation 1:11 immediately comes to mind. "Write on a scroll what you see and send it to the seven churches: to Ephesus, Smyrna, Pergamum, Thyatira, Sardis, Philadelphia and Laodicea." To fully understand the significance of this verse, consult a Bible map of Paul's third missionary journey. Notice that the seven churches mentioned in Revelation are all in Asia Minor (modern-day Turkey) and form a cluster around Ephesus. They are each within a hundred-mile radius of Ephesus. Colosse, yet another church, is about ten miles from Laodicea.

Although we do not know for certain how these churches were established, we do know that Paul never personally visited Colosse or Laodicea and that this was true of other churches as well. A reasonable explanation for how the churches of Asia were planted is that the disciples in whom Paul invested his life at Ephesus were instrumental in multiplying themselves in other disciples and consequently establishing churches. Evidently, Epaphras, who was originally from Colosse, spent time with Paul at Ephesus and then went back to his hometown to plant the Colossian church.

If indeed the emphasis of spiritual multiplication was a key ingredient in Paul's approach to ministry and church planting, we would expect to see models as just described. We would also, however, expect to find Paul instructing others in this philosophy if it was important to him.

PRIORITY OF BUILDING MULTIPLYING DISCIPLES

In 1 Thessalonians 1:6–8, we read, "You became imitators of us and of the Lord; in spite of severe suffering, you welcomed the message with the joy given by the Holy Spirit. And so you became a model to all the believers in Macedonia and Achaia. The Lord's message rang out from you not only in Macedonia and Achaia—your faith in God has become known everywhere."

Paul is commending a very young Thessalonian church, with whom he has spent a limited amount of time, for their faithfulness in following his own example of living the Christian life and passing it on to others. Paul goes on in chapter 2 to explain how he ministered to the Thessalonians with both the loving nurture of a mother and the exhortation and encouragement of a father. It seems that through modeling and coming alongside people, Paul's goal was to build disciples or laborers who could pass along to others the good news of Christ.

How Paul viewed the process of discipling others is further articulated in his letters of instruction to the churches. In Colossians 1:28, he says, "We proclaim him, admonishing and teaching everyone with all wisdom, so that we may present everyone perfect in Christ. To this end I labor, struggling with all his energy, which so powerfully works in me."

Paul begins by proclaiming the gospel, then focuses on helping every individual to grow to maturity by admonishing and teaching them. All this is energized by God's power at work in his life. In Ephesians 4:12,13, Paul describes the purpose for the gifts given to the church: "to prepare God's people for works of service, so that the body of Christ may be built up until we all reach unity in the faith and in the knowledge of the Son of God and become mature, attaining to the whole measure of the fullness of Christ." Paul's passion seems to be to help every individual in the church to become mature in their faith so that out of this maturity they can use their gifts to proclaim the gospel to the nonbelieving world and admonish and teach each individual believer to grow toward maturity.

Finally, as Paul nears the end of his ministry, he clearly instructs his faithful disciple Timothy to do what Christ had assumed would be the natural fruit of abiding in the vine. Paul instructed Timothy, "The things you have heard me say in the presence of many witnesses entrust to reliable men who will also be qualified to teach others" (2 Timothy 2:2). What is clear, from both Christ's prayer for His disciples and Paul's instructions to church leaders toward the end of his ministry, is the priority of building disciples who will multiply themselves in the lives of others. One could conclude that both Jesus and Paul saw spiritual multiplication through the lives of their disciples as the key to the fulfillment of the Great Commission.

STRATEGY MAKES A DIFFERENCE

Why is this conclusion important to the Church today? We live in an age where success is measured by the size of the crowd. It is always tempting to lay aside what is often perceived as the slow-moving task of building individual disciples for what seems to be a faster, more exciting approach to ministry. If the church could only gain a hearing in the media or fill the stadiums of the world, the Great Commission could be fulfilled more quickly.

The following calculation helps to visualize why investing time in multiplying disciples produces more fruit than spiritual addition.

Addition

Based on one person reaching 10,000 persons per day, 365 days per year = 3,650,000 per year

3,650,000 persons per year for 33 years = 120,450,000

Multiplication

With multiplication the number of people doubles each year. At the end of one year there are two people; at the end of two years, four people, etc. At the end of 33 years there are 8,589,934,592, more than the population of the world.

Spiritual Addition vs. Multiplication

	Addition No. of new Christians by winning 1 person to the Lord each year	*Addition* No. of new Christians by winning 10,000 to the Lord each year	*Multiplication* No. of Christians by winning 1 new believer per year, training him to win others, and each believer doubling himself the next year.
Year 1	1	3,650,000	2
Year 2	2	7,300,000	4
Year 3	3	10,950,000	8
Year 4	4	14,600,000	16
Year 5	5	18,250,000	32
Year 6	6	21,900,000	64
Year 7	7	25,550,000	128
Year 8	8	29,200,000	256
Year 9	9	32,850,000	512
Year 10	10	36,500,000	1,024
Year 11	11	40,150,000	2,048
Year 12	12	43,800,000	4,096
Year 13	13	47,450,000	8,192
Year 14	14	51,100,000	16,384
Year 15	15	54,750,000	32,768
Year 16	16	58,400,000	65,536
Year 17	17	62,050,000	131,072
Year 18	18	65,700,000	262,144
Year 19	19	69,350,000	524,288
Year 20	20	73,000,000	1,048,576
Year 21	21	76,650,000	2,097,152
Year 22	22	80,300,000	4,194,304
Year 23	23	83,950,000	8,388,608
Year 24	24	87,600,000	16,777,216
Year 25	25	91,250,000	33,554,432
Year 26	26	94,900,000	67,108,864
Year 27	27	98,550,000	134,217,728
Year 28	28	102,200,000	268,435,456
Year 29	29	105,850,000	536,870,912
Year 30	30	109,500,000	1,073,741,824
Year 31	31	113,150,000	2,147,483,648
Year 32	32	116,800,000	4,294,967,296
Year 33	33	120,450,000	8,589,934,592

This diagram contrasts the long-term effectiveness of spiritual multiplication through disciples, as defended in this article, with a more traditional approach of spiritual addition. The diagram demonstrates what could happen if I lead one person to Christ this year and disciple and equip him or her so that the next year we could both lead someone to Christ and disciple them. If this multiplication process could be repeated each year for 33 years, 8,589,934,592 people would be discipled. This well exceeds the earth's population at this time.

Suppose, in contrast, I chose to preach the gospel to 10,000 people each day, 365 days per year, for 33 years. Although such an undertaking would be physically impossible, during this time I would be able to preach the gospel to 120,450,000 people.

In the multiplication model, not only would people hear the gospel, but they would be followed-up, discipled to walk with Christ, and equipped to multiply themselves in the lives of others. Of course, we know that not everyone who hears the gospel will respond by becoming a disciple. Thus, while a disciple looks for other disciples, he will share the gospel with a number of people who may not be ready to respond to the gospel. Every person on this earth could hear the gospel in a much shorter time than 33 years if each of us were consistently looking for another disciple. On the other hand, the 120,450,000 people who were reached through the addition approach would only hear the gospel once and would not even have the luxury of having their questions answered. Spiritual multiplication is the only way God could possibly use me as an individual believer to fulfill His command to preach the gospel to every person on earth.

We should not conclude from this discussion that discipling a person takes only one year. Discipleship, as Paul described it in the passages mentioned earlier, is a lifelong process. However, it is possible to bring people along in their faith in one year to where they can begin to pass along to others what they have learned. This process of passing our faith along to others and helping them grow toward maturity serves to increase our own desire and motivation to grow. This kind of spiritual growth and involvement can be used by the Spirit of God to create the kind of vibrant, growing, unified body of believers for which Christ prayed in John 17.

DISCIPLESHIP AROUND THE WORLD

The principle of spiritual multiplication has been at the heart of Dr. Bright's vision as he expanded the ministry of Campus Crusade around the world. One practical expression of this principle can be seen in Campus Crusade's approach outside the United States. Each ministry was encouraged to raise up national leadership who could be equipped to multiply themselves in the lives of others in their country.

To assist and accelerate this process, Campus Crusade for Christ staff members in the United States committed themselves to give 5 percent of all the support they raised toward the support of raising up national leadership around the world. Although these overseas leaders were at first assisted financially, with time they were trained and encouraged to raise their own financial support within their own countries. The result is that today Campus Crusade ministries on all continents of the world are involved in sending laborers to the harvest around the world and American staff are in the minority.

Maiwa'azi Dan Daura, one of the original Campus Crusade leaders in Nigeria, began his ministry with seven men. The goal of this group was to find and disciple twelve others. Throughout the past twenty years, this little group has grown to a vast leadership network that has given birth to more than 1,200 churches across Nigeria.[1] This is but one example of what has happened all around the world.

This commitment to leading people to Christ, building them up in the faith, and equipping them to multiply themselves in the lives of others has been a primary motivation for me in ministry over the past thirty years. Recently, I was able to compile an alumni list of former students who were involved in my ministry of spiritual multiplication at the University of Michigan during the 1970s. Now, 20 to 30 years later, it is so encouraging to find many of them working as pastors, as church planters, as missionaries with different mission agencies around the world, and as laymen actively giving spiritual leadership in their churches. Many have shared how they continue to actively disciple others.

There is a special need in the Church today to embrace the biblical principles of spiritual multiplication. In our media-driven culture, it has become very attractive to have large mega-churches with polished programs. In such an environment, it can be easy to remain anonymous and never really grow in faith. It is important that as leaders in the church (whether large or small), we are deliberate in developing a ministry process where individuals can grow in the basics of their faith and learn how to multiply themselves in the lives of others.

Certainly, Jesus ministered to the multitudes; but in the midst of the crowds, He spent time teaching and developing His disciples. Large crowds can be used by God to expose people to the gospel and to motivate them to take steps of obedience. Yet in the midst of these large events, we need to be involved in discipling and equipping those whom God will use to reach others with the gospel. Jesus, the Son of God, and Paul, an apostle of the early Church, knew that the only way any generation could be responsible to complete the Great Commission was to send forth laborers who would abide in the vine and bear fruit that would multiply.

NOTES

1. Larry Stockstill, *The Cell Church* (Ventura, CA: Regal Books), 95.

CHAPTER 14

Reaching Leaders

SWEDE ANDERSON
On Staff since 1959
Founding Director, Christian Embassy

On Friday, June 17, 1972, Explo '72 was drawing to a close in Dallas. More than 85,000 people, mostly students, had come to the week of training and inspiration, meeting together in the Cotton Bowl and in hundreds of smaller venues for discipleship and training. Around 280,000 came to the closing rally with Bill Bright, Johnny Cash, and Billy Graham. The entire event broke molds and blasted faith barriers for those who attended and for the hundreds of us who had worked to put it all together.

That noon I sat in on a luncheon hosted by a Dallas businessman at his club on top of the Southland Life building. It was an opportunity for Bill Bright to say thank you to the political leaders of the Dallas/Fort Worth area for all that the cities had done to welcome the delegates and to make Explo '72 possible. About two dozen attended.

Because the purpose of the luncheon was to express thanks, I was both surprised and ministered to by what Bill did. Bill graciously and meaningfully thanked the leaders at the luncheon, but then he transitioned into what was really the heart of Explo '72: faith in Jesus Christ. He shared his story of how he had come to know Jesus and clearly explained the gospel.

As usual, Bill did this in the spirit characterized by one of his favorite quotes from Dr. James Stewart, New Testament scholar of Edinburgh, Scotland:

> If we could but show the world that being committed to Christ is no tame, humdrum, sheltered monotony, but the most thrilling, exciting adventure the human spirit could ever know, those who have been standing outside the church and looking askance at Christ would come crowding in to pay allegiance, and we might well expect the greatest revival since Pentecost.[1]

Bill gave each of those present an opportunity to receive Christ right then, leading them in a prayer. (He prayed aloud, giving them a chance to pray silently.) What marked me that afternoon? I realized that I would not have been so bold. Fear of man would have made me hesitant to speak so clearly and give each person an opportunity to receive Christ. I learned that Bill doesn't hesitate to share Christ in the presence of powerful people! He knows they need Christ as much as anyone.

Since 1972, I have participated with Bill on a visit to a Latin American president's office, in outreach dinners in the early days of the Christian Embassy ministry in Washington, and in visits with members of the Parliament of the Soviet Union. I always saw the same pattern in Bill's conversations:

- A winsome testimony
- A lovely exaltation of Jesus Christ and what an adventure it is to follow Him
- An explanation of the cross, that Jesus is alive, that He can be known personally
- A request for a response

Because in those instances I was with Bill around the clock, I saw that with cab drivers, with bellhops, in conversations on the telephone, and in personal appointments, each person with whom Bill spent a few moments was given a loving opportunity to hear about our Lord. He didn't just share with the prestigious or powerful. Yet on each continent, people whom society considers powerful have met the Master during a conversation and prayer with Bill Bright.

WHY IS BILL SO FRUITFUL IN MINISTRY AMONG LEADERS?

Bill is utterly convinced of each person's spiritual need and of how attractive our Lord Jesus Christ is, thus he shares with all with whom he has opportunity. In addition to these characteristics, I will advance four reasons why I think Bill is so fruitful in ministry among leaders.

First is his view of God. Michael Richardson, in his biography of Bill, records Bill's thoughts as follows:

> Who or what is at the center of your concentration and your ideals? When one focuses on the God of the Bible,... such a God releases power to the individual to accomplish activities that are in harmony with

> His own thinking. How much power?...Far more than we would ever dare to ask or even dream of! Let your mind race,...let your prayers be without limit; and yet whatever you believe, whatever you think, whatever you pray for—God's power is infinitely beyond it all...This God who is so powerful has proven His personal concern for human beings ...Think of it: The omnipresent Creator God, who created the heavens and the earth and the vastness of billions of galaxies, has come to die on the cross for our sins and to take up residence within us![2]

Without question, a large view of our great God underlies all of Bill's fruitfulness. In that there is hope for all of us. Because each of us can look out to the galaxies, down at the flowers, and into the Bible, and thus grow in our comprehension of God's greatness.

There is much to learn from Bill, but this is number one. All of us—and Bill would say this about himself, too—risk the danger captured in the title of J. B. Philips's book, *Your God Is Too Small*.[3]

Second, I believe God prepared Bill for ministering to leaders through his personal experiences and his spiritual experiences. In his family, college, and early business experiences (read this fascinating story in *Amazing Faith*[4]), Bill grew up around confident men who conquered big challenges. He was elected to leadership in every conceivable area in college, and he had great business success early.

While most of us in our human nature struggle to share Christ with persons we perceive as more powerful than ourselves, we often feel more comfortable sharing the message with our peers. Although Bill is shy, influential leaders were Bill's peers. He had been around them from childhood, and he accomplished enough in early adulthood to be comfortable among persons perceived by society as prominent.

Third, and significantly more important, is his spiritual preparation. Evangelism is a spiritual and supernatural process. People must be born again from above. Yet this is a process in which we can be the agent of God's work through our witness.

Bill was not only overwhelmed by the greatness of God and the love of God for him, but he also made clear his response to God's love. At Forest Home Conference Center in June 1947, he heard Dr. Henrietta Mears say,

> God is looking for men and women of total commitment. During the war, men of special courage were called upon for difficult assignments; often these volunteers did not return. They were called "expendables." We must be expendables for Christ...If we fail God's call to us tonight, we will be held responsible.[5]

The phrase "expendables for Christ" was riveted in Bill's mind and heart. As you and I look at Bill's example, we can certainly qualify in this third area. We, too, can choose to be "expendables" for Christ.

What about the second area? Most of us are not from backgrounds where we lived among the so-called "important people." We overcome that background by going to those people anyway. What will perhaps shock us and will certainly embolden us is the discovery that the spiritual need and responsiveness are as great or greater than what we have found among those with whom we feel more comfortable.

I remember one of my first Bible studies with a small group of congressmen in Washington after several years of campus ministry. In the course of the study, a congressman knit his brow and said in a serious tone, "I don't know if you have ever thought about this before, but I wonder about the people in Africa who never heard about Christ. What will happen to them?" How many students had asked this question in the preceding several years! It struck me with great force that though I was wearing a dark suit and sitting in a room in the United States Capitol building, I was hearing exactly the same intellectual questions and trying to meet exactly the same spiritual needs as I had done wearing Levi's in a dorm on a campus!

Fourth, I believe Bill has been fruitful in ministering to leaders because, working alongside others, he has developed strategies that specifically target leaders and provide them an opportunity to both hear and respond to the gospel.

Shortly before Campus Crusade for Christ was born, Bill was leading 120 dedicated young men and women from Hollywood Presbyterian Church in ministry teams to approximately thirty locations a month, visiting jails, hospitals, skid row missions—wherever they felt invited or needed. Bill recalls:

> We had to wait our turn to go to jail services and skid row missions because many other churches were covering this area of service as well. One day it occurred to me that there were no waiting lines to reach college students or the top executives of the city. Here were the neglected leaders of our world, both today's and tomorrow's.[6]

His experience in both the student world and the executive world taught him that those people were just as needy and just as open as others were, and there were no waiting lines. Thus, in the first year of the ministry of Campus Crusade for Christ at UCLA, among the 250 students who opened their lives to Christ were the student body president, the student newspaper editor, and a number of well-known athletes. Ministering to those who could influence others just made sense (2 Timothy 2:2)!

IS A MINISTRY TO LEADERS BIBLICALLY VALID?

First Corinthians 1:26 says, "For consider your calling, brethren, that there were not many wise according to the flesh, not many mighty, not many noble" (NASB). James wrote, "My brethren, do not hold your faith in our glorious Lord Jesus Christ with an attitude of personal favoritism. For if a man comes into your assembly with a gold ring and dressed in fine clothes, and there also comes in a poor man in dirty clothes, and you pay special attention to the one who is wearing the fine clothes, and say, 'You sit here in a good place,' and you say to the poor man, 'You stand over there, or sit down by my footstool,' have you not made distinctions among yourselves and become judges with evil motives?" (James 2:1–4, NASB). Can we truly be obedient and yet invest time, money, and effort into reaching leaders with the gospel?

The argument of 1 Corinthians 1:18–31 is not about social levels but about the power of the cross to save, even if so-called "wise" humans believe this message is foolish. "Has not God made foolish the wisdom of the world?... We preach Christ crucified,... Christ the power of God and the wisdom of God" (NASB). These are central to Paul's preaching. "Not many wise..., not many mighty, not many noble" describes the particular group that received Paul's preaching in this case. These verses are not a directive against reaching leaders.

In fact, the Bible frequently shows God touching the lives of leaders. There is much talk in the Old Testament about pharaohs, kings, and political leaders. When Jesus called Paul, He made it clear that Paul was to bear His name "before the Gentiles and kings and the sons of Israel" (Acts 9:15, NASB). The statement "Gentiles and the sons of Israel" would suffice if the point were to refer to all people. But God mentions kings specifically.

In Acts, we see Paul before the proconsul Sergius Paulus (Acts 13:6–12). Paul was a friend of the "Asiarchs," political leaders in Ephesus (Acts 19:31). He witnessed before the Roman governor Festus and King Agrippa (Acts 25:23–26:26). Many were spared death because of his friendship with a Roman centurion (Acts 27:37,42–44). We assume that Paul appeared to witness before Caesar, probably Nero (Acts 27:23,24). He seems to have influenced Caesar's household through the witness to the praetorian guard (Philippians 1:12–14; 4:21,22). Paul later bore witness to Christ at another trial (2 Timothy 4:16–18), and we assume that he bore witness again at his final trial when he was condemned and then beheaded.

Also, the instructions in Paul's pastoral guidance letter to Timothy juxtapose prayer for those in authority with evangelism:

> First of all, then, I urge that entreaties and prayers, petitions and thanksgivings, be made on behalf of all men, for kings and all who are in authority, in order that we may lead a tranquil and quiet life in all godliness and dignity. This is good and acceptable in the sight of God our Savior, who desires all men to be saved and to come to the knowledge of the truth. For there is one God, and one mediator also between God and men, the man Christ Jesus (1 Timothy 2:1–5, NASB).

As we pray for leaders, we cannot help but pray for their salvation, for God "desires all men to be saved." The Great Commission passages that end each Gospel and begin Acts send us to all persons.

Space does not allow opportunity to write about the great difference it makes when leaders are obedient to and seeking wisdom from our Lord Jesus Christ, but Scriptures, history, and contemporary experience all demonstrate the multiplying influence for good that such leaders have.

For example, a British executive gave a copy of the *JESUS* video to all 1,100 partners in his global firm and received back one hundred positive replies. An American entrepreneur, now dead, left a legacy of more than a dozen CEOs and professionals who not only are influencing their companies and communities but also have helped establish ministries in Africa, Eastern Europe, Cambodia, and Thailand. A Polish executive couple reach hundreds for Christ each year by hosting outreach dinner parties.

Campus Crusade for Christ International has strategies, staff, and volunteers in place to share the gospel with leaders. But as strategically important as we feel these ministries are, the resources allotted to them do not begin to compare with the resources allotted to Campus Crusade's ministries to those not viewed as mighty and noble.

In addition, these who minister to leaders conform to James 2, in that there is no motive or action designed to dishonor the poor, but rather a passion that those with means and power use those resources to minister to the poor. This passion drives our calling toward leaders.

One dramatic example is the *JESUS* film. Is there a tool that has brought the love of Christ to more people, more remote people, more poor people, more children than this? The creation of the film, begun in 1974, was funded by a $5 million gift from one couple who were friends and supporters of the ministry. In subsequent years, hundreds of others, members of History's Handful, have enabled the distribution of the *JESUS* film so that by century's end more than 4 billion people have heard of the Lord through this tool. In the Bible, in Bill's life, and at the heart of our movement, passion for the lost is expressed without an attitude of personal favoritism.

HAS BILL ENCOURAGED OTHERS TO MINISTER TO LEADERS?

In the context of sharing the love of our Lord with everyone, Bill has been the Lord's instrument to help launch many effective strategies for reaching leaders. All those strategies conform to Crusade's core values of "win" (sharing the gospel in the power of the Holy Spirit, leaving the results to God), "build" (lovingly helping people grow in their faith and obedience), and "send" (training, equipping, and motivating people to share their faith with others).

For example, in a message he was giving at a conference at Arrowhead Springs in 1974, Bill said, "We need a Christian Embassy in Washington!" A prominent attorney approached Bill after his talk and said, "I agree!"

Those two men and their wives gathered others to form a board and to procure a property. Bill selected staff to form the ministry team. During 1975–1977, he and Vonette averaged a week per month of personal ministry in Washington doing evangelism, setting the pace, coaching the staff. Washington-trained staff then launched the same ministry at the United Nations in New York. Canadians rapidly developed a multiplying ministry in Ottawa among political leaders and diplomats, which has had enormous impact worldwide as foreign diplomats in Ottawa have worked with Canadian political and business leaders to create outreaches to leaders back in their countries. Then came Bonn. Then London.

Meanwhile, Campus Crusade for Christ board members and friends of the Brights, Arthur and Nancy DeMoss, developed a means of effectively winning executive couples to Christ in Philadelphia. This became a cooperative action, with Campus Crusade supplying mature staff to help executive couples in ministries to their peers in various American cities. Now this pattern of staff working alongside leaders in politics, business, the arts, and the professions has spread to more than fifty countries.

Yes, Bill has enabled and encouraged others to follow his example of being bold and clearly inviting leaders to follow the Lord of lords.

WHAT DO WE LEARN FROM BILL?

What can be learned from all that Bill has taught us about ministry, especially to leaders? First, we learn that a clear vision of God and who He is provides the proper foundation for all of life and ministry. God is a great God to Bill Bright. Nothing is too difficult for Him. No person is beyond God's ability to reach. So if we go in faith in a mighty God and in the power of the Holy Spirit, we can expect God to do great things. Therefore, God is no different when we are seeking to reach leaders or followers.

Second, we learn humility from Bill's example. Bill never comes to people in a cocky, arrogant manner. Whether he is talking to a taxi diver or to a senator, he has a spirit of humility that people can sense. This opens them to the message of Christ that he brings. In keeping with our Lord's teaching (Luke 22:24–27), Bill is a humble, servant leader. And humility is dependence on God rather than on ourselves.

A third thing we can learn from Bill is the need for much prayer. Bill is dependent on God through prayer. At the founding of the ministry of Crusade, before any steps of outreach were taken, Bill and Vonette formed a 24-hour prayer chain. People were praying around the clock. Before Bill undertakes a new ministry, it is bathed in prayer by Bill and Vonette and others they recruit to join them in prayer. Prayer also undergirds every meeting and every appointment that Bill has. He is convinced that God works in answer to believing prayer. So he asks God and is not surprised when God answers. This is also true when Bill is working with the leaders of society.

A fourth lesson from Bill's example in working with leaders is boldness. Although Bill is shy, he is not timid. He gets to the point: the gospel of Jesus Christ. He has prayed for God to use him, so he expects God to work. He knows people are lost and in need of Christ, so he does not want to miss an opportunity to share the gospel and to give people a chance to respond and receive Christ as Savior and Lord. He knows that Christ has said, "If anyone is ashamed of me and my words . . . , the Son of Man will be ashamed of him" (Mark 8:38), and, "Whoever acknowledges me before men, I will also acknowledge him before my Father in heaven" (Matthew 10:32). He does not want to miss an opportunity to share Christ, so he is bold. Because of his boldness many leaders have heard the gospel and have responded. Without his boldness in Christ, he would never have had the impact he has had on leaders.

Often people perceived as powerful are even more open than others are. Perhaps many leaders respond so readily to Jesus Christ because they have achieved so much of what this world offers, hoping that would satisfy, only to find that material success and power do not fill the "God-shaped vacuum" in their hearts.

Former U.S. Senator Bill Armstrong illustrates this point. He describes his experience this way:

> I had all I ever dreamed of—now what?
>
> I had reached all my goals. I had set a target of how much money I

wanted to make by the time I was 30 years old, and had achieved that. I had a fine family, a nice house, some businesses, and served on some boards. Now I had been elected to the U.S. Congress, to go back to serve in Washington and whisper advice in the ear of the President of the United States. Fortunately, he did have other sources of advice, as well. But can you imagine how it felt inside to have achieved this level of success?

I felt great, right? Actually, it didn't happen that way. My experience was exactly the opposite. Having achieved the things I had dreamed of, the things I knew were important and counted for success, I didn't feel successful. I felt terrible. Inside I was crumbling. On the outside, everything seemed fine: wonderful family, children, success in business, and success in politics. Inside, however, I was despondent.

That was my frame of mind when a fellow came to call on me. He was not a clergyman or a constituent, but a dentist from Alabama who came to call on me at my office in the Cannon House Office Building. He asked me a completely unexpected, and somewhat confrontational question. He asked, 'Bill, where do you stand with Jesus Christ?' I don't know about you, but where I come from that is not a question we ask people. The last thing we would do is go over to someone and say, "How's everything between you and Jesus?" And we particularly don't go visit people in their offices and raise that kind of question, especially with perfect strangers, which he and I were.

In retrospect, it's interesting how this situation turned out because his question was a little embarrassing—and congressmen know how to get themselves out of embarrassing situations. I had a perfect opportunity to terminate this conversation because as we were talking the bells rang and lights on my wall lit up to signify a vote was about to occur in the House of Representatives. All I had to do was say to this guy, "Look, I've got to vote. Thanks for dropping in. I'm going to go do my duty and go across the street to cast my vote." But for reasons I didn't understand, but which in retrospect are absolutely clear, I didn't say that. Instead, I said, "I've got to vote. Walk over with me, and then we'll go down to the coffee shop, drink a cup of coffee, and continue to talk." So that's what we did. I voted, and then we went down into the Joseph Martin Dining Room, which is a little chamber under the House of Representatives. This dear guy, who was then a stranger, but as you can now imagine, has become a wonderful friend, shared with me a little pamphlet, which he called *The Four Spiritual Laws.*

After that discussion, we bowed our heads and said a little prayer. As I did so, without fully understanding what was transpiring, I became a

Christian in the biblical sense of the word—that is, a person in whom Christ lives.

A fifth lesson we learn from Bill is going: just do it. Bill hasn't waited for leaders to come to him. He has gone to them, starting on the UCLA campus to the present. He has intentionally sought them out. He has people who know leaders arrange appointments with them. He encourages people to sponsor leadership breakfasts, luncheons, and dinners. He organized the Christian Embassy in Washington, D.C., then encouraged the staff there to help set up additional such embassies. Bill and Vonette have constantly used their home and Vonette's gift of hospitality to entertain others. This definitely has included entertaining leaders: student leaders, business leaders, political leaders, Christian leaders, leaders of all kinds. Bill has taken the initiative in ministering to leaders, and they have greatly responded.

So finally, sweeping all the above into our hearts, minds, and wills, we learn from Bill Bright:

Vision of God
Humility
Prayer
Boldness
And finally, Going—do it!

Will you take ten minutes right now, just ten minutes, and review before our Lord your current status on these five crucial parts of your Christian walk? As you pray, ask God to give you a specific person, perhaps someone you consider a leader, to approach? Then in light of these principles, do what God leads you to do.

NOTES

1. James Stewart, *The Strong Name*, cited by Michael Richardson in *Amazing Faith* (Colorado Springs, CO: WaterBrook Press, 2000), 31,32.
2. Michael Richardson, *Amazing Faith* (Colorado Springs, Co: WaterBrook Press, 2000), 131.
3. J. B. Philips, *Your God Is Too Small* (New York: MacMillan Publishing Company, 1961).
4. Richardson, 1–18.
5. Richardson, 36.
6. Richardson, 53.

CHAPTER 15

The Involvement of Women

GWEN MARTIN
On Staff since 1960
Coordinator, Partners in Ministry, International School of Theology

Why include a chapter on women in ministry in a book such as this? Why examine some of what women have done throughout the history of the Church to advance the cause of Christ? Why examine what women have done and are presently doing in the ministry of Campus Crusade for Christ?

It is no secret that women have been left out of books on Church history, despite their involvement. Ruth Tucker and Walter Liefeld tell us that this has happened even though "in numbers women have dominated the church and the source material relating to their ministry and status is simply overwhelming."[1] They suggest that the main reason for the virtual omission of women's activities from Church history is that the contribution of women has not been as noteworthy as that of men—it is mainly men who have led church councils, preached, and written theology. Tucker says that the history of religion is "probably the only field of history where women have had such an influential role—even though they were systematically denied positions of authority."

Women need heroes—positive role models—and they need vision as to how their own lives can be significant in the kingdom of God. When women read about women who are faithful to God, they are challenged to be faithful. When women read about women whose adornment is their sterling character, they are motivated to become women of character. When women read about women who have taken risks to serve God, they are challenged to take risks, and to demonstrate what faithfulness to God really means. When women see what other women have done against countless odds and in difficult circumstances, they are challenged to see what God can do in and through them in their circumstances. It is refreshing and encouraging for all of us to see some of what God has been doing "behind the scenes" through women who love Him. God continues to work in and through the lives of women today, as will be seen by the vignettes of women ministering today within the ministry of Campus Crusade for Christ.

Another reason to write about women's involvement in ministry is to motivate men to do what they can to encourage women under their leadership to increase their involvement. It is interesting to note that, historically, leaders even within the same culture have not agreed on the why, when, and how of the ministry of women. Some have actively discouraged the ministry of women. Others, including our Savior, encouraged women to reach out to others with the good news of the kingdom of God.

JESUS AND WOMEN

Jesus showed us how to treat others, men and women. In contrast with those of His day, He treated women as "whole" human beings, deserving of dignity and honor. Women were not omitted from His ministry, nor did He discount their ministry to Him and to others. It is amazing that women are even there, at His feet, or involved in ministry to or with Him. For in the time in which He lived, a typical prayer of most Jewish rabbis was, "Thank You, God, that You have not created me a gentile, an infidel, nor a woman."[2] A Jewish man was encouraged not to speak to a woman in public—and not to speak to his wife any more than was necessary. Few women were educated (unless their fathers taught them) because the rabbinical schools were only for boys.

Jesus initiated a conversation with a woman—and not only a woman, but a Samaritan woman (the Jews did not speak to Samaritans)—surprising His disciples. He expected women to learn from Him, telling Martha that Mary, who was learning at His feet, had chosen the "one thing [that] is needed"—that learning from Him was *more* important than preparing food. Women traveled with Him and His disciples, "helping to support them out of their own means" (Luke 8:1–3). He chose Mary Magdalene to go and tell His disciples that He was risen, asking her to be a witness of His resurrection, at a time when the Jewish historian Josephus said that a woman's testimony could never be used in court because of the "lightheadedness and brashness of the female sex."[3] Facts like these prompted Dorothy Sayers to write:

> Perhaps it is no wonder that the women were first at the Cradle and last at the Cross. They had never known a man like this Man—there never has been such another. A prophet and teacher who never nagged

> at them, never flattered or coaxed or patronized; who never made arch jokes about them, never treated them either as 'The women, God help us!' or 'The ladies, God bless them!'; who rebuked without querulousness and praised without condescension; who took their questions and arguments seriously; who never mapped out their sphere for them, never urged them to be feminine or jeered at them for being female; who had no ax to grind and no uneasy male dignity to defend; who took them as he found them and was completely unself-conscious.[4]

THE APOSTLES AND WOMEN

Luke, writing the Book of Acts, gives us a picture of the involvement of women in the early Church. Following Pentecost, when the Holy Spirit came upon each believer, man or woman, we see the New Testament Church meeting from house to house, eating together, praying together, worshiping together. "They all joined together constantly in prayer, along with the women and Mary the mother of Jesus, and with his brothers" (Acts 1:14). This was very different from the current worship habits of the Jews, who separated women and Gentiles from Jewish men for a time of worship.

Ruth Tucker remarks that Peter's sermon in Acts 2 shows very clearly "that the gift of God's Spirit and the ensuing prophetic ministry in the church was now bestowed fully and equally on women as well as men." There is a "double force" here, she says, because Joel 2:28–32, a prophetic text from the Old Testament, emphasizes the role of women ("your sons and *daughters* will prophesy,... and even on the male and *female* servants I will pour out My Spirit in those days," NASB). Peter, filled with the Holy Spirit, chose this text to describe and explain the inception of the age of the Spirit.[5]

Paul constantly mentions women in his letters to the early churches, women who were ministering, whom he considered his "fellow workers." Priscilla and her husband Aquila worked with Paul as tentmakers. It was this couple who took Apollos aside to explain "the way of God more adequately," and Priscilla seems to be the more prominent of the two. In two different cities, the church met in their home. In the last chapter of Romans, Paul commends his fellow workers. Of the 29 people mentioned, 10 are women. Phoebe, called a "servant of the church," may have been a deaconess because the Greek word "servant" is often translated "deacon" in other places. Paul also calls her a "helper of many." Priscilla is mentioned here. Mary "worked hard for you." Junias, along with Andronicus, is said to be Paul's kinsman, fellow prisoner, and "outstanding among the apostles."

Tryphaena, Tryphosa, and Persis "the beloved" are said to have worked hard in the Lord. Paul, writing to Titus, emphasized that the older women were to be teaching "what is good" to the younger women. The involvement of women in ministry to believers and to unbelievers in New Testament times gave great impetus to the spread of the gospel throughout the known world.

THE ORGANIZED CHURCH AND WOMEN

As the Church developed, spreading throughout the Roman Empire and east to India, only certain men were ordained for liturgical ministry. As the Church moved out of the home and into buildings to worship, women's gifts and acts of hospitality were no longer key factors in the advance of the kingdom—although women who were widows could be appointed (not ordained) for ministry, especially the ministry of prayer. Theologians such as Augustine taught that only men were created in the image of God. The Council of Tours (A.D. 567) blamed women for luring men into sin. The Council of Macon (A.D. 585) only narrowly affirmed—30 to 29—that women had souls. The office of deaconess, established in the early years of this period, was abolished.

As the Roman Empire became the Christian Roman Empire, wedding the church to the state, there was an increased separation of clergy and laity. Clergy were elevated and laypeople, both men and women, were removed from public ministry, a situation that continued even beyond the Reformation. People who wanted to know and serve God were recruited to a life of contemplation—men went to monasteries, women to cloisters (140 in England). Being part of a cloister gave women opportunity to commit their lives to God and be supported by the church. A few ministered to the people in nearby communities by caring for the sick and providing places of refuge for the poor and needy, but most were isolated from the world. The average woman practiced her religion by participating in religious holidays, pilgrimages, and by worshiping saints. Sadly, Christianity had turned into a religion of works and rituals. With the expansion of Islam at the beginning of the 13th century, women welcomed the opportunity for ministry and joined the Crusades, making pilgrimages to the Holy Land to save Jerusalem from the infidels.

With the invention of the printing press in 1440 by Johannes Gutenberg, for the first time common men (and women) had access to a copy of God's Word—*if* they could read and *if* they could read Latin or had access to Luther's German translation of the Bible. But it wasn't until King James had the Bible translated from Greek and Hebrew into English in 1611 that the Bible became more available for the common folk.

THE REFORMERS AND WOMEN

Many think that the Reformation, begun by Martin Luther in 1517, came about because of the availability of the Scriptures. With the Reformation came many new perspectives, the chief one being Luther's "The just shall live by faith." Luther, formerly a celibate monk, married Katie Von Bora, whom he helped escape from a nunnery. Katie was a wonderful "pastor's wife," a manager extraordinaire. The government deeded a monastery (with forty rooms on the first floor) to them jointly, and she and Martin proceeded to fill their home with eight children, numerous nephews and nieces, four orphan children, other relatives (some of whom came to help Katie), and the students and guests who came and went. She was a wonderful partner to Luther, showing hospitality to hundreds, joining in discussions with her husband and his students and friends, managing and caring for their own farm and animals, as well as a farm she owned in Zulsdorf—"for Katie it was a retreat from the hubbub in the Wittenberg monastery."[6] Martin said that he thought it might be necessary for women to preach if no man was available. A woman, he said, should not be excluded from "any honor that human beings enjoy, even though she is the weaker vessel."[7]

Calvin's view of women is not completely clear. One student of his Institutes says that he upheld the traditional view of women's subordination to men. Another student says that he did something new in systematic theology by shifting Paul's advice on women's silence in the church from the context of eternal, divine law to the context of Christian freedom, of human law which is open to change.[8]

Generally, the Reformers' view of women elevated marriage and motherhood, but actually curtailed the possibilities for public ministry. It is interesting to consider that the Reformers did not see (apparently) what had happened to the church when the separation occurred between the clergy and the laity. The emphasis on the authority of the clergy continued, thus the priesthood of *all* believers continued to be neglected. Not only were women excluded from public ministry, but men, unless they were ordained, were excluded as well. This separation of clergy and laity continued to greatly hinder the advancement of God's kingdom.

Weary of the restrictions placed on freedom of conscience to worship according to one's beliefs—and of persecution for those who did not follow the beliefs of the current ruler of England—the Puritans sailed for America in 1620. Generally, they opposed public ministry for women unless there was evidence of "special anointing." However, they did view men and women as spiritually equal and encouraged equal education and freedom of conscience. The Quakers and other sects gave women more freedom than did the mainline denominations.

THE FIRST GREAT AWAKENING AND WOMEN

When the First Awakening (1740–1742) began in Jonathan Edward's church, he was perplexed—the show of emotion was troubling to him (and to many others). He kept careful records of the people who were converted or especially blessed, to see if their lives really changed. When his own wife became involved, he was open to saying that the expression of emotion was valid—but one still had to wait to see if there were real changes in folks' lives. Sarah Edwards evidenced such change. She no longer exhibited the anxiety that had plagued her before. An estimated 50,000 people came into the churches of New England as a result of this awakening.

The Awakening was occurring in England, as well. There are scholars who have documented that the Awakening in England under John Wesley and George Whitefield saved England from complete collapse such as occurred in France at that time, and that the formation of what John Wesley called "class meetings" succeeded in re-parenting those who had no families. Women led many of these class meetings. John Wesley had observed his mother's ministry to the parish in his father's absence, and he knew how God could use women. He was known to have told one of his woman leaders to "preach, but don't sound like it." Wealthy men were known to tell their wives not to hire a Methodist maid because she would convert the cook, the cook would convert the governess, and the governess would convert their children, and their children would convert them. Thousands became Christians in England, changing the face of English society, as women (and men) began establishing hospitals, schools, orphanages, and Sunday schools, eventually even abolishing slavery.

EARLY MISSIONS AND WOMEN

William Carey, often called the "Father of Modern Missions," sailed for India from England in 1761, providing many with the vision and the challenge of a world without Christ. Moffat sailed for Africa in 1800, Judson for Burma in 1812.

In the United States, missionaries went West to reach the native Americans. Mary Richardson Walker, newly married to Elkanah, went with him to the Indians of the far West in 1838. Sadly, her journals reveal that she was distressed at her lack of interest in the Indians; she was uncertain of her salvation, and she even questioned her calling.[9]

Following another Awakening after the Civil War, a wave of missionaries departed. Hudson and Maria Taylor and Jonathan and Rosalind Goforth went to China. For a time most of the women who went were wives; then single women began following the call of God to enter foreign missionary work. Hudson Taylor encouraged the ministry of single women, knowing that they were free to reach the women of China: "We are manning our stations with ladies," he wrote.[10] So many went from so many denominations that the provinces of China had to be divided up, the Presbyterians taking one area, the China Inland Mission another, etc.

Women were involved in establishing and teaching in the Sunday School Movement on both sides of the Atlantic. Eventually, many were involved in the temperance movement. Catherine and William Booth focused on reaching the masses with the gospel, cofounding the Salvation Army in England in 1877. Catherine, a better preacher than her husband, had opportunities to speak to congregations all over England, persuading men and women to make a commitment to Christ. Thousands made a personal commitment to Christ under her preaching. One of her writings, a pamphlet on "Women in Ministry," pled for all to consider setting women free to help advance God's kingdom. All their children followed them to minister in the Salvation Army. While some denominations were open to women in ministry (Methodists, some Baptists, Free Methodists, Christian and Missionary Alliance, Church of God), others were not.

Foreign missions had begun to capture the imaginations of women. Up to this point, women who wanted to serve God could teach Sunday school or work in orphanages and hospitals, but other ministries were not open to them. Going to the mission field presented an opportunity for women to serve God with their entire lives. In the U.S., hundreds of societies were formed by women to send women to the foreign field. Ralph Winter of the U.S. Center for World Mission (USCWM) says that by 1905 there were 150,000 Women's Missionary Societies in American Churches.[11]

THE MODERN MISSIONARY MOVEMENT AND WOMEN

We have personal writings from many of the women who went overseas during the Modern Missionary Movement. These biographies are sources of encouragement and vision to me. My heroes are the women who trusted

God when far from family and friends, women who risked all to follow Jesus. Priscilla Studd responded in a godly way when her husband, C. T., at age 54, went to Africa, leaving her an invalid in England. Rosalind Goforth moved from village to village in inland China with four small children, preaching the gospel to the women as her husband did to the men. Amy Carmichael founded Dohnavur Fellowship, and at one time was caring for more than 1,000 children and Indian workers, living by faith, not asking anyone for money. Her character and her poetry draw me to Jesus.

Granny Brand left India when her husband died, but returned to reach people in the mountain ranges she and her husband had planned to reach together. And she did it by riding a horse from village to village until age 94! Isobel Kuhn went to China despite the strong opposition of her mother, who told her that only women who can't get married go to the mission field. Gladys Aylward, turned down by the China Inland Mission as being too old to learn the language, went to China on her own and preached to the women in the villages about Jesus while being on the government payroll as a "foot inspector."

Margaret Laird went to Africa as a single woman, married an American engineer-missionary, and raised several children in Africa. It was the stories she told of God's miraculous working in her life at a missions conference in 1959 that assured me of God's love for me wherever I might go and prompted me to give my life fully to Jesus. Helen Rosaveare's courage when she returned to the place in Africa where she had been beaten and raped, and Elisabeth Elliot's forgiveness when she took her tiny daughter and went into the Huorani tribe who had killed her husband are examples for me. Dr. Henrietta Mear's discipline, love for Jesus, emphasis on the Word, and her influence upon hundreds of young men and women as their teacher make her a person to emulate.

CAMPUS CRUSADE FOR CHRIST AND WOMEN

Then we come to history-in-the-making—the lives of women presently engaged in full-time ministry through Campus Crusade who are making history day by day as they seek to trust God and obey Him. Their stories will be available to encourage and motivate other women to believe God, to take risks, to give all they have for Jesus and the fulfillment of His Great Commission. Hundreds of others could have been included in this chapter. I've included a few women I've known for years—women who were willing to write their stories for me.

Campus Crusade for Christ, founded in 1951 by Bill and Vonette Bright, has provided opportunities for women to minister—in the United States as well as around the world—that are almost unprecedented. Single women have joined the staff by the hundreds, welcoming the opportunity to "live by the gospel" as they share the gospel. Married women (considered full-time staff along with their husbands) have found opportunities to truly be "partners in ministry" with their spouses. While those who have children do not have a job description, they are strongly encouraged to care for their families *and* to reach out to those who need Christ. Standing on the shoulders of those who have gone before, Campus Crusade women are taught the Word of God and how to rely on it for direction in their lives. They have assurance of their salvation. They are taught how to be filled with the Spirit and to walk with Him moment by moment. They are trained in how to share their faith and how to disciple the people who receive Christ.

The evangelical community in the U.S. is divided on where, how, and in what context women should minister. Some would say that the Bible teaches that a woman belongs only in her home. On the other end of the spectrum are those who interpret the Scripture passages that appear restrictive as intended for the New Testament culture only—thus paving the way for women to preach and teach and lead men and women. Campus Crusade for Christ has no written policy on this matter, but appears to follow a course somewhat in the middle. Women, single and married, are encouraged and expected to be involved in fulfilling the Great Commission—in taking the initiative to see where God would have them minister, showing hospitality in their homes, reaching out to those who don't know Christ. There have been single women who have left Crusade staff, frustrated because their gifts and abilities have not been recognized and used—but men have left staff for similar reasons. Have women "led" men? In certain cases, women have been campus directors, and in two cases, women have been directors of countries in Europe. Have women "taught" men? Women regularly speak at campus meetings to both men and women. In these cases, the women have been responsible to a man in leadership over them, who has delegated to them the responsibility to perform these tasks of leading, teaching, and speaking.

Opportunities to minister in a significant way abound in Campus Crusade. Godly women who desire to serve God find abundant opportunities to do just that. As you read the rest of this chapter, notice how God worked in the life of each particular woman. Also notice the hand of God behind the scenes, using women to bring lost women, men, and children into His kingdom, then discipling and training them to obey the Great Commandment and the Great Commission.

Vonette Bright

Any discussion of the life and ministry of women in Campus Crusade for Christ needs to begin with Vonette Bright, the wife of Dr. Bill Bright and the cofounder of Campus Crusade. Vonette has provided, and continues to provide, a very positive model for all Crusade women, as well as for Christian women everywhere.

Bill told Vonette on their honeymoon that he wanted her to be his partner in everything they did, that he knew her perspective was different, and that he wanted her viewpoint. He asked her to take a look at his business (at the time he was a businessman in California) and give him suggestions. She was very surprised since she had been cautioned by an uncle "to let that young man run his own business." When God gave the vision of Campus Crusade to Bill, he shared this with Vonette, bringing her gently along to see what this would mean. She had to ask herself, "Am I going to get on board, or am I to be on the sidelines?" Fortunately for Bill and the entire movement, Vonette chose to "get on board." At early staff conferences, I remember her challenge to each wife to ask the Lord for the strength and courage to respond to her husband, to give her a heart to go along with what God was showing her husband and to be equipped for ministry herself. More than once I have heard her encourage wives to do all they can to "get behind their man and do what they can to make him successful in God's sight."

As she and Bill began the ministry on the campus at UCLA, she continued teaching school. When she saw several women from the Navigators discipling new believers, Vonette decided that she wanted to be working alongside Bill doing that rather than teaching. So she quit her job and began doing evangelism and discipleship on the campus. She remembers times (after Zach and Brad came along) when the Crusade moms cared for each other's children while they took turns on the campus. Other times they even met with students in the park where they could push their strollers. When training for new staff became necessary, Vonette wrote some training manuals. She was faithful to her parenting responsibilities (Zach is now a pastor, Brad on Crusade staff) while she continued her involvement in training staff and encouraging hundreds of staff women through her talks at conferences, her gracious hospitality, her personal conversations, and books she has written.

When the Campus Crusade organization became very large and God sent some men with MBAs from Harvard to give Bill needed support, Vonette asked the Lord what her role should be. At that point, she began the Great Commission Prayer Crusade, encouraging women to pray for our country and our world and to pray that God would mightily use the huge gathering of Explo '72 (planned for summer of 1972) in the lives of thousands of college students and laymen and women. In 1988, as Chairman of the National Day of Prayer Task Force, she introduced legislation that was signed into law, making the first Thursday in May a permanent Day of Prayer. "Prayer," she believes, "is the greatest resource we have to bring about change."

Vonette often travels with Bill. She speaks to large groups of women, always challenging them to trust God and to believe that He will work in and through them if they are available to Him. In a conversation years ago, she and I were talking about the Consciousness Raising Groups developed by women in the feminist movement. "Well," she said, "we need to raise the level of consciousness of Christian women so that they see who God is and have confidence in Him that He can use them to advance His kingdom and fulfill the Great Commission." This is her message and her heart's desire, and this kind of encouragement is what she will continue to give to the women with whom she comes in contact. A recent book, *100 Christian Women Who Changed the 20th Century* by Helen Kooiman Hosier,[12] includes portraits of Mary Lee Bright (Bill's mother), Dr. Henrietta Mears, and Vonette Bright. Read Hosier's book to discover the honors Vonette has received and the books she has written.

Judy Downs Douglass

Judy Downs Douglass never imagined that she would, in 2001, be the wife of the new president of Campus Crusade for Christ, Steve Douglass. As a single woman, she had broken an engagement and given up a dream of hers—to be a writer and editor—when she came on staff in 1964, having been involved with Campus Crusade at the University of Texas. She was shocked and surprised when Bill Bright called her to his office and asked her if she would be interested in working on an evangelistic magazine designed for college students (*The Collegiate Challenge*). When the focus of the magazine changed to challenge believers to be involved in what God was doing, Judy was delighted again, because now she could use her gift of exhortation to motivate 100,000 believers to become involved in the advancement of God's kingdom. She eventually became the editor of this magazine, *The Worldwide Challenge*, and continued to work with various other publications for fourteen years, even after her marriage in 1975 to Steve Douglass, then Vice President for Administration.

Then their daughter Debbie was born, with Michelle coming along a couple of years later. Judy concentrated on being a full-time mom but remained involved in ministry as much as feasible outside the home. Together, Steve and Judy ministered through their church where they taught a college class. (Judy still keeps in touch with some women from that group.) Steve coached a soccer team, and both of them ministered to the families of the girls on their team. Some of these girls and their parents became Christians.

When Steve became the Director of U.S. Ministries for Campus Crusade in 1987, Judy asked, "How can I be the best partner with and for my husband?" God directed her to minister to the moms of Campus Crusade, encouraging them by writing to them, providing them with resources, and arranging seminars to encourage them at the Staff Conference every two years. Her book, *What Can a Mother Do?*, was written to encourage mothers that God can use them to reach others—in their homes and out of them, with their children and husbands, or alone, as God gives opportunity. More recently, she has sought to minister to all the Crusade women. She limits the time spent in her office at Crusade's headquarters in Florida so that she can adequately care for her family. Her girls are in college, and she is homeschooling their son Josh, who is in high school.

As I am writing this, Judy is again asking herself, "How can I be the best partner with my husband?" as she considers being the wife of the new president of Campus Crusade for Christ. Judy's obvious love for God and her confidence in Him—that He knows what He is doing when He gave her *this* job—will enable her to stand strong. They will enable her to continue to motivate and encourage all believers in her sphere of influence to trust and obey God and to reach others with the gospel. I know, too, that her ability to be "real," to share her heart in times of challenge, difficulty, and rejoicing, will be a factor in helping staff women to trust and obey God where they are.

SINGLE WOMEN

Single women have found a significant place of ministry in this Movement and have made valuable contributions. **Lianne Roembke** (now Dr. Lianne Roembke), a graduate student at Wheaton, was planning to teach overseas in the field of Christian Education when her sister suggested that she join Campus Crusade for Christ for two years to "round out her skills in evangelism." Lianne had heard Bill Bright speak, and the vision for the world and the excitement and dedication of the staff were drawing points, as was the emphasis on the ministry of the Holy Spirit. She found that the emphasis that God was at work in her to empower her to live a holy life gave her a new sense of freedom, where in her background, the letter of the law had prevailed.

In her first months on staff on the college campus, she experienced shock upon shock—"opportunities to trust the Lord," others called them. She was sent to evangelize the radicals on the campus at the University of Wisconsin who were throwing tear gas and bombs. After other assignments, chiefly to develop the training of staff, she moved to Basel, to work in the European Training Office with Finns, Swiss, Dutch—and later Germans, British, and Canadians.

As Lianne worked with people from other cultures, she noticed that the minority cultures on the team were often misunderstood—and had the least to say, not only within Crusade, but in other missions as well.

She began researching the topic of "multicultural teams" for her doctorate while she kept up with speaking and training responsibilities. She discovered some freeing principles, which, when applied, left everyone with their identity intact but able to move harmoniously in the same direction. Her dissertation, *Building Credible Multicultural Teams* (published in the U.S. by the William Carey Library, and in Germany as well) presents these principles. Lianne says, "One doesn't have to 'go native' to identify with the people group one wants to reach with the Good News of Christ. One does have to be willing, however, to give up things which are a barrier to the credible communication of the gospel in a given cultural context. And the direction of the cultural adjustment of the team is not to be governed by the majority represented, or the leadership or even the 'mother mission,' but by the cultural group to which the gospel is being communicated."

Lianne's current ministry is worldwide (and reaches beyond Campus Crusade to other missions) as she travels, teaching, advising, and caring for staff members.

Ann Bowman, Th.M., presently teaches Greek, Inductive Bible Study, and New Testament at the International School of Theology in Southern California. Her journey to being an assistant professor in a graduate school began years before, when, as a missionary in West Africa with another mission board, she saw two distinct needs. First was the need to know how to do evangelism and discipleship, and second was the need to understand the ministry of the Holy Spirit in the life of the believer. Returning to the U.S., she found some Crusade staff members in Houston to talk to about these things, was promptly hired as their secretary, and discovered the principles of "spiritual breathing" which, Ann says, "changed my life!" Sometime later, Ann realized that God wanted her to serve Him in Campus Crusade for Christ.

Ann has been on the staff of Crusade for thirty years, serving in many capacities—designing cross-cultural training, training staff in the Philippines, managing offices, teaching Sunday school, teaching in Leadership Training Conferences. For a time, she studied at Dallas Theological Seminary. Because Dallas's Th.M. degree was not open to women at the time, she finished up at Talbot.

Besides teaching Greek and Inductive Bible Study at the International School of Theology, Ann was a section editor for the Women's Study Bible and is one of the authors of a forthcoming book on women in ministry. Her pastor appreciates the fact that she is a "team player." He recognizes and utilizes her pastoral, administrative, and teaching gifts through home fellowship groups, home Bible studies, and prayer counseling. In all the discussions of what women should and should not do, biblically, in the local church, Ann's desire is that women be allowed and encouraged to use their spiritual gifts to advance the kingdom of God.

Mary Graham currently is associate Crusade staff and the president of Women of Faith, a weekend conference ministry designed to encourage women spiritually (presently drawing 10,000 to 20,000 women regularly). She joined staff in 1969 after being personally challenged by Bill and Vonette at a college reception. She says, "The surprises that awaited me included developing my own financial support, taking *all* the initiative on the campus in evangelism, and being in over my head for the next 25 years." (We can identify, Mary!) Mary's time on staff has included working on a campus, being a traveling women's representative, working on the national U.S. team, and being the director of Women Today, including the radio broadcast with Vonette Bright. Following a meeting with Luci Swindoll, who explained how God was using a new nationwide conference "Women of Faith," she was encouraged by Vonette to see how Crusade could help with the tremendous response to the conference. She became directly involved in this conference ministry, planning how to follow-up the women (sometimes more than 1,000!) who said they had received Christ at the conference. Her involvement continued to grow until Bill and Vonette actually encouraged her to leave staff. God was working, they said, and He had opened this particular door for Mary. It didn't make any difference that Crusade's name wasn't on this ministry. "Our responsibility is to work in His vineyard," Bill said. Again, Mary wasn't certain what she was getting into, but the Brights had instilled in her the confidence to believe God and take her eyes off herself. "This is," she says, "one of their great legacies in my life."

Ney Bailey is another single woman whose ministry has touched lives all over the world. She first came in touch with Crusade at a Leadership

Training Institute in Mound, Minnesota. The godliness of the staff made her hunger and thirst to know the Lord like they did, but she felt she could never qualify. God, however, had other thoughts, and a year or so later Ney joined Crusade. She wanted to be part of a group of people who were taking the Lord seriously, obeying His Great Commission. She says, "I remember my heart was inflamed to hear Bill Bright talk of the world." She remembers Bill showing them a world map that was divided into regions —actually making the Great Commission seem "doable."

For a number of years Ney traveled, encouraging staff members. When she was home, she helped to plant several new churches. During this time, Ney also learned that "faith is not a feeling" (and she has written a book by that title). "Great faith" is simply taking God at His Word, and His Word is true. Ney says, "I learned that His Word is truer than how I feel, His Word is truer than any circumstance or situation that will ever be in my life. These truths have been life-changing for me." As she shared these truths at conferences and evangelistic meetings, they have changed the lives of hundreds of people in the U.S. and in other countries. She remembers arriving at a huge ballroom in Warsaw at 8:30 on the morning of a women's conference in 1991. "No one was there. Then the trains started arriving from cities all over Poland, and a steady stream of women soon filled the ballroom to capacity. The media people who were there covering the conference were astonished: 'Where did all of these beautiful young women come from?' We knew that they had come from the far reaches of Poland because our Crusade staff had been in there for years quietly and secretly ministering to them. Now they could worship openly. What a memorable and historic moment for all of us!"

Harriet Smith heard about the need for a bilingual person with a heart for reaching Hispanics at her first training conference. After working with Hispanics in the U.S. and in Mexico for fourteen years, she began ministering to the Chinese. She tells about her "switch" from one people group to another: "I was translating a Missions Class for Dr. Roy Rosedale in Mexico City when he quoted a statistic that totally blew my mind: '97% of today's Christian workers are working in areas that are culturally *close* to Christianity, but only 5% of Christian workers are reaching out to the rest—more than half—of the world's population.'" She had trouble even translating this, not because she couldn't say it, but because of the impact it had on her life. She thought, *Who is going to tell the rest of the world?*

Leaving Mexico briefly to renew her visa, she found herself in a prayer meeting in Atlanta, where the focus was on prayer for unreached people groups, especially those of East Asia. At the end of the evening, she thought,

How could anyone be here tonight and not just want to pack her bags and go on the next plane to Asia? She began praying and moving in that direction, but it took four years before she arrived at her Asian assignment. Harriet's ministry grew to be so successful—with so many folks meeting Christ—that she had to leave, because too many people (and people in power) knew her main reason for being in China.

Returning to the U.S. and having God's heart for the unreached people of East Asia, she began working with another Crusade ministry that reaches out to students from Mainland China with the gospel while they are in the U.S. While her main role is in the office, she prefers opportunities to work directly with Chinese students. She networks with students, helping them connect with people who can continue the process of evangelism and discipleship as they move from one location to another. Harriet's influence for the kingdom has been, and continues to be, invaluable!

WIVES AND WIDOWS

Wives of men in the Campus Ministry of Campus Crusade for Christ (Crusade has 106 ministries) have opportunities to do evangelism and discipleship with the women on campus as their husbands work with men.

Sue Michels became a Christian through the ministry of Campus Crusade at Eastern Michigan University and then went on a summer project that "changed my life." She married Dave Michels following graduation, and they joined Crusade together.

Sue wanted to be on staff because she knew she did *not* want to become a complacent Christian. She wanted the CCC environment where her faith would be stretched and where she would be challenged to grow spiritually. Being in the front-lines has caused her to depend on the Lord and to follow Him faithfully. Following their time at the International School of Theology in California, Sue decided that she really wanted to get back on campus, sharing her faith (she had been home with three small boys, one a new baby). Dave offered to stay with the boys one day a week so she could go on campus, teach a Bible study, and go witnessing with some key students.

In 1983, the Michels packed up their household and moved to Moscow to serve with the CoMission for one year, a huge faith stretcher for the whole family. Sue saw one neighbor come to Christ, was able to go into some schools and an orphanage to teach, and led a Bible club for 10 to 12 children —all while keeping Dave and their household going in a foreign situation.

Sue admits to experiencing some tension between being a wife and mother and working with the students on campus. But she has come to realize that she needs to depend on God and His power and focus on what He wants, rather than worrying about how others think she should spend her time. She says, "As I look at being with CCC for these past 22 years, I have no regrets about my calling. It has been a privilege to be in ministry and to be a part of what God is doing."

Some of the women on the staff of Campus Crusade are widows. **Jerri Younkman** lost her husband, Chuck, in 1992, in a car accident in Southern California. She and Chuck, a faculty member at Ohio State University, had come on staff in 1967 after hearing Bill Bright speak at a Faculty Lay Institute in Chicago. Assigned to headquarters, Chuck became the director of Mass Media, and Jerri continued her homemaking tasks, seeking to reach her children's friends for Christ. When Chuck began working with pastors under the auspices of Church Dynamics, Incorporated (a Campus Crusade ministry), Jerri began discipling the wives of those pastors.

When Chuck was killed, Jerri felt definitely that God wanted her to remain with Campus Crusade. Indeed, they had previously decided to remain on staff no matter what might happen. Because the youngest of her four boys, Chris, was still in high school, she looked for a place to serve that would allow her to stay in San Bernardino. Her life experience—both as a mom and as a discipler of women—qualified her to work with Partners in Ministry, a program designed to encourage wives of graduate students at the International School of Theology. In 1997, she completed a MAPS (Master of Arts in Pastoral Ministry) degree and is presently pursuing her M.Div. to be better prepared to teach enrichment classes on campus and online. The dream that she and Chuck had together—to minister within Crusade—has become her own personal dream.

Another woman who remained on the staff of Crusade following her husband's death is **Shirley Hinkson**, now living in England. Bud had been the director of all of Campus Crusade's work in Eastern Europe.

Shirley began working with Crusade early in the 1950s as a college student. She was already talking to fellow students about Christ, so she fit right in with the brand-new movement of Crusade, helping to write materials. One thing that amazed her was that Bill's ideas were put into action at once. She came on staff full-time in 1956 and began serving at the University of Texas, where she claimed Joshua 1:3: "Every place on which the sole of your foot treads, I have given it to you." Shirley said that she talked to 250 people about Christ before anyone responded to the gospel, but once there was one response, many, many came to Christ. When she told Bill that "we need someone to travel around to campuses and encourage us," he said, "You're the one!" So she became the first "women's rep," traveling to many campuses to encourage women in the Word and in their ministry to students.

Following her marriage to Bud Hinkson in 1961, they ministered in Oregon and then in England, where they took the first "University Ambassador" team to begin a movement. Moving to Africa, Austria, and Germany, they ministered to all of Europe, including the then Soviet Union. Bud became the director of Campus Crusade in Europe. She occasionally traveled with him, teaching in Lay Institutes for Evangelism and having evangelistic teas for women, but mostly she stayed at home, providing stability for their two children.

As their children grew and returned to the U.S. for college, she began traveling regularly with Bud. She remembers one incident in the Soviet Union (during *perestroika*, but before the Iron Curtain came down) as being particularly amazing. While Bud met with church leaders, she went sightseeing with a language teacher/translator who took her to a political rally, complete with soldiers with machine guns. Impressed that she should talk with this woman about Christ, she shared *The Spiritual Four Laws* with her and then gave her the *JESUS* video. Surprisingly, the woman was very open. "This is good; this is the time of *perestroika!*" She showed the video to her father, who then invited Bud to come to his "Club" and give five lectures on Christianity. Bud and Shirley were astonished to discover that this "Club" was the Soviet Academy of Science! Not knowing what to expect, Bud boldly shared who Christ is and what He came to do. When he finished proclaiming the truth of the resurrection, the men stood and cheered! Bud stayed and answered questions for two hours. Shirley had the joy of leading her language teacher and the teacher's mother to faith in Jesus.

Following Bud's death in a bicycle accident in 1992, Shirley relocated to England and has continued to minister through Bible teaching, Bible conferences, and evangelistic events in Europe and Russia. One of her greatest joys is ministering with her grown children, Jon and Joi, and their spouses —all on Crusade staff.

WOMEN FROM COUNTRIES OTHER THAN THE U.S.

Lois Seruyange joined the staff of Campus Crusade when she married Lazarus in 1974. Lois remembers being impressed that the Crusade staff were loving, caring Christians. ("Bill and Vonette sent us a gift when we got married!") Following a training time in Kenya, they began sharing their faith on the campus of Makerere University in Uganda and in their neighborhood. When Lazarus came to the International School of Theology in California to get his M.Div., Lois entered the Partners in Ministry Program.

Following graduation, they went to Western Seminary so Lazarus could get his doctorate, and Lois graduated with an MA in Christian Education.

When Lazarus was appointed the principal of the International School of Theology in Nairobi (NIST), a sister school to ISOT in the U.S., Lois designed a Women's Program for those women whose husbands were graduate students. Some community women have participated in this, as have wives of pastors.

Her ministry through NIST has been remarkable. While raising their three children, she has coordinated the Women's Program, taught classes, and trained many women in evangelism and discipleship—women who will be passing this training and a vision for outreach on to those in the African churches their husbands will be pastoring. She designed and instituted conferences for pastors' wives. More than 130 pastors' wives attended in March 2000; in May about 100 attended, and more conferences are planned. Lois rejoices for the opportunity to be part of the team that is training and developing women as servant leaders to love others and fulfill the Great Commission in the African church.

Miriam Motta recalls with sadness the years in her Central American homeland, Guatemala, when hundreds of students went out in the streets seeking social justice and equality. Many fell under the bullets that silenced their claims—claims she felt were justified, although she didn't agree with their methods of violent protest. Recognizing that the only way things could change would be through the power of Jesus Christ, she began to share her faith. Often, however, she just became involved in fruitless religious discussions. Impressed by the way some young leaders shared the gospel so aggressively in a Campus Crusade student meeting ("Jesus is the greatest revolutionary you can know"), she decided to join the staff of Campus Crusade in 1970 to help reach her country for Christ.

She began working with university students in Mexico. When she married Lionel (a Crusade leader from Guatemala), they continued together to win and disciple students in El Salvador, Costa Rica, and Mexico. Eventually, they came to the International School of Theology to receive further training and education. Miriam took the opportunity to participate in the PIM Program and appreciated the encouragement in finding a balance between ministering to her family (two girls) and to others outside her family.

After working with the Executive and Embassy Ministry in Latin America for four years, they developed Crusade's Family Ministry in Latin America. When their two daughters got married, they had the freedom to travel together to seventeen countries, teaching couples' seminars and parenting seminars to more than 1,000 couples. They have also trained 115 couples to do this ministry in their own countries.

Miriam says, "I am so grateful for Dr. Bright's vision—for his obedience and availability to be used by God to expand that vision to reach the whole world for Christ. Someday he will be so happy to see how many Latinos are going to be in heaven as a result of his obedience." She is also grateful to be a part of what God is doing in Latin America.

Myung-Hee Kim, her husband, Paul, and their children came to the U.S. to the International School of Theology from Hungary (where they were Korean Campus Crusade for Christ missionaries) for further training. Holding a masters degree in literature in her native Korea, she nonetheless became part of the enrichment program, Partners in Ministry, taking as many classes as possible while learning to speak English, caring for her children, helping her husband with classes, and participating in their Korean church (many miles away). Through an English-as-a-Second Language class in the community, she became acquainted with numbers of other internationals and planned occasions to share the gospel with them. Several trusted Christ. She was a writer who was published in Korea, but was very self-effacing about her writing. Her second book, designed to encourage Koreans to share their faith, was written while in the States. They have since returned to Hungary to share the gospel.

MY OWN EXPERIENCE

When my husband, Ted, suggested we work briefly with Crusade before going to the foreign mission field, I agreed, not realizing that our two-year commitment would extend to more than forty years. Our first staff conference was a stretching experience. Although we talked a lot about witnessing in the solid evangelical church of my childhood, it was something we virtually never did. At the staff meeting I not only learned how to share my faith, but a young woman I talked to actually responded to the simple message and placed her faith in Jesus. I was challenged to be a "woman after God's own heart" by Shirley Milligan Hinkson, and Diane Ross Hutcheson's encouragement to *expect* God to work (faith!) was another challenge. I slipped into a small prayer meeting with some staff women and was absolutely startled to hear them thank God because He was *going* to answer the prayers they were praying. Bill's emphasis on the ministry of the Holy Spirit in my life really hit home—the need to be continuously filled with the Spirit moment by moment. I began thanking God in all things, confessing sin immediately, and I began to expect Him to work in and through me.

At the University of Minnesota (our first assignment), we had students continually in our home, and for a time, I went on campus one day a week to talk to students about Christ. Moving from a campus to a regular neighborhood in San Bernardino (so Ted could work at Crusade headquarters) was a definite challenge. Another move to the San Bernardino Mountains eventually provided the opportunity for our kids to be discipled by some Crusade staff who were assigned to work with students at Rim of the World High School. God used this ministry and the ministry of others—some with Crusade, some not—in their lives. Three of our children are presently on the Crusade staff, two working in East Asia, one recently returned with her husband from assignments with the International Leadership Academies (a ministry of Campus Crusade) in Mexico and Costa Rica.

For the past 23 years, I have worked with the Partners in Ministry Program at the International School of Theology, encouraging the wives of the graduate students to be true partners in ministry with their husbands. The PIM Program, by the way, was the idea of Bill and Vonette Bright, who have always encouraged every wife to be involved with her husband in whatever ministry God has called them to serve.

And what more shall I say? I have mentioned just a few of the women from history and a few of the women presently engaged in the ministry of Campus Crusade (which, as Bill Bright says, is "only a leaf on a twig on a branch of the tree that is the Body of Christ"). With great courage, many mothers constantly struggle to balance family and ministry to others, so that God's kingdom might be advanced. I think of women like Elizabeth Marks, Judy Anderson, and Lois Mackey who have followed their husbands all over the globe, raising children on-the-go, leading women to Christ, and discipling them. The time will come when *all* the women of Campus Crusade for Christ, including the small number mentioned in this chapter, will be honored by their Lord and Master for seeking to be faithful to Him and doing what He has called them to do. It is my prayer that these examples will motivate women of all situations—single, married, with or without children, of all ages and races—to seek the calling that God has for them and, as women who are chosen to receive God's amazing grace, to be faithful to share that grace with others.

NOTES

1. Ruth Tucker and Walter Liefeld, *Daughters of the Church* (Grand Rapids, MI: Zondervan, 1987), 15,16.
2. Leonard Swindler, *Women in Judaism* (Metuchen, NJ: The Scarecrow Press, Inc., 1976), 80.

3. Swindler, 115.
4. Dorothy Sayers, *Are Women Human?* (Downers Grove, IL: Intervarsity), 47.
5. Tucker, 64.
6. William J. Petersen, *Martin Luther Had a Wife* (Wheaton, IL: Tyndale House, 1983).
7. Tucker, 174.
8. Tucker, 175.
9. Cathy Luchetti, *Women of the West* (St. George, UT: Antelope Island Press, 1982).
10. Pearce R. Beaver, *All Loves Excelling* (Grand Rapids, MI: Eerdmans, 1968), 116.
11. Ralph Winter, *Mission Frontiers* (August 1999), 4.
12. Helen Kooiman Hosier, *100 Christian Women Who Changed the 20th Century* (Grand Rapids, MI: Revell, 2000).

CHAPTER 16

Sowing Broadly

PAUL ESHLEMAN

On Staff since 1966

Director, The JESUS Film Project

One of the most important philosophies of Bill Bright and Campus Crusade for Christ has been the principle of "sowing broadly." In 2 Corinthians 9:6, the Scriptures say that "whoever sows sparingly will also reap sparingly, and whoever sows generously will also reap generously." Although this passage refers primarily to giving, the principle is the same for evangelism. Jesus sowed broadly. He and His twelve disciples, and later the seventy, went throughout Galilee and parts of Samaria, presenting His kingdom and calling men and women to repentance. The Scripture records crowds of four and five thousand who heard Him teach.

But then Jesus withdrew to teach those who were willing to follow Him and prepare them for their "work of service." Dr. Bright has always had the philosophy that it is our responsibility to sow, but the results are up to God. He also believes that among those who respond to the message are those who will become 30-, 60-, and 100-fold producers. He has often commented that the "cream rises to the top." It was these men and women that he wanted to disciple as leaders in the work force—those who would also sow broadly and bring in the harvest.

One of the great legacies that Dr. Bright has brought to the Christian endeavor is his unflagging commitment to the Great Commission. Early in his ministry, he began signing all of his letters, "Yours for fulfilling the Great Commission in this generation."

Two thousand years ago, Jesus gave His Great Commission to take the gospel to the whole world. He was very definite about it. In fact, He gave us the same command five times in the first five books of the New Testament. Each time, He gave us a slightly different insight into what He has asked us to do:

- Matthew 28:18–20 defines the *depth* of the Great Commission.

> Then Jesus came to them and said, "All authority in heaven and on earth has been given to me. Therefore go and make disciples of all nations, baptizing them in the name of the Father and of the Son and of the Holy Spirit, teaching them to obey everything I have commanded you. And surely I am with you always, to the very end of the age."

In this passage, Jesus tells us to make disciples in every nation and teach them all things that He has commanded us. Sometimes the scope of this commandment seems overwhelming and, perhaps, never-ending. However, He is clear that it is more than just proclaiming the gospel. And He assures us that all authority in heaven and earth are His and that He will always be present with us. He is the Lord of the Great Commission.

- Mark 16:15 emphasizes the *breadth* and *quantity* of the sowing.

> He said to them, "Go into all the world and preach the good news to all creation."

Sowing should be widespread. We have a God who cares about "all" and "every." In fact, these words are used more than 6,000 times in the Scriptures. For example: He is not "wanting anyone to perish, but everyone to come to repentance" (2 Peter 3:9).

- Luke 24:46,47 shows the *surety* of the Great Commission.

> He told them, "This is what is written: The Christ will suffer and rise from the dead on the third day, and repentance and forgiveness of sins will be preached in his name to all nations, beginning at Jerusalem."

For those of us involved in evangelism, this is perhaps the most comforting. Jesus is saying that just as surely as He rose from the dead, so we may have the same confidence that His "good news" will go out to the whole world.

- John 20:21 shows Jesus as the *model* of the Great Commission.

> "As the Father has sent me, I am sending you."

Jesus said in Luke 19:10, "The Son of Man came to seek and to save the lost." Certainly a legitimate reading of John 20:21 could be: "As the Father sent me into the world to seek and to save the lost, so I am sending you into the world to seek and save the lost."

- Acts 1:8 speaks of the *extent* of the Great Commission.

  > "You will receive power when the Holy Spirit comes on you; and you will be my witnesses in Jerusalem, and in all Judea and Samaria, and to the ends of the earth."

  In this passage, Jesus says that after the Holy Spirit comes upon you, you will be His witnesses in Jerusalem (people near you), Judea (people in the local areas surrounding you), Samaria (people who are different from you), and the uttermost parts of the world (those in the farthest corners of the globe).

Certainly, to reach the far corners of the globe, it is essential to do broad sowing. In John 4:35, Jesus instructs His disciples (and us), "I tell you, open your eyes and look at the fields! They are ripe for harvest." This verse contains the principles that lie at the heart of the Campus Crusade for Christ philosophy of broad sowing—repentance, vision, and faith.

Open Your Eyes (Repentance)

First of all, Jesus says, "Don't be blind to the needs of the world. Open your eyes." The KJV says, "Lift up your eyes." Everything in the Christian life begins with repentance, vision, and faith. Jesus says that our eyes are either closed or looking down. Physically, when we are looking down, we can see only what we are doing or what our hands are doing. We tend to pray only about our ministry and our needs. Our scope is so small, our vision so puny, that we don't really need anyone else in the Body. We seem to be saying that if God would just help us a little bit, we could be quite self-sufficient. We need to repent of looking only at our own ministries or interests.

Look at the Fields (Vision)

Second, Jesus says, "I want you to look at the fields." He didn't ask us to find a nearby tree or bush where we could harvest. He painted us a picture of vast fields ripe for harvest. Our problem is that we tend to look at only a very narrow part of the harvest field. Every Christian needs to become aware of many other fields where it would be possible to sow and reap.

Realize the Harvest Is Ready Now (Faith)

This is sometimes a difficult principle for us to accept. We have tried to harvest in some fields that just don't seem to be ripe. But Jesus says they are ready to harvest. He tells us, "If you'll just open your eyes and look up at the fields, you'll see that the harvest is ripe in North Korea, Kuwait, Saudi Arabia, and Iran."

Since the first year of ministry on the UCLA campus, Bill and Vonette have always stressed the need to talk to groups of people. As an individual, Bill has been an ardent personal evangelist. I have watched him share *The Four Spiritual Laws* with taxi drivers, bellhops, stewardesses, bus drivers, hotel maids, and many others. During his fifty years as president of Campus Crusade for Christ, he has set an example of personal evangelism that is unlike any that I have seen. His consistency "in season and out" has been a model to our entire staff.

But Bill is also a visionary, and so his burden has always been to reach more people to give groups of people a chance to hear the message. This culminated, in terms of numbers, when he spoke to more than 2 million people at Yoido Plaza in Seoul, Korea, in 1980, and more than 1 million people indicated decisions to receive Christ.

In 1951, Bill began to speak in fraternity and sorority houses at UCLA. After the evening meal, he would give his testimony and a presentation of the gospel to the entire student group. In those days, he would invite those who wanted to know more about Jesus and how to receive Him personally to attend an "after-meeting" in the living room. Sometimes, three-fourths of the students would come to the second meeting, and most would indicate decisions to trust Christ. Then, in the days that followed, he and Vonette would meet with each of the new converts personally to begin the follow-up process.

Bill saw very clearly the principle of using a "filter" to find the ripe fruit that God had already prepared. In the years that followed, this idea of presenting the gospel to large groups of people to find the ripe fruit began to grow and expand across the country. In 1966, Hal Lindsey began speaking on prophecy and his book *The Late Great Planet Earth*. Hundreds of students turned out weekly to hear him speak. And there was always an opportunity to receive Christ. André Kole, an illusionist, began drawing big crowds using his skills in magic and attracting students who were looking for an entertaining evening. What they found was the profound truth that Jesus was no illusion and that His resurrection from the dead was the greatest event of history. Jon Braun drew thousands with his three-night series on Sex and the Single Swinger. Josh McDowell packed auditoriums with his talks on Maximum Sex. And always, always, the goal was the same: to attract students through their interests and turn them to the One who could meet the real and deep needs in their lives. Not every staff member was a great speaker, but each one could speak to a dormitory group, or an athletic team, or a campus club.

In Wisconsin and Northern Michigan, where I directed the ministry for a time, we held 63 team meetings in one week at Michigan Tech and Northern Michigan University. We spoke to every fraternity, every sorority, student groups on almost every floor of every dormitory, the athletic teams, several clubs, and numerous classrooms. Some students heard the presentation two or three times. But in one week, we contacted more than 3,000 students in small group meetings and saw more than 500 indicate decisions to trust Christ.

Meanwhile, the idea of broad sowing began to reflect not only the principle of filtering out the "ripe fruit," but also the principle of "going where the fruit is."

During 1966–68, three or four other thrusts were begun. The idea of a blitz on a campus was launched at the University of California at Berkeley and later at UCLA. The results at Berkeley were awesome, culminating in a final rally in the Greek Theater where Billy Graham addressed 8,000 students. I spent my week at that very radical campus, ministering in the Forum Restaurant on Telegraph Avenue—the hangout for those in the drug culture. Two young men prayed with me to receive Christ.

I was intrigued with the idea of trying to find crowds that were already gathered for another purpose and to see if we could present the gospel to them. At Wisconsin State University in Eau Claire, all first-year students—about 2,000—were required to attend Freshman Forum. I asked to speak to the group. I gave my testimony, talked about the need for a spiritual foundation in life, and gave an "eyes-open" invitation to "say to God the words I said when I accepted Jesus as my Savior." Four hundred thirty-two students indicated on comment cards that they had received Christ. Doug Radunzel was one of those freshmen who responded. Three years later, after graduation, he joined the staff of Campus Crusade for Christ and later served for a number of years in Russia.

Every spring, college students head for the beaches of Florida, Texas, and California for Spring break. In line with the principle of going where people are, Eddie Waxer put together our first big beach project. While Dick Day was organizing the outreach at Newport-Balboa in California, Eddie was bringing in hundreds of Christian students to witness to the thousands of college students drinking and partying at Daytona Beach. The results were astounding! Many responded. Christian students were having personal conversations with three or four students a day. In one week, I personally talked to 22 students and saw four of them make decisions to receive the Lord. In the evenings, the Christian coffeehouse, The Hunger Hanger, was jammed with non-Christians. And the Campus Crusade for Christ music groups, The New Folk and The Armageddon Experience, performed in the Daytona Beach Bandshell for crowds as big as 10,000.

In the summer of 1967, Dave Hannah launched Athletes in Action (AIA). I was privileged to be the first field staff worker. The idea was to launch competing athletic teams in various sports who could not only perform well, but also give a personal witness for Christ during the intermission times. During that spring, I traveled through the Midwest sharing Christ with wrestlers who had won NCAA national championships in their respective weight classes. Almost all of those I spoke with responded to receive Christ, and I invited them to join our AIA wrestling team for a tour of Japan. For three weeks, the eleven-man team toured Japan, wrestling against the best of that country. At each match, the more mature Christians would give their personal testimonies. John Klein, a long-time ministry veteran, began his years with Campus Crusade for Christ as part of that team. In later years, scores of teams were formed and the Athletes in Action ministry would reach millions of people each year by using sports as a platform to present the gospel.

THE VALUE OF LITERATURE

Bill Bright always placed a great value on the importance of literature. "What people hear is sometimes forgotten," he reminded us. "But what they hear *and see* will be retained much longer." So the ministry of Campus Crusade for Christ reflected his philosophy.

One of the first tools developed for evangelism was the Van Deusen letter. Written to a skeptical doctor, it presented very clearly the essence of how one could become a Christian. This letter became the source of the content that was later put into the little booklet called *The Four Spiritual Laws*. In my early years of campus ministry, we would write out *The Four Spiritual Laws* on the back of the Van Deusen letter, and then leave the letter with them as a means of follow-up. Many who initially heard the gospel without response actually made their decision to receive Christ later as they read the letter and reflected on its challenge to receive Christ.

So for Dr. Bright, literature was important. Soon after the founding of the ministry, he wrote the booklet called *Jesus and the Intellectual*, which was based on a conversation with a student who wondered if there was a basis for rational belief in Christ. This and many other pieces of literature were written over the years to reinforce this philosophy of sowing broadly. His point was always to get the gospel out as widely as possible. "Give a piece of literature to everyone you meet," Bill would say. "Share *The Four Spiritual Laws* if there is opportunity."

During my first year as campus director at the University of Wisconsin at Madison, anti-war protests broke out daily. No one went to class except a few freshman and the foreign graduate students. During one period after the U.S. bombed Cambodia, 3,000 National Guard troops were sent to the campus to try to keep peace. It wasn't enough. Fifteen thousand students, radical organizers, and militant protestors bussed in from other cities charged the administration office of the university on Bascomb Hill. Outside the Student Union on Langdon Street, I watched as beat-up VW buses with peace symbols unloaded grocery bags filled with rocks brought in from a nearby gravel pit.

With my fellow staff member Jack Sims, I stood next to the administration building, behind the troops, watching the milling mob and listening to the taunts. He was new to the radical scene, direct from the fraternity-sorority society of Texas. Suddenly, the student mobs did an end-run on the National Guard troops and got behind the lines. In an effort to keep them out of the buildings, the troops fired tear gas everywhere. Jack and I found ourselves lying on the ground with our eyes burning. We looked up just long enough to see a *Newsweek* photographer capture our pictures for a cover shot of the protesters in Madison.

Personal ministry was tough. But with the campus in turmoil, the opportunity was great. I began to think of what we might do to take advantage of the chaos. During the next several days, we began to gather the Christian students on campus to organize an anti-protest. And with it, I began to draft a piece of literature called "Where We Stand." I enlisted my friend and director, Jim Green, for his help. My idea was to say that the present protest was not radical enough. It talked only about changing political systems. It didn't change people inside.

Here is what we wrote:

WHERE WE STAND

1. We believe that poverty, racism, and social injustice are symptoms of man's basic problem: ego-centeredness and rebellion against the infinite-personal God.
2. We believe that if we are to solve these problems *man must be changed from within!*
3. We believe that involvement in the present conflict is a decision. We are not religious dictators. We judge no one. Responsible convictions must be respected.

4. We believe that the revolution occurring today is not revolutionary enough! It seeks to change the system, but does not deal with the *self-centered attitude* of man.
5. We believe that it is not enough to merely end the war; we are also concerned about man's problems of greed; lust; hate; prejudice; anger; anxiety; boredom; bitterness; sexual, social and economic exploitation; dishonesty; purposelessness; frustration; fear; lack of peace; jealousy; strife; envy; impurity; bigotry; intemperance; insolence; materialism; pride; and self-righteousness.
6. We believe that only Jesus Christ has the power to permanently change man from within and to produce true peace, love, and fulfillment.
7. We believe that religion in itself is not the answer to man's basic problem. Many have said, "Religion is the opiate of the people." Jesus of Nazareth said, "If therefore the Son shall make you free, you shall be free indeed."
8. We believe that religion and philosophy are man's best attempts to find God. Jesus Christ is God's best effort to reach man.
9. We believe that a relationship with Jesus the Christ begins when a person receives Him into his life as his personal payment for sin. Jesus then gives liberation from self-centeredness, inner power for life, and complete forgiveness from sins. As Jesus said, "Behold, I stand at the door [of your life] and knock; if any man hears my voice and opens the door, I will come in to him . . ."
10. We believe that the solution to man's problems lies in "Spiritual Revolution." "When my people, who are called by my name, shall humble themselves, and pray, and seek my face, and turn from their wicked ways; then I will hear from heaven and will forgive their sins, and will heal their land"—God (2 Chronicles 7:14).

We then printed up thousands of bright yellow flyers. There was a picture of "Jesus, the Revolutionary" on one side and the article on the back.

The next afternoon, a rally was being planned by the Students for a Democratic Society on the lawn area in front of the Student Union. We gathered our small band of Campus Crusade students to make signs for our anti-protest. Many of them were young believers.

The staff members were not exactly prepared for radical protesting. The "How to Dress for a Fraternity Meeting" sessions at staff training had reminded us to buy Gant shirts, Gold Cup socks, and Bass Weejun penny loafers. Nobody said anything about combat boots and red bandanas tied around our heads.

By late morning, our signs were ready and we headed for the rally site. The crowd was in the thousands and growing rapidly. We took the fliers and began to pass them out. But we needed more help.

Finally, I began to approach students coming to the rally as if I were one of the organizers. I'd say, "Look, we need your help. We need to get these out to everyone here. Take that sidewalk on the side and make sure everyone gets one." They assumed it was some anti-war literature, and most of them helped get it out.

Then, as the rally began, we surrounded the podium with our signs. They said things like:

> Only Through Christ Can There Be Real Peace
> Death Through War; Life Through Christ
> Real Peace—Only Thru Christ
> Support Minority Groups—Accept Christ
> Inner Peace Before World Peace
> Stopping The War Is Not Enough

To the television and news reporters who were there, the protest against the war in Vietnam was old news. But our demonstration was new, and we made the evening TV news as well as the papers.

In the next several days, our students began to share Christ with even more boldness. We put out fliers telling how to deal with tear gas and minor injuries. Our Campus Crusade students went throughout the campus wearing yellow armbands, helping to wash out the eyes of protestors who had been tear-gassed. They would then have a chance to share Christ with them.

At our early morning prayer times at the Sims's apartment on Langdon Street, we found ourselves in tears. The pepper gas used the night before to break up that protest had settled in their basement apartment. It was just one of the hazards of campus ministry during those days.

But that was not the end. Campus ministry leaders in the national office of Campus Crusade decided to publish an activist evangelization newspaper that could be handed out. More than 5 million were printed, and we set out to distribute the paper ourselves to the campuses of Wisconsin. On the back page was the article "Where We Stand."

We divided our team into four groups and set out to the 35 campuses in our state. At Carthage College, Lawrence College, and other small private schools, we recruited the cashiers in the lunch halls to distribute the fliers at the checkout counters. We headed out to other schools, and then called back after lunch to make sure all the papers had been distributed. By the end of one week, we had distributed some 500,000 papers. It was a huge task, but in line with the philosophy of broad sowing.

Soon the results started coming in. A student at Oshkosh State found the paper in the trash and filled out the coupon for more information. We went to meet him, and he prayed to receive Christ. On another campus, we visited a student after receiving his coupon. It turned out that his roommate had filled out the coupon as a joke, but when we invited him, he also received the Lord. It was a fall of harvest.

As the new year began, our Madison, Wisconsin, campus team received word that the Athletes in Action basketball team had scheduled a game with Northern Michigan University. I told the staff that we needed a break after the Christmas Conference in Chicago. I suggested that we drive to Marquette and see if we could find some local churches that would follow-up the results of the sharing at the basketball game. The team members give their testimony at half-time along with a prayer of invitation. There is usually a good response. As we packed the car, I suggested we take our remaining bundles of the Student Action newspapers with us to distribute at Northern Michigan University Student Union. The rest of the story is amazing.

For almost a year, four Christians at Northern had been praying that God would send someone from InterVarsity or Campus Crusade for Christ to help them grow in their faith. When they walked through the Union, they spotted the newspaper and said, "They're here! God has answered our prayer!" Bill Malick and some of the others began to search for us and put out the word to their friends. At about 2:00 in the afternoon, they ran into some of the gals on our team in a dorm and the connection was made. We agreed to hold a leadership training clinic that night, and 33 students showed up for the first meeting—and the ministry at Northern Michigan was begun. All of this came as a result of broad sowing.

But perhaps the greatest and best-known example of widespread sowing has been the use of the *JESUS* film.

As a young Christian in 1947, Bill Bright felt a strong urging from God to produce a film on the life of Jesus that could be used for worldwide evangelization. Living in Hollywood at the time, he began to approach various producers to discuss the project. Among those he met was the great director Cecil B. DeMille, who had produced the historic film on Jesus called *King of Kings*. But lack of funds kept delaying the making of the film. Perhaps it was not yet God's timing. However, Bill's burden to produce the film on the life of Jesus continued to grow. Year after year, board members of Campus Crusade for Christ discussed the need for a film on the life of Jesus. Yet more than thirty years would pass before God was ready to make this vision—the vision He had placed in Bill's heart—a reality.

The first opening came in 1976. In the San Bernardino Mountains of California in a cabin near Lake Arrowhead, several of us involved in the national leadership of Campus Crusade for Christ gathered for a day of prayer. The "I Found It" (new life in Christ) campaign was under way all across the United States. But in some cities this enormous evangelistic media effort was in serious trouble and in danger of collapse. There were too few workers to follow-up those who called in for counsel; several television stations had declined to carry our spot announcements; and we were running out of money. The obstacles seemed endless.

We set aside the entire day for prayer. But in the middle of the morning, we received a call. The voice on the telephone said that Dr. Bright wanted us to take time out to meet a man who had some Bible films. "I'm sorry," I said, "but we just do not have the time to see him today. We're in the middle of a crisis. Maybe some other time." And I hung up.

A few short minutes later, the phone rang again and the same voice said simply, "Dr. Bright wants you to see this man *now*. He'll be there within the hour." And *he* hung up.

In less than an hour, I heard a knock at the cabin door. The tall, slender man standing on the porch was loaded down with projector, films, and cords. I took an armload of film canisters from him, and he stuck out his hand.

"I'm John Heyman," he said. "Thank you for taking the time. I know you're busy."

"We are." I grasped his outstretched hand. "We'll have to limit you to thirty minutes, John. I hope you'll understand. Especially after the long drive up here."

He set to work threading the projector. Explaining briefly his credentials and what we were about to see, John hoped that we would be willing to help him reach some of the 30,000 churches Campus Crusade was in touch with in America. I listened to his presentation, but as hard as I tried, I could not get my internal clock to slow down. It ticked impatiently as John spoke. Why now? Why today when we had so much to do? It was so important that we use the day wisely. Reluctantly, I drew the shades and found a seat toward the back of the room.

But as we sat together in the half-darkened cabin, something happened. I found myself drawn into what I was seeing on the screen—and I forgot all about being impatient. The simple but dramatic portrayal of Creation was refreshing and wonderful. The time had been used well. Everyone in the room sensed that something special had taken place. In the providence of God, He brings men and organizations together to accomplish the goals and visions that He gives to them. As with any birth, the *JESUS* film was not brought to life without pain, struggles, and a few nervous moments.

Dr. Bright, ever a catalyst in evangelistic effort, was eager to assist any endeavor that would bring his years-long vision of a film on Christ's life to fruition. I was placed on special assignment with John Heyman's production company in New York, and plans were launched for the production of a two-hour, full-length motion picture. But financing would be the key. Since the Campus Crusade ministry was not in a position to underwrite the entire film, perhaps some of the major studios would get involved. There was a lot of work to be done.

The first question was the story line. Should we simply choose one of the gospels to portray? If so, which one? Matthew presents Jesus as the King, Mark as the Servant, Luke as the Son of Man, and John shows Him as the Son of God. We considered compiling all four accounts, but that meant we would have a ten-hour movie on our hands, and who is wise enough to weigh the value of one segment of Scripture against another to decide what to leave out? We sought the counsel of religious leaders around the world, and the unanimous recommendation was that we use Luke's account because of its completeness.

Deciding how to tell the story of Jesus was a key question. Since this film was to be as authentic as possible, shooting was to be done on location in the places where the events originally took place, or as close as we could get. Bernard Fishbein prepared a screenplay from Luke's Gospel. There were no liberties taken with the text, no invented dialogue. Nearly every word that Jesus would speak would come from the Scriptures. Within a month, we sent the completed script to more than 450 religious leaders and scholars asking for their input. Their response was positive and enthusiastic, with several providing excellent suggestions that improved the screenplay.

Co-producer Richard Dalton began working on the cross-plot, calculating production costs for the film. His final projections came to nearly $6 million for production. Another $3 to 4 million would be needed for distribution.

Assistant producers Omri Maron and Mati Raz immediately immersed themselves in the process of locating just the right people for the parts. They spent long hours poring over the biographies and photographs of actors in Israel. Auditions were held in London and Tel Aviv. Key questions included: Who would play the part of Jesus? What would Peter look like? What kind of voice should he have?

We began plans for distribution in the U.S., trusting that the production funds would soon be available. Key religious leaders were contacted.

Marc Tannenbaum, head of the American Conference of Christians and Jews, bestowed his blessing and backing. "My primary concern," he said, "is that we don't add to existing anti-Semitism by portraying the Jews as Christ-killers again." That thought had never crossed my mind before; the Jews had not killed Christ. It was my sin that kept Him on that cross. It was true that the Jews were the ones who asked Pilate to crucify Jesus, but it was a Roman prosecutor who sentenced Him, and Roman soldiers nailed Him to the cross. It was the world that crucified the Savior. But we decided that to help prevent the Jews from being blamed for Christ's death, we would introduce Pilate with the following words: "He was handed over to Pontius Pilate, the most vicious of all Roman procurators, alone responsible for the crucifixion of thousands." Marc showed his appreciation for our efforts and gave his endorsement to the film.

Archbishop Fulton J. Sheen personally gave us his warm approval. "You have taken no liberty with the Gospel text," he stated, "and have surrounded the figure of Christ with either credible or authentic characters who blend into the history. You have produced a masterpiece. Not only will all Christian churches support a masterpiece of this kind, but so will all who love history and the portrayal of a life that has affected millions."

But everything hinged on finding the necessary finances for production. After weeks of contacting studios in Hollywood, New York, and London, we were nowhere. Every door we tried in our attempts to raise the production funds was closed and barred. Without the money, the film would never become a reality. There seemed only one remaining possibility.

Campus Crusade for Christ had scheduled several weekend meetings designed to raise funds for world evangelism. John and I were scheduled to lead a special seminar on the first weekend. The topic was: how a film on the life of Christ could be used to help reach the world. John had also been asked to talk about his faith at a dinner that Saturday night. Perhaps when those who attended heard of the need, someone's heart would be stirred to back the project financially. We prayed, expecting the Lord to do great things.

Only a handful of people attended our seminar, including one man who monopolized the time arguing his personal views against any man portraying the Son of God on film. A gray pallor of discouragement settled over the room.

"Maybe someone will see the need tonight," I said to John as we left the seminar. "At least you can tell them about it in your talk."

John spoke to a large and attentive audience that night. In just a few words, looking beyond his own discouragement, he opened up to them and revealed his love and his heart for the God of Abraham, Isaac, and

Jacob—the God John Heyman had learned to love and lived to serve. Many in the room wept openly as they stood up to applaud the soft-spoken man before them.

In a corner of the room, Bunker Hunt, touched deeply by John's words and spirit, shared his feelings with his wife, Caroline. That night, they talked for several hours with Dr. Bright. By morning, Bunker and Caroline Hunt had made the decision to underwrite the film. John and I drove down the mountain with a $3 million guarantee and a dream that would become reality because one couple was committed to world evangelism enough to fund a movie, *JESUS*. Thousands of people throughout the world want to make films with a Christian message. But few people are willing to take the financial risks. It would be the faith and generosity of Bunker and Caroline, and other supporters of Campus Crusade for Christ, that would make this film on Christ's life available to millions.

On the production side, John Heyman proved to be a master. He came from years of experience in the film industry, having produced or gathered the financing for such films as *Saturday Night Fever, The Longest Yard, Heaven Can Wait, Black Sunday, Ghandi*, and many others. Uppermost in his mind was to make a film that stayed true to the Scriptures, and therefore would be usable by the whole Body of Christ.

All the filming was done in the Holy Land, as close as possible to where events took place 2,000 years ago. Every attempt was made to be accurate. All the cloth used in the film was handwoven. Costumes were designed to look like the drawings found on the pyramids of Egypt showing captured Hebrew slaves. Only 33 colors were used because that was the number of dyes available at the time of Christ. Finally, Yemenite Jews were selected as actors because their facial features have changed least over the past 2,000 years.

Playing the role of Jesus was Brian Deacon, an English actor with the Royal Shakespearean Company in London. He was selected because of his ability to portray Jesus as a man of warmth, care, and compassion.

The film was distributed initially by Warner Brothers and opened its theatrical release in October 1979 in the United States. It eventually played in 2,000 theaters in North America and then moved to Showtime, HBO, and The Movie Channel. In 1980, Campus Crusade for Christ began international translation and distribution of the film, and the first showings in the Tagalog language of the Philippines began in July of that year.

In 1981, The JESUS Film Project was formed to handle the distribution of the film internationally and charged with raising whatever funding would be necessary for the effort. The Project staff has now grown to 325 serving in support roles in the United States and 6,250 workers internationally on 2,862 full-time teams. The JESUS Film Project quickly became a servant to the whole Body of Christ, taking as its mission statement "to show the *JESUS* film to the people of the world, in an understandable language, near where they live."

By the close of the year 2000, this vision was rapidly becoming a reality. The total viewers increased by almost 3 million people per day. Even with incomplete reporting, here are some of the results of the film's distribution as of October 1, 2000:

624	Language translations complete
282	Language translations in process (one new translation completed every 3 days)
2,380	Full-time film teams showing 2 to 3 nights per week
6,250	Film team workers
233	Countries of the world where the film has been shown
3,910,095,456	Viewers of the film
121,481,585	Indicated decisions
110,000	New churches established
1,186	Partnering organizations
24,322,269	Videos distributed
11,900	Film prints distributed

But statistics alone cannot tell the story. Only the Lord knows the real impact. Because so many denominations and missions use the film, it is impossible to even know all that is taking place through its use. But here are a few highlights:

- Eleven million students saw the film in Russian schools as a result of the CoMission initiative.
- It has been distributed to every Member of Parliament or Congress in the Ukraine, New Zealand, Mongolia, and several other countries.
- One man in Alabama mailed a video to every house in his state—4.2 million copies.
- When it was first screened in Mongolia, there were fewer than 15 known believers. The film has now been shown in every village of more than 250 people, and there are 30,000 believers worshiping in 400 churches.
- Before she died, Mother Teresa asked for the film to be shown in all her homes for the dying in Calcutta, India.
- Screenings have been done in some 400,000 villages of India in 51 languages.

- Fifty-three language translations are available to be downloaded from the Internet. Besides English, the most-requested language is Arabic.
- More than 1 million videos and audiocassettes of the *JESUS* film have been distributed in North Africa in the last 24 months.
- Newspapers in Brazil are selling the *JESUS* film as a special promotion to new buyers of their paper; 250,000 were distributed during the year 2000.
- Stories of healing are a regular part of reports from the field. As viewers see Jesus heal people in the film, they ask Him to heal them as well—and He does!
- One of the 1,100 partnering organizations, the Church of the Nazarene, showed the film to more than 7 million people in three years. Of these, 1.1 million indicated decisions and 389,000 people were involved in follow-up.

It is wonderful to read the statistics regarding the progress of the film, but even more heart-warming are the stories of those whose lives have been changed forever as they have met the Savior. Here are just a few glimpses of God's miracles from several parts of the world.

South Pacific Cannibals

Some time ago, a film team was sent to an island in the South Pacific where the first missionary who had gone there had been killed and eaten by cannibals a hundred years ago. The film team was a little bit worried, but we said, "It's all right, there are no more cannibals there." Then, as the showing was conducted, those who wanted to receive Christ were asked to come to the front. The first man to come forward was a 104-year-old man who had been alive when the cannibals killed the missionary. With tears streaming down his face, he said, "God is so good to let me live 100 years so that I could find Christ."

A Rape in Liberia

A visitor to the Ivory Coast walked into his hotel room in the capital city of Abidjan and began to share Christ with the girl who was cleaning his room. She said, "I know about Jesus. I am from Liberia. Let me tell you my story: One night some gangsters came into our house. They tied up my brother; they shot my father as he tried to resist, and then they beat my mother and me and raped us. Over the next several days, my brother nearly went crazy because of the shock of what had happened before his eyes. My mother was desperately sick, so when some men came by and offered me a job in the Ivory Coast, I took it.

"When I came here, I found that they had brought me here to work in a brothel. After several days, I finally escaped. As I was running down the alley, I heard some music, and I ran into the building where the music was playing. It was the music from the *JESUS* film. I stayed and watched the whole film. At the end, I accepted Jesus as my personal Savior. One of the counselors who was there said he would help me, and he got me the job here in this hotel. So I'm very happy to know that you also believe in Jesus."

The Pagans of Borneo

Not long ago, I took a canoe six hours into the middle of the jungles on the island of Borneo. We visited a little village called the Munkubaro, where our film team had been conducting showings. The previous six months, the film teams had covered 435 villages in this section of Borneo, going along the river banks, holding showings for these people, many of whom had never before seen a film.

As we got to the village of Munkubaro, the chief of the village invited us to come to his little house. He had made a sign in our honor that said "The Religions of Munkubaro: Christians—26 [they had just become believers as a result of the film showing]; Muslims—91; Pagans—127."

I said, "I'd like to meet some pagans." He said, "Oh, we have lots of pagans here! Come outside with me." He saw a couple of men a few feet from us and waved them over. He said, "These men are pagans." As he introduced us, I said, "I'd like to know what you pagans believe." So they took us down to the center of the village where there was a little spirit house. It looked like a dollhouse up on stilts. In the spirit house was a pie tin, and on the pie tin were five smooth stones. "These stones came to this village all by themselves," they told us. "We pray to these stones, and these stones protect us from the evil spirits." I said, "What will happen to you when you die?" They said, "When we die, our body must be placed in a tree. Then it will shrivel up, and afterwards, someone must come and get our bones from the tree, and put the bones in the spirit house." I said, "What if someone forgets about you when you are in the tree, and doesn't put your bones into the spirit house?" He hung his head and he said, "Then we cannot go to the spirit world."

I thought, *Imagine, 2,000 years after Jesus Christ came and died for their sins, there are people still praying to stones. They are people who have never heard that Jesus died that they might live forever.*

An Indonesian Blind Lady

Some of the interesting things about the showing of the *JESUS* film all over the world are the reports that we get about people who are healed physically as they watch the *JESUS* film. Perhaps, in our society, we're too sophisticated to believe that Jesus still heals physically. Perhaps it's just the fact that Jesus honors the simple faith of those who come to Him, and, as they pray, decides to grant them physical healing so that the Word of God might go forth in a greater way in that area of the world.

In the village of Pawangari, Indonesia, there was a Muslim lady by the name of Mrs. Pahni. She had been blind for a number of years. One night the *JESUS* film came to her village. She had heard about the film, and about the fact that in the film Jesus heals a man who is blind. So when the film came to her village, she asked her daughter to lead her to the showing.

When the film came to the part where Jesus asks the blind man, "What do you want me to do for you?" and the blind man says, "I want to see," Mrs. Pahni shouted, "I want to see too. I want to see too!" As the nails were being driven into the hands of Jesus, suddenly, Mrs. Pahni's eyes were opened and she could see. She began to rejoice and tell everybody that she could see and that Jesus had healed her.

Not too long after that the Muslims were having a festival. There was a town meeting of sorts held in a central hall, and Mrs. Pahni was sitting in the back of the room. The Muslim leaders were quite irritated that she kept talking about Jesus having healed her. So they asked her to come up to the front of the hall and to light the candles at the ceremony. Mrs. Pahni got out of her seat, walked to the front, took the matches, lit them, and lit the candles. Instead of being a put-down of Christianity, everyone wanted to talk to Mrs. Pahni. They invited the *JESUS* film team to come to the village, and 3,500 people came out to see the film. Hundreds received Christ. A few months later, Mrs. Pahni was baptized, along with twelve others, six of whom she had led to Christ. Many, many people in that area now have come to Christ because of the faith of Mrs. Pahni.

A Crippled Buddhist in Thailand

One day, I was in the northeastern part of Thailand visiting villages where new groups of believers were just getting started. As we went to a little village, our staff member in that area said, "The people we were visiting all received Christ at the film showing last week, and we're having the first follow-up meeting today." We walked over to the house (the houses in Thailand are on stilts), and meeting underneath one of these houses was a group of 12 to 14 believers. Seated on the mats was a lady I will never forget.

Someone pointed her out to me and said, "This lady was healed by the Lord last week." I went to meet her. She said (through an interpreter), "For over thirteen months, I laid on that hammock over there. I couldn't walk." She took me over and showed me the hammock where she had lain.

She said, "One of the people who was from the other village that knew about Jesus came and talked to me and told me that I should believe that Jesus was the Son of God. He said that Jesus had died for me and that I could live forever. But I was skeptical. All of my life, I have been a Buddhist. All my family are Buddhists, and everyone in my village is a Buddhist. But I said to them, 'If Jesus can heal me, then I will come to see the film about Jesus, and then I will be a believer in Him.' Well, this lady who had come to talk to me said, 'Well, I don't know very much, but maybe I can pray, and ask Jesus to heal you so that you will believe in Him, and that you will be able to go to heaven.' So she just prayed and said, 'Lord, will you heal this lady to show her how strong you are, and your power so that she can live forever in heaven?'"

After thirteen months in her hammock, the woman got up and began to walk! As I watched her walk around that day, I was amazed. She wasn't ready to roller-skate yet, but she was walking around with a beautiful smile on her face. God had healed her, and she was gaining her strength back after thirteen months of not walking.

Martyrs in Uganda

Sometimes the distribution of the *JESUS* film throughout the world has resulted in paying the ultimate price—one's life. Not long ago, we were recording the Iteso language for a tribe in Uganda. We had finished the first week of recording and had returned to the village to pick up more people from that tribe to bring them into the city where the recording was taking place. On the return trip to the city, a band of guerrilla fighters opened fire from the side of the road and riddled the truck with automatic-weapons fire. One of the men was shot through the head and killed instantly. A young girl was shot in the leg, and the man who had played the part of Jesus, John Aluru, was shot through the heart. The guerillas shot out one of the tires, but the driver kept going anyway—driving more than a mile and a half on just the tire rim. They managed to get away from the guerrilla fighters and drove directly to a hospital. The man who was killed was taken to the morgue; the little girl was taken to the emergency room, as was John Aluru.

That night as John lay dying, in deep, deep pain, our film technician, Abraham Kasika went in to see him. John rose up in obvious pain and said, "Abraham, don't stop the dubbing. Uganda needs this film. I have done my part, but don't stop, and don't ever be afraid."

The next morning, John Aluru died. Today he's with the Lord, and I imagine that he is looking down over the battlements of heaven. Every time the Iteso film is shown in Uganda, it's the voice of John Aluru as Jesus that is telling thousands and thousands of his own people how to know Jesus. The very first showing of the film was in the high school where John had been the principal. The day it was shown in his school, at the very first showing, the voice of John Aluru, playing the character of Jesus, helped scores of young men and women to come to know Jesus in a personal way. John Aluru is dead, but his voice lives on in the *JESUS* film, and many thousands will come to know Jesus because of it.

Jesus in the Clouds of India

Many people pay a very heavy price to take the message of Christ to the world. A young couple and their three-year-old son from the southern part of India, who worked with Friends Missionary Prayer Band (FMPB), felt God was calling them to the Bihar region in the north to take the gospel to an unreached people group, the Maltos. For several years, they worked there with no visible results. Everything they tried was opposed. The government leaders told the people that if any of them believed in Jesus they would not receive their monthly subsidy from the Indian government. In addition to the lack of response to everything they did, the couple experienced continual sickness. The water was infected with disease. Very often the entire family was sick. One day the father was feeling especially ill, so he went to the doctor to see if he could get something to ease his pain. When he came home from the doctor that night, he collapsed in the doorway of his home and died. The mother was distraught, trying to figure out what to do. When she went in to check on the three-year-old little boy, she found him dead in the crib as well.

She returned to her home in south India. It seemed that there had been no results from the giving of these lives for the kingdom. But several weeks later, a *JESUS* film team came into this area. While he usually prevented anything having to do with Christianity, the governor of the area was quite impressed with the film and gave it permission to be shown and said it should be protected. The film team came to the village where the missionary had died. When they showed the film in this village, people began to respond. They said that on the night the missionary had died, some clouds appeared in the sky, and on the clouds was a man walking. He went to a tree and picked from it a branch and the branch withered, and finally the picture of the man faded from out of the sky. The villagers thought that perhaps God was displeased with them because they had not accepted the message of the missionary. The incredible thing was that when they saw the *JESUS* film, they said, "That's him; that's the one, the man who was walking in the clouds!" Because of that, hundreds came to Christ, and there are now more than 130 new believers meeting in seven different churches that have been established in that area.

A Guatemalan Lady Who Cursed Jesus

Many cooperative efforts using the *JESUS* film have been launched throughout the world. Recently, in Nicaragua and El Salvador, Guatemala Christian Broadcasting Network and the *JESUS* film launched a combined effort to field forty *JESUS* film teams that would travel throughout the jungles. In just eight months, more than 2 million people saw the *JESUS* film, and hundreds of thousands responded.

One of these film teams went into a little village in Guatemala. As the workers entered the village, they began to announce with their sound horns that the *JESUS* film would be shown that night. About the same time, a lady was cooking by a fire and talking to some Catholic nuns who had been holding a class nearby. This woman began to curse the Christians: "I curse them; I curse this film!" The nuns turned to her and said, "You shouldn't curse the film. This is about God's Son. This is a wonderful film. It tells people how they can live forever and how they can know Jesus." A short time later, the woman fell dead by the fire. Word began to spread throughout the village that the woman who had cursed the film was dead. People turned out by the hundreds to see the film that night. Fifteen hundred came the next night. More than 3,500 came during the two nights the film was shown, and more than 1,000 indicated a decision to receive Christ.

A Tijuana Man Shot by Cocaine Runners

People don't always respond to receive Christ the first time they see the film. But because the film is based on the Word of God, it does not return void. Sometimes there's a span of time as they think, consider, and begin to really understand what Jesus is saying. We had a film showing in the mountains outside of Tijuana where there was no electricity. We started the portable generator, ran the power lines to the projector, tied down the screen with ropes, and began showing the film. About 500 people had gathered on this hilltop to see this film on the life of Christ.

As the film was ending, I took out my Spanish *Four Spiritual Laws* booklet. The leader of the film showing that night had said, "If tonight you would like to become a follower of Jesus and to receive Him as your personal Savior and Lord, come to the light." (Those who respond then come to the front of the crowd where a string of lights is lit up.)

I went up near the lights where the men were gathered. I began to talk to a young man in his twenties and asked, "What did you think of the film?" He said, "I liked it very much. I saw it before." I said, "Oh, really? Where did you see it?" He answered, "In Tampico, about 700 miles south of here. It was about five or six months ago." I asked him, "Well, did you invite Christ to come into your life then when you saw the film?" "No, I didn't," he replied, "but tonight is my night." So I opened *The Four Spiritual Laws* booklet, and we read through the booklet step by step. At the end, he said he would like to pray a prayer of invitation and receive Christ as his personal Savior.

After we had finished, I asked him, "Why didn't you receive Christ the last time you saw it?" He said, "I don't know; I didn't think I needed God. But let me tell you what happened after I left there. I got involved in drugs, and not too long ago, was shot by cocaine runners who were delivering drugs from Colombia to the United States." He opened his shirt and showed me the scars from four bullet holes in his chest. He said, "There's no possible way that I should be here today. As I lay on the ground with the blood running out of my body, I said, 'God, save me'—and He did. The only reason I'm here is because of God, and I want to give my life back to Him right now."

After we prayed together, I said, "Let me show you what it says in the Scripture. It says in John 1:12 that when you receive Him, you become His son, that you become a child of God." I asked, "Did you receive Him tonight?" He said, "Yes." I asked, "Well, what does that make you?" He said, "His son." I said, "I made this same commitment a number of years ago. What did I become?" He said, "You're a son of God." I said, "What's our relationship then to one another?" He said, "*Somos hermanos*" ("We're brothers"). He smiled, and I shook his hand and said, "Welcome to the family! Let me introduce you to some of the other brothers and sisters." I took him to meet some of the other counselors. About thirty minutes later, after he finished talking to several of the counselors, he turned to leave, and said, "*Adios, familia!*" He understood what it meant to be in the family of God.

KGB Listening Room

The *JESUS* film is shown not only in the jungles and the far reaches of the world, but also in commercial theaters and on national television. The initial negotiations in the Soviet Union to show the film in their commercial theaters began while the Communist Party was still in power. The negotiations had to be conducted with people in the government, and I was being closely watched by the KGB. During one of my first negotiating trips to Moscow, I was being followed, and, of course, our room was monitored. It happened to be very hot in Moscow at the time, and one of the days when we were riding up in the elevator, we rode up with the KGB agents who were assigned to the listening room. The listening room was about two doors down from our room. As we got off the elevator, they went into their room and put on their earphones. We could see all of their equipment because, due to the heat, they had been forced to leave the door open. We went down to our room, closed the door, and said, "We'd just like to say 'good morning' to those of you there in the listening room. We're going to take some time before we start our day to read the Bible. If you have a Bible, we'll be reading from Psalms." So during the week we were there, every morning we gave them an hour of Bible reading straight out of the Scripture. It was wonderfully refreshing to read the Scriptures out loud and praise the Lord. At that time, the KGB, who didn't have much access to the Scripture, were getting an hour a day of the Word of God.

Soviet Schools

During a meeting with the Ministry of Education of the former Soviet Union, we offered to provide a *JESUS* video for every one of their 130,000 schools so that teachers could show it to all of their students. As we met to consider how this might be done, we also offered to help their teachers to present a course called "Christian Ethics and Morality—A Foundation for Society." Officials of the Ministry of Education said, "I believe we want to consider this proposal very carefully. We don't know how many holes there are in the foundation of our society after 70 years without God." As a result of the agreement that was signed, conferences were eventually held in 142 cities for 42,000 teachers.

Georgia, USSR

The first showings of the *JESUS* film in the Soviet Union in 1989 took place in the Republic of Georgia. The response was absolutely phenomenal. When an invitation was given at the close of the film, you could hear people weeping softly. For the first time in 70 years, people were learning how they could know Jesus in a personal way.

At the close of a showing in Batumi, a small city located on the shores of the Black Sea just a few miles from the border of Turkey, I talked to some of those who had seen the film that night. One young woman was close to tears. She said, "I have felt all of my life as though my soul has been ripped from me. After these years under communism, tonight you have given us back spirit in our lives." A man who was 84 years old came to say that in all his years, these had been the most meaningful, powerful two hours of his entire life because tonight he had a chance to know God. At each of the showings, we passed out comment cards so that those in attendance could tell us what they thought of the *JESUS* film, if they were interested in being in a Bible study, or whether they had made a commitment to receive Christ. One man wrote on his card, "We need this film more than we need bread, which is not so easy to get." Another one said, "This is the film of our century." Another wrote, "Thank you for this film which heals our souls. Thank you, America!"

Sabah, Indonesia

In the northern part of the island of Borneo is an area of East Malaysia known as Sabah. The jungles that rise up out of the blue Pacific were at one time inhabited by cannibals. As we went there for the premiere of the *JESUS* film in the Kadazan Dusun language, I was assured that the cannibals were long since gone. However, it happened that the day we arrived in the capital city of Kota Kinabalu, the headline of the paper read, "Headless Corpse Found in Kota Kinabalu."

During the next three days, more than 8,000 people came out for the premiere showings of the *JESUS* film. Of these, more than 3,000 indicated a decision to receive Christ. We had large showings in some of the major cities. Then one night, we went to a very rural village. That night only about 300 came to watch the film. The screen was just a bed sheet hung on the side of a barn. Cattle and the caribou used to pull plows through the rice paddies were feeding nearby. But as the sun sank in the west, people began to walk across the little dikes, through the rice paddies, to this hillside where the barn was located, and seated themselves in the soft grass. It began to rain, so the projector was quickly hustled underneath a covering. The people sat in the rain anyway, so we began the projection of this film on the life of Christ. At the end of the film, we asked those who wanted to respond to come to the light so that they could make their commitment to follow Jesus of Nazareth as their Savior.

One of those who came was an 80-year-old woman. A counselor who spoke English brought her to me and said, "This lady would like to meet you because she knows that you are the one who helped to make the film and bring it here tonight." She said, "Many, many years ago as a small girl, a missionary came through my area and talked about Jesus as the way that you could know God, but I never knew how I could be sure that I could accept Jesus. Tonight you told me that I could open the door of my life and invite Him to come in. I'm so happy tonight, and I wanted you to know that tonight, I have opened the door of my life." I looked down at her. She was about 4 feet 10 inches tall. Her face was wrinkled, and her skin paper thin, but she had a glow and a radiance on her face that could only come from having discovered at this late time in her life how she could be forgiven and live forever.

Sometimes we talk about the great numbers of people who have come to know Christ through the *JESUS* film. But what it's all about is one person who finds out that she can know Jesus, that she can have her sins forgiven, and that she can have eternal life because of what He did for her on the cross 2,000 years ago.

A Pile of Human Skulls

One day I was in the Karamoja region of Northern Uganda. As our plane landed on a grass airstrip, we were greeted by native tribesmen with their spears. Because of fighting in the area, the cattle belonging to the Karamojong had been stolen, and 185,000 of the people died within the last year due to starvation. We went to a field where I saw a pile of skulls, maybe five feet high. I picked up two skulls, one in each hand. As I looked at them, I realized that six months earlier these people had been living human beings. As I held their skulls in my hands, I wondered whether they had ever had one opportunity to hear the message of Christ. I wondered how many people in this region knew who Jesus really is.

That afternoon in a small village, I said to my interpreter, "Could we find out what people really know about Jesus?" So we lined up 14 or 15 individuals, and I asked them one at a time, "Tell me, just what do you know about Jesus?" One by one they shook their heads and said, "I don't know him." "Where does he live?" "No, I've never heard of him." Finally, there was only an eight-year-old boy left. I said to the interpreter, "Just ask him to tell me anything, anything at all he's ever heard about Jesus." A big tear ran down the little boy's face, and the interpreter said, "Sir, he would like to tell you about Jesus, but he has just never, ever before heard His name." I thought that day, "I am only one person, but whatever I can do, I want to make sure there are no little boys or girls, or men or women who don't get one opportunity, one chance, to hear who Jesus really is."

The year 2000 saw some of the biggest showings ever conducted—and the release of a new version of the film, *The Story of Jesus for Children.*

On Saturday night, August 19, 2000, *JESUS* was shown to an estimated 1 million young people following Pope Paul II's address at the World Youth

Day in Rome. In the preceding four days, 694,000 videocassettes were distributed to young Catholics at 85 locations throughout the city.

During the Christmas and Easter season of 1999–2000, more than 500 million people saw the telecasts of the *JESUS* film on national television in 122 countries as a part of "A Millennial Tribute to Jesus."

And on February 10, 2000, 7-year-old Amber watched the new *Story of Jesus for Children* on TV in her living room and prayed the prayer at the end to receive Christ as her Savior. The film was a gift from new parents who had just adopted her.

ON A PERSONAL LEVEL

The stories of the impact of sowing broadly go on and on. But how can we apply this principle in our own lives? How should we implement it in our local church?

You, too, can have an impact on the people around you—or on people in places where you'll never travel. Take the following steps to begin sowing broadly:

- Increase the number of nonbelievers for whom you are praying.
- Give gifts of the *JESUS* video to your friends, relatives, and employees for Christmas.
- Think of every creative way you can to demonstrate the love of Jesus to every person with whom you have regular contact—workers, neighbors, service professionals, etc.
- Give financial support to ministries that are sowing broadly.
- Give gifts of *The Story of Jesus for Children* video to all the families you know who have children ages 4 to 14.

IN YOUR CHURCH OR MINISTRY

Beyond your personal life, there are additional areas to consider. Use the following suggestions to help you spread God's good news:

- Set a goal each year for how many nonbelievers you as a church want to hear the gospel.
- Consider distributing a *JESUS* video to every home in your area.
- Look for opportunities to speak to groups already gathered. Talk about the spiritual dimension of life to meetings of expectant mothers, senior citizens, social workers, etc.

- Launch programs that reach out to people in crisis and need.
- Use the media to present the gospel. Go where non-Christians gather.
- Make your group or church a friendly place to gather for nonbelievers.

Does God care about numbers? Absolutely! He is not willing that any should perish. He loves the whole world. Therefore, it is consistent with the heart of God to give everyone everywhere at least one chance to hear of His love and forgiveness. That is the essence of sowing broadly.

CHAPTER 17

Creative Evangelism

J. STANLEY OAKES, JR.
On Staff since 1972
President, International Leadership University

Countless people have heard of Campus Crusade for Christ and its evangelistic efforts, but many millions of them have never heard of Bill Bright. Even though he heads one of the largest Christian organizations in the world, he has never been enamored with his success. In my own case, I was involved with Campus Crusade for Christ for several years before I ever heard him speak.

FIRST ENCOUNTER

The first exposure I had to the ministry was in the living room of my parents' home. My mother had just returned from a weekend conference in Minneapolis, Minnesota, when she told me that she had learned something really interesting at the conference and wanted to share it with me. A typical high school student, I was a bit impatient but consented. She brought a booklet from her purse entitled *Have You Heard of the Four Spiritual Laws?* and asked if she could read it to me.

I don't remember much about the experience except for her final haunting question, "Is there any good reason why you wouldn't want to receive Jesus Christ as your Savior right now?" Two questions went through my mind: *What was I doing wrong that motivated her to share it with me? And how did she know all of these things about God?*

The conference turned out to be a Lay Institute for Evangelism, and my mother's life changed quite dramatically in the ensuing months. Until then, she had been beset by both melancholy and anger, but after the weekend conference, she was filled with a love that was genuine and unrelenting. So even though the message of the booklet was lost on me, the changes in her life were not.

SECOND ENCOUNTER

My second encounter with Campus Crusade for Christ was at the University of Minnesota. My sister, after a summer of babysitting children of the Crusade staff at the former headquarters in Mound, Minnesota, recommended that I attend their College Life meetings on campus. So in the fall of my third year, I finally agreed and went to a meeting on a Friday night at Coffman Memorial Union, which was the main student gathering place on campus.

I was amazed when I walked in the door. There were hundreds of students in the room, probably more than a thousand. And they were so attractive, so normal—athletes, fraternity and sorority students, and others like myself. The music was trendy; the atmosphere wasn't somber or stifling; the speakers were magnetic and not judgmental or paternalistic.

It is hard to describe what I expected because my mind was filled with so many misconceptions about religion and church. From the clothes they wore to the words they used and the way they acted, the leaders of the meeting were so completely different from my expectations, it was jarring. As for the content of the meeting, I have only one memory, and it is vivid. These people spoke about Jesus Christ as if He was alive and could actually do something for them in this life. In fact, before the main speaker's presentation, two students discussed the makeover that God had worked upon their lives. The entire audience was as attentive as I was, and I wondered how many of them were also admitting to how little they knew about God.

I started attending the Campus Crusade meetings regularly and still did not know much about Bill Bright, but it didn't matter because I was getting so much out of each meeting and every speaker. Tuesday evenings were devoted to Leadership Training Class. It may seem an odd pairing, but the only groups that I heard talking about leadership were the campus radicals of Students for Democratic Society (SDS) and Campus Crusade for Christ. I attended both meetings but found SDS bombastic and hateful, whereas Crusade was entertaining and had a plan to help change the world with God's love. In sum, the meetings repeatedly drove home one lesson: Not only did I know very little about God, I knew even less about following Him, and almost everyone I knew was as badly informed as I was.

After one of the classes, a staff member of Campus Crusade introduced himself and asked me if we could get together for lunch. I willingly said yes to what was to be a casual meeting, but what I received instead was an insight into God and the meaning of life. As we met together regularly after that, one of the surprises in store for me was his question about whether or not I would like to go with him to share my faith. Would I like to go with *him* to share *my* faith? Wait a minute. What about going with *him* to share *his* faith? Aside from the fact that I didn't have much to share, I had no idea how a person actually went about such an atypical activity. Today I realize that I was being challenged to go beyond a personal belief that might be helpful to me to a Truth that underlies the destiny of every living human being.

The first time that the staff member and I spoke with a student on campus in Minnesota, it took me one-and-a-half hours to get through the gospel. In fact, I am not even certain if I knew what the gospel was because I started with ramblings from the Book of Genesis, touched on predestination, and ended with a dose of eternity and the glowing fires of hell. That student was unmoved. Then my staff friend pulled out a gold booklet with the same title as the one my mother had read to me. Within a few minutes, the student received Christ as His Savior. As you can imagine, I was captivated. Moreover, what was said in those few minutes applied as much to me as it did to that unbelieving student. Until that encounter, I was still uncertain as to whether or not I myself would go to heaven if I died.

I ultimately concluded from this experience that I knew less than nothing about Christianity because what I did know was a combination of hearsay and blather.

THIRD ENCOUNTER

Some weeks later, a staff member and I met with another student who immediately started yelling at us. I didn't much like that, and, indeed, it was downright embarrassing because there were about 25 people within earshot. This had never happened to me before. My parents had yelled at me, but I deserved it. To be yelled at and embarrassed when you could avoid it seemed really stupid. But again, something strange happened. In the process of being yelled at, I believe that I was inadvertently developing a conviction. I was a college student who was discovering something for which it was worth being yelled at in public. Until that very moment, I didn't have one single conviction in my life that wasn't simply borrowed from my parents or from my peers, and my friends did not have any more to spare than I did.

After all of this, I still knew almost nothing about Bill Bright, and yet I knew everything about him. I was hooked. My own life was changing before my very eyes, and God was using me to help others understand how to know God personally as well. Although I had never met him, God was extending Bill Bright's influence to me through those he had inspired and taught. I am convinced that many hundreds of students at the University of Minnesota experienced the same things I did. It is intriguing to realize that this impact upon so many aspiring students resulted from reading or sharing a simple little booklet.

DRAMATIC CHANGES

Looking back over the past thirty years, a revolution has taken place in America and around the world—and Bill Bright has been at the center of much of it. I am not the only one who has been transformed and enlisted in the cause; it would be fair to say that I am one of millions. But just exactly what is it—aside from his contagious love for Jesus Christ, of course—that has captivated so many people and so positively influenced the world?

I cannot consider every turn in this revolution, but there is one characteristic of Bill Bright's ministry that far outstrips most other considerations. Bill Bright has made it appealing for the average person to talk about Jesus Christ in public. He has so dramatically changed the face of evangelism that millions of followers of Christ now have a dozen or more attractive ways of sharing their faith themselves rather than being constrained to send friends and family to church or to others to do the job.

The secret to this creativity is that Bill Bright accepted the biblical mandate to give everyone in the world a chance to say yes to Jesus Christ. Or better said, he understood that God did not want His servants to simply "labor in the harvest field of lost souls," but to actually take the responsibility for finishing the task of reaching the world with the gospel in each generation. In other words, get the job done.

It may not be obvious why I think that embracing the correct goal was the key to Bill Bright's creativity. And yet it makes perfect sense when you think about it.

When he devoted his life to this challenge, Bill Bright's mind and heart opened to any creative idea that could help accelerate the task. Many of those who joined in this effort are likewise driven to inventiveness. Thus, it was his choice of the correct objective—reaching the world with the gospel *in his lifetime*—that fostered new ideas. After all, if the goal is just to labor in the harvest field, accomplishing it doesn't require striving and imagination.

BILL BRIGHT'S METHODS

Even so, not everyone appreciates Bill Bright's methods. Over the years, occasionally I have had conversations with people who were critical of him. "He uses canned presentations," they say. Or, "He's just interested in numbers." Or, "He is simplistic." Knowing him as I do, he is guilty on all counts. Nonetheless, the question remains as to whether or not he's wrong in using canned booklets, or being interested in all 6.2 billion people in the world, or in being simple. I think, in fact, he is not wrong, and these criticisms embody very bad thinking.

First, the Bible itself is a canned presentation. There are and never will be more than 66 books in the Bible, and this book includes everything that the billions of people who have ever lived since the beginning of time have needed to know about God and living a godly life. Are all of the answers to life really contained in this one small book? Then the Bible is the ultimate canned presentation, and the criticism of Dr. Bright's canned presentations can apply equally to God Himself.

Second, it confounds me that some people are bothered by Bill Bright's fixation on numbers. To begin with, it was not his idea. He believes that the Bible talks about numbers all the time. Anytime it mentions *the world*, God is counting out really big numbers.

- "For God so loved the *world*..." the Bible reveals to us.
- "The Lord is not slow in keeping his promise, as some understand slowness. He is patient with you, not wanting *anyone* to perish..." the Bible consoles us.
- "Go into all of the world and preach the good news..." the Bible commands us.

The idea of reaching everyone in the world was God's idea. Furthermore, whenever He gives us a task, He entrusts it to us with the expectation that we will finish it. He discusses this stewardship plainly in Matthew 25:21: "Well done, good and faithful slave. You were faithful with a few things, I will put you in charge of many things; enter into the joy of your master" (NASB). If this argument is correct, and I believe it is, then a person ought to be very careful with this criticism.

THE WORLD OF COMPLEXITY

Before I take up the issue of simplicity, I should explain that for seventeen years, I worked with college and university professors. They are, of course, the ruling elite in the world of complexity. My colleagues and I assembled a network of more than 14,000 faculty from almost a thousand universities. We sponsored conferences, published books and journals, and shared the gospel with many of the most educated people in the world. If we were the kind of people who bragged about such things, we would claim that we know as many educated men and women as anyone in the world. But we are not the bragging kind.

As a result of this experience, I had more than my share of encounters with the concave world of complexity. Because of this familiarity, I must digress for just a moment and share about my secret life as the founder of The International Institute for Mankind.

It is a great name for an organization. It stood for almost nothing, and yet academics loved it. A few weeks after we founded the organization, I met a philosopher who had just flown to the United States from England with her husband and several others. When I told her the name of the organization that I represented, she whispered to me that she had always admired the work of *The Institute*. The name was pure magic.

The first event we sponsored after establishing The Institute was a conference at Yale University on the topic of Artificial Intelligence and the Human Mind. We organized the meetings in honor of the distinguished Yale physicist Henry Margenau, colleague to Heisenberg and Schroedinger, who for forty years held court in New Haven.

We invited everyone. And they came. Who could turn down an invitation from *The Institute*? Hans Moravec, inventor of the first vision-equipped robot, was there. So was the diminutive Eugene Wigner, the Hungarian-born scientist who helped develop the first atomic bomb. Nobel Prize winners Brian Josephson and Sir John Eccles spoke. Marvin Minsky, the founder of the Artificial Intelligence Laboratory at the Massachusetts Institute of Technology, came in aluminum-colored tennis shoes with a rope belt holding up his pants.

Anthony Flew, the leading atheist from Britain, was not about to miss this conference. My first contact with him, however, got off to a shaky start. When I called and invited him to come, he was really quite adamant that he would not even consider coming if we did not pay him an honorarium of $250. When I agreed to this amount, he was elated, and from then on was positively delightful to work with. Apparently, this sum of money was all he needed to assure him that we understood his status as a philosopher. For the longest time, I did not have the heart to tell him that we were paying all of the other participants $750 to speak. His stature as a philosopher certainly outstripped his stature as a negotiator.

Flew was my personal favorite at the conference. He had a certain flair, like the scholars of old, and apart from his own, he was able to sniff out humbug wherever he spied it. He was an avowed, even ornery, atheist, who, even though he was an atheist, was conservative in his politics and had no use at all for liberal Christians. "Have-their-cake-and-throw-it-away Christians," he called them. At each of the lunches during the conference, he flitted from table to table, telling stories like a comedian to all who would listen and even to those who didn't. I treasure the picture taken of the two of us. It is one of my favorites. (I did hear a rumor—I do not know if it's true —that he threw his copy of the photo away the day he heard the story about the $250.)

Another speaker, Hans Moravec, was a professor at Carnegie-Mellon University and considered himself an expert in applied artificial intelligence. After listening to him sound off for several days, I quite agreed. In all of my interaction with scientists, he was the person I found who most epitomized it. Moravec married a hapless woman who, as he described it, was a born-again Christian. I could not ascertain whether he knew she was born again before he married her or she had called upon God later in life after years of marriage to the venerable Hans.

When it was his appointed time to speak, Moravec put forward a fascinating theory on artificial intelligence. Actually, it was more like science fiction than science. He was, of course, a monist, meaning that he believed that there was no such thing as the mind, only the brain, and that the brain is nothing more than the sum of its electrical charges. As a Christian dualist, I take the opposite position. I have both a brain *and* a mind. From the moment I learned that Hans was a monist and did not have a mind, I have not ceased to worry about him. I tried to set him straight, but no amount of bioelectrical persuasion could convince him otherwise.

In all, four scientists who had been awarded the Nobel Prize attended, along with six scholars who had delivered the prestigious Gifford Lecture Series in England. Bill and Sue Garrison, a wealthy Texas lawyer and his wife, sponsored the conference. Bill was one of a kind. He was a businessman who thought deeply about his faith in God and endlessly cajoled others into the same kind of depth. Few listened, but they all respected him for his vibrant intellect and farsighted leadership.

When a friend of mine, Roy Varghese, and I first planned this conference, I told Roy to call Bill Garrison to see if he might like to support it. Roy emigrated from India and should be counted among the best of those that have left the land of the *rajahs*. He had the uncommon gift of telling you about an idea in such a way that at the end of an hour you felt like it was your own creation. At the end of another hour, you not only took complete credit for the plan, but of course you were going to pay for it as well. When all was said and done, Bill Garrison told Roy he wanted him to go put on a conference at Yale and send him the bill. Bill spoke of the week in New Haven with genuine delight.

BILL BRIGHT'S APPROACH

Without my knowledge, Roy invited Bill Bright to give a lecture at this esoteric conference on artificial intelligence, which was going to be attended by the world's preeminent scholars and scientists. I knew we were in trouble a short time later when Dr. Bright arrived at the hotel. When we were alone, he asked me what he should speak on. I had worked closely with university professors for years, just like the ones who were going to be in the audience. When they give a scientific paper, they frequently work for weeks to prepare the presentation. Then they let their colleagues read it and subject it to withering criticism. Finally, to avoid any chance of error, they slowly and tortuously read it to the longsuffering attendees. I reflected for a few moments as to how I should respond to this renowned Christian leader's question. In a few moments, like a bolt of lightening, it came to me; I knew exactly what to say. I told him that I had no earthly idea. Later, I learned that he always asked this question even though he had something already prepared, but it did provide a bit of excitement for me at the time.

A short time later, Eugene Wigner appeared out of nowhere. He could not have been more than 5 feet tall, and yet he was a giant in his field and a distinguished professor at Princeton University. In his charming and humble accent, he thanked me and, of course, The Institute for sponsoring a marvelous convocation. He told me that his wife would have come, but she was quite ill and could not travel. Then, as people moved away, he grabbed my arm, and almost with a look of desperation, begged me to answer a question that had been troubling him ever since we extended him the invitation. "Mister Oakes, Mister Oakes," he pleaded. "Please. Can you tell me, just what exactly *is* artificial intelligence?" Somehow I knew that Dr. Bright was going to do just fine.

When the time came for Dr. Bright to speak, I tried to find something else to do. But I knew that was the coward's way out. Visions of the Roman Coliseum danced in my head. By far the best dressed person in the audience—he was probably the only person with a matching tie in the entire lecture hall—Bill strode confidently to the front and opened his Bible. He looked around the room and then read purposefully from the timeless first chapter of Ecclesiastes. In fact, he read the entire chapter! He closed his Bible and sat down. No one said anything. No one moved. No one dared ask a question for long moments—except, of course, for Hans Moravec, who broke the silence by wondering aloud how this could be compared with his own groundbreaking research and that all of this sounded vaguely reminiscent to what his selfless wife had told him.

One might conclude that I am flirting with an insult of Bill Bright. My aim is the opposite. I could not have done any better. Indeed, few have ever really tried to do something like this before, that is, to bring the gospel to the elite scientists of the world. And rather than do nothing, which is the temptation when you do not know what to do, Bill went into the "belly of the beast" and took his chances. We were all better informed on how to improve in the future. And nearly every scientist there heard the gospel. Yet it was Bill Bright who was at the epicenter of the criticism. If we are not willing to endure criticism, how else can we figure out what to do and what not to do? Most scientists who could have done a much more suitable job were too afraid to take the first step out of the closet even though they are the only ones left in it. But I digress from my digression.

COMPLEXITY AND SIMPLICITY

Scientists come primarily in two varieties: the Hans Moravecs in the world, pompous and condescending, who believe that history memorializes egos and not simply accomplishments; and others, like Eugene Wigner, who are shy and gentle and so secure that they are willing to ask any question and then allow their endeavors to speak for them. Every scholar or scientist who came to Yale that week fell into one of those two categories. Marvin Minsky concluded that Moravec did not really understand the true meaning of pomposity and gave him a lesson. Sir Alfred Ayer, barely able to see over the podium, dismissed Minisky as a rank amateur. On the other hand, Nobel laureate Brian Josephson barely said a word. Painfully shy, like a boy at his first dance when all of the girls have been taken, he actually looked like he was at the wrong conference. After years of studying quantum mechanics, he concluded that some strange force held the atom together. It was for this reason that he embraced the paranormal world of the occult, concluding that it was a primitive spiritual force that was at work at the sub-atomic level. So close to the truth and yet so far.

Some weeks after the conference concluded, a graduate student wrote a ten-page article for the journal *Artificial Intelligence*, published by MIT. He referred to the conference as the strangest one he had ever attended. I have to agree. Roy and myself, a Catholic and an evangelical, sponsored it. A lawyer who always wanted to be a theologian paid for it. More Nobel laureates came to Yale than had ever been on campus at one time before. Scientists spent a week considering a watershed issue, an issue that would never see the light of day in most universities. Are humans unique? Is there a mind that is distinct from the brain? Are we more than our chemistry and biology?

In all of my years of working with professors, I have seen too many of them worship at the altar of complexity only to miss the simplest of truths. Hitchhiking on what my good friend Friedhelm Radandt says, I have to ask if a person can be truly knowledgeable if he does not understand that before knowledge existed, there was, according to John 1:1, THE WORD who was with God and was God.

Complexity is overrated. Yes, it appeals to the few intellectuals, but God's message is for everyone. Yes, it strokes the ego, but complexity is not the *lingua franca* of a message that is for everyone. It frequently becomes a barrier to those who very much want to know more about God, whereas simplicity opens a portal into the mind and heart of God. As Jesus says in Mark 10:15, "I tell you the truth, anyone who will not receive the kingdom of God like a little child will never enter it."

Simplicity, then, is a revolution all its own, and despite the criticism of Bill Bright that it has evoked, this insight of his points out hidden boundary markers into the souls of the many who want to know God.[1]

INTO THE HEART OF THE CAMPUS

Of course, there are still too many followers of Christ who think that evangelism is essentially "buttonholing" people or even pushing beliefs on those who aren't really interested. Witnessing certainly isn't for everyone, they say, because it takes a special gift—probably the gift of being obnoxious. On the other hand, over the last three decades, I have seen the most amazing ideas surface regarding evangelism. At the risk of giving witnessing ("sharing" as Bill calls it) an entirely new image, I'll include a few of the ideas that I have found to be the most engaging. (I could go on at some length since we are thinking about making it a major research project of The Institute.)

In the early 1950s, quite a few missions were established to reach out to the "down and outers" of society, the unfortunates on skid row. And yet God led Bill and Vonette to establish a ministry to college students. Their stated goal was to "reach the campus today; reach the world tomorrow." They started by setting up speaking engagements in the Greek houses on the UCLA campus in Southern California.

No one had really done this before. Instead of waiting for students to come to them, they went to the students. And they went right into the heart of the campus and spoke out loud about God in a social setting rather than a religious one—that is, in the fraternities and sororities. This strategy is one of the reasons why so many students who would never have crossed the threshold of a church found Christ on the UCLA campus.

This effort was so successful that Bill could have devoted his entire life to speaking in fraternities on colleges and universities all across the country. And yet he could never have helped lead the effort to reach the entire world if he had done so. So what did he do instead? He multiplied himself. He developed others into leaders by challenging and training them to take up the cause. This process was frequently unpredictable and always exciting—at least it was in my case.

One of the more wacky things that happened to me occurred when I spoke to the SAE fraternity at Southern Methodist University some years ago. It was after rush week, when the pledges—those students who were seeking to join the fraternity—were expected to serve the active members as well as undertake certain madcap deeds that had the inevitable result of making their college career memorable.

We were invited to dinner at the house and afterwards to speak to the entire fraternity during the regular chapter meeting. Dinner was an omen of things to come. At an earlier time, fraternity members wore sport coats and khakis and dinner was formal, but that era was a distant memory. Dinner was now a buffet in which food was piled on top of food until a great heap resulted.

At any given moment, an "active" could ask a "pledge" to fulfill some crazy requirement, which happened during the meal. Right in the middle of the pledge's recitation, he made a mistake, perhaps purposefully. Just then, a piece of broccoli flew past my face and slapped up against the side of the pledge's head. He said something under his breath just loud enough for a few actives to hear. That was it. Some things just could not be tolerated. With one movement, all of the actives leaped out of their chairs and began chasing down the pledge. They quickly caught him and, for his punishment, they took him outdoors, stripped off all of his clothes, and began tossing him up and down on a blanket for the whole world to stare at.

With great pride, the actives strode back inside and immediately proceeded upstairs for the chapter meeting at which I was the first item on the agenda. I began my message by saying that we were happy to be present on a night when not that much was happening. About fifteen minutes later, after telling a joke or two and talking about how Christ provides an abundant life of peace, power, pardon, and purpose, more than 25 of the 85 men present indicated decisions to receive Christ as their Savior.

Once you have seen something like this happen, you'll never be the same, nor will you think about evangelism in the same way. And it was Bill Bright who pioneered this idea.

FOCUS ON LEADERSHIP

While many leaders expend great efforts to appeal to Christians and church attenders, it was Bill who said that our standards would be higher if we could learn to communicate effectively with those who do not follow Christ. They will not put up with sloppy thinking, mediocre presentations, or smarmy attitudes.

As most everyone knows, many Christian organizations are committed to reaching the world with the gospel. So what differentiates Campus Crusade for Christ's role in the church from the others? If you ask Bill Bright this question, he will tell you, as he did me, that Campus Crusade is not primarily an evangelistic organization but is rather a discipling movement. It exists solely to disciple leaders who are committed to reaching and discipling other leaders to fulfill the Great Commission in this generation.

Consequently, the focus of Campus Crusade is leadership, leadership, and more leadership. So instead of Crusade reflecting the creativity of one person, it reflects the ingenuity that God has instilled in the minds of thousands of leaders from every nation in the world. This simple innovation works itself out in a variety of powerful ways.

Bill Bright challenged some of these leaders to establish ministries in other countries. One was Dr. Joon Gon Kim. As the founder of Campus Crusade for Christ in Korea, Dr. Kim has helped to evangelize his entire country. In one week in 1974, he organized a conference in Seoul for more than 300,000 Koreans, with large evening meetings reaching more than a million in attendance and hundreds of thousands indicating decisions for Christ. Now Dr. Kim sends Korean missionaries to the toughest parts of the world, and he is one of the most famous men in the entire country.

David Hannah, an athlete who held several world weightlifting records, was inspired by Bill Bright to establish Athletes in Action. He developed a ministry to professional and college athletes in which they use their platform of popularity to share the gospel with hundreds of millions around the world. Whether it is traveling basketball teams, Super Bowl breakfasts, or chaplains to major league teams, Hannah's influence is felt all across the sports world.

Then there's Dennis Rainey. Some years ago, I privately wondered what Dennis Rainey was thinking when he took over the FamilyLife ministry of Campus Crusade. But today, twenty years later, more than 100,000 people attend his conferences each year, thereby saving or strengthening their marriages. The stories are heartrending. Not a conference is organized where the staff do not see people become believers. Somehow, Dennis and Barbara knew that the breakdown in the family would accelerate and that the heartache that resulted would create openness to the gospel. Now with his own radio program, a stable of books, and the *Homebuilders* Bible study materials, he too utilizes his many talents alongside Bill Bright to help fulfill the Great Commission.

If you were to ask Bill Bright for the one or two persons who have done more than any other to help take the gospel to the rest of the world, you are going to hear about Bailey Marks. Raised in affluence in Birmingham, Alabama, Bailey and Elizabeth left the family business almost thirty years ago and a salary of $50,000 per year for a massive salary of less than $500 per month. He started out as Bill's assistant, but very quickly Bill saw his potential and asked Elizabeth and him to leave the United States and to help build the ministry around the world. Under their leadership, the staff grew from a few hundred to more than 15,000. The creativity that God has unleashed through these thousands of staff is a primary force in missions work today.

Working with Bailey, Henri and Ruthie Aoun live in Paris, where Henri is the Director of North Africa and the Middle East for Campus Crusade. In recent years, he has seen hundreds of thousands of North Africans and Middle Easterners respond to Christ through radio, satellite television, and literature distribution. To circumvent the impossible problems of access, letters are mailed directly to people all over several major North African cities, places where people cannot attend a Christian meeting. They are given the opportunity to locate a radio broadcast in their language and correspond with a believer outside their country. Today, a dozen communication centers have been established across the Arab, Turkic, and Persian world. Thousands of those who responded are being discipled.

In another classic example of creativity, a missionary observed that thousands of North Africans return to their homes each summer from employment in European countries. En route to the ten port cities, they must pass through control points before boarding ferries to their destination. This gives our staff leaders the opportunity, in cooperation with twenty other organizations and numerous churches, to distribute millions of packets, including Bibles, *JESUS* videos, and children's books, as well as audiotapes and CDs in dozens of languages. The response has been supernatural. Today, the correspondence centers are overwhelmed with respondents requesting Bible studies and further discipleship. These kinds of victories are gained only when obstacles become the stimulus to creativity and cease being roadblocks and excuses.

Not to be outdone, Thomas Abraham's protégés in India pulled off a coup. When the blockbuster movie *Titanic* hit the world stage, the staff in India utilized the themes of life and death as well as love and romance to share the gospel with university students. This evangelistic tool grabbed the attention of the elite, upper-class students on university campuses. Known as *Titanic and Beyond*, it engages students in a dialogue about the disaster and the movie and then challenges them to think about their own destiny.

In the past, it had been very difficult to reach out to Hindu and Muslim students, but the *Titanic and Beyond* strategy broke new ground. In less than a month, several thousand difficult-to-reach students heard the gospel and more than 6 out of 10 ended up indicating decisions to receive Christ as their Savior. One student leader, Priscilla, was able to share the gospel with all her classmates in one course. While holding faithfully to the essence of the gospel, the staff are finding creative, culturally relevant inroads into the hearts and minds of others.

Anywhere in the world, even if they've never heard of Bill Bright or Campus Crusade for Christ, people have probably viewed the *JESUS* film. At the latest count, the film has been translated into 635 languages and seen by more than 3.9 billion people. Thirty-five years ago, of course, the film was just a vision that God had put on the heart of Bill Bright. And he literally had to wait for Paul Eshleman to grow up to fulfill that vision.

In my opinion, you cannot appreciate all that God is doing in the world if you haven't heard Paul share "war stories" from every continent and nearly every nation and from remote villages with names you've never heard of. (When you see him, ask him to tell you about the time his staff showed the film in the "village of thieves.") And this does not even touch on the creative ways in which the film has been used, including the children's version, radio versions, sports versions of the film for the Olympics and the World Games, and the Millennium Tribute to Jesus Christ. This fellow is a genius, and yet he, like the rest of us, built his life and ministry upon the groundwork of Bill Bright's ideas.

In a story that will live on in the lore of Campus Crusade for Christ, a magician by the name of André Kole contacted Bill Bright and asked if the ministry in some way could use his act. When Bill polled the staff, they responded with resounding apathy. What could an illusionist possibly do to expand the kingdom of God? No one had ever heard of such a thing. In spite of the opposition, Bill gave an enthusiastic "yes" to André with the confidence that God had a plan. Now, some three decades later, magic is unbelievably popular, and André Kole has had the privilege of sharing the gospel before millions of people. And several of the most famous magicians in the world consider him a friend or mentor.

Josh McDowell, known to many simply as "Josh," proved that college students would listen to well-reasoned arguments. Probably no other person has spoken to as many students on college campuses as he has. And he must be working on his umpteenth book. One of them, *Evidence That Demands a Verdict*, has sold millions of copies and for years has helped students to appreciate the reliability of the Bible. Another book, *More Than a Carpenter*, did much the same regarding Jesus Christ, helping students all across the world grasp His uniqueness as the Son of God. Whether it was speaking or writing books or touring with music groups or helping parents teach their children right from wrong, Josh is another one of those staff members who could have done anything he set his mind to do. Yet he chose to utilize his creativity alongside Bill Bright to help fulfill the Great Commission.

LEADERSHIP AND THE CAMPUS

As you can tell, although all of us in Campus Crusade for Christ share the vision for the world, I am convinced that Bill and Vonette's decision to establish the ministry on college campuses was from God. Colleges and universities provide the pool of leadership to accomplish the task. Nearly every ministry leader I have mentioned was introduced to Jesus Christ or discipled in the Campus Ministry of Crusade. For fifty years, the college and university campuses have been central to all that Bill Bright and Campus Crusade have accomplished. Nowhere is the need for cultural relevance and creativity more acute than among students.

It is remarkable the way in which the campus teams have continued to innovate year after year. Under Steve and Christy Sellers' leadership, the U.S. Campus Ministry continually initiates creative and effective evangelistic outreaches. Concerned that Christianity was increasingly becoming marginalized on campus, a team of campus staff developed the Every Student's Choice campaign. The idea was to develop ads on issues that were prominent on the campus, and then take out full-page advertisements in student newspapers to address them. A toll-free number was included for those who wanted to know more. Staff and committed students would take a follow-up article personally to each student who inquired.

These ads are not always for the faint-hearted. Most people who have not been back on the college campus except for football games do not fully comprehend what is going on. Whereas student radicals ruled the campus in the late '60s and '70s, gay radicals and post-modernists rule the campus in the new millennium. Even so, the vast majority of students are still interested if approached in a nonjudgmental, culturally relevant fashion.

When business leaders and others get to know the staff of Campus Crusade, they often ask how Bill has been able to attract so many talented and creative leaders. In fact, it is this one gift of his, more than any other, that has fostered a phenomenal energy and creativity in the organization. To tell you the truth, it is amazing even to me as I consider the contributions of my friends on staff: Bailey and Elizabeth Marks and family, Thomas Abraham and his protégés, Josh and Dottie McDowell, Dennis and Barbara Rainey, Steve and Christy Sellers, Paul and Kathy Eshleman, Warren and Diane Willis, Mike and Susie Duggins, Scott and Jan Luley, Walter and Ann Bradley, and other friends whose names are not so well-known to the world but who, in any other organization, would be celebrated. Just knowing them inspires me.

WRITING A CHAPTER OF HISTORY

I love to read biographies of great men, people who have changed the world for good or for ill. No doubt, my favorite is Churchill. Or at least he was until I read the speeches of Lincoln.

Abraham Lincoln is usually presented as the log-splitting bumpkin who failed in nearly every bid for election until somehow he became president. Without formal education, no one could really understand how he could have led the effort to free the slaves. And yet he did.

The real story is different from the myth. One of Lincoln's first speeches was in favor of laying down the first transatlantic telephone cable. Another one of his speeches, this one to the Washington Temperance Union, is a classic in teaching future generations how moral issues that have repercussions in the world of public policy ought to be handled. And his "House Divided" speech provoked the Civil War to protect the Union and the rights of all to reap the fruits of their own labor.

Over the years, I am certain that I have read hundreds of accounts of people who have played an important role in forming our world. This is man's historical account. But there is another history—a truer and more important history of the world—that is being written. And God is doing the writing. When this history is read, one of the central figures for all of time and eternity will be Bill Bright. I do not say this casually. In fact, if you think about it, this entire chapter has not said much about Bill Bright directly. I have written mostly about my own experiences, and the experiences of a few others. The point is that millions credit Bill, like I do, with helping them to find the purpose for which we were created. Every one of these will write a chapter. Each chapter will be our own story, and yet in the end it will all be about the way in which God has used Bill to inspire each of us.

Bill Bright's life serves as an example of so many positive virtues: his commitment, his faith, his vision, his standards, his success, his walk with God, and many others. Yet I believe the thing that has moved the world is that he helped inspire so many leaders who have inspired so many others. The obvious results include changed lives, books, videos, Internet sites, audiotapes, CDs, articles, pamphlets, seminars, conferences, organizations, training—on real issues for real world people in the language of real life. For those of us who have been immersed in this effort, we will carry on in his footsteps. Fulfilling the Great Commission in *our own generation* means that the leaders whom God is raising up right now will continue to be a mindspring, relevant for our own era and for the glory of God.

NOTE

1. Sometimes the commitment to simplicity can create a misconception that complexity is the enemy of the gospel. This is not the case, and a simplistic understanding of simplicity has led to a prejudice against higher education, elite universities, and science. Complexity, properly understood, allows the learner to plumb the mind of God and nature in ways that simplicity introduces but cannot fathom. It is only when complexity is used as a tool to undermine the profound that it ceases to be complexity and becomes deception.

CHAPTER 18

The Use of Technology

J. RAYMOND ALBREKTSON
On Staff since 1974
Associate Professor of New Testament/Church History,
International School of Theology

One of the defining characteristics of the American contribution to the twentieth-century mission movement is the concept of applying industrial standards of productivity to the world of missions. Few individuals in history have succeeded like Dr. William R. Bright, and consequently Campus Crusade for Christ, in adapting the tools of industrial expansion to the task of worldwide evangelism.

The concept of using technological advances for the sake of expanding God's kingdom has always been controversial, despite such New Testament examples as the apostle Paul's. He regularly took advantage of his era's most advanced technology, primarily Roman roads and Greek sailing ships. The complete lack of self-commentary on this fact by Paul or other New Testament authors seems to imply an unquestioning affirmation of the use of technological means to reach the lost.

IN THE TRADITION OF WILLIAM CAREY

The assumption that technological advances should be used in evangelism was seriously challenged at the dawn of the great age of technological innovation, the eighteenth century. William Carey, considered by many as the founder of the modern era of world missions, found himself sternly rebuked for suggesting that the Christians of his age should use the technology of his century to promote world missions. Some thought that when God wanted to convert the heathen, He would sovereignly do this without the use of human means. Carey argued in his famous work, "Enquiry Into the Obligation of Christians To Use Means for the Conversion of the Heathen," that we are *obligated* to use whatever tools we have available to advance Christianity. His efforts led to the founding of a dozen missionary societies by 1824.

Dr. Bright stands very much in the tradition of William Carey in his concern to use new methods to extend the proclamation of the gospel in ways that had not been foreseen before the twentieth century. While Carey was a child of the dawning of the age of colonialism and saw Britain's colonial possessions as the great new roads for reaching the world's multitudes, William R. Bright is a son of twentieth-century American industrialism. Industry, not colonies, was the inspiration for much of Dr. Bright's innovations in mission methodology.

Those close to Dr. Bright in the years prior to the founding of Campus Crusade for Christ recognized him as an ambitious individual. He was determined to make "Bright's Delights," a kind of preserved fruit candy, a nationwide success. He had drunk deeply from the American well of industrial progressiveness that had enabled the United States to take the lead in every conceivable category by the mid-century. From agriculture to industry, from shipbuilding to highway construction, the Fabulous Fifties were a time when the hard-won proficiency that had fought powerful enemies on two fronts in World War II was finally put to work for the sake of building a better America. While Dr. Bright left behind the candy industry when he founded Campus Crusade for Christ, he did not abandon the industrial values of energy, productivity, and efficiency that were the basis of the postwar economic miracle.

One of the great concepts of nineteenth-century industrialization was brought to near-perfection in the automobile industry under the vision of Henry Ford. The concept of precision-made parts of standard size were extensively used in the production of high-precision products ranging from firearms to timepieces. Under Henry Ford, however, the concept of standard parts was melded to the theory of standardized assembly procedures, and the modern automated assembly line was born.

While Dr. Bright had used these procedures in the manufacture of "Bright's Delights," it was his novel application of these industrial concepts to the work of campus ministry that revolutionized evangelism in the twentieth century. Dr. Bright became convinced that the key to developing a highly productive campus ministry lay in quickly and efficiently training ordinary laypeople in simple, standardized methods of evangelism, follow-up, and spiritual growth. The first great breakthrough in this area was *The Four Spiritual Laws.*

REPRODUCIBLE EVANGELISTIC TRAINING

Like others before him, Dr. Bright noticed that the message of God's love and forgiveness—the gospel—could be boiled down to a few simple elements. Yet the task of training ordinary laypeople to communicate these essentials in a straightforward, repeatable, and comprehensible way was anything but simple. His first attempt to produce a standardized presentation required that the trainee memorize a lengthy presentation, then reproduce it from memory (complete with accurately quoted Bible verses) on paper.

Dr. Bright noticed that staff trained in this new method could present the gospel in a clear and repeatable manner, often with many individuals in a single day. The bottleneck, however, was the difficulty in training laypeople until they mastered the presentation.

The great breakthrough in productivity occurred when Dr. Bright reduced the lengthy, memorized evangelistic message to a simple booklet introduced with the positive yet biblical message, "God Loves You—and Has a Wonderful Plan for Your Life." Rather than memorize the contents of *The Four Spiritual Laws*, the trainee simply learned how to read the booklet and how to negotiate a simple decision-tree to effectively share the gospel. Dr. Bright quickly discovered that new converts, with almost no training, could frequently lead others to Christ the same day that they themselves had become believers.

The printed form of *The Four Spiritual Laws* was produced in multiplied millions and has become the backbone of the evangelistic ministry of Campus Crusade for Christ. Countless variations on *The Four Spiritual Laws* soon became essential tools in hundreds of denominations and other mission agencies.

In addition to making it possible for untrained laypeople to share Christ in a direct and non-threatening manner, *The Four Spiritual Laws* made it possible for new converts to become evangelists. What began as training experiences—one believer showing another how to share his faith using *The Four Spiritual Laws*—ended with unbelievers coming to faith in Christ when the trainee practiced his new skills.

Dr. Bright became convinced that simple, transferable, standardized tools such as *The Four Spiritual Laws* could easily be developed, and he believed that they could have an enormous impact on the growth of the Crusade ministry. Helping Christians learn how to be filled with the Holy Spirit and to appropriate His power in their life was already an important concept in the movement. Therefore, in short order a booklet explaining how to be filled with and controlled by the Holy Spirit was developed and became widely used in the Campus Crusade ministry. It was called *Have You Made the Wonderful Discovery of the Spirit-Filled Life?*

One of Dr. Bright's most deeply held beliefs is that God wants every individual to share his faith in Christ. What stands in the way of all Christians living fruitful, satisfying, and productive lives? The key, as Dr. Bright repeatedly affirms, is that every Christian needs to know how to be filled and controlled by the Holy Spirit. Such a Christian would naturally and successfully share his or her faith on a frequent basis. The result would not only be more evangelism (and hence more new believers), but a happy and satisfied life for the believer.

DISSEMINATING THE TRAINING

Having developed these key tools, the greatest remaining task was clarified: How can the greatest number of Christians be exposed to the training for using the tools? In an effort to find the most highly productive methods of disseminating this training, several concepts arose within the movement, but few had greater impact than the Lay Institute for Evangelism.

The key to promoting mass evangelism, Dr. Bright believed, was to enlist the rank-and-file believer, the churchgoer, the "man in the pew," in the task of world evangelism. While Campus Crusade for Christ had been begun as a campus ministry, the Lay Institute for Evangelism was developed as a seminar that targeted local churches. Why not train the millions of Christians who already trusted Christ and were being spiritually fed in a nourishing church? By this one step, the highly productive training of the campus could be taken to the churches and grafted into the lifestyle of millions of churchgoing Christians.

When training seminar leaders, Dr. Bright often pointed out that many who attend church are not even sure that they are Christians. As a result of this training, each participant could have an opportunity to be sure that he has personally put his faith in the Savior. The result was that many church members heard for the first time how they could put their faith in Christ.

The Lay Institute for Evangelism was a standardized presentation that could be multiplied indefinitely through leadership training seminars. In an effort to extend this training to many thousands of churches in an evangelistic effort coordinated with the 200th anniversary of the founding of the United States, the training seminars were condensed into a "mediated-training" package. These were footlockers packed with tape recorders, slide projectors, and many hours of audiovisual training courses. In theory, a completely untrained individual could unpack the materials, read the Leader's Guide, and conduct the mediated equivalent of a Lay Institute for Evangelism not just for one church, but for many churches.

While some pointed to these mediated training packages as the essential keys for multiplying training for thousands of churches, others criticized them for being excessively impersonal. Some detractors deplored the "one size fits all" approach to evangelism represented by *The Four Spiritual Laws*, and these critics also felt that mediated training represented an unacceptably mechanical approach to Christian education.

These critics failed to grasp the driving force of Dr. Bright's passion, a zeal illustrated with every letter that he signed: "Yours for the fulfillment of the Great Commission in this generation." Dr. Bright was not enthusiastic about evangelistic productivity simply for its own sake. He was not driven only by greater productivity, like an evangelistic Henry Ford. His goal was to take the gospel to *every* nation, *every* tribe—and ideally, to *every* human being during his lifetime.

MASS MOVEMENTS

Faced with such a goal, Bill Bright constantly experimented with more and more effective methods of reaching that objective. Even before the movement had reached its twenty-first birthday, he and his leadership team had envisioned enormous rallies in which mass movements of training and evangelism would create the kind of momentum that would have far-reaching consequences for entire nations. The first of these was Explo '72, which was held at the Cotton Bowl in Dallas, Texas.

Those who heard the plans for Explo '72, which were announced during the summer of 1970, were typically either amazed or appalled at the prospect of 100,000 youth jamming a major sports venue for most of a week. Some felt that it was a useless publicity stunt at which "Jesus freaks" would gather for a few days of "getting high on Jesus." The staff who participated in organizing the transportation, housing, program, and countless other details found themselves, for the first time in Christian history, organizing a mass meeting of the type that in the past had been the sole prerogative of totalitarian governments.

The outcome of Explo '72 more than vindicated Dr. Bright's commitment to harnessing the power of mass movements for the cause of world evangelism. A far larger international training conference was held in Korea two years later—a conference that some see as the key event in catalyzing the modern mission explosion in the Korean church. Less than a decade later, Dr. Bright organized a simultaneous multinational conference linked via live-satellite connections—one of the first in history and dedicated to the single goal of training and motivating many thousands for world evangelism.

A HIGH LEVEL OF COMMITMENT AND PRODUCTIVITY

Staff members of Campus Crusade for Christ often heard the slogan "work hard—play hard." In actual practice, Dr. Bright found it very difficult to play at all. His passion for world evangelization meant that every resource—time, talent, and treasure—must be used to the fullest extent to achieve that goal. That commitment guided Dr. Bright in many of his life choices.

Dr. Bright once described a time before the founding of Campus Crusade for Christ when he was invited to go with other young men and women of Hollywood Presbyterian Church on a skiing trip in the California mountains. At first, he made enthusiastic plans to attend, but then he reflected on the many injuries that a person could incur while skiing. Realizing that a few hours of pleasure could jeopardize his ability to reach the world for Christ, Dr. Bright decided not to go.

The high level of personal commitment Dr. Bright brought to his lifestyle rubbed off on those with whom he worked. He attracted bright individuals, and he challenged them to live up to the high standards of dedication that he himself set. He was personally willing to work very long hours, and the culture that he defined within Campus Crusade for Christ resulted in a high-pressure, high-productivity lifestyle that many found invigorating. Others, however, found that intense level of commitment unsustainable for the long term. As a result, many leaders left Campus Crusade for Christ over the years. Ironically, many of those who left the movement launched their own Christian organizations and found themselves unintentionally emulating Dr. Bright's lifestyle.

In the early years of Campus Crusade for Christ, the movement was so small that administrative overhead was almost unnecessary. The ministry leadership knew what all the members were doing. With growth, the overarching goal of fulfilling the Great Commission led to a significant innovation in missions: the survey. Just as the average businessman of the period had to cope with production reports, time-management statistics, and customer satisfaction surveys, so did the typical staff member. These reports helped keep track of ministry success.

Since the early days of the movement, Campus Crusade for Christ staff had collected statistics. One of the most productive methods of meeting people to share *The Four Spiritual Laws* was by taking a survey about a person's religious views. Not only did many come to Christ as a result of these surveys, but the results were used in many ministry settings. The statistics gathered consistently demonstrated that most people surveyed were not sure they were Christians. Furthermore, the reports confirmed that many who participated in the survey were, in fact, very interested in having a personal relationship with Christ. These two facts alone motivated laypeople to overcome their initial hesitations about being involved in evangelism.

A much less appreciated statistical report highlighted the movement's zeal for productivity: the staff member's weekly report. This much-disliked account of the week's activities asked questions such as: With how many persons did you share *The Four Spiritual Laws* this week? How many prayed to receive Christ? How many follow-up sessions did you conduct? With how many persons did you share the Holy Spirit Booklet? How many hours did you spend in evangelism? These, and questions like them, constantly kept the goals of the movement before the eyes of the staff in straightforward and quantifiable terms.

These statistics were compiled and analyzed, and Dr. Bright paid close attention to them. In the first few decades of the movement, staff were counseled and even terminated on the basis of poor productivity as determined by these reports. The seeming sterility of summarizing a ministry of evangelism in a few numbers discouraged some, but the personal example of Dr. Bright's productivity went a long way to lighten the burden of those reports.

LEADING BY EXAMPLE

All who knew him realized that Dr. Bright was a tireless witness. He never asked of his staff any more than he consistently demonstrated in his own life. Even after a brutally long period of travel and ministry, he would somehow find the reserves to share the gospel with a hotel maid or taxi driver. All he asked for in others was what he demanded of himself—ceaseless productive labor for a very simple goal, the fulfillment of the Great Commission in this generation. Dr. Bright took as his model the apostle Paul, who wrote, "I worked harder than all of them—yet not I, but the grace of God that was with me" (1 Corinthians 15:10).

The biblical basis of Dr. Bright's zeal was often summarized by this simple poem repeated on countless occasions to his assembled staff: "Only one life, 'twill soon be past; only what's done for Christ will last." Frequently, when speaking to groups of students who were involved in ministry with

Campus Crusade for Christ, he would challenge them to dedicate their "time, talent, and treasure" to the task of world evangelization. What's more important, he would challenge his listeners: You can either achieve worldly success in this life or receive a warm welcome from Jesus, hearing the words, "Well done, good and faithful servant" (Matthew 25:21, NKJ).

Dr. Bright has received considerable recognition for his achievements in this world. In 1996, he was honored as the recipient of the Templeton Prize for Progress in Religion, which included a seven-figure cash prize that he promptly gave away to promote prayer—for world evangelism! In the official statement of the Templeton Prize, Dr. Bright was described as "God's super salesman who has utilized the technology of his day to 'go and make disciples of all nations.' The number of people that Bill Bright and his coworkers in Campus Crusade for Christ have reached with the gospel would be the envy of any advertising agency's report to a client." Sir John Templeton later said privately of Dr. Bright, "He's just the kind of man I had in mind when I started the program twenty-five years ago."[1]

Many industrialists of the past century are credited with introducing innovations that greatly increased productivity. Dr. Bright stands alone among the spiritual leaders of the twentieth century in his willingness to call forth productivity in evangelism and discipleship. While he modeled the high standards of great Christian leaders through the centuries, Dr. Bright uniquely harnessed the raw and impersonal tools of the modern industrial age for the cause of world evangelism. Even his greatest critics would have to concede that the tools he devised and popularized have been copied, adapted, and assimilated into the toolboxes of almost every modern denomination and mission. As for his detractors, he has always dismissed criticism by his peers, however unfounded or unjust, in favor of hearing those much-anticipated words, "Well done!"

NOTE

1. Michael Richardson, *Amazing Faith* (Colorado Springs, CO: WaterBrook Press), 214.

CHAPTER 19

Raising Money

DAVE HANNAH

On Staff since 1961
Senior Vice President, Campus Crusade for Christ
Executive Director, History's Handful

It seems that all Christian ministry depends upon money. In the Old Testament, the building of the tabernacle under Moses relied on the contributions of the Israelites. They gave abundantly (Exodus 35:4–36:7). Later, much money was needed to build the wonderful Temple of Solomon (1 Kings 6–7). Also, the priestly tribe of Levi was chosen of God to serve Him in a special ministry. The Lord said that He was their inheritance and that He would provide for them (Numbers 18:20). They did not receive any land on which to produce food as the other tribes did. So how did God provide for them? He required the other tribes to give a tithe—a tenth of the produce of their land, grain, wine, and oil—to support the Levites and their families (Numbers 18:21–24).

Did you ever wonder how Jesus and His disciples were supported as they traveled and ministered around Galilee, Perea, and Judea? Jesus, the Son of God, depended on the financial contributions of God's people. Out of their private means, a group of women who had been healed by Jesus either of demons or of sicknesses and who were evidently also women of some wealth contributed to the support of Jesus and His disciples (Luke 8:1–3). Because Jesus had ministered to them, they in turn gladly ministered to Him financially. The apostle Paul also teaches that believers should minister in material ways to those who minister to them in spiritual ways (1 Corinthians 9:8–11).

So throughout the history of the Church, spiritual ministry has depended on the giving of God's people. Campus Crusade for Christ is no different. One of Bill Bright's major responsibilities has been raising the finances for the ministry.

MY FIRST EXPERIENCE WITH FUND-RAISING

I first met Bill Bright about six months after I gave my life to Christ. He came to Oklahoma State University, and I remember sitting across the table from him, listening as he challenged me to make my life count for Christ. Even at that first meeting, he challenged me to dream big and to ask God for impossible things. My faith was stretched.

I had the opportunity to talk with Dr. Bright several more times before I graduated from college. Two years later, when I joined Campus Crusade staff, I felt I had some special inside friendship with Dr. Bright so I figured I didn't have to go through all the procedures set up for new staff. But the director of personnel quickly set me straight.

One of my first responsibilities was to raise my own personal support—in those days all of $200 a month. Because my parents were well off and had many wealthy friends, I felt that this would be no problem. But as I contacted these people, to my surprise, none of them supported me. My support came from humble, faithful believers who joyfully gave to the Lord's work.

During my first year on full-time staff, I was appointed the campus director at the University of Oklahoma where I had nine full-time staff reporting to me. As I look back, this responsibility helped me prepare for the years ahead when I would give leadership to Athletes in Action. As campus staff, we decided to have a spring break conference at Arrowhead Springs, California, for the students who were involved in our ministry at the University of Oklahoma. I called Dr. Bright about the concept of bringing 100 students to Arrowhead Springs. He challenged me to bring 500 students. We didn't get the 500 students, but we did get 292, which was way beyond what our faith had been. To bring those 292 students to Arrowhead Springs, we had to raise nearly $25,000. For a young staff director, that was an enormous amount of money. For the first time, I had to trust God for a large amount of money, and I had to meet with business leaders from all over Oklahoma City. God blessed; the people gave; and the event was a great success. This was my first real learning experience at what we often call fund-raising.

THE BEGINNING OF HISTORY'S HANDFUL

Dr. Bright shares that when he first started Campus Crusade, he thought he could support all the staff through his business and through various fund-raising efforts with which he would be involved. But later, he realized that there were limitations to this policy and that "many hands make for light work." As a result, Campus Crusade started asking all staff to raise their own personal support. One of the greatest benefits was that staff members learned how to generate funds.

Our donor partners are a huge part of Campus Crusade for Christ's success. We now have more than 20,000 staff. Over the past fifty years, staff supporters have given more than $4 billion to help us take the gospel to the world. Donors have also given generously to various projects like the *JESUS* film, the Million Population Target Areas (MPTAs), and the "Freshman Survival Kits."

When Dr. Bright was trying to figure out how to fund taking the gospel to the entire world, he reasoned that for every $1 given, we could share Christ with five people. Of these five, usually one would pray to receive Christ, and there would be pocket change left over from the dollar for follow-up. But even with the minimal cost of a dollar for every five people and 5 billion people in the world, Campus Crusade would need to raise $1 billion to help take the gospel to the entire world. So Dr. Bright asked a question: How do you raise $1 billion? The answer: Find a thousand people who will each give $1 million! That would provide the billion dollars needed to take the gospel to the entire world. Bill named this concept History's Handful.

During the early years of the History's Handful movement, Merrill Oster, a History's Handful member, asked me, "What kind of people become members of History's Handful?"

I said, "Most of History's Handful people are entrepreneurs who have aggressively built their own businesses."

Merrill suggested, "Then why don't you recruit those kind of people?"

So from that time on, we have aggressively built the History's Handful movement around entrepreneurs. The beauty of entrepreneurial leaders is that they are risk takers. They like to go after the big challenges, so when we challenged them with an idea as big as seeking to take the gospel to the entire world by the end of the year 2000, they responded.

MINISTERING TO DONORS

As staff, we also realized that if we are going to get people to give $1 million each to the Lord's work in the right spirit, we need to minister to our donors. When we hold conferences for new History's Handful people, the first night Bill tells them that we will be asking each of them to give $1 million to Campus Crusade for Christ. Later that night, I tell them that we actually want them to give much more than $1 million: We want them to give *themselves* completely to the Lord. Then we seek to minister to their needs.

We try to make sure that they each know Christ personally, that they understand the ministry of the Holy Spirit, and that they know how to live by faith. We train them in how to share Christ with others. We take them on vision trips to different parts of the world. As Christ transforms their lives and gives them a vision for reaching the masses of the world, their pocketbooks gladly follow. They have gone; they have shared Christ; they have given.

During the last ten years, Campus Crusade's large donors have given more than $1 billion to help take the gospel to the entire world. More than $1 billion more has been raised jointly by the efforts of the International Ministry, U.S. Ministries, The JESUS Film Project, and History's Handful.

Dr. Bright's concepts of getting donors involved with Campus Crusade and the staff committed to fund-raising have paid off through the years. At the time it was instituted in Campus Crusade, the idea of the staff raising their own support was a revolutionary concept. So was the idea of raising $1 billion.

Sometimes, as recipients of necessary financial help, we do not appreciate our donors as much as we should. We do not always give them the recognition and thanks they deserve. But without the investments of donors, big and small, who live in wealthy America and in the poorer nations of the world, God could never have accomplished the things He has through Campus Crusade. To all of you who have invested in this ministry, we say, "Praise God for you!"

FINANCIAL INTEGRITY

Bill Bright is not ashamed to share the gospel because he knows it is the power of God for salvation (Romans 1:16). In the same way, Bill Bright is not ashamed to ask for money because he knows that spreading the gospel to the world depends on money, and money only comes through people who give.

But Bill Bright is not personally enamored by money. He wears the garment of materialism very loosely. In addition to raising money for the movement, Bill and Vonette also raise their own personal support through friends who designate gifts specifically for them. They receive the same salary scale as every other staff member. This means that some staff who have more children than the Brights actually make more money per year than they do. The Brights have never owned a home. They have paid rent in every place they have lived. They do not own a car. Over the years, a friend who owns a car dealership has allowed them to drive his demonstration cars. They do not even have a savings account.

Bill gave away his Campus Crusade retirement package as an investment in the ministry in Russia. When he received the $1 million for the Templeton Prize, he immediately invested it in the fasting and prayer ministry. Bill has never personally accepted any royalties for his many books. This all goes back into the ministry. He is a most generous person, personally giving to the poor and to others in need. He plans to leave no inheritance. He has laid up his treasures in heaven.

As you read these pages, how do you view money? It is necessary for ministry. Do you use it for ministry? Do you need extra money for the ministry in which you are involved? Are you completely honest and open in your financial dealings before God and before man (2 Corinthians 8:20,21)? Are you bold in asking God to supply the money needed? Are you bold in asking the right people to give to God's work? Are you grateful to God for those who give to God's work? Are you laying up for yourselves treasures on earth or in heaven (Matthew 6:19–21)?

May God bless, guide, and use you in this important area of life and ministry.

CHAPTER 20

Fasting and Prayer

BEN JENNINGS

On Staff since 1983

International Coordinator, Great Commission Prayer Movement

In 1995, Dr. Bill Bright made an unusual announcement to the Campus Crusade world headquarters staff. "God has impressed me," he said, "to begin a forty-day fast. The terrible spiritual and moral decline of our country and the overwhelming world opportunities for the gospel compel me to extended fasting and prayer. I may not fast for forty days. I may fast for only thirty days, or ten. But my goal is forty."

Bill's goal became an immediate challenge to me. Should not I, as the ministry's international prayer coordinator, be the first to join him? Forty days loomed before me like Mount Everest. Yet Bill's options gave me an escape should I need it. He might not complete a full forty days! I decided to try.

The fast was a liquid fast with lots of water and non-acidic juices. Bill graciously checked with me on occasion and provided valuable coaching. We each carried out normal activity schedules. I realized several benefits in the fast. I found more time for prayer, particularly during meal times. I grew more sensitive to the Spirit's prompting and guidance. And fasting strengthened in me an awareness of God's presence and a longing for the fulfillment of Christ's Great Commission.

The fast carried a small amount of discomfort but was not overly difficult. Occasional twinges of hunger became reminders to pray. After four or five days, my digestive system settled into a non-eating mode. For most of the time, it was not hard to avoid eating at a luncheon or banquet because I experienced almost no hunger. The Lord became increasingly real to me. I continued to experience His presence in larger measure. Advances in ministry have resulted as have increases in biblical insights, spiritual growth, material resources, faith, strength, and synchronizing of circumstances.

Heavenly riches have become a valuable exchange for short-term sacrifices.

EXTENDED FASTING WITH PRAYER

During his first fast, Dr. Bright envisioned 2 million Christians seeking the Lord in extended fasting and prayer. That fast did indeed launch a new era in evangelical Christendom that, from my perspective, has far exceeded his expectation.

The closing years of the twentieth century witnessed a remarkable resurgence of fasting and prayer. Prayer with fasting began expanding worldwide. Fasting conferences in the United States began gathering tens of thousands of believers annually. Multitudes participated through televised satellite locations.[1]

At the time of this writing, at least five massive international prayer movements with fasting are underway. For the last seven years, October has been devoted to prayer for the 10-40 Window,[2] drawing 40 million or more people. America's National Association of Evangelicals observed forty days of fasting leading up to Reformation Sunday. Pray!USA gathered 15 million intercessors during the forty days of Lent. I was honored to coordinate PrayWORLD!2000, a multi-organizational annual spreading of fasting and prayer to all nations. Up to 100 million people took part during the forty days prior to Palm Sunday 2000. Youth With A Mission observed the first forty days of the year in fasting and prayer in the nations in which they serve. Nations of Africa prayed with fasting from November 1 through December 10, 2000. Two forty-day emphases for young people were launched in Europe—one for children and one for teen-agers.

Fasting and prayer seem to be surging toward global tidal-wave proportions. Prospects soar beyond mere human projections. The movement is a harbinger of revival in the churches of the world. It presages spiritual awakenings and healing among nations, in line with 2 Chronicles 7:14. It signals completion of the Great Commission of Christ.

THE IMPORTANCE OF FASTING TODAY

As a result of his first fast, Dr. Bright wrote a book titled *The Coming Revival.* He anchored his prophetic expectations in 2 Chronicles 7:14: "If My people who are called by My name will humble themselves and pray and seek My face, and turn from their wicked ways, then I will hear from heaven, and will forgive their sin, and heal their land." Incredible, timeless principles were given by God to Solomon in this verse. They were an answer to the king's prayer of dedication for the temple. The verse is a complex covenant expressing the Lord's heart for people of all times. It anticipates times of spiritual decline and suffering. It prescribes a people's return to God's favor.

"Fasting," Dr. Bright wrote, "is the only discipline that meets all the conditions of 2 Chronicles 7:14. When one fasts, he humbles himself; he has more time to pray, more time to seek God's face, and certainly he would turn from all known sin. One could read the Bible, pray, or witness for Christ without repenting of his sins. But one cannot enter into a genuine fast with a pure heart and pure motive and not meet the conditions of this passage."[3]

Fasting means "going without food or drink voluntarily, generally for religious purposes," explains one Bible dictionary. Moses, Samuel, Jehoshaphat, the inhabitants of Ninevah, David, Nehemiah, and Esther are examples of people who practiced powerful fasting in the Old Testament.

Fasting is also recorded in the New Testament. Anna served God in the temple with fastings and prayers night and day (Luke 2:37). John the Baptist led his disciples in fasting (Mark 2:18). Jesus, after His baptism, fasted for forty days and forty nights in the wilderness (Matthew 4:1,2). He also anticipated that His disciples would fast after His departure (Matthew 9:14,15; Mark 2:18–20; Luke 5:33–35). Cornelius was fasting at the time of his vision (Acts 10:30, KJV). The leadership of the church in Antioch was fasting (Acts 13:1,2) when the Holy Spirit sent Paul and Barnabas off on their first missionary journey with additional fasting and prayer (Acts 13:3). Paul and Barnabas prayed with fasting when they appointed elders in churches they planted (Acts 14:23). Paul included fastings among his credentials as a minister of God (2 Corinthians 11:27).

In his excellent book on the subject, historian Elmer Towns chronicles Christian leaders in history who stressed the benefits of fasting and prayer.

> Each of the sixteenth-century reformers also practiced fasting, as did the leaders of the evangelical revivals in the centuries to follow. Jonathan Edwards fasted for 22 hours prior to preaching his famous sermon, "Sinners in the Hands of an Angry God." During the Laymen's Prayer Revival in America in 1859, Christians fasted during their lunch hours and attended prayer meetings in churches near their places of employment...Many revival movements have advocated a return to the early Christian practice of fasting two days a week.[4]

Bill Bright writes that "John [Wesley] and his brother, Charles, with their friend George Whitefield and other fellow believers, regularly fasted and prayed while students at Oxford University in 1732." Having experienced the spiritual power of fasting and prayer, they carried this discipline into their historic ministries. "John Wesley so believed in this power that he urged early Methodists to fast every Wednesday and Friday. He felt so strongly about fasting those two days a week that he refused to ordain anyone in Methodism unless they agreed to do it."[5]

Dr. Bright further quotes Wesleyan preacher William Bramwell. This man wrote in 1809 that the reason many do not live in the power of their salvation is because "there is too much sleep, too much meat and drink, too little fasting and self-denial, too much [taking part in] the world... and too little self-examination and prayer."[6]

EIGHT FACTORS FOR REVIVAL

As you can see, fasting with prayer has been an integral discipline practiced by many godly leaders over the span of history. Eight factors can be observed in 2 Chronicles 7:14, all contributing to revival of God's people and spiritual awakening in a nation. They include humility, prayer, devotion, repentance, response, forgiveness, healing, and appeal. The first four are human actions. The next three are divine. The eighth is mutual. These factors elevate fasting from a mere physical discipline to a spiritual movement, both individually and corporately. They show that God works through His people in spiritual awakenings. Let me describe each factor.

Man's Part in National Spiritual Awakening

The first of these factors is in our relationship to God. We must take appropriate action to open ourselves to God's Spirit.

1. Humility. "If My people... will humble themselves."

The very weakening effect of fasting produces humility. In so doing, fasting attacks pride, one of the strongest barriers to heavenly blessing. Human arrogance is a sin that God hates (Proverbs 6:16,17).

The humbling nature of fasting confronts the kind of independent spirit that precipitated the sin of Adam and Eve in Eden. The results of such confrontation can be miraculous. Author Ronnie Floyd writes, "The command of God is laser clear: The people of God are to return to him humbly, with their whole hearts—with fasting, weeping, and mourning... We must enter the Father's presence one way only—humbly, with our whole hearts, grieving for our sins, and with prayer and fasting. It is neither a prerogative nor luxury to suggest compromises when God has told us what is necessary for us to return to Him."[7]

2. Prayer. "If My people will... pray."

Fasting is a biblical way to increase and intensify prayer. It transfers our attention from the material world to God. Well-known Christian author Edith Schaeffer writes:

> Is fasting ever a bribe to get God to pay more attention to the petitions? No, a thousand times no. It is simply a way to make clear that we sufficiently reverence the amazing opportunity to ask help from the everlasting God, the Creator of the universe, to choose to put everything else aside and concentrate on worshiping, asking for forgiveness, and making our requests known—considering His help more important than anything we could do ourselves in our own strength and with our own ideas.[8]

Wesley L. Duewel adds, "Fasting in the biblical sense is choosing not to partake of food because your spiritual hunger is so deep, your determination in intercession so intense, or your spiritual warfare so demanding that you have temporarily set aside even fleshly needs to give yourself to prayer and meditation."[9]

3. Purpose. "If My people will... seek My face."

Prayer with fasting enters into a dual exercise for the earnest intercessor. It waits *for* the Lord, seeking His face; and waits *on* the Lord, claiming His answers (Psalm 37:7,9). Elmer Towns explains:

> Now that the bridegroom [Jesus] has been taken from us, we should be engaged in disciplines of self-denial enabling us to enjoy something of the closeness to Him enjoyed by the original disciples when they walked and talked daily with their Lord.
>
> I know fasting can not only draw us closer to the bridegroom, but it can also accomplish beneficial results in the lives of others who have deep needs. Fasting has transpersonal or social benefits.[10]

4. Repentance. "If My people will... turn from their wicked ways."

Concerning a fasting intercessor, Dr. Bright writes, "Certainly he would turn from all known sin." The physical discipline of fasting works against appetites that lure us from godly living.

Bright further points out that "fasting wars against the flesh... Bible scholar Adam Clarke... defines 'flesh' in his New Testament commentary of 1825 as the old carnal nature, that tendency in every person to gravitate toward the 'evil propensities' of the soul.

"As fasting and prayer brings surrender of body, soul, and spirit to our Lord and Savior, Jesus Christ, it also generates a heightened sense of the presence of the Holy Spirit; it creates a fresh, clean joy and a restored determination to serve God. In short, it brings personal revival."[11]

God's Part in National Spiritual Awakening

Prayer is the key to all of God's action on earth. Therefore, He regards the believer's sincere attitude toward seeking His face as an essential element in His work. As we fast with a heart of love toward Him, He awakens us to His purpose for us.

5. Response. "Then I will hear from heaven..."

God, by His loving nature, guarantees to answer the sincere, concentrated, holy call of His children. By meeting God's loving, mandated conditions, the principle of fasting and prayer seizes upon divine rescue from evil conditions.

Fasting with prayer produces two kinds of supernatural developments. The first kind is *when heaven comes down*. Anna was an old widow who served God with fasting and prayer in the temple most of her life. God showed her the infant Christ (Luke 2:36–38), and to her was given the historic privilege of announcing Him to God's expectant people.

The second kind is *when hell breaks loose*. Do not be surprised or afraid if intensified prayer arouses Satan. Nehemiah, when he was fasting and praying for his home city, received a commission to return and build it. Enemies harassed and opposed the workers, but the work was completed in a remarkably short time (Nehemiah 1,2).

A major challenge for intercessors is to directly track the results of fasting and prayer. Parallel chronology of events may indicate a cause-and-effect relationship. I have observed seven major developments during recent prayer-fasting years which I view as related to fasting and prayer because they are so closely integrated in time.

1. An explosive sowing of the gospel in restricted-access areas such as North Africa.
2. Outbreaks of college and church revivals with extended times of repentance and commitment to Christian service. Locations include Brownsville, Texas; Wheaton, Illinois; Ft. Collins, Colorado; Modesto, California; Pensacola, Florida; and others.
3. Large numbers of young people dedicating their lives to Christ at school

flagpoles, assemblies, and conferences.

4. Unprecedented numbers of men and women filling arenas with worship, praise, and salvation. Promise Keepers is a phenomenal, historic demonstration of this movement.
5. An outburst of church planting among previously barren populations, evidenced by large, new moves of this kind in North India.
6. A revolutionary increase in Great Commission missionary partnerships. Two instances of this enlargement are a cooperative effort among major Christian radio networks (HCJB, TWR, and FEBC) to reach all major remaining language groups, and an over-arching networking among missions networks, called Great Commission Global Round-Table.
7. Increased persecution against Christians in many nations experiencing rapid church growth in answer to much prayer. At this writing, among the most vicious onslaughts are those occurring in Sudan and Indonesia.

Be prepared for the active workings of God when you seek Him with all your heart. And be assured that in all results, He is fulfilling His promise to hear from heaven, forgive and cleanse sin, and to heal the lands of His people.

6. Forgiveness. "Then I will . . . forgive their sin."

Sin within nations is always enormous. It ravaged and savaged the world in the days of Noah, will do so at the Lord's return, and has characterized all intervening ages. "Then the Lord saw that the wickedness of man was great on the earth, and that every intent of the thoughts of his heart was only evil continually" (Genesis 6:5, NKJ). Isaiah, however, recalls God's passion to spare people from wrath. "Unless the Lord of hosts had left to us a very small remnant, we would have become like Sodom, we would have been made like Gomorrah" (Isaiah 1:9, NKJ). A small praying minority—even a praying man like Abraham—moves God's heart.

Old Testament prophets underscored the role of fasting and prayer in God's forgiveness and cleansing from sin. Joel appealed to the wayward nation of Judah. "'Now, therefore,' says the Lord, 'Turn to Me with all your heart, with fasting, with weeping, and with mourning.' So rend your heart, and not your garments; return to the Lord your God, for He is gracious and merciful, slow to anger, and of great kindness; and He relents from doing harm" (Joel 2:12,13, NKJ). In response to Jonah's preaching, the king of ancient Nineveh called for nationwide repentant fasting and prayer to God. "Then God saw their works, that they turned from their evil way; and

God relented from the disaster that He had said He would bring upon them, and He did not do it" (Jonah 3:10, NKJ).

7. Healing. "Then I will... heal their land."

Promises to Israel cannot automatically be applied to modern nations. Yet God never changes. His principles are eternal. Even today, intense, biblical, sustained prayer on a broad scale turns nations back to God. The history of North America, for example, closely parallels that of Israel and Judah. In their book *The Light and the Glory*, Peter Marshall and David Manuel detail the "finger of God" in the early history of America. When the people walked with God, the nation was blessed with good crops, good weather, health, and peace with the Indians. When the people forsook the Lord, they suffered floods, drought, epidemics, and massacres.[12]

"God is able to make all grace abound toward you," says Paul to the church in Corinth (2 Corinthians 9:8, NKJ). God's favor and providence upon His people is an accomplished fact. He has "blessed us with every spiritual blessing in the heavenly places in Christ" (Ephesians 1:3, NKJ). The challenge He gives now is that we, His people, reposition ourselves to receive the riches of His goodness—for ourselves and for our nation. The larger our need, the more earnest our petitioning should be. As I heard the late Armin Gesswein once pray, "Lord, save us from that slavish working *for* Thee, and teach us that powerful working *with* Thee."

A MUTUAL COVENANT

The last factor combines the work of God and the efforts of believers. It is the culmination of the other seven points.

8. Appeal. "If My people will... then I will."

Like an eternal Master Composer and Conductor, God is imparting to us the very responses He wants from us. We call it His *prevenient* grace. "It is God who works in you both to will and to do of His good pleasure" (Philippians 2:13, NKJ). God works through us so that His appeal becomes our appeal to our world. We become like the violin played by the Master Violinist, producing the beautiful melody of His composition. That music then draws the world to the feet of God.

Dear reader, heed the words of the Lord. Is trouble surrounding your life, family, ministry, country? Have you received His Son, Jesus, and become one of "His people"? If not, you need not wait any longer. He is knocking now at the door of your heart. He is saying, "If anyone hears My voice and opens the door, I will come in" (Revelation 3:20, NKJ). The moment you receive Jesus, you become a child of God (John 1:12)! Just this quickly, you are numbered with the people of God and qualified for the blessings of His marvelous provision.

To all who are His people through Christ Jesus, God extends the same promise He gave Solomon. It boils down to this summary of God's invitation to us: "Your future as My people is assured. You are in My care and control, guarded by My presence within you. I design, however, that we work together. I understand your human nature. I will work with you as you are. You can regard future hard times—shortages, challenges, afflictions—as further harmonizing your life and ministry with Me. Make it your priority to abide in Me. When you stray, get back to Me. I have given you 2 Chronicles 7:14 as your way to come back. I do not regard your fasting and prayer as works of merit. These cannot extract greater favor from Me. I have already given My full favor to everyone who is in My Son. When you fast and pray, you are simply opening your channels to receive My limitless grace. I love you!"

Bill Bright's message to the Christian world is a call to heed God's voice and humble ourselves through fasting with prayer. The Master Himself appeals to us through the encouragement and vision of this godly leader. The call is a major legacy that Dr. Bill Bright has bequeathed to Campus Crusade for Christ and to the Body of Christ throughout the world.

NOTES

1. To read more of my research into the Fasting and Prayer movement, see my book, *The Arena of Prayer* (Orlando: New*Life* Publications, 1999).
2. A geographical area lying between the 10th and 40th parallels north of the equator, from the Atlantic coast of Africa to the Pacific coast of Asia.
3. Bill Bright, *The Coming Revival* (Orlando: New*Life* Publications, 1995), 17.
4. Elmer Towns, *Fasting for Spiritual Breakthrough* (Ventura, CA: Regal Books, 1996), 27.
5. Bright, 92.
6. Bright, 96.
7. Ronnie W. Floyd, *The Power of Prayer and Fasting* (Nashville: Broadman and Holman Publishers, 1997), 30.
8. Bright, 117.
9. Ibid.
10. Towns, 12.
11. Bright, 96–99.

12. Peter J. Marshall, Jr. and David B. Manuel, Jr., *The Light and the Glory* (Old Tappan, NJ: Fleming H. Revell Co., 1977), 14.

CHAPTER 21

Using Large Events for Momentum

E. BAILEY MARKS

On Staff since 1967

Vice President, International Affairs

In the thirty-five years that I have been associated with Bill Bright, one phrase has been the theme of his strategy formulation: "small plans do not inflame the minds of men." A staff member or close associate who hears this phrase repeatedly cannot help but be infected by it in the same way as Bill Bright.

He does not believe that God is a small God, and he is willing to believe God for the impossible. He knows that believing God for the impossible pleases Him, and Bill delights in pleasing God.

As I have studied Bill Bright's leadership style and learned from him, I have concluded that he is the most consistent person I have ever met. He is loving, gracious, compassionate, sympathetic, and a fabulous encourager; yet at the same time, he never wavers in his commitment to the fulfillment of the Great Commission at all costs. He evaluates everything he does in light of helping to fulfill the Great Commission. At times, one may question some of his plans and ideas in the beginning stages, but eventually realize in the outcome that helping to fulfill the Great Commission was the objective all along.

A BALANCED APPROACH

When speaking of the Great Commission, Bill always refers to Matthew 28:18–20: "Then Jesus came to them and said, 'All authority in heaven and on earth has been given to me. Therefore go and make disciples of all nations, baptizing them in the name of the Father and of the Son and of the Holy Spirit, and teaching them to obey everything I have commanded you. And surely I will be with you always, to the very end of the age.'" Then Bill usually goes on to say, "The Great Commission is the greatest plan ever given to man, by the greatest person who has ever lived, concerning the greatest power ever revealed, involving the greatest promise ever recorded." His emphasis has always been on evangelism, both personal (one on one) and mass evangelism, with an equally strong emphasis on teaching, training, and discipleship.

He insists that a balanced approach to evangelism and discipleship must prevail. If it's merely evangelism, then it is spiritual addition. If it is all discipleship, very soon you would run out of people to disciple. Discipleship and spiritual multiplication must be involved in evangelism to have adequate numbers. The balance is always present as Campus Crusade for Christ disciples and evangelizes in every nation, playing a strategic role in helping to fulfill the Great Commission.

Having observed Bill Bright for 35 years, one thing is obvious about him. He expects God to initiate great things through his life and ministry and is never surprised when God does so. A verse that he continually quotes is Philippians 2:13: "It is God who works in you to will and to act according to his good purpose." As a new staff member and a relatively new believer in my early thirties working closely with Bill Bright, I often wondered why he quoted this verse so much.

One day the light came on. Bill was saying that if he was walking in the power of the Holy Spirit, with no unconfessed sin in his life, believing God for the impossible, then God would anoint his mind with thoughts, plans, and strategies that would relate to the fulfillment of the Great Commission.

With this kind of dependency upon God to do the supernatural in and through his life, it is easy to see how so many great things and events have taken place through his ministry. Even though Bill's life can be characterized by supernatural faith, it is equally characterized by strict obedience to God and His Word and a work ethic that has rarely been paralleled. It is because of his great faith, total obedience, and hard work that the mega-events in this chapter and their impact upon the Body of Christ around the world have occurred.

WHY MEGA-EVENTS?

Bill has no trouble with big numbers or large events, and he is quick to point out to those who may question them that Jesus was interested in numbers and that the Bible is full of such illustrations. For example, the various feast days of Israel where the entire nation was encouraged to come together were large spiritual events. When Solomon dedicated the temple, it was "in the presence of all the assembly of Israel" (1 Kings 8:22, NASB). That was a lot of people. When Jesus fed the multitude, there were 5,000 present on one occasion and 4,000 on another. Acts 2:41 says, "So then, those who had received his word were baptized; and there were added that day about three thousand souls."

The apostle Paul was concerned about large numbers of people, and he always seemed to have a plan and strategy. Frequently, the Lord changed these plans and Paul was sensitive to the leading of the Holy Spirit. But you cannot read the Book of Acts without appreciating that he was a man with a vision who applied plans and strategies to that vision.

Many more recent events—Berkeley, a New Kind of Revolution; Explo '72; Explo '74; Here's Life, America; Here's Life, World; KC '83; Explo '85; New Life 2000; and numerous smaller events in different parts of the world—have helped to generate momentum toward fulfilling the Great Commission. Did Bill Bright sit down and plan out all of these great events in detail? No! Then one might ask: How did they all happen and what was their role in the overall movement of Campus Crusade for Christ?

Years ago, I heard Bill say that he constantly thought about ways and means to help train, motivate, and mobilize the Body of Christ. So many of the organizational and management practices and principles that we read volumes about today come naturally to Bill because of his faith, obedience, common sense, and hard work. At the same time, he has always been open to radical and new ideas and has tried to surround himself with individuals who could think "outside of the box."

Through the years, Bill Bright's vision and faith have helped him attract this kind of people—people who do not wish to be just ordinary Christians, but who want to make a difference in the world. Thus, the movement God called him to found and lead for fifty short years has had a profound impact upon the world.

I will attempt to take these mega-events and place them into the context of the last half of the 20th century and explain how they helped in the development of the movement of Campus Crusade for Christ, as well as influence the world and the Body of Christ.

The big events sponsored by Campus Crusade for fifty years have always had an objective—not big events for the sake of holding large meetings, but stepping stones in the development of the movement and the fulfillment of the Great Commission.

Management experts who study successful companies and organizations write about cycles of momentum, vision casting, creating an environment for growth, etc. These concepts come naturally to Bill. He saw a need; he addressed it. In turn, his effort became a momentum builder, enlarged the vision of the staff, and created an environment for learning.

The question that needs to be asked is: Why are big events necessary? Could not the same objective be achieved without all the time and effort used to make a big event happen? The answer is no! The big events provide momentum and place Christianity in a very positive light.

It is true that there is usually a downside to the mega-events, possibly a temporary loss of momentum or at times fallout, such as a loss of staff. I believe this is a result of leaders failing to catch the vision for the large event and to see how the event fit into the overall plan. But in the long run, any major event provides a major boost. In the two to three years following each event, the Lord would take the ministry to a new level.

This momentum also provides benefits. *Leadership is multiplied* as staff are placed in positions of trusting God to use them in unusual ways and as they use their administration and managerial skills to the maximum. For example, a 28-year-old staff member named Paul Eshleman directed Explo '72. He went from there to direct the U.S. Ministry, and ultimately became the Director of The JESUS Film Project, which has touched the lives of billions of people around the world.

Rapid mobilization of manpower is another benefit of the momentum process achieved through the large events. A broad geographic spread of manpower is mobilized to help fulfill the Great Commission. Many more people are raised up with expanded vision, believing God to do great things in their communities and being challenged to be used in other parts of the world.

Let's look back at some of the mega-events sponsored by Campus Crusade and the momentum they inspired.

BERKELEY, A NEW KIND OF REVOLUTION

In the 1960s, the United States was facing its greatest internal struggles since the Civil War. Vietnam War protests, the battle over integration, and a new theology stating that God was dead were sweeping university campuses. This new philosophy created a situation that found many at a loss about how to cope. If God was dead, then all restrictions were removed. The result was the rapid infusion of the drug culture and the decline of religious and moral teaching. Fortunately, not all university students fell into this category, but most were seeking answers to issues in their lives.

Bill Bright and the leadership saw this unrest as a golden opportunity to challenge Christians to stand up for Jesus and to make Him known as the solution to all problems. A plan was conceived to bring together committed Christian students, as well as laypeople from the communities, for a week-long blitz on a major campus. The most radical university in the country was chosen—the University of California at Berkeley.

For one week during the winter of 1967, Jesus Christ became the central issue on that campus as 600 staff and students, whose theme was "Solution—Spiritual Revolution," invaded the Berkeley campus with the good news of Jesus Christ. The result: More than 700 athletes, student leaders, faculty members, and students made commitments to Jesus Christ and approximately 2,000 others indicated they would like to know more about Him. Two major television networks commented that, while an action by the California Board of Regents caused student unrest on all the other University of California campuses that week, Berkeley was the quietest campus in the whole system because of the influence of Campus Crusade for Christ.

In the three years following the Berkeley event, more people joined the staff of Campus Crusade for Christ, including Elizabeth and myself, than at any other time during its history. This was no coincidence. University graduates and others alike caught the vision and wanted to be a part of a movement that was truly involved in helping to fulfill the Great Commission.

EXPLO '72

Bill was sitting on the platform at a Billy Graham conference in 1970 when God gave him the idea of bringing students, laypeople, and professionals from across North America to a massive training conference in evangelism and discipleship. Once again, he was applying Philippians 2:13 in his walk with the Lord.

At that moment, the seed of Explo '72 was planted. Bill then presented the Campus Crusade leadership with the most faith-stretching experience they had ever faced. Through trying hours, God began working in their lives to lead them to commit themselves to the massive undertaking.

Billy Graham and others had held many large evangelistic meetings in big cities. But how could any one group plan for an interdenominational conference of 100,000 people from all across North America to meet in Dallas, Texas, to be trained in personal evangelism and follow-up, and then to send these people out to evangelize their campuses and communities? Many Christians would not walk across the street to be trained in personal evangelism, much less come from across the country. Would this work? The staff had to be convinced and become enthusiastically supportive.

Bill needed to cast the vision. He says, "Vision casting is the work of describing the future in emotionally powerful terms. It paints a picture of the future. What has God called us to do? It involves hearing the Lord and speaking passionately about it." Few people can cast a vision like Bill Bright, but his work was cut out for him. The staff did catch the vision, were brought into the objective, and began to put together the structure to make Explo '72 a reality.

The major objective of Explo '72 was to plant Spirit-filled, Christ-centered witnessing Christians on university and high school campuses and in churches all across North America. One hundred thousand did not show up, but eighty-three thousand did. One then-staff member writes of the event:

> The year is 1972. Two Apollo 16 astronauts spend 71 hours exploring the moon's surface... President Richard M. Nixon announces an agreement with the People's Republic of China premier Chou En-lai on increased Sino-U.S. contacts... At the University of Michigan, students vandalize ROTC offices, an incident that reflects the unrest that continues on America's college campuses.
>
> And for six days in Dallas, 80,000 college students, high school students and laypeople converge for a demonstration of a different kind...
>
> Friday, June 16. The Cotton Bowl, ablaze with light only moments before, is blanketed in darkness. High school students sit cross-legged on the plastic-covered Astroturf of the stadium floor; college students, businessmen, community-minded women and families fill the stadium's seats.
>
> Tiny points of light begin to appear throughout the concrete and steel structure as the flames from a few candles are passed from delegate to delegate. Bill Bright's words are still echoing in their ears: "Light a spiritual fire here that could sweep the world."
>
> As the light multiplies, the delegates' singing swells in intensity:
>
> *It only takes a spark to get a fire going. And soon all those around can warm up in its glowing.*
>
> The stadium grows brighter as thousands of candles are lit. The flickering candlelight illuminates not just the Cotton Bowl, but faces that are gleaming with conviction, inspiration and determination.
>
> *That's how it is with God's love. Once you've experienced it;*
> *You spread His love to everyone; you want to pass it on.*
>
> This was Explo '72! One of the largest Christian gatherings in Amer-

ican history, Explo '72 involved inspiration and training in evangelism on an unheard-of scale.[1]

The significance of one candle lighting another throughout the stadium is a clear picture of the momentum spread by Explo '72!

EXPLO '74

The momentum from Explo '72 carried from Dallas to other parts of the world. During the conference, God was working in Dr. Joon Gon Kim's heart about what He desired to do in Korea. Dr. Kim, National Director of Campus Crusade for Christ in Korea, kept praying and discussing the matter with only his wife and the Lord. Although the Korean ministry of Campus Crusade for Christ had come to Explo '72 with a sizable delegation, he did not discuss the matter with any of his leadership. Then one evening when he was addressing the audience in the Cotton Bowl stadium, Dr. Kim announced from the platform that in August 1974, Explo '74 would be held in Seoul, Korea, and before he realized it, he invited all to come to Korea in two years!

A vision had been caught by a faithful Spirit-filled Christian, and there was no turning back. Explo '74 did occur, and there were 323,000 registered for the weeklong conference, most of whom lived in tents during the event, with more than one million in attendance at most of the evening meetings. It was quite a ride with one faith-stretching experience after another. Dr. Kim comments,

> Ever since Explo '74 concluded, I have been pressed with the question, "What did Explo '74 really accomplish?"
>
> Volumes could be filled with the wonderful details of all that God did through this congress. Explo '74 was not only an international Christian conference, but from the Korean point of view, it was a movement from the grassroots of Korean Christianity, and it deeply affected hundreds of thousands of lives.
>
> It was of course very thrilling to all of us who had been preparing for this event for two years, because a number of "firsts" in Christian history were set during Explo week:
>
> 1. The largest Christian gathering in recorded history (at least two of the evening mass rallies exceeded 1.3 million according to the official police estimate).
> 2. The largest number of Christians trained in discipleship and evangelism during one week (a total of 323,400 delegates registered from 78 countries).

3. The largest number of decisions for Christ at one time (an estimated 70% of the first-night audience of 1.3 million people indicated that they had received assurance of their salvation by faith as a result of the message, which explained how they could receive Christ and know that He was in their lives).
4. The largest all-night prayer meetings in the history of the Christian church (spontaneous prayer meetings occurred six nights in a row, with several hundred thousands in attendance each night).
5. The largest personal witnessing campaign ever conducted (more than 420,000 heard the gospel in one afternoon, and a recorded 274,000 indicated decisions for Christ).
6. The largest number of Christians to appropriate the filling of the Holy Spirit at one time (an estimated 70% of the 1.3 million audience one night responded to this invitation).
7. The largest number of Christians to commit their lives to the fulfillment of the Great Commission at one time (a response of 90% was estimated among the Sunday afternoon audience of 650,000).

These and at least 15 additional "firsts" were recorded at Explo '74, to God be all of the glory and praise.[2]

Our organization jumped to a new level of faith because of what God did during Explo '74. It was one thing to see big conferences take place in the United States, but something else to see one the size of Explo '74 taking place in South Korea, which was still suffering from the Korean War. Explo '74 also set the Korean church into an unprecedented growth cycle and put the International Ministries of Campus Crusade for Christ on the map around the world. Staff returned to their nations with a new level of faith, commitment, and zeal. It was as if the staff were saying, "If God could do that in Korea, He can do something similar in my country." We opened new ministries and saw older ministries grow and expand in an unprecedented way. In the next few years, our movement experienced rapid growth in Asia, Africa, and Latin America.

HERE'S LIFE, AMERICA

It wasn't long after Explo '74 that God began to speak to Bill Bright about truly making Jesus Christ relevant in every community and home in America. The ministry was well established and growing across the U.S. The campus movement was expanding, and a large number of churches were using Crusade's training in evangelism and discipleship. Yet the question remained: How can thousands of churches across the country train their congregations to reach out into their communities? Then the idea arose about how much more effective laypeople would be if they knew that they would be reaching out to "ripe fruit," in other words, to those who probably were interested in hearing the gospel.

Keep in mind that big events are for creating momentum and vision and for getting more and more people involved very quickly, resulting in the maximum number of people being exposed to the claims of Christ. Since its inception, Campus Crusade has always desired and attempted to work through the local church. This includes the big events it has sponsored. Those who were trained in the big events were trained in initial follow-up and discipleship, which were designed to lead people to become involved in Christ-centered churches. Thus, Here's Life, America was born.

Atlanta, Georgia, was chosen as a test city to launch the campaign. The strategy was really quite simple: recruit the maximum number of churches within a city to participate in the campaign. The congregations of those churches were trained in evangelism and initial discipleship. A media strategy called a "teaser campaign" was launched over a weeklong period. On billboards, television, radio, newspaper, and every place a person could look, someone was saying, "I Found It, You can find it too!" Finally, after the suspense level was high, the "reveal campaign" was launched. It stated "I Found It, You can find it too: New Life in Jesus Christ," and included a phone number and address for people to respond. People in Atlanta responded by the thousands. The campaign was a success.

Now we had to launch similar campaigns in every major media market in North America and duplicate what had taken place in Atlanta. Bill traveled across the continent speaking to groups of church leaders in city after city, casting the vision for Here's Life, America. As a result, almost every major media market in North America participated in the campaign.

Late in 1976, Bill Bright was interviewed about the results of Here's Life, America.

> *Dr. Bright, as you review Here's Life, America in 1976, would you say the movement has been a success?*
>
> I would say that the Here's Life movement is phenomenally successful. In approximately 250 cities across America, many thousands of churches have already been mobilized. Hundreds of thousands of Christians have received training and they are in the process of continuing to train others in discipleship and evangelism. As far as I have any knowledge, this is the most remarkable movement of its kind in history. More

people in our country are in the process of hearing the gospel of Jesus Christ and making their commitments to Him as Savior and Lord than ever before. More people are involved in discipleship and evangelism training than ever before in the history of this country.

Also, one of the most important aspects of the movement, according to the pastors and laymen I meet, is the phenomenal feeling of brotherhood that exists between denominations. For the first time, many of them are discovering brothers and sisters in other denominations and in other local churches. They are working together, witnessing together, praying together, and demonstrating the love of Christ together.

Many pastors have told me that, if there had not been one single decision for Christ, what has happened through Here's Life, America in removing barriers between individuals, churches, and denominations would have been worth all the investments of time and money.[3]

The following are comments by others who were involved:

"One of the highlights of the campaign was the unity of churches from different denominations all working together," said Tom Calahan, a lawyer who worked with the movement in the Washington, D.C. area.

Faith barriers were also shattered in the West. "One of the highlights was the cooperation of the churches," said Jim Burke, city coordinator in Portland, Ore., where 230 churches cooperated during the campaign. Many pastors and laymen commented about how so many churches were working together to reach the city.

"I believe our greatest strength has been our weakness," said Col. Nimrod McNair, another worker in the Chicago campaign. "Our media effort was weak due to lack of funds, plus we could not get on the major networks. Then on November 19, the *Chicago Tribune* hit the streets with a story on the second page. Negative, yes; but the results were positive." In the wake of the *Tribune* article came live interviews with NBC, ABC, and CBS news and an article in Chicago's *Sun-Times*. As a result of the publicity from these sources, the awareness of Chicagoans about the campaign leaped from 20% of the population to 60%.[4]

HERE'S LIFE, WORLD

With the vision of a man like Bill Bright, you can well imagine the logical progression following Here's Life, America. Naturally, Here's Life, World! At first, there was resistance in many parts of the world because Here's Life, America had used sophisticated media and large telephone banks in every city, and numerous other means not available in developing countries.

However, the International leadership began to look at the principles that were applied during Here's Life, America. First, churches needed to participate, and that was not a problem. Second, people within the churches needed to be trained in evangelism and discipleship, and that was not a problem. Here's Life, America used a suspense campaign involving high-tech media, but many alternatives were available: placards, signs on automobiles, signs on buses, motorbikes going to villages in rural Africa. In Latin America, people went up and down the streets in villages with megaphones saying, "I Found It, You can find it too." In several Asian countries, so many creative ideas came forth that it is impossible to describe them all. In the Philippines, the suspense campaign was so successful that some commercial companies adapted it into a new form of advertising.

Next came the reveal week of telling people that they could find new life in Jesus Christ. Some telephone banks were available, but they were quickly maxed out. So people were encouraged to come to central locations and put response cards into boxes on street corners. By the hundreds of thousands, people from many different religious backgrounds indicated decisions for Christ. People were standing up and taking notice of Jesus Christ. Christians were beginning to get out of their little shells where they felt like a defeated minority and were recognizing that they truly were the ambassadors of the King of kings and Lord of lords.

The seeds for world evangelization were truly being planted in the hearts and minds of Christians all over the world in the mega-cities, small hamlets, and villages. Christians were beginning to pray that people would supernaturally intercede in their country and do the impossible.

As plans were formulated for Here's Life, World, Thomas Abraham, the National Director of India Campus Crusade for Christ at that time, believed that the gospel could be taken to every single home in his native state of Kerala. Apart from Thomas and Molly Abraham, no one in Kerala believed it could happen. But the Abrahams began to encourage their staff, who began to train people in churches and recruit rural evangelists to be involved in taking the gospel into every home. By the end of 1978, every home in Kerala had had a gospel presentation or a piece of literature received at the front door, and people were responding to the gospel by the scores.

The momentum that the Kerala campaign generated laid the foundation by enlarging the vision for Christians in India to believe God that their entire country could some day be reached for Christ. And so the cycle has gone on through decades of casting the vision, increasing the faith, and building momentum so that more people would be trained and more exposed to the gospel in order that the Great Commission might be fulfilled.

Just read some of the ideas used to lift up Christ in difficult situations.

Then there's the problem of manpower shortage. One city, for example, has 120,000 Buddhists and only one Christian church—with 50 members. In addition, in some places the penalty for sharing one's faith could be a beating, prison sentence or even death.

If these sound like insurmountable obstacles, then you are beginning to see why Here's Life, Asia has had to adapt the original Here's Life, America format.

These adaptations have enabled Here's Life to "reach its fruition," according to Asian Here's Life coordinator Jerry Sharpless. "Right now I know of no other strategy that is more applicable to Asia," he said. "It's the only strategy in which a small number of Christians can have an impact on a large number of non-Christians."

Of the campaigns that have been conducted already—44 by last month, including a whole state of India—each has been as individual as its locale.

For example, the first campaigns in Asia were held in Manila and in Baguio City, Philippines. Here, the corner response box made its debut. Many Asians do not have telephones, so comment card drop boxes supplemented the telephone response system, one of the mainstays of the U.S. Campaign. In some cases, the response boxes were used alone.

Media saturation also took on a new look as signs posted on jeepneys, taxis, and horse-drawn calesas augmented the traditional buttons, bumper stickers, banners, billboards, newspaper ads, television spots, and radio announcements.

Cities like Hong Kong, Singapore, Jakarta, Kuala Lumpur, Taipei and Bangkok each added their personalities to the Here's Life story by altering the campaign format to suit their needs. In Jakarta, if the reveal portion of the campaign (in which "I Found It!" is explained) had mentioned the name of Jesus Christ, campaign workers would have participated at the risk of their lives, so a partial reveal strategy was adopted. In Okinawa, where the Bible has appeared on the best-seller list, the phrase "new life as described in the Bible" answered the curious who asked, "What did you find?"

In Taegu, Korea, strong social action measures were added—campaign workers were asked to give blood to take part in the campaign. The blood was given to the city and labeled so that those handling and receiving it knew it had been donated in the name of Christ.

Hong Kong added typical Chinese thoroughness to its campaign by training some 15,000 Christians as campaign workers, having 1,100 telephone workers and holding evangelistic meetings in 300 churches. Also, in an amazing balloon parade, 46,000 people carried balloons printed with the "I Found It!" message in both Chinese and English.[5]

Banners, radio spots, sound cars, and newspaper ads make "I Found It!" the best-known phrase in the city. In San Cristobal, the "I Found It!" craze reached such a point that people in the community began spontaneously to call numbers in the phone book. The caller would simply say, "Good evening, I found it!" and hang up.

As a final touch, a pilot and light plane were hired to circle over the city for an hour with a large banner streaming out behind the plane that read (of course), "I Found It!"

At the sound of the plane, people began to fill the streets, necks craned upward, calling out to one another, "I can't believe it. It's on the walls, in the newspapers, on the radio and now in the sky." The pilot was so entertained watching all the ruckus he was causing down below that he stayed aloft three hours instead of one![6]

Information centers, located primarily in Nairobi's church buildings during the Kenya prototype, moved to crossroads, bus stops and market places in largely rural Swaziland. Publicizing the campaign took on new forms, such as a hot air balloon proclaiming "I Found It!" to draw the Benoni community's attention to the "*Ke bo fumane*" campaign.[7]

The use of innovative methods further showed how vital vision is to the spread of the gospel.

KC '83

The original vision that God gave to Bill Bright in 1951 was to launch a ministry on the university campuses of the world, thus the name Campus Crusade for Christ. Knowing that the students of today are the leaders of tomorrow, Campus Crusade for Christ has attempted to launch its ministry in most every country of the world, beginning on the university campuses. This establishes a leadership base and develops the manpower source to carry on other strategies throughout a particular nation.

For years, Campus Crusade for Christ had been holding major regional conferences all across North America, both at Christmas and during the summer. Tens of thousands of students were involved, resulting in a high percentage of leadership in churches today who were involved in the ministry of Campus Crusade for Christ during their university days. However, in the early 1980s, the Crusade leadership felt that it was time to hold a nationwide student conference to build momentum and link students from all across North America.

More than 17,000 college students and staff members spent part of their Christmas vacation braving arctic conditions and icy roads in Kansas City to receive evangelism and discipleship training. The weather was terrible, but the bonding was terrific.

EXPLO '85

The next event following KC '83 was a worldwide student conference. The idea was to bring together 30,000 students from around the world for the largest international student conference that had ever been held. My wife, Elizabeth, and I had just passed over the responsibility of the Asian leadership to Dr. Thomas Abraham and Dr. Joon Gon Kim, and I had stepped into my present position as the Vice President of International Ministries. Therefore, Dr. Bright asked me to take over the responsibility of this worldwide gathering.

As soon as I began some preliminary planning, it became obvious that the costs would be prohibitive because the vast majority of the students would be coming from developing countries and would need scholarships. Therefore, the initial budget was in the tens of millions. If we had that much money, which we did not, God would not want us to (nor would we) spend it all on one mega-conference.

My initial response was, God does not want us to have it. That was not Bill Bright's response! To him, it was quite obvious that we needed to have the conference and that God had another plan. Bill became fairly persistent about asking me what I was doing to prepare for the Worldwide Student Conference. My only response was, "I am praying."

After some weeks of prayer, God impressed me one morning with the fact that I was approaching the conference the wrong way. Rather than taking the students to the conference, we needed to take the conference to the students. My response was, *How?* Then I seemed to hear a still, small voice saying, "By satellite." I have a hard time turning on my TV and I know absolutely nothing about electronics, but within two days God put things into motion to formulate a plan and raise up people we had never met before who enabled Explo '85 to take place.

Billy Graham called Explo '85 "one of the historic events in the history of the Christian church." In a remarkable series of satellite teleconferences, 300,000 Christians (rather than 30,000) around the world locked arms and pledged to "Come Help Change the World." Here is one example of what happened all over the world at Explo '85:

> Daniel sat inside a huge bamboo shelter covered by palm leaves, his eyes fixed on a video screen before him. Approximately 2,500 others seated around him in Trichur, India, watched with equal fascination. Outside the shelter, a large metal satellite-receiving dish arched toward a black and starry sky.
>
> On the screen, Daniel saw Christians gathered in such faraway places as Seoul, Berlin, Manila and Mexico City. He marveled that the world had seemingly come to Trichur.
>
> "It is my first experience to see people all around the world worshiping, singing, and hearing the Word of God," he said. "I would not have believed it, but I have seen it with my own naked eyes."
>
> What Daniel saw with his "naked eyes" was a historic series of broadcasts viewed by approximately 300,000 Christians around the world. The broadcasts, which linked 94 sites simultaneously for two hours a day on December 28-31, were the centerpiece of Explo '85, the most ambitious training conference yet organized by Campus Crusade for Christ. The conference was, according to Campus Crusade founder and president Bill Bright, "the single most important event in the history of this movement."[8]

Explo '85 focused on motivating and training Christians of more than 160 nationalities to "Come Help Change the World." At each conference site, delegates learned how to witness to others, how to walk in the power of the Holy Spirit, how to pray effectively, how to disciple others—in short, the basics of the Christian life.

Dr. Bright says, "Conferences like Explo '85 are momentum builders. They keep fresh in our minds the need for aggressive action for the cause of Christ."

But what made Explo '85 unique were the daily broadcasts, which experts called a technological marvel. The largest closed-circuit satellite videoconference in communications history at that time allowed ordinary Christians to realize that they are not alone, that God is raising up believers around the world to help fulfill the Great Commission of Matthew 28:18–20. Participants understood that they are part of a worldwide movement for Jesus Christ. The encouragement combined with the training the conferees received helped produce a well-equipped and unified force of future Christian leaders all around the globe.

On one occasion in London, the audio power in the anchor room was suddenly cut off just before the program was to begin. Then, miraculously, power was restored at the last minute. Our Lord demonstrated His power and honored our faith and obedience to bring together the greatest event in the history of this ministry.

According to Bill Bright, here are the results of Explo '85:

- Three hundred thousand people from at least 160 countries were trained at 98 conferences. Many additional millions were involved on worldwide satellite and national cable networks. To think of so many people around the world receiving training in discipleship and evangelism is mind-boggling. Just think of the impact they can have as they reach out for Christ to millions of others in their local areas!
- Hundreds of thousands of people were introduced to Christ on the worldwide day of witnessing.
- Many Christians in countries where they represent a very small minority of the population now recognize that they are part of the vast worldwide body of Christ. They have seen what God is doing around the world, and they realize that through Christ they can be part of a great movement of believers who can change the course of history for the glory of God and for the good of mankind.
- Thousands of churches and Christian organizations participated in Explo '85. Their involvement helped build bridges of love and mutual ministry.

- Campus Crusade for Christ staff members, delegates and volunteers are following up on Explo by teaching others what they learned. For example, the Campus Crusade ministry in Korea is planning to use the 70,000 trained Explo delegates to take the basic training to others in 2,000 Korean cities and rural areas.
- Explo '85 and the ministry of Campus Crusade for Christ received favorable worldwide publicity.
- Many Christian leaders throughout the world were enthusiastically involved in and responsive to Explo '85. Though I have not yet received final statistics, we have reason to believe that many thousands of people will join this and other ministries as full-time or associate staff or as volunteers.
- Delegates will be starting ministries of Campus Crusade for Christ in several new countries, 13 in Africa alone.[9]

The benefits of Explo '85 were numerous. Christians all over the world began to realize how small the world truly is, how rapidly information can be transferred from one area to another, and how Christians can be united in prayer at one single moment throughout the entire world. God used

Explo '85 to launch our ministry into a new orbit and to truly prepare us to help bring the Body of Christ together for the sole purpose of world evangelization. Momentum was generated spontaneously throughout the entire world. Hundreds of thousands of Christians had a new vision of what could happen if a sufficient number of believers took God at His Word and believed Him to do the impossible.

At the same time Explo '85 was occurring, God gave the movement the *JESUS* film. Under the able leadership of Paul Eshleman, The JESUS Film Project ministry was beginning to grow; languages were being dubbed in large numbers, and film teams were being positioned in most every country in the world.

NEW LIFE 2000

With the momentum that was achieved through Explo '85 and the introduction of the *JESUS* film, God impressed the leadership under the direction of Bill Bright that another momentum event was not needed. What was needed was to launch a global strategy that would give everyone on earth the opportunity to hear and understand the gospel and to respond by inviting Jesus Christ to come into their lives. Thus in 1986, New Life 2000 was launched with a plan to give every person at least one chance to hear the gospel, one chance to see the *JESUS* film and hear the news of Jesus' love and forgiveness, or one chance through many other strategies.

Here's what Bill Bright had to say about New Life 2000 in 1986:

> Since its inception, Campus Crusade for Christ has focused on the fulfillment of Christ's Great Commission. That massive task involved taking the gospel to the world—a world whose continents will embrace 6.5 billion people by the year 2000. Campus Crusade seeks to work with the body of Christ to win people to Christ, build them in their faith and send them out to win, build, and send others.
>
> No goal of such magnitude could be accomplished without specific, prayerfully considered plans of how to reach that goal. Campus Crusade has crafted plans of how to work with churches and other Christian organizations around the world to win and disciple people in every country by the end of this century.[10]

Large denominations and other para-church organizations were also beginning to realize that we each have unique gifts, abilities, and strengths and that we need each other. During the last ten years of the 20th century, there has been a greater cooperation within the Body of Christ throughout the world than at any other time in Church history. Our organization has established thousands of partnerships to see the Great Commission fulfilled. The Berlin Wall fell; the Soviet Union dissolved; China became more tolerant of religious activities; technology increased opportunities to present the gospel in the Middle East. Therefore, the *JESUS* film could now be taken to the world!

Latin America: Julio Campos clutched the guide ropes as the hanging bridge swung in the wind. Only 50 more yards to go, but the weight of the generator in the homemade backpack was throwing him off balance. He gazed through the rotten wooden slats at the Lempa River far below. "We're not going to stop showing the *JESUS* film until every last centimeter of territory in El Salvador has been covered by the gospel!" he had declared. Some of the mountain villages he and another Campus Crusade worker would visit on this trip were so remote the people had never seen a film, never had electricity, and most importantly, never heard that Jesus alone forgives sin. So Julio forced himself forward.

Asia: The fields are nearly ready for harvest. This year's is expected to be one of the most plentiful anyone in these parts can ever remember. The prospects for spiritual harvest are equally encouraging. Two students are reading through *The Four Spiritual Laws* booklet with willing listeners while Ongkit reads to the village headman from John 3. Ongkit, director of the Sisaket New Life Training Center, has brought some of his 37 trainees here to practice explaining the gospel to the villagers.

Europe: *JESUS* drew sellout crowds and top government officials in Bulgaria, a country which, in the not-too-distant past, has been called the "little Russia" for its hard-line Marxism. Attendance by Bulgaria's new president, vice president, and prime minister was a first in film history for any premiere, according to the Bulgaria Film Industry Corporations. Prime Minister Dimiter Popov had seen the film years before in Holland and wanted to see it again and bring his children. Afterward, he expressed interest in using the film in the country's schools and prisons, as well as the churches.[11]

Russia: [In] perhaps one of the most historic events to happen in Russia since the fall of communism, the gospel is being taught in Russian schools.

Created in response to Former President Boris Yeltsin's decree to celebrate the new millennium and 2,000 years of Christianity, the *Story of Jesus* audiodrama brings to life the person of Jesus for Russian school children. In a captivating way, it retells His life, death, and resurrection. Russian education officials worked closely with Campus Crusade staff and the Russian acting community to see the project accomplished.

"The *Story of Jesus* was invaluable help," said Yelena, a teacher in Tverskaya. "I used every minute of the tape and every page of the curriculum in my Literature lessons and out of curriculum activities."

Every school in Russia, some 67,000 plus, was encouraged to implement this curriculum in their classrooms. Teachers were given a preview of the *Story of Jesus* at their training conference between terms. Already these teachers are sharing the materials.

Middle East: "I want this country to be an open country. Do not put your freedom on a shelf. Use it!"

When a Campus Crusade staff member in the Middle East heard those words spoken by his national leader, he thought, "Okay, a good Christian ought to submit to his leaders." So the very next day, he and a friend went to the local newspaper offices and took out an ad, offering the *JESUS* film and Bibles. To be exact, he put 17 ads in daily and weekly newspapers, telephone books and an airline magazine. They expected 50–60 people to respond to the listed address, yet in the first week, more than 1,200 people sent letters to our Communication Centers.

India: Patna is considered the birthplace of both the Hindu and Buddhist faiths. One would think with such a history, this regional capital would be a difficult place to be a Christian and have an evangelistic ministry.

Ray of Hope, or *Asha Kiran* as it is known in Hindi, broke new ground as an evangelism outreach to this city.

"Never before in the known history of Christ's Church in this city has such a complete gospel saturation campaign been done," said Preetam Putro, co-chairman to the outreach and an "on-fire" businessman. "We virtually blanketed our city. Every nook and corner was reached. The excitement among believers is very high and even our skeptics are expressing surprise."[12]

Millions of stories such as these have happened in almost every country of the world during New Life 2000. Christians have prayed and fasted, received a heavenly vision for their countries, and believed God for the impossible—and God has worked.

CATCHING A WORLD VISION

Developing staff, providing vision, stretching one's faith, creating momentum, multiplying leadership, rapidly mobilizing manpower, distributing massive amounts of materials, developing clear objectives, creating the proper environment, exposing millions to the gospel, equipping the saints, boldly proclaiming the gospel, modeling Christlike character, giving every person one chance to hear the gospel, establishing partnerships, recognizing that nothing is impossible with God—all are part of mega-events in the history of the ministry of Bill Bright.

Have mega-events been necessary? I think so. I believe that the mega-events paved the way and prepared the soil for the phenomenal things that have happened through New Life 2000. In every single country of the world, the gospel has been presented. People have prayed for every area of the world for years, and now the harvest is being reaped. To me, the role that Campus Crusade for Christ has played in this process would not have been possible in this short period without these mega-events that have led to distinct cycles of momentum.

This is a Ministry Summary of what has happened as a result of large events as of December 2000:

- Campus Crusade for Christ has 24,823 staff members and 553,700 trained volunteers.
- Campus Crusade for Christ has either full-time staff or a ministry presence in 191 countries, representing 99.6% of the world's population.
- In 2000, more than 1.2 billion exposures to the gospel took place through Campus Crusade for Christ and partnership activity.
- In 2000, more than 23.1 million people indicated decisions for Christ in "live" evangelism situations through Campus Crusade for Christ and partnership activity.
- Since the ministry began in 1951, there have been approximately 6.1 billion exposures to the gospel worldwide through Campus Crusade for Christ and partnership activity.
- There is a Campus Crusade for Christ ministry active in 4,639 Million Population Target Areas (MPTAs), in 476 strategic urban centers, and on 1,423 priority university campuses.
- There have been 4.1 billion exposures through the *JESUS* film. The film has been seen in 234 countries and has been translated into 638 languages.

No matter who you are or what ministry you are connected with, it is important that you wisely use large events that are attention-gathering and attractive, programs that will move people to action, events that the people of your church can be involved in. Perhaps you could take your men to a large Promise Keepers event or encourage church members to become involved in the nationwide Lighthouse Movement. Perhaps you can work together with other local churches. Your people need to catch a world vision. Vision trips, praying for unreached areas, and large events will stretch your people's vision.

NOTES

1. Chuck McDonald, "Where Were You in '72?" *Worldwide Challenge*, June 1982, 6.
2. Joon Gon Kim, "Stage Set for Awakening," *Worldwide Challenge*, September 1974, 8.
3. "An Interview with Bill Bright," *Worldwide Challenge*, December 1976, 29,30.
4. Chuck McDonald, "America's Famous Phrase," *Worldwide Challenge*, April 1977, 21,22.
5. Vickie Kyte, "Here's Life, Asia," *Worldwide Challenge*, February 1980, 9,10.
6. Kathy Long, "Ya La Encontre," *Worldwide Challenge*, February 1979, 10,11.
7. Donna Bahler, "Here's Life, Africa," *Worldwide Challenge*, February 1979, 15.
8. David Boehi and Jim Morud, "A Call to 'Come Help Change the World,'" *Worldwide Challenge*, March/April 1986, 8,10.
9. Bill Bright, "Looking to the Future," *Worldwide Challenge*, March/April, 1986, 57.
10. "Here's Life World," *Worldwide Challenge*, November/December 1986, 49.
11. Linda Anderson, Donna Bahler, Bill Hunt, Bill Sundstrom, Jim Tulloch, Anne Marie Winz, "And Around the World," *Worldwide Challenge*, May/June 1991, 48.
12. *World Today*, International Ministries, Campus Crusade for Christ, Spring 2000, 1.

PART THREE

Special Issues

CHAPTER 22

Reaching the World Through the Universities

JON HINKSON

On Staff since 1985

Research and Teaching Fellow of Rivendell Institute for Christian Thought and Learning, a special project of the Campus Ministry at Yale

Let me begin by expressing my great gratitude to Dr. Bright for so many years of fatherly friendship. We shall greatly miss his godly leadership. As the Carthaginians inscribed upon the grave of their beloved leader Hannibal: "We vehemently desired him in the day of battle."

Dr. Bright's motto from the inception of Campus Crusade for Christ has been "Reach the campus for Christ today, reach the world for Christ tomorrow." When he first sounded this note of reaching the world through the universities, it had an ancient and august heritage. A fitting beginning for our historical caper is Alexandria—metropolis and center of Hellenistic culture during the first spread of Christianity. It was also the site of the far-famed "Museum," a kind of academy of learned men which boasted the greatest library in the ancient world. At this great meeting point between east and west, the arts and sciences flourished and every type of philosophy and religion had its distinguished representatives.

By the second century, a Christian community had grown up in the bosom of this great university town, and yet the educated elites remained largely unbending and contemptuous of the Christian witness. But God raised up disciples with the vision and learning to meet the challenge of penetrating the elite pagans of the academy. A catechetical school was established, which abutted the university and had the ambitious goal of engaging the reigning pagan philosophies and commending Christianity as alone rational and worthy. This catechetical school was blessed with gifted apologists. In Clement and Origen, Christianity had ambassadors to the academy who in learning and acumen were second to none of their pagan counterparts and in the gracious winsomeness of their lives, typically their superiors.[1]

While the clear aim of Clement and Origen was to draw men to Christ by demonstrating the contradictions and imperfections of all rival systems, they were not controversial in any petty or ignoble sense. "They looked up to the great masters of the Hellenistic schools with a generous admiration, and infused the same spirit into their disciples."[2] Many pagan seekers were drawn to the open lectures and discussions, attracted by the thoughtfulness, sincerity, and congeniality of these Christian apologists. Not a few who became part of that community of learners soon became part of the community of Christ.

The catechetical school became a great success, not only in penetrating the elite educated and cultured society of Alexandria with the gospel, but also in spawning similar philosophical missionary schools through its many disciples who went out from the parent project. And of course, master apologists like Clement and Origen were as much a product of this project as they were its forgers. Taking the university culture seriously helped to fashion thoughtful, passionate Christians of such caliber. Origen and Clement became the premier Christian thinkers of their age.

THE BEGINNINGS OF UNIVERSITY MINISTRY

While we may legitimately speak of Origen and Clement's work as "university" ministry, technically the "university" began in the medieval ages. No sooner did universities evolve than their strategic importance was at once discerned. One thinks of the Spaniard Dominic Guzman's ambition to forge an order of itinerant preachers who would go out two by two to extend the Christian faith both at home and beyond.[3] Dominic's own dream was to personally evangelize the Cuman Tartars in Easter Europe. But Dominic never reached the Tartars himself. He died, not on the foreign field, but in the university city of Bologna, for he had recognized that the vitality of the movement he had founded would, among other things, pivot on successful recruitment at the universities. Accordingly, Dominic sent his first recruits to the great universities of the day, such as those in Paris and Bologna. Here those optimally fitted to take up the cause—students—would be found, those gifted and already trained in some of the requisite skills of the missionary—learning and teaching.[4]

Although Dominic himself never reached the Tartars, his strategic thinking paid off, for some of his university boys did, along with many other "uttermost parts," while he was still alive.

One of the reasons the university is so critical in reaching the world is that the world's students gather at the university, then typically return to their far-flung places of origin, disseminating whatever they acquired around the globe. This dynamic is well illustrated by the ministry of John Wycliffe, dubbed the "evangelical professor."

Not a few foreign students were drawn to study at Wycliffe's famed university, including quite a coterie from Bohemia. One of their number, Jerome of Prague, returned home with not only Wycliffe's spirit in his heart, but also several of his books in his satchel. In turn, they became powerfully inspirational for one of Jerome's Prague fellows, Jan of Hussenitz, more widely known as John Huss, whose impact is well known. With Huss, we are on the doorstep of the Reformation.

UNIVERSITIES AND THE REFORMATION

The Reformation has been aptly called "a university movement" and amply illustrates the theme of reaching the world through centers of learning. The drama resulting from Luther's rediscovering of the gospel put Professor Luther very much in the news, so students flocked to Wittenberg from near and far to attend the fledgling university.[5] Upon completion of their "gospel" studies, they typically returned to their native lands. Thus, this Saxon university became the epicenter of successive waves of gospel impact.

The brothers Peterson, Olaf and Lars, came from Sweden, kindled their torch, and returned to ignite their nation with the gospel. Olaf is often called the Martin Luther of Sweden. Hans Tausen made the trek from Denmark and returned to sow the gospel seed in his land—with abiding fruit. He was appointed royal preacher. Johannes Bugenhagen left the spores he acquired in the Wittenberg lecture room all across northern Germany, Scandinavia, and the Baltic territories. Scholar Gerhard Ebeling aptly remarks about Luther's academic influence: "It is no exaggeration to say that never in the history of the university has the work of a scholar, in the study and in the lecture-room, had so direct and so extensive an influence upon the world, and changed it so much. If we ask what is the utmost that can be expected from a university, Luther provides the answer."[6]

Perhaps the best known foreign student with a passion to reach his homeland at Wittenberg was William Tyndale. He had made Luther's gospel his own and was its great advocate with tongue and pen. Well remembered for his gift of the Scriptures in the language of his people, a daring service which cost him his life, his prefatory comments to assist the reader contain a good bit of "verbatim Luther" in translation. One of Tyndale's chief haunts in England was the White Horse Tavern in the heart of Cambridge University. The tavern came to be known as "Little Germany" for the intense absorption of some of its regulars with the evangelical ferment emanating from Luther's Wittenberg. This group of university men played the courageous part of fuglemen of the English Reformation. Almost every one of them would seal their witness to the truth in the flames. We know of 25 Cambridge martyrs. Indeed, for the singular role of that university, historian E. G. Rupp suggests that the English Reformation may be known as "the Cambridge Movement."[7]

Universities educated practically every significant religious leader of the Reformation. Indeed, not a few of the principal leaders—Bucer, Melanchthon, Vermigli, Oecolampadius—were university professors. It was vitally important to have well-educated spokesmen for the evangelical message as its progress in several places hinged on the outcome of debates. In the first Zürich Disputation, reformer Ulrich Zwingli championed the gospel cause against all challengers. Before him lay open a Greek New Testament, a Hebrew Old Testament, and a Latin Vulgate. They were not for ostentation, but for use.[8]

On a heated point, an opponent claimed to have confuted the Reformers from Scripture.

"Oh, really?" responded Zwingli, "What chapter and verse?"

The bluff was exposed by the embarrassed silence.

"Ha!" concluded the burgomaster, "You fail to produce the pike by which you allegedly poked the pig."

Another university-honed reformer made his debut at the Lausanne debate. For his diminutive stature and French origin, he was dubbed "the little Gaul." At a critical point in the debate, in which Farel, Viret, and the little Gaul were arrayed against 174 opponents, a skillful gambit caught Farel and Viret—men more stormy than studied—without a response. But the until-then silent junior partner stood to respond. From a seemingly miraculous memory, he quoted huge swathes of Augustine, Chrysostom, and other church fathers, clinching the case. Silence filled the hall. Even the ignorant sensed the decisiveness of the words spoken, and another canton (Geneva) had declared itself for the Reformation, thanks in no small part to the well-marshaled learning of a university trained scholar—the young John Calvin.

Scarcely a finer instance of reaching the world through the university can be offered than Calvin's Geneva. In the words of John Knox, its reputation for being "the most perfect school of Christ since the day of the apostles" drew pilgrims from across the continent. There they were trained (it was said you could stop any citizen in the street and they could give an account of their faith "like a doctor of the Sorbonne") and then they were sent out as missionaries. A special college was established for this enterprise, which was so close to Calvin's heart that he was often seen going door to door soliciting funds for its support. In the first year of the college (1555), two missionaries went out, in the next, three, then 11, then 22, then 32, and so on. In the year 1562, more than 100 missionaries were sent out from Geneva to declare the glad tidings of the gospel. It was from Geneva that the first Protestant missionaries carried the gospel to the Americas!

UNIVERSITIES AND THE PURITAN MOVEMENT

Just as the university was at the heart of the Reformation, so also was it the center of the Puritan Movement. It would surely take a life's work to tally the impact of even Cambridge University alone in the spread of the gospel under the Puritans. In its cluster of colleges, Scripture was studied, the Word preached, convictions crystallized, and disciples made and given the mandate to go and multiply.

Walter Mildmay's foundation of Emmanuel college tells the story well. His vision for the college is enshrined in the founding statutes of 1585. His desire was that the colleges of Cambridge might be "opened like fountains, that arising out of the Paradise of God, they may as with a river of gold water all the regions of the land, with a faith of the purest doctrine and with a life of the most holy discipline."

"I have set an *acorn*," he told the queen, "which when it becomes an *oak*, God alone knows what will be the fruit of it."[9]

The fruit of the foundation was impressive. From Emmanuel's door went out many a godly minister, indeed many of the great Puritan leaders of the age. From the college to the countryside, they poured into "the dark corners of the land," bringing in "a very great Harvest into God's Barn."

Not only across England's green and pleasant land did Sir Walter's acorn send out its shoots, the branches of the oak stretched farther, for many sons left their alma mater to cross the sea. Indeed, 96 Cambridge men migrated to New England between 1620 and 1645—35 from Emmanuel![10]—and one of them bore the now famous name of John Harvard. So crucial was a university viewed for the flourishing progress of the gospel that the establishment of one was considered the first task beyond securing physical survival in the new land. As Cotton Mather expressed it, the "other hemisphere" would never send enough learned and able ministers to answer our necessities. "Without a nursery for such Men among ourselves, darkness must have soon covered the land."[11]

It was no coincidence that they called the spot "Cambridge," for Harvard College merely transplanted Mildmay's kingdom enterprise onto American soil.[12] Within 25 years of its foundation in 1636, 91 graduates had gone out from her portals, and this was only the "first fruits" in "a succession of a learned and able ministry."[13]

The aim of one of the dorms at Harvard College (not only to pervade the land with the gospel, but also to propagate the gospel beyond its borders) reflects the missionary spirit of its founders. The dormitory was furnished to host native Americans in accordance with the express design in the charter to educate "English and *Indian* youth in knowledge and godliness." Incidentally, Dartmouth College was founded (1769) chiefly to serve this same strategic ambition—reaching out to the natives by drawing them into a college.[14] Eleazar Wheelock, the founder, fittingly took as the college motto, "Vox Clamans in Deserto," a voice crying in the wilderness, and the college shield on which it is inscribed depicts Indians hearing the gospel.[15]

The first Indian trained by Wheelock was the Mohegan Samson Occom, who returned as a missionary to his tribe. So successful was his evangelism among the Montauk people of Long Island that the local presbytery ordained him. After further labors among the Oneida Indians in upstate New York, Occom was so convinced of the strategic significance of Wheelock's school that he set aside his evangelistic efforts and traveled to England to raise the funds to put the college on firm footing. Occom raised more than 12,000 pounds sterling, and Dartmouth is with us to this day.

Eleazar Wheelock was a graduate of Yale College, and through Yale, the thread works all the way back to the influence of Mildmay's acorn. Chaderton's missionary mantle of mastership of Emmanuel fell upon John Preston, whose gospel-rich corpus of writings were reverently edited by John Davenport. Davenport went on to found the New Haven colony and laid the first plans for a college. Historian Benjamin Brook writes: "The first public service observed in this new plantation was on the Lord's day April 18, 1638, *under a large spreading oak*."[16]

No sooner had the Pilgrims disembarked upon the shores than Davenport began to gather up a collection of books—the first fruits of what would become Yale's library. The full fruition of Davenport's dream was not realized in his lifetime, but when it did transpire, the vision was no different. As the founding trustees put it, the college was to serve the purpose "both to plant and under the Divine Blessing to propagate" pure worship of God.[17] From her founding in 1701 down to 1748, about half of Yale's 483 graduates went out from the classroom to the pulpit and parish. In her earliest days, the proportion was greater. A full four-fifths of those who sat under Abraham Pierson, the first rector, became ministers of the gospel.[18]

So strategic was the university for the progress of the gospel that when Yale began to flounder in its function, a new collegiate enterprise was ventured as replacement: the College of New Jersey, later called Princeton.[19] From its inception, Princeton exercised a significant role in imparting vital Christianity to numerous young men and in taking the gospel to those who had not heard. Jonathan Dickinson, Princeton's first president, was the representative of his early successors in the description which comes down to us of him as a "friend of revivals and a zealous promoter of missions among the aborigines of this country." But Princeton's vision for getting out the gospel extended further than the local "aborigines." Given the concentration of resources—human, intellectual, informational, imaginative—universities are great places to dream dreams and concoct schemes for the kingdom. In the correspondence of Samuel Davies, the fourth president, we find a record of a plan to secure three or four Africans "who still retain their native language, are pious and of good abilities" to be educated at Princeton to return as missionaries to their own land. Whether this happened, I do not know. It may well have. Interestingly, twenty years later, Yale adopted a similar scheme. Two African youths were selected, but it was judged expedient for them to receive their tuition at Princeton.[20] Here, again, we know little of the outcome, but clearly it was out of the bosom of the university that many of the great plans were hatched to bring the gospel to the world.

In Princeton's cemetery, there is a small stone with an inscription now only scarcely and partially decipherable. It hints at the budding of another gospel scheme out of the college, but also serves as a metaphor for how much more there must be to the stories than we can retrieve. From the words not yet lost to us we read:

> In memory of Guy Chew, a Mohawk Indian, who departed this life just... aged 21 y. and 8 mo. This youth continued in pagan darkness until his 18th year... experienced the renewing grace of God... became eminent for his... desire to proclaim the gospel to his countrymen. Providence called away in the morning of his days. Reader, pray for the Indians.

But we have lingered long on colonial colleges and must hasten on.

THE UNIVERSITY OF HALLE

We have cited Cotton Mather, the Puritan patriarch, in connection with the founding of Harvard. One of his correspondents who was acutely interested in the progress of the gospel among the Indians was August Hermann Francke, one of the outstanding figures of the Pietest Movement in Germany. Francke directed a galaxy of associated institutions at Halle—an orphanage, a Paedagogium,[21] a printing press, a Bible Institute, etc.—all clustered around a university founded in 1694 to serve the growing Pietist Movement. Under the leadership of Philip Jakob Spener and his colleague and successor Francke, the influence of the university grew rapidly and spread far and wide. At the height of its fame, 1,200 students passed through its theological faculty every year—the largest in all of Germany!

The significance of Halle for supplying missionaries for foreign fields is well known. One need only mention the labors of Bartholomew Ziegenbalg and Henry Plütschau, who departed from Halle in 1705. They were the first Protestant missionaries to reach India from Europe.

But Halle illustrates the strategic nature of the university in some additional ways. One that immediately suggests itself is the *scholarly* contribution to reaching the world for Christ which the university is uniquely poised to make. It was, for example, Halle which supplied the church with the pioneer of missiology as an academic discipline—Gustav Warneck. He held the chair of missions at Halle (the first of its kind in Germany) from 1897 to 1908 and is rightly regarded as the founder of the science of mission studies. His vast scholarly productivity (of typical Germanic proportion) and especially his monthly missions journal helped to inform and direct much missionary energy. His corpus of writings cover virtually the whole range of the theory and practice of missions. He was also the first to promote effective coordination and cooperation in missions by means of conferences on local, regional, and national levels. One can only conclude: Thank God for scholars and the universities that nurture them![22]

Halle illustrates a crucial point. The strategic nature of the university is made crystal clear when one observes the effects of the withering of a credible gospel witness. The gospel must sustain its most aggressive and powerful intellectual critique at the university. If the gospel fails to stand in this arena, it will not last long in the wider culture.

When the icy blast of rationalism blew across Europe, it struck Halle with a vengeance and brought a severe numbing of Christian zeal and missionary impulse. Biblical criticism descanted its corrosives upon the once full wealth of conviction. It seemed as if confidence in the Scriptures must shatter beyond repair and the fabric of faith of many a student looked fated to fray at every point. In this critical moment, God raised up a servant in the heart of the university to contend valiantly for the faith. His name was Friedrich August Gottreu Tholuck (1799–1877).

Signs of his acumen were evidenced early. At an early age, he was inseparable from books—not all of them in his native tongue.[23] Before he reached the age of seventeen, he had already acquired facility in nineteen languages—several of them exceedingly exotic. In his twentieth year, while a student, Tholuck was brought to vital faith in Christ through pietism. Becoming professor of dogmatics and exegesis at Halle when spirituality and orthodoxy were at low ebb, he remained there for nearly fifty years until his death, laboring patiently to win back the university from the icy grasp of rationalism. A bachelor all his days, Tholuck devoted much personal time to his students. Each day he would select a student to accompany him on his lunchtime walk and a few others to join him for dinner. As they walked or dined, he would inquire into their spiritual state and intellectual doubts. His marvelous mix of fervent faith and able answers rescued a vast number of students from the abyss of skepticism. Tholuck stemmed, then turned, the tide of rationalism at Halle in both the faculty and student body and saved a generation of students in Germany. One shudders to think how different things would have been had God not raised up such a servant in such a critical time and place. May God send us many more Tholucks to contend for the gospel in the severest and most fateful arena—the university.

SIMEON AND CAMBRIDGE

Tholuck has been called "the Charles Simeon of Germany." The comparison is apt in many ways because Simeon's labors in Cambridge show the strategic nature of the university exploited to remarkable degree.

After taking his degree at King's College, where as a fresher he had experienced a sound conversion, Simeon stayed on as a resident fellow until his death in 1836. Thus, he was an insider to the university for 57 years! While his early years were fraught with severe opposition, Simeon stayed the course and weathered the adversity until it withered against his evident character and genuine care for students. In Simeon's day, half the students who went up to Cambridge did so intending ordination, and the ministers launched from that university comprised half the clergymen in all the land! Those who did not go into ministry filled other stations of influence, such as government, law, or education. Cambridge was like the narrow neck of an hourglass—strategic ground to occupy with the gospel. "I look upon my position here as the highest and most important in all the kingdom," confessed Simeon, "nor would I exchange it for any other."[24] Simeon likened his situation at Cambridge to the spring into which Elijah administered the salt: "Cry mightily to God that the cruse of salt may be cast into this foundation from whence so many streams are issuing; that being rendered salubrious they may fertilize this whole land, and be the means of diffusing life and salvation to the remotest corners of the globe."[25]

The horizons of Simeon's vision were "the remotest corners of the globe," and the fields to which he lifted up his eyes were not only domestic but distant. In fact, Simeon reserved his best and brightest disciples for the honor of the foreign field. The roll of those he sent is lengthy, and they *were* his very best. One thinks of Samuel Marsden, called "the apostle of New Zealand," or Henry Martyn, who, in the words of his memorial, "translated the Holy Scriptures into the Oriental languages" and "defended the Christian faith in the heart of Persia against the united talents of the most learned Mohametans."[26] Simeon sent so many of his "Sims"—as his disciples were called—to India, he came to call it "my diocese."[27]

Despite being so strategically placed, Simeon's influence did not simply settle about him as an unbidden fog on the Cambridge fens; it was as deliberate and contrived as the nascent railways. To draw certain types of students (like bright, but poor evangelicals) from certain areas (like those underrepresented or greatly in need of some gospel witness), Simeon established specifically designated scholarship funds. At the other end, he would network and strategize to place his graduating "Sims" where they could have singular impact—near the inns of court, for example, where they might influence judges or in large cities lacking any gospel witness. Crucial, of course, was what happened in between matriculation and graduation when Simeon imparted a vision for ministry and equipped students to fulfill it.

The meat and potatoes of his student ministry (or should we say the bangers and the mash) was a rich fabric of relational discipleship. I have leafed through many collegiate diaries of the period and frequently turned up the repeated entry: "Tea with C. S." Also at the heart of his student ministry were his famed "Conversation Parties" with an open invitation for all to gather in his spacious rooms and ply him with queries. Every Friday in term, shortly before 6 p.m., a trail of students would ascend the stairs to the top of the Gibbs building and seat themselves on the benches and chairs supplied for the occasion. Simeon would take his accustomed seat, a mahogany stool to the right of the fireplace, and open the proceedings: "Now if you have any question to ask, I shall be happy to hear it and to give what assistance I can." As two servants passed out tea, queries were posed and solutions offered with constant reference to his small quarto Bible "until the clock struck seven."[28]

So Charles Simeon had what has been perhaps the greatest ministry to students in the history of the Church, and for a span of more than half a century, dramatically displayed how singularly strategic the university is for reaching the world with the message of Christ!

PRINCETON AND MISSIONS

We left Princeton at a gravestone and the story it told of a Mohawk student's desire to reach the unevangelized with the good news of Christ. We must now return to Nassau Hall to tell the story of another of her sons and similar dreams, which came to more than imagined fruition. It is a tale that attests to student power in world evangelization.

One of the features that invests any university with such a potential for advancing the kingdom is that it is largely populated with young men and women who are in a unique season of life. The university years tend to represent a convergence of maturity and opportunity. Prior, many are too often immature; past these years, often too preoccupied. But meet them in that moment with a challenge worthy of their life which will call for all their skill and ardor, and you may well release a spate which becomes a tide.

In 1884, a little band of Princeton students began meeting every Sunday evening in the home of a retired thirty-year veteran missionary to India, Royal Wilder. It was his son, Robert, a junior at Princeton, who had founded a little society called "the Princeton Foreign Missionary Society." Its constitution read: "The object of this society shall be the cultivation of a missionary spirit among the students of the college, the information of its members in all subjects of missionary interest, and especially the leading of men to consecrate themselves to foreign missions work."

The meetings were open to all who had an interest in missions, but to become a member, one had to subscribe to a covenant. It read simply: "We the undersigned declare ourselves willing and desirous, God permitting, to become foreign missionaries." This covenant came to be known as the "Princeton Pledge." The watchword this little posse of—at the time five—pledgers adopted was gloriously audacious: "The Evangelization of the World in this Generation." Week after week they met with their maps and on their knees, the old missionary veteran often contributing from his wealth of experience and conviction.

As the meetings were held, Robert's sister, Grace, was on her knees in another room of the house, asking God's blessing upon the little group of consecrated students. And every evening brother and sister prayed together that from this little beginning, 1,000 volunteers for missionary work would be raised up from the colleges of America.

Then came the invitation to attend D. L. Moody's first "College Students' Summer School for Bible Study" at Mt. Hermon. Delegates were to be selected from colleges across America and Canada.

Two hundred and fifty-one delegates attended from 86 colleges, among them Robert Wilder. Although the topic of foreign missions was not part of the program, Robert brought his burden before many fellows as they hiked, swam, or ate. Soon those possessed of the same passion found each other and began to meet daily to pray for more volunteers. Another, then another, put his name to the pledge Wilder had brought with him from Princeton.

With a week remaining in the month-long conference, Wilder presented the cause of missions before all the delegates. He hastily gathered from those in attendance seven internationals and three children of missionaries (himself included). Each was given three minutes to present the spiritual needs of his land and a plea for missionaries. Each address concluded with the words "God is love" spoken in the tongue of his people. The effect was unforgettable. That night, many delegates withdrew to their rooms or went out under the stars to seek God's guidance.

"There were great searchings of heart and great resolves," recalled Wilder. By the end of the conference, 99 had signed the pledge. A farewell meeting was held for a final season of prayer before the pledgers separated for their colleges. As the 99 knelt in prayer, one last student quietly slipped in the back and joined them, filling the ranks of what was to be known as the "Mt. Hermon One Hundred." But compared to what would come, the "Mt. Hermon Hundred" was merely "a cloud the size of a man's hand."

Within twenty years of the first Mt. Herman conference, 3,000 volunteers had sailed as missionaries to foreign lands. In the next 20 years, more than twice as many departed for far-flung shores at a rate of more than one a day! As Princeton President James McCosh remarked: "Has any such offering of living men and women been presented in our age, in our country, in any age, or in any country, since the days of Pentecost?"[29]

GREAT LEADERS FROM THE UNIVERSITIES

We have so far highlighted the great *numbers* the universities gave to the cause of missions, but it is equally true that the universities gave great *leaders* to the cause. One thinks of the leadership of Luther Wishard or Robert

Speer of Princeton, or Tracy Pitkin or Bill Borden of Yale. The universities supplied a brilliant constellation of women and men of unequaled gifts, all consecrated to the cause of Christ.

But a single illustration must suffice. Among the delegates at the historic Mt. Hermon conference was a junior from Cornell. He too was among the 100 who signed their names to Wilder's pledge. It was clear that he was "willing and desirous to become a foreign missionary." But it also became clear that John Mott—for that was the junior's name—was one of the most gifted men of his generation.

Charles Ober, who had organized Moody's Summer Conference, had been watching the young Mott. It did not escape Ober's notice that when Mott returned to Cornell and assumed the presidency of the Christian Association, its membership rapidly jumped from about 100 to 330 out of a total of 800 at the university! Ober was convinced that this sort of leadership ability must be used on a national scale. He proposed that Mott *not* go as a foreign missionary, despite the pledge, but to stay and instigate and organize the whole process of getting more to the field.

Christian Associations existed on only 300 of the 1,200 colleges in the U.S. and Canada. If collegiate fellowships like the one Mott had forged at Cornell could be established and mobilized across North America, the impact for the gospel could be incalculable.

Mott took up Ober's challenge for a one-year trial and discovered what many suspected: God had given him a singular gift for leadership and organization. As one who knew Mott aptly observed, "If he faced a church or a state, a mob or a world, he organized it."[30] First Mott took the fervid rush of students volunteering to evangelize the world and turned it into a movement. It was like harnessing a gusher! Under his leadership from 1888 to 1920, 16,000 student volunteers were sent. And by 1940, 18,000 volunteers had reached foreign fields.[31] Little wonder it was said in his time, "More than any other, [John R. Mott] was used of God to draw together and organize the Christian forces of our generation."[32]

If the university can supply the cause of the gospel with leaders like Mott—and it has—then the university is surely a principal place we will want to be recruiting with all our might for the sake of reaching the world for Christ. Let us not leave the great leaders to merely build Microsoft or Goldman Sachs, let us call them to build the kingdom.

THE UNIVERSITY'S CENTRAL ROLE

This is, alas, a poor place to leave off our tour of some of the historical territory. Present constraints prevent telling the story of the emergence of InterVarsity Christian Fellowship out of the loins of Simeon's Cambridge[33] or its influence upon a veteran missionary returning from India, Doc Fullerton, who was prompted to establish at Princeton a vital missionary-orientated student fellowship which supplied some of the early staff for Dr. Bright's fledgling Campus Crusade in its early years. This tale of God's wonderful providence among universities must be saved for a sequel. In our present account, we have traversed the centuries in a rather erratic cadence, tarrying only briefly over some scattered episodes in a long heritage of the university's strategic role in reaching the world. Perhaps it would be helpful, in concluding, to draw together the collage of anecdotes into some thematic strands. How has the university been so critical in fulfilling Christ's Great Commission?

By its offering of *students*: The university years often represent a moment in life where zeal meets opportunity. Thus, it has afforded a great pool of laborers to go out into the harvest.

By its gift of *leaders:* Among this pool are a high proportion of leaders. The university has typically supplied the officer corps for the army of laborers.

By its formation of *influencers:* The universities produce the influencers of society—the women and men who sit in the cultural cockpit. Culture goes where they steer it. This is so across the board from politics and law to media and entertainment. If we wish to effectively influence the influencers, we must be at the university.

By its concern with *ideas:* It is at the university that the perennial questions are posed and pondered. What is true? Good? Just? Who are we? Where do we come from? Where are we going? How should we then live? If the gospel has no voice which credibly and winsomely engages these questions precisely where they are most decisively engaged, they will inevitably be answered without any reference to Christ. And the answers the university gives are pervasively influential.

By its wealth of *scholars:* Those typically most equipped to engage ideas are scholars and thinkers. And they are most commonly found and nurtured in the university. We must harvest such scholars for our cause and encourage them in it, for great thinkers and apologists are required by each generation in the task of commending the gospel with insight and imagination. If we neglect their cultivation, we imperil our task.

By its abundance of *internationals:* The typical university is like Jerusalem at Pentecost, full of "Parthians, Medes, Elamites, Mesopotamians, Cappodocians..." We are greatly helped in reaching the world when the world comes to us, then returns home. This happens all the time at the university.

These are among the reasons why the universities are so critical—perhaps uniquely critical—for fulfilling our Christian commission.

Since the university is so critical, what have been some of the principal features of effective university ministry over the centuries? Does our story suggest anything that might inform our present efforts and exploits? I think it does.

First, our account impresses us with the value of *influential insiders*. The university, it seems, is most susceptible to impact by those who are part of her community. There is a natural suspicion of those who come from the outside and seek to exert influence. Accordingly, becoming an insider is a definite need. The cost may be high, but the payoff is substantial—being recognized as a legitimate presence, someone who belongs. Much of the ministries of several of our subjects were made possible, or at least augmented, by being insiders: Tholuck as faculty, Simeon as fellow, Chaderton as master.

We are also struck by the fruitfulness of *longevity* in campus ministry. Partially because becoming a true insider may be a lengthy process, one may not enter a season of harvest for some time. Simeon felt he had made no inroads for ten years! But from then on, influence seemed to be compounded year after year—for another 44 years. It was his latter decades that were his true harvest years. Thankfully, he did not miss out on them by restlessness or weariness after a mere decade.

Conspicuous also is a pattern of *genuine engagement* with the thought of the university—fully entering into the field of discourse; taking seriously the academic world; respectfully listening and thoughtfully challenging. One thinks of the noble pattern that marked Clement and Origen, men who did not ignore or minimize the obstacles to faith in their hearers, who knew every rock and rapid that littered the course toward Christianity for the pagan, and who could act as skilled and sympathetic pilots. Neither can one imagine Tholuck's impact apart from his hard-won capacity to give solid answers to the substantial questions of his day. That he lived to see rationalism replaced by gospel conviction in both faculty and student body was in no small measure due to his own willingness to enter the intellectual arena and prevail.

Finally, I cannot help but feel on the part of these ministers, a *loving affirmation* of the university. Its presence is profound. I mean "love of the university" not in any idolatrous way, but in the sense of genuinely affirming the life and labors of the university and participating in them with joy and thankfulness. This as opposed to a purely instrumentalist attitude which values the university only for how it might forward world missions. This loving affirmation surfaces in a relation to the academy. It is not simply a prophetic posture of speaking truth but also involves a priestly posture of loving service. For example, Simeon offered to help keep the college financial books. They had a need, and he had a knack for it. I think this ethos is a vital part of effective university labors. It is telling that when Cambridge was to receive a royal visitation, the university heads invited Simeon to join them as hosts for the grand occasion. They knew he loved the university, and the university loved him back.

We have shown what has *marked* some of the great university ministers, but what has *made* them what they were? Doubtless many things (principally among them things of the Spirit), but one of the formative factors has been the university itself. These great ambassadors for Christ to the academy were in no small measure shaped and sharpened by the very universities they labored to reach.

Why is the university so significant? It helps to form and fashion the very ambassadors required to effectively reach it.

May God once again raise up, from the university and for her, a Simeon, a Tholuck, a Mott in our generation. Reader, pray for the university.

NOTES

1. Clement's writings contain references to more than 400 different pagan authors, and not typically in an undigested superficial form. Origen's capacity for intellectual output was staggering. He is easily among the most prolific writers of all time. Jerome and Eusebius estimate his productions at 2,000; Epiphanius, though implausibly, asserts 6,000! Little wonder he was soon given the sobriquet "Adamantios," man of steel. We are told Origen was able to keep seven stenographers going at full tilt, often dictating different compositions simultaneously! Among his works, the "Hexapla"—six parallel columns of comparative texts of the Old Testament—was a literary labor of 28 years and has been called "the greatest textual enterprise of ancient times." It covered fifty great rolls of parchment and was probably never copied in full. But Origen was by no means always at his desk. He was supremely an evangelist. His debating prowess took him to Athens where he took on the highest caliber of opponents; his fame brought invitations to speak before royalty.
2. Charles Bigg, *The Christian Platonists of Alexandria* (Oxford: Oxford University Press, 1886), 43.
3. This ambition was spawned in an inn where Dominic stopped for the night. But he never got to bed, for the innkeeper, it turned out, had recently fallen away from the faith, so Dominic stayed up all night seeking to win him back for Christ—which he

did. He emerged from the experience, no doubt sleepy, but with the conviction that more were needed who could preach the gospel.

4. The Constitutions of Dominic's order permit that any preacher in training may stay up the entire night for the purpose of study if so inclined, a habit most obviously honed during university days.
5. It is worth observing that the Reformation itself originated in a scholar's—a university professor's—insight into the meaning of the Scripture. How, fretted Luther, in no small agony, could the gospel be "good news" at all if, as Romans tells us, it is a revelation of the righteousness of God? Surely a righteous and just God can mean only wrath and judgement for a sinner whose own righteousness even on a good day is partial and paltry. But Luther did not give up pondering this page of Paul until a light dawned and he grasped that the ominous phrase "righteousness of God" in fact meant a righteousness *from* God—one that God Himself supplied as a gift. At that moment, the terror of the Law turned to the sweetest of gospels. As Luther himself put it, "With this opened the very doors of paradise."
6. Gerhard Ebeling, *Luther: An Introduction to His Theology* (Philadelphia: Fortress Press, 1970), 17.
7. E. G. Rupp, *Studies in the Making of the English Protestant Tradition* (Cambridge: Cambridge University Press, 1949), 15.
8. He had copied out the entire Pauline Epistles by hand and memorized them.
9. Cited in Benjamin Brook, *The Lives of the Puritans* vol. 2 (London: James Black, 1813), 446 fn. [emphasis his].
10. Cf. Winthrop Hudson, *The Cambridge Connection and the Elizabethan Settlement of 1559* (Durham, NC: Duke University Press), 1980.
11. Cotton Mather, *Magnalia Christi Americana* vol. 2 (Hartford, CT: Silas Andrus & Son, 1852), 8.
12. The College Laws announced the pole star of the endeavor: "Let every student be plainly instructed and earnestly pressed to consider well the main end of his life and studies is to know God and Jesus Christ which is eternal life, John 17:3, and therefore to lay Christ in the bottom, as the only foundation of all sound knowledge and learning."
13. Mather, 8.
14. Or as the charter states: "the education and instruction of Indian Youth . . . and Christianizing Children of Pagans."
15. Interestingly, Wheelock's strategy included native American women who also received instruction and accompanied male graduates back to their people.
16. Brook, vol. 3, 449 [emphasis mine].
17. The Yale College Rules specified: "Every student shall consider ye main end of his duty to wit, to know God in Jesus Christ and answerably to lead a godly sober life."
18. I suppose one might as well have chosen that vocation, for whether one was a candidate for ministry or not, the curriculum was the same for all: Greek New Testament, Hebrew Psalter, Westminster Catechism in Latin, and William Aims's *Marrow of Theology!*
19. One wonders if the earliest recorded alumni bequest to Yale reflected the desire to

buttress it against theological wobbliness and stave off the onset of tergiversation, for Charles J. Smith, class of 1757, directed in his will that "six Spanish milled dollars" be paid yearly to support three annual lectures before the student body upon: "The Nature and Necessity of Regeneration," "The Nature and Necessity of Justification by Faith Alone," and "The Dignity, Utility, Greatness and Importance of the Gospel Ministry." I have diligently watched for these lectures, but fear they have alas been discontinued.

20. My conjecture, of course, is that the transfer was impelled by a sound intuition as to the superiority of a Princeton education.
21. The young Nicholas Ludwig von Zinzendorf, the later leader of the mission-minded Moravian Brethren, got his start at Halle. From the age of ten, he attended the Paedagogium conducted by Francke, and it was there that he formed, with five other students, the "Order of the Grain of Mustard Seed," a spiritual secret society. Among the aims of the society was that of carrying the gospel of Christ across the seas to those who had never heard. Zinzendorf never lost sight of this purpose, which was crystallized at Halle. The Moravian missionary movement was the fruit of that mustard seed.
22. This point might have been made by any number of figures. One thinks of the Yale scholar Harlan Page Beach (1854–1933) whose work as a statistician and compiler of atlases of foreign missions rendered a huge contribution to the cause. Beach made it his ambition to build a missions library and soon had made the Day Missions Collection at Yale certainly the largest in America, probably in the world. Its service in the cause of Christian missions continues to be incalculable. It certainly afforded Harlan's successor as librarian, Kenneth Scott Latourette, ample material from which to fashion his monumental seven-volume *History of the Expansion of Christianity*, which inspired so many to enter the vanguard of bringing the gospel of Christ to the world. It was, in turn, K. S. Latourette who prompted J. Edwin Orr to take up the scholarly study of the role of revivals in forwarding missions. How much has Orr turned the archival work of his three doctorates to the inspiration of Campus Crusaders! Perhaps I should reiterate: Thank God for scholars and the universities that nurture them!
23. By the time he was 12 years old, he had already devoured some 2,000! In fact, from 14 he kept a diary which for secrecy sake he inscribed in numerous foreign languages typically switching in mid-sentence from among English, French, Arabic, Polish, Hebrew, Latin, Greek, Dutch, etc. Occasionally, his native German appears, but invariably in Greek or Hebrew characters!
24. Abner Brown, *Recollections of C. Simeon's Conversation Parties* (London: Hamilton, Adams, & Co., 1863), 176.
25. Charles Simeon and Jean Claude, *Horae Homileticae* (London: Holdsworth and Ball, 1833), Sermon #359.
26. Chancel, South Wall, Holy Trinity Cambridge.
27. Among Simeon's most prized possessions was a portrait of one Abdool Messeh—Henry Martyn's first and only convert. The portrait was a gift of Messeh inscribed "to C. Simeon, my spiritual grandfather."
28. Whenever serious illness prevented Simeon from holding forth at these gatherings,

he would call on some of the more mature disciples to field the questions, "no trifle," as one of them later remembered. "Simeon and water" was the good-humored verdict pronounced by those present, and this came to be the name by which this expedient was subsequently known.

29. Cited in Timothy Wallstrom, *The Creation of a Student Movement to Evangelize the World* (Pasadena, CA: William Carey International University Press, 1980), 9.
30. Sherwood Eddy, cited in Jon Hinkson, "Ivy Profiles: John R. Mott," unpublished mss. delivered at Ivy Leadership Conference, November 5, 1998.
31. As to campus Christian fellowships, Mott soon created a vital organ of 778 student associations comprising some 75,000 members, with 38,000 in Bible studies and active in evangelism! From America, he turned to organize Christian students around the world. Soon Mott had established a network of more than 3,000 University Christian Fellowships, comprising more than 300,000 students spread over more than forty countries representing every continent of the world.
32. Sherwood Eddy, cited in Jon Hinkson, "Ivy Profiles: John R. Mott," unpublished mss. delivered at Ivy Leadership Conference, November 5, 1998.
33. For this inspiring tale, read Oliver Barclay's *Whatever Happened to the Jesus Lane Lot?* (Leicester, Eng.: InterVarsity Press, 1977).

CHAPTER 23

Being an Arm of the Church

DR. EDWARD G. MURRAY

On Staff since 1973

Teaching Fellow of the Institute for Biblical and Theological Studies

Director of Moldovan Ministries, Eastern Europe and Russia

WITH DAN CLEMENT

On Staff since 1981

Christian Leadership Ministries

We would like to begin this study by expressing our deepest gratitude to Campus Crusade for Christ and its staff members for being God's instrument in bringing us to salvation and being the vehicle that has allowed us to serve Christ for more than fifty years of combined service, most of that working in the area of Eastern Europe. We have had at every step of the way encouragement to trust Christ, help in discovering the gifts God has given us, and encouragement to use those gifts. Bill Bright's vision of winning, building, and sending has found fulfillment in our lives for which we will literally be eternally grateful. What is reflected here has been, however, carefully considered and is not simply sentimental attachment to an organization. It has been forged in the crucible of helping to reach the world for Christ as an evangelistic arm of the church in the Eastern European part of the world.

Campus Crusade for Christ has made an enormous contribution to the cause of world missions in the latter half of the twentieth century and is poised to continue that contribution on an even greater scale in the twenty-first century. While many factors have made that contribution possible, not the least of which is the sovereign choice of God in raising up this ministry, it is not an unworthy task to consider some of the theological and philosophical foundations that have allowed God to work through this movement in such a fruitful way.

Certainly, the Spirit of God has the freedom to move as He wills; nevertheless, distinctives such as initiative evangelism, transferable training, a strong emphasis on life in the Spirit, and spiritual breathing have played significant roles. One often-overlooked aspect, however, which we believe has been critical to the impact of Campus Crusade for Christ, has been Dr. Bright's focus on being "an evangelistic arm of the church." Organizations and ministries like Campus Crusade for Christ are often referred to as "para-church" organizations. In this chapter, we would like to question the concept and designation of "para-church" and examine from the analogy of the Body of Christ prevalent in the New Testament the validity of the existence of Campus Crusade for Christ as an "arm" of the church. First, we will look at this from a theological perspective and then examine more closely philosophical and historical precedents for God's work done in this way.

BIBLICAL CONSIDERATIONS

In looking ahead at what would take place after His departure from this earth, Jesus Christ introduces something unique. In Matthew 16:18, Christ, in reply to the discussion about His identity and the forthright answer from Peter that He is the Christ, the Son of the living God, affirms what Peter says and then offers a glimpse of the implications that confession would ultimately stand for: "...and on this rock I will build my *church*"—for the disciples, this was certainly a new word in this context. They were familiar with the synagogue, the place of meeting for the people of God, and they knew the temple, the central focus of national religion. They were the people of Israel, the people of God, but this strange word in this context anticipates something new, something unique.

The Greek word *ecclesia*, usually translated "church" in the New Testament, is made up of two root words: *ek*, "out" and *kaleo*, "to call." The word was used in secular Greek culture before it was given its specialized meaning by the writers of the New Testament when they referred to the body of people who had trusted Christ for salvation and who followed Him. In the centuries before Christ, Alexander the Great spread the Greek language and culture throughout Europe and the Middle East. Among the Greeks and in their city-states, some citizens had special rights not afforded non-citizens.[1] At times, important news *for citizens* needed to be communicated. A messenger would enter a city and convene the *ecclesia*, calling out a gathering in the city center. Those to whom the message was applicable, in this case the citizenry, would assemble *out from among* those who had no right or interest to be in the assembly.[2]

The Gospels record just two occasions when Jesus spoke of the *ecclesia*. In Matthew 16:18, Jesus said that He would build *His ecclesia*—and one must wonder what picture came to mind for His disciples. What would Jesus' *ecclesia* be like? What would be the defining parameters of this special group of people? The second use comes in Matthew 18:17 where Jesus speaks of a sinning brother or sister and how they are to be treated in the context of the special group called the *ecclesia*. What kind of new paradigm was Jesus promoting?

The rest of the New Testament develops and expands the concept of the Christian *ecclesia*. In the New Testament, *ecclesia* takes on the specialized meaning of "believers in Christ among an unbelieving world." These *people* become the "church" of God.[3] The church is *people*. It is a functioning body of people called for the purpose of reflecting God's character and making His plan of salvation known to the world. Wherever the people of God are gathered together to honor God in their lives by doing the will of God, the church becomes present in one form or another.

The New Testament refers to the Christian *ecclesia* in two ways: universally and locally. The universal church—in other words, the universal gathering of believers in Christ called out from the world—includes all who ever have or ever will believe in Christ in all places. In Paul's letter to the Ephesians, which is so often used to describe local church life, every reference to the *ecclesia* in the letter refers to the universal church, the entire body of believers who are held secure in the hand of God by His magnificent salvation. In his seminal work on the church, Earl Radmacher gives this perspective on Paul's concept of the universal church:

> The doctrine of the universal church arises out of an inductive study and systemization of the metaphorical usages of *ecclesia* in the New Testament. When the Apostle Paul comes to the metaphorical use of the *ecclesia* (predominantly in Ephesians and Colossians), he conceives of an entire world of individual Christians immediately related to Christ apart from local *ecclesiae*, and he terms them simply the (only) *ecclesia*. Thus, the concept of the physical assembly gives way to the spiritual assembly.[4]

Given the universal expression of the Body of Christ, how does the local church express itself and how should we define it? This proves to be a much more difficult question than it might seem. The expressions of church in our culture are many and changing with the rise of new and different forms of church for the modern world. In reality, the New Testament speaks of the local gathering of believers with the word *ecclesia* in 90 of the

114 occurrences of the word. Nevertheless, a clear picture of what that church looks like eludes even the astute reader. It appears first to be related to a local area. The churches of cities and regions are addressed (e.g., "To the church of the Thessalonians," "To the church of God in Corinth," or "To the churches in Galatia"[5]). John is instructed to write to the seven churches, but we are told very little about their structure and organization. Paul refers to things he teaches in every church everywhere.[6] In other words, the local gathering of believers in Christ called out from the world can refer to an entity of true believers in Christ, irrespective of size or organization in a geographical place, who are bound together by the awareness that their redemption in Christ is their sole uniting factor. From a human perspective, it is possible that the local gathering may also include some nonbelievers, "tares among the wheat" in Jesus' words,[7] but the focus of the group is Christ and promoting God's kingdom in the world.

Theologians differ somewhat concerning what is necessary to qualify as a local church. Perhaps it can be articulated most basically in the following way: A group of believers constitutes a local church when it chooses to be "a local expression of the body of Jesus Christ, with all its privileges and responsibilities." At a minimum, these "privileges and responsibilities" include evangelism, teaching for edification, worship, fellowship, social concern, and the ordinances of baptism and the Lord's Supper; but even these can transcend the boundaries of a *local* group of believers.

This definition focuses on the *function* of the church and does not say anything about the *form* in which these should be carried out. The New Testament consistently focuses upon the *functions* that believers are to fulfill and not the *forms* through which that function is to be fulfilled.[8]

The church of the New Testament was a dynamic, growing, and changing organism with apparently a minimal, adapting organization. It was truly "the body of Christ."[9] In the beginning of the New Testamental period, the local gathering of believers in Christ called out from the world was indistinguishable from Judaism. All the believers in Christ were Jewish. Those who believed that Jesus fulfilled the prophecies about the Messiah met in the Jewish Temple in Jerusalem; but they also met from house to house, both of which were Jewish social customs.[10]

But as the church expanded and grew, it also added new and different forms to respond to new challenges. Acts 6:1–7 relates the incident of the widows of Hellenistic Jewish background being neglected in the serving of their food to the advantage of the native Hebrew widows. The twelve disciples were summoned and a decision was made to implement a new way of handling this problem. Special servants were designated to fulfill this responsibility and ensure that it be done properly. It was not enough that these men simply be servants, but they must also be spiritually capable people because, as we shall see later, they themselves directed the work. The result is recorded in verse 7: "The word of God kept on spreading; and the number of the disciples continued to increase greatly in Jerusalem, and a great many of the priests were becoming obedient to the faith" (NASB).

We see illustrated here an issue that is critical to our discussion: the church freely adapted its *forms* as necessary to fulfill its necessary *functions.* The apostles were unable to fulfill their necessary *function* of assuring daily teaching both in the temple and from house to house (Acts 5:42) and at the same time carry out the *function* of meeting the needs of the widows and needy of the new group of believers. Therefore, the *form* of designated table-servers (deacons) was developed. *Organizational structures* were created *in response to needs.* This new organizational form, growing out of need, was, nevertheless and without question, considered to be a part of the church, not something auxiliary to it. It was not something that existed alongside of the church (para-church), but something that grew out of the need of the church that was an integral part of the functioning of the body of believers that made up the church.

Looking at one of the most significant passages on the function of the local church in the New Testament, in Ephesians 4 we discover that the concept of serving is germane to the nature of the church. The New Testament assumes that those who make up the church will also be those who serve in various capacities to help proclaim and build the kingdom of God. In other words, and most significantly, *all* believers are called upon to *serve:*

> And He gave *some* as apostles, and *some* as prophets, and *some* as evangelists, and *some* as pastors and teachers, *for the equipping of the saints* for the *work of service* [deacon-ing], to the building up of the *body* of Christ; until we *all* attain to the unity of the faith, and of the knowledge of the Son of God, to a mature man, to the measure of the stature which belongs to the fullness of Christ. As a result, *we* are no longer to be children, tossed here and there by waves and carried about by every wind of doctrine, by the trickery of men, by craftiness in deceitful scheming; but speaking the truth in love, *we* are to grow up in all aspects into Him who is the head, even Christ, from whom the *whole body*, being fitted and held together by what *every* joint supplies, according to the proper working of *each individual part*, causes the growth of the *body* for the building up of itself in love (Ephesians 4:11–16, NASB, emphasis added).

Some Christians have an ongoing, specific role of service (evangelist, pastor-teacher, etc.), but *all* Christians are called to serve believers and non-believers, thus extending the kingdom of God (the reign and rule of God) on earth and participating in the fulfillment of what Jesus prays in His model prayer, "Thy kingdom come, Thy will be done" (Matthew 6:10, NASB). This service could take on as many different forms as there were gifts and avenues of expression for those gifts. In one place, it was serving tables; in another, making clothes; in another, offering hospitality; in another, extending mercy and grace to the rejected of society; in another, reaching out to leaders of the day; etc. All that was done was considered an expression of the church of Christ. It was truly the church at work to touch a needy world with the forgiveness of Christ.[11]

The usage of the English word "church" serves as a simple and clear example of what has happened, however, in our current understanding of church. The word "church" is derived from the Greek word for Lord (*Kyrios* or in its possessive form, *Kyriakos*, meaning "those who belong to the Lord"), a fitting, accurate, and biblical picture of how the church/*ecclesia* was understood for much of the first three centuries of the church's existence. First, whoever belonged to the family of faith in Christ was a part of the "church/ecclesia," but wherever those who belonged to the Lord gathered to worship and serve Him according to His Word, the church was present. It reflected something that was active and dynamic rather than static. However, in the third and fourth centuries, as Christians began to gather in meeting places that were more permanent and exclusively used for worship purposes, the meaning of the word shifted *from those who belong to the Lord to the place where those who belong to the Lord meet.* As Christianity became the religion of the Roman Empire, the building became more prominent as the local expression of "church." As Christianity was spread to the English-speaking world, this became the common usage. So today, in the English language, we speak of "going to church." In the New Testament, however, the local *ecclesia* of Christ was never used to describe a building or place, but rather people in a geographical area bound together in their life with and service for Christ. In essence, we have redefined the biblical word into something that is foreign to the biblical concept of church. This, we will see, plays a significant role in defining movements and organizations involved in the service of Christ today.

PHILOSOPHICAL CONSIDERATIONS

So, how does an organization like Campus Crusade for Christ and the modern expression of the church of Christ fit into the New Testament pattern? Does it fit? Is Campus Crusade for Christ an expression of the church of Christ, an extension of the church of Christ, or something other than and parallel to the church of Christ (para-church)? The most common term used today for movements like Campus Crusade for Christ is "para-church." The question is, however: Is this a proper description of what this movement and others are, or have we invented something that doesn't really exist because we have started from a presupposition of definition that was faulty in the first place? We believe that our problem with defining movements and organizations like Campus Crusade for Christ stem from the fact that we have defined too narrowly what the church of Jesus Christ actually is and how it expresses itself. Where has this term "para-church" developed, and how is it understood?

The term "para-church" was coined primarily to describe the phenomena of the last half of the twentieth century. After World War II, due to several factors beyond the scope of this discussion, interdenominational groups and mission organizations began to proliferate at a rate unknown in previous church history. The local church retained its traditional *form*, which had changed very little since the days of the Reformation. Most people viewed the church primarily as a place to meet rather than the dynamic functioning of a body of believers in Christ. For most people, the local church meant a meeting on Sunday morning for worship, another on Sunday evening for what was perhaps called an evangelism service, and on Wednesday evening for a Bible study/prayer meeting, which, in many places, retained much of the same form as the Sunday meetings. The church was delineated by the *form* it then manifested rather than by the *functions* it was biblically mandated to fulfill, which is, as we have seen, the biblical definition of the church. When analysts observed this phenomenon, the term "para-church" (literally, "beside the church") was coined to describe certain ministry manifestations which did not fit easily into the predominant understanding of the local church. Something that was clearly related to the church was labeled "para-church" because it did not have the same *form*.

A similar use of the prefix "para" occurs in other domains and may help us to understand the issue more clearly. A "paramedic" is a person who works in a health field in an auxiliary capacity to a physician. The concept of "physician" is the more basic of the two, and therefore a paramedic is defined after one has established specifically what is a "medic." If one incorrectly defines "medic," it is impossible to correctly define "paramedic."

A function that is essential to the definition of the church cannot, however, be considered "auxiliary." Yet the so-called "para-church" became and is often considered to be auxiliary to or alongside of the church. However, according to the New Testament, what Stephen and the other six did in Acts 6 was an *essential* ministry of the church. When that ministry grows larger than one local fellowship, it does not cease to be a ministry of *the* church, it simply ceases to be the ministry of *just one* local church. The ministry to the widows was not "para-church," but rather the broader church of Jerusalem relating to the needs of the people.

What should we call something clearly related to the purpose of the church but that does not fulfill *all* of its "privileges and responsibilities"? What designation seems most proper for a structured and organized group of people committed to promoting the kingdom of God, but that still may not do all of the things we see being done in the context of one local church? Should it be considered a church even though it does not fulfill all the functions of the church, such as baptism and the Lord's Supper? What should we call Campus Crusade for Christ or other similar organizations?

To answer this question, notice that the New Testament term *ecclesia* was used to describe a variety of configurations of gatherings of believers.

- It can refer to the church in a house (Romans 16:5).
- It can refer to the church in a city (1 Corinthians 1:2).
- It can refer to the church in a region (Acts 9:31; 1 Corinthians 15:9).

When the New Testament used the sense of a "church in one home," it is easy to imagine how the organizational structure might have looked. There would have been some gifted, competent leaders perhaps even appointed by an apostle, but not necessarily so, who gave spiritual direction to the believers, building them up in their faith so that all were able to serve the needs (physical, emotional, and spiritual) of the believers and nonbelievers in their area. There were some believers in their fellowship who had regular ongoing roles of service, and therefore were named "deacons" for a specific task.

But when the New Testament referred to the church of a whole city or a region, it becomes more difficult for us to imagine their organizational structure. Obviously, the churches of a city or region had some interrelatedness or else a letter could not have been sent to them, instructing them how to relate to one another. But what did the organizational structure (form) for leadership or service look like for a whole city or region?

Let us consider the situation in the city of Jerusalem. There were perhaps 20,000 believers[12] with more being added every day. There was a significant problem of widows not getting fed. Seven servants from the "church of Jerusalem" were chosen to feed them. Suppose that each of those seven were from different household churches. What were the chances that all the widows were from just *those* seven household churches? It is unreasonable to conclude that all the widows came from the same households as the deacons; therefore we conclude that the seven deacons served many widows throughout the city of Jerusalem. This does not fit our current model of church organizational structure. Nowadays, deacons serve only their own local group. But *those* deacons served as a ministry to "the church," not just in the midst of their specific congregation, but also to the entire Body of Christ in the city.

What was the nature of this ministry to the widows? Let us return to Acts 6:1–4 for some key insights:

1. A legitimate unmet need (serving widows) became the mandate for this work of service (verse 1).
2. The apostles appreciated the importance of that need, but saw it as a calling distinct from their own, which was spiritual leadership in the church (verse 2).
3. There was no struggle for authority, and there was no great problem of structure and form. They observed a specific need and they organized themselves to meet it (verses 3 and 4).
4. This organized group did not do everything the church did—it was a *ministry* of "the church."

Let us consider an analogy from today's world that can shed light on this issue. Suppose that a Christian feels a burden for unwed mothers. The elders in his or her church agree with the need but have little time for the actual ministry. So the Christian begins to help the mothers with food, clothing, shelter, and education. Word spreads about these services and more and more women in difficult situations show up at his or her doorstep. A neighbor who attends the same local church begins to help. He or she is chosen to help on the basis of burden, but also on spiritual qualification. Together, the two believers minister to unwed mothers. Several Christian friends contribute financially to help cover expenses. At this point, this service would be considered a grassroots ministry of *one particular* local church.

Now, suppose that still more unwed mothers hear about this assistance and come for help. Five more Christians from several different local churches in the city begin to help with this ministry. As even more unwed mothers ask for help, this loosely organized band of Christians draft some policies to manage their limited resources and growing responsibilities for greater efficiency and solicit the services of a board of godly, mature believers to give them wisdom and advice for the broader ministry. At this point, this service clearly no longer qualifies as a ministry of one local church as we typically define it today.

According to the contemporary definition, this ministry would be called a "para-church" organization. They're not from one local church. They have organized their action around one limited need in their community and do not fulfill all the functions of the church. But in reality, the work being done is a service extension of the church of the city in which it takes place and not something different from the church.

Now let's expand once more to an even larger ministry—Campus Crusade for Christ. By its own definition, it is an interdenominational ministry of the church of Christ with the goal of helping to spread the gospel to all the nations, winning people for Christ, building them in their faith, and sending them to reach people around them even to the ends of the world. As with the *diaconia*, the spiritual qualifications to join this movement are high. The human resources department employs a battery of tests and references are gathered. Veteran staff interview every candidate about personal and theological matters. Every staff member is expected to be active and involved in a broader ministry where he or she lives through a local body of believers. Every effort is made to put people in positions that are commensurate with their spiritual maturity and with their gifting and abilities. Through its School of Leadership, Campus Crusade also provides ongoing theological education of high caliber for its staff. In other words, very important functions of the church are carried out to assure that God's work is done properly.

My own (Edward) experience is an illustration of this. As a young freshman at Northwestern University far away from my home and traditional religious upbringing, I had decided that religion was a thing of the past for me. My last years of high school had been increasingly characterized by a lack of purpose in my life, and the church I attended regularly and in which I was very involved provided me with no clear answers. I slowly came to the conclusion that church was irrelevant to the modern world. I wanted to be a nuclear physicist, so there would certainly be no room in my life for some metaphysical idea that had no meaning to my life. I was satisfied to pursue my search without the aid of pastor, Bible, or institutional religion.

My first encounter with the possibility of a relationship with Christ that transcended religion came in my first semester of college. A friend of mine had become a Christian and invited me to a Bible study. I went out of duty and respect for my friend. There I met someone who invited himself to my room the next day to share with me something he had found meaningful in his own life. He had no booklet (they hadn't been printed yet), but took a piece of paper and began writing down the Four Spiritual Laws. I was familiar with most of what he said, but when he told of the possibility of a personal relationship with God through Christ, I realized that I knew nothing about what he was talking about, and I knew I wasn't interested; at least, not yet.

Some months went by and my search for meaning and purpose in life in science and my studies began to turn sour on me. As I watched my colleagues and my professors, I realized that most of them knew nothing about a meaningful and abundant life. They had everything I wanted, but many of them still lacked a true reason for living. My search became more intense. In the spring of my freshman year, I heard a knock at my dormitory door. It was a friend from across the hall with another man who introduced himself, and we made an appointment.[13] He returned and began sharing with me the same thing I had heard some months before. I searched in my desk drawer and found the piece of paper I had kept from the earlier conversation and showed it to him. He took the paper and proceeded to share the gospel with me using the Four Spiritual Laws that someone else had written. At the end of his presentation, my heart was questioning. He asked if there was any reason why I wouldn't want to trust Christ right now. I thought of a few smoke screens, but he realized I was seriously searching and together we considered God's love again. He read John 3:16 with me and then encouraged me after he left to pray a simple prayer of faith and trust Christ with my life.

I did just that... but nothing happened. I saw nothing, felt nothing, heard nothing; another religious fix that did not take. Just as I had suspected, irrelevant! But this man came back to visit me two days later. He mentioned something about a movement on campus called Campus Crusade for Christ, but that was in the background. He asked me if I had taken that step of faith. I said I had tried, but nothing had happened. He opened his New Testament and had me read John 3:16. He asked me if Christ would ever lie to me, and I knew somehow that He never would. He turned to 1 John 5:11–13, and we read together of the assurance we could have based on the Word of God and not on feelings or experience. As we discussed the trustworthiness of God, a calm assurance came over me based upon God's promise that I had indeed become a child of God and that God was now and would always be my Father in heaven. That sense of assurance I have never doubted. The tracks were laid early in my Christian experience for confidence in God's Word and its relevance for me.

That person was a staff member of Campus Crusade for Christ, and he did his job well. He came back every week, and we read together, drawing me into the faith. At his invitation, I attended a weekend conference and saw several hundred students excited about their faith and desiring to share it. I became more interested and began attending weekly meetings and then signed up for a leadership-training course to learn how to share my faith. Within two months of having trusted Christ for my own salvation, I was leading friends and colleagues around me to Christ. Bible studies grew and others became involved. My roommate trusted Christ along with several good friends. That was only the beginning of a life that I have never regretted and that has taken me around the world in serving Christ.

As my involvement grew, I became aware of my need for deeper biblical training. Our local staff worker suggested enrolling in what was then called the Institute of Biblical Studies (IBS): a three-year program for four weeks every summer, offering twelve basic courses for doing Christian ministry. For a total of twelve weeks spread over three years, I was exposed to some of the most significant teachers in the evangelical world and their teaching has shaped my life since. I was highly motivated, and not an hour was wasted as we studied late into the night to learn how we could take God's Word and use it effectively in winning, building, and sending people on our campuses. Although I went on to graduate from a four-year Master's of Theology program, I have always considered that initial IBS training the most significant twelve weeks ever spent in theological training.

I had a group of friends "closer than a brother" with whom I shared my burdens and concerns. We prayed together and saw God answer. We discussed each other's gifts and encouraged each other in love and good works. We creatively dreamed together about what we wanted God to see happen.

My story is a typical Campus Crusade for Christ story. I was reached because someone came to me; someone took the initiative when I had given up all desire and hope. The traditional church *form* could never have reached me, but I was reached by someone functioning in the name of Christ for the sake of His church and drawn into the kingdom. I can only praise God for the church, a living *organism*, which, in response to the needs of the culture, spawned a *new form* of outreach suited to my culture and time. Thousands like me have been reached by this movement that has dared to be aggressive and creative about the way the church should do business of reaching the lost for Christ. An *evangelistic arm* of the church reached out and took me in when the normal expressions could never have done so.

A HISTORICAL PARADIGM

Even before the twentieth century and its proliferation of mission organizations, we find several examples of similar ministries that may help us to gain better perspective. One significant movement that merits our attention is the Renewed Moravian Brethren movement of the eighteenth century under the leadership of Count Nicholas Ludwig von Zinzendorf.[14]

The history of the Moravian Brethren reaches back to the early part of the fifteenth century when John Huss, a professor of theology at the University of Prague in Moravia (the modern Czech Republic) began teaching and preaching that salvation was to be found by faith and that God's Word was the sole and ultimate authority upon which faith should rest. His views came into direct conflict with the Roman Catholic Church, of which he was a representative, and in 1415 he was condemned by a church council in Constance, Germany, and burned at the stake as a heretic. The blood of this martyr for the faith became the nourishment for a movement that swept across the land, and by the end of the century, the Moravian Brethren had established themselves as a major participant in the spiritual life of Moravia. In the sixteenth and seventeenth centuries, however, the movement did not fare well at the hands of its persecutors, and at the turn of the eighteenth century, the movement had almost died with only a small remnant of people remaining in northern Moravia.

At the beginning of the eighteenth century, a young German nobleman named Nicholas Ludwig von Zinzendorf, who had devoted his life to Christ and the work of God from an early age, renewed his commitment to Christ and the spreading of His kingdom. He had initiated what was called "the order of the Mustard seed." The members of the small order pledged themselves to remain true to the teachings of Jesus and to conduct themselves accordingly; to love their fellow men; to refrain from worldly things; to seek at all times the welfare of others; to work especially for the conversion of the lost. Each member wore a ring with the inscription in Greek, "No one lives unto himself."[15]

In a similar way, before Campus Crusade for Christ was born, Bill Bright formed, along with others who became lifelong friends in the cause of evangelism, "The Fellowship of the Burning Heart."[16] Both Zinzendorf and Bright were young men of promising influence in their respective worlds, yet both chose to follow Christ with everything they possessed. Zinzendorf gave all of his wealth as a nobleman to the cause of Christ, just as Bill and Vonette Bright have given every ambition and possession to the cause of Christ as expressed in their "contract with God."[17]

Upon hearing of the Moravians and their persecution, Zinzendorf invited them to come to his estate in southeastern Germany and build a colony, offering a new start for the group. Just a few short weeks later in June 1722, a small band of ten people arrived, and the first building was erected on the site that eventually became the center of a worldwide missionary movement. The settlement became known as *Herrnhut* or the "watch of the Lord."

In its initial years, the colony attracted not only persecuted Moravians, but also dissidents who were being persecuted by even the Lutheran Church of which Zinzendorf was a member. Nevertheless, Zinzendorf's great heart and love for Christ and the people of Christ gave him the freedom to accept anyone who truly loved Christ. By 1727, however, this variety of beliefs threatened to destroy the colony with internal dissension over petty doctrinal matters. Zinzendorf became concerned, and what grew out of his personal pastoral work among the people was called "The Brotherly Agreement." This became the basis for what is now called the Renewed Moravian Brethren. But an agreement was not enough. Zinzendorf knew they needed the anointment of the Spirit of God, so that was his earnest prayer. On August 13, 1727, as the group was preparing to worship together, God began to speak to individual hearts, and a time of reconciliation and repentance began that brought healing, forgiveness, and restoration to the small band of people.[18]

In 1731, two of the men of the colony were called to go to the Virgin Islands to tell of the Savior. In 1733, others went to Greenland; in 1734, some to Lapland and Georgia; in 1735, the mission was opened in Surinam; in 1736, in West Africa, and in 1737, in South Africa; in 1738, missionaries went to Estonia and to the Jewish quarter of Amsterdam; in 1739, to Algeria; and in 1740, to Ceylon, Romania, and Constantinople. In 1742, the most effective missionary movement to the American Indian was commenced in what would become Bethlehem, Pennsylvania, as a colony of Moravians settled there. By the time Zinzendorf died in 1760, there were Moravian missionaries on every continent of the world, and by the turn of the century almost 1,000 Moravian missionaries were scattered around the world.[19]

Among many others, three things stand out as parallels of the Moravians and their leader, Count Zinzendorf, and Campus Crusade for Christ and Bill Bright:

1. From the beginning, the work of the Moravians transcended all denominational boundaries. Zinzendorf was a visionary who had a broad faith

that would tolerate many expressions as long as Jesus Christ was the primary focus and love for Him was the main motivation for life. His Moravians were not interested in establishing a certain kind of church, but rather in establishing the church of Christ wherever they went. In the same way, Dr. Bright and Campus Crusade for Christ have maintained since its inception a clear interdenominational stance, serving the entire body of Christ particularly in the realm of evangelism, but also with training and vision for a lost world.

2. Their highest desire was to testify of the saving power of Jesus Christ and to bring others into relationship with him. Zinzendorf called his theology of missions the theology of "First Fruits," and as such he headed the first movement since the second century to emphasize personal and spiritual conversion in contrast to political or national conversion. In this sense, Zinzendorf was the true father of modern missions.[20] They took the initiative to reach out to those whom they desired to reach with a message that was clearly understood. They had no political ambitions such as most missionary endeavors before them had. They did not go in the name of a king or a land. They ventured forth under the banner of Christ and His kingdom. The missionaries would spend the long hours they endured on the boats traveling to their stations in learning language and culture, studying the topography and structure of the peoples and lands to which they were going.

   In comparison, Campus Crusade for Christ has maintained for fifty years a clear focus on the need for the personal salvation on the individual. Training for workers has centered on creative ways of reaching out to a secular and lost world. Campus Crusade international workers are subjected to rigorous "Agape International Training," a three-month program of preparation for cross-cultural service that is now used by several other mission organizations for the training of their workers.

3. For the Moravians, everyone was a participant in the service of proclaiming Christ to the nations. There was no division between the clergy and the layperson. Each was encouraged to discover and use his or her gifts to reach out and help build the kingdom of God. Unique for that day, women were considered equal workers and encouraged to use their gifts in creative ways to spread the gospel. Women were included in the leadership structure of the movement, and their contribution was valued. Leadership was not considered a position from which to wield power, but a gift to be used to empower each member of the movement for the service he or she was to contribute.

In the same way, Campus Crusade has recruited its workers not primarily from the seminaries and Bible colleges of the land, but from the ranks of those converted through the ministry or those who in the course of their professions have been touched with the significance of sharing the gospel with the world around them. Similar to the Moravians, women have found a place of service in the American culture on campuses, in the business world, at the political level reaching others for Christ that, at its inception, was unique and that simply was not found in more formal church settings. As normal as it seems today, it has been a groundbreaking focus for women in ministry. Many people who are truly concerned about doing God's work in this world have often found it difficult to find a place in traditional church forms where their gifts can be properly expressed. Campus Crusade and other similar ministries have been able to offer everyone a place of service to advance God's work. In very creative ways, Campus Crusade has utilized the talents of thousands in music, drama, the arts—even the art of illusion has been used to share the good news of Christ.

4. The highest motivation of the Moravians was their love for Christ and the desire to allow His Spirit to guide them and empower them for service. In his "Method for the Conversion of the Heathen," the last of 25 points states, "The central figure from whom everything derives meaning and the one who is always in our speech is Jesus, the Lamb, the Saviour." Probably no other motivating factor in the life of Bill Bright shines forth more than his love for Christ and his desire to serve Christ because of His great love for humanity. This is an oft-repeated theme at training conferences and is a main thread of several books Bill has authored. Nothing is more important to him than loving and serving his Savior.

Zinzendorf, like Bright, was not a trained theologian. He was an influential man of his day who chose to give up his ambitions and the dreams of his family to serve his Savior. With vigor and vision, he led the movement of the Renewed Moravian Brethren until his death at age 60. He loved Christ above all and was motivated only by the joy of the Spirit of God in bringing others to a knowledge of Christ. Years hence, it may well be said of Bill Bright as it has been said of Zinzendorf:

> Zinzendorf was an incomparable person. His time, his culture and its issues, his noble heritage, but above all, his Lord, seem to have called him to his role. One will not find in Zinzendorf all that is modern. He could not have anticipated all of the modern questions and the issues

> related to them. Yet he responded to a world which was giving birth to our world; his response to his times was a response for God, for his Saviour, in his times...He listened to the sciences and movements of his time, but he also listened to his heart and affirmed that ultimately the issues of life are resolved in relationship to the God of the wounds... His response to his times was mission. This mission encompassed the world, but this mission was God's, not his.[21]

Who would argue that the Moravians and Campus Crusade for Christ were something auxiliary to the church or parallel to it? In the same tradition of the Moravian movement we have examined, it can justly be said that Campus Crusade for Christ is not something auxiliary to the church or parallel to it, but something that is integrally a part of the church of Christ and is genuinely an arm of the church both local and universal. The Moravians saw themselves as an extension of the Body of Christ seeking to evangelize a lost world for Christ. They neither wanted nor strove to be a separate branch of the church. In many places they were forced to be that, but it was never their intention.

A CALLING FROM GOD

The explosion of missionary activity that began after World War II appeared to be a new phenomenon, but in fact its uniqueness lay in its magnitude, not in its essence. Had Zinzendorf lived and served in our century, his activity would have been right at home among the so-called parachurch ministries such as Prison Fellowship or Joni And Friends. Had Campus Crusade for Christ appeared two centuries earlier, it would have been viewed for what it is—believers who are part of Christ's church who are mobilizing themselves to fulfill a *function* of the church and organizing in an efficient *form* to accomplish the task.

Biblically speaking, Campus Crusade for Christ qualifies as a focused ministry of the church. Philosophically, Campus Crusade for Christ adheres to the values and reality of New Testamental service. Historical precedents exist for organizations such as Campus Crusade for Christ—organizations which, prior to this century and the coining of the phrase "para-church," have simply been viewed as ministries of Christ's church without much of the contending and arguing about definition that we see today.

About ten years ago I (Dan) heard that Mrs. Bright was scheduled to visit a city very near the seminary I was attending. I contacted her office and was able to arrange for her to address the seminary chapel service. After her message, as I drove her to her next engagement, I profited from her perspective on a variety of issues. On the church/para-church issue she shared with me, "Dan, we never sought that designation, but for some reason, others felt a need to apply that term to this movement. We've always simply viewed ourselves as an evangelistic arm of the church."

We believe that biblical, philosophical, and historical factors reveal that Bill and Vonette had it right all along—and that their humility and vision to serve in an oft-misunderstood form has been an honor to Christ and a major contribution and blessing to the church they so dearly love.

Christian organizations need to determine what God wants them to do, and therefore how they will relate to the broader concept of church, to local churches, and to denominations. All Christian ministries need to recognize that they are a part of the Body of Christ that has received a specialized, targeted calling from God. Workers in those ministries should be and can be confident that they are functioning as a part of the Body of Christ, the church, not simply as something alongside the church.

At one time, a group of Campus Crusade campus staff wanted to make Campus Crusade for Christ a church. They reasoned, "We do evangelism and discipleship; we do preaching and teaching; we do everything a church does, except baptism and the Lord's Supper. Why not also do these things, and become a church?" Bill Bright would not hear of such a thing. He correctly understood that God raised up Campus Crusade for Christ, and other organizations with specific callings, for the particular purpose of assisting local churches and denominations everywhere in the accomplishment of specific ministries within the spectrum of the church's total mandate. No Christian ministry can accomplish the job alone, but as a part of the church, the Body of Christ, together they can be a catalyst to the rest of the Body of Christ, the church, in helping to fulfill the Great Commission of our Lord. Christian ministries are not local churches or denominations, but neither are they separate from the church. It is not ours to abdicate or to "edit" God's calling to the various ministries of the Body of Christ. As we embark on this new millennium, let us "embrace" and fulfill it with the variety of ministries He has established with all the power He supplies, to His glory and the advancement of His kingdom.

NOTES

1. See Acts 22:25,29 for an example from the life of Paul.
2. Acts 19:32–41 presents a clear use of this word in this secular context. Demetrius, a silversmith, was losing business to the effects of Paul's preaching. He called out an assembly *(ecclesia)* of tradesmen to discuss the issue. Their assembly eventually

caused a great disturbance in the city, and in verse 32 the *ecclesia* was in confusion. The assembly was obviously made up of only men, but had no official significance noted by the call of the city clerk for a "legal" *ecclesia* in verse 39, after which the *ecclesia* is dismissed in verse 41.

3. The special term "church of God" is used eight times: Acts 20:28; 1 Corinthians 1:2; 10:32; 11:22; 15:9; 2 Corinthians 1:1; Galatians 1:13; and 1 Timothy 3:5.
4. Earl D. Radmacher, *What the Church Is All About* (Chicago: Moody Press, 1978), 187.
5. See 1 and 2 Thessalonians 1:1; 1 Corinthians 1:2; 2 Corinthians 1:1, Galatians 1:2, etc.
6. 1 Corinthians 4:17; 1:2.
7. Matthew 13:24–30,36–40, NASB; Revelation 3:1,4.
8. For an excellent discussion of this *form/function* paradigm, see Gene Getz, *Sharpening the Focus of the Church* (Wheaton, IL: SP Publications, 1984, orig. 1975); Howard A. Snyder, *The Problem of Wineskins: Church Structure in a Technological Age* (Downers Grove, IL: InterVarsity Press, 1975), as well as *The Community of the King* (1977); and Linus Morris, *The High Impact Church* (Houston, TX: Touch Publications, Inc., 1993).
9. The metaphor most used by Paul to describe the *ecclesia* is the "body." See Romans 12:5; 1 Corinthians 10:16,17; 12:12–27; Ephesians 1:22,23; 4:11–16; Colossians 1:24.
10. See Acts 2:46; 5:42; and 20:20.
11. See Stacy T. Rinehart, *Upside/Down* (Colorado Springs, CO: NavPress, 1998) for an excellent discussion of the right and privilege of every believer to be involved in the ministry of the kingdom of God.
12. Acts 2:41 (NASB) speaks of 3,000 *souls* and Acts 4:4 records 5,000 *men* who believed. If women and youth are added to this sum, along with others who might have believed, the number 20,000 is not unrealistic.
13. That person was Linus Morris, who was then a Campus Crusade for Christ staff member and who now leads Christian Associates International, a ministry to begin culturally relevant, high-impact churches around the world.
14. During a ministry sabbatical from 1993 to 1995, after turning over the leadership of the ministry of the country of Austria, where we had lived and worked for nineteen years, to an Austrian, we were given the privilege to prepare more fully for the work we are doing now in theological training for some 1,000 full-time workers in Eastern Europe and Russia. The Renewed Moravian Brethren became the focus of my [Edward] dissertation, and I was strongly encouraged by the parallels I saw between that pioneering movement of modern missions and the work of Campus Crusade for Christ. Space will allow me to share only a glimpse of those parallels. I would also like to express my deepest gratitude to Dr. Bright and the human resources department of Campus Crusade for Christ for allowing my wife and me the privilege of this time of study, family ministry, and "Sabbath" rest. It was an investment made by the organization and the supporters who so faithfully stand behind our work that has reaped great benefit for our continuing ministry, as well as the spiritual well-being of our marriage and family.

15. *Regeln des löblichen Ordens vom Senffkorn*, Erich Beyreuther, Gerhard Meyer, and Amedeo Molnar, eds. (Büdingen: Johann Christoph Stöhr, 1740; reprint in *Zweiter Sammelband über Zinzendorf*, Hildesheim: Georg Olms, 1975), 125–40.
16. Ibid., 37.
17. See Michael Richardson, *Amazing Faith* (Colorado Springs, CO: WaterBrook Press, 2000), 53–60.
18. Of the English literature available on the Moravians and their history, I recommend John R. Weinlick and Albert H. Frank, *The Moravian Church Through the Ages* (Bethlehem, PA: The Moravian Church in America, 1989); John R. Weinlick, *Count Zinzendorf* (Bethlehem, PA: Moravian Church, 1989); and Fredrick E. Stoeffler, *German Pietism during the Eighteenth Century* (Leiden, Netherlands: E. J. Brill, 1973).
19. A complete history of the Renewed Moravian Brethren and their mission activity can be found in J. Taylor Hamilton and Kenneth G. Hamilton, *History of the Moravian Church* (Bethlehem, PA: The Moravian Church in America, 1967).
20. William Carey, who is often given that title, once said, "Look at what the Moravians have done!" And they had done it almost a century before he began his missionary work.
21. Arthur J. Freeman, *An Ecumenical Theology of the Heart* (Bethlehem, PA: The Moravian Church in America, 1998), 67,68.

CHAPTER 24

Doctrinal Convictions and Persuasions

ALAN SCHOLES
On Staff since 1969
Associate Professor of Theology, International School of Theology

I sat in a large open-air amphitheater at Arrowhead Springs, then the headquarters of Campus Crusade for Christ, surrounded by more than a thousand of my fellow staff members. It was a balmy summer evening in the early 1970s.

Bill Bright rose to introduce the main speaker of the evening. The president of Campus Crusade spoke enthusiastically about the man's years as a prominent pastor and his contribution as the president of a major evangelical seminary. He talked of the many books the man had written and his other contributions to the progress of evangelical Christianity. By the time the guest speaker took the podium, I was excited with anticipation. What was this important man of God going to say to us?

The speaker spent the next 45 minutes telling of his own experience with the ministry of the Holy Spirit and explaining several passages of Scripture that he felt supported his view. The longer he spoke, the more agitated I became.

His view of the ministry of the Holy Spirit is quite different than Bill Bright's, I thought to myself. *Some of these points are in serious tension with what Bill himself taught us just last week!*

I had recently joined the staff myself, and I was not sure what Bill would do. Would he interrupt the man before he could do any more damage? Would he let him finish, but then take over the podium and correct the speaker's errors?

After the speaker closed in prayer, Bill did return to the podium. To my surprise, Bill renewed his praise of the speaker, thanked him for his wonderful message, and urged each of us on staff to take the things we'd heard and apply them to our own walk with God. Bill even repeated some of the language about the Holy Spirit that had been new to me and had seemed in conflict with Bill's own previous teachings.

Bill Bright's response that evening was my first experience of what I believe has been his consistent approach to the theological distinctives of Campus Crusade. That approach might be summarized by the following statement: "Hold strongly to a small number of the historic doctrines of Christianity, but be gracious and supportive of all true believers, even when they disagree in non-essentials." Both strength and grace have characterized Bill's and the movement's stance toward theology.

INCLUDING CONVICTIONS AND PERSUASIONS WITHIN BOUNDARY STATEMENTS

My observation of this approach in Dr. Bright's ministry and in the movement of Campus Crusade was the inspiration behind my own development of a series of technical terms for dealing with different levels of belief. Although I have written more extensively concerning these terms elsewhere, I will briefly review them for the purposes of this chapter.[1]

Convictions. As I have defined them, convictions are central beliefs, crucial to salvation, over which we should be willing to denounce someone in serious disagreement and (if there is no repentance) eventually divide fellowship. These are the historic doctrines of Christianity that separate it from non-Christian world religions and from pseudo-Christian cults. Some examples of convictions would be the Trinity, the deity of Christ, and salvation by grace through faith.

Persuasions. I use the term "persuasions" for beliefs about which we are personally certain, but which are not crucial to salvation. We should accept those with differing persuasions as members in good standing of God's family, even when we are certain they are wrong. These may include some doctrines based in biblical teaching, but concerning which true believers have differed through the centuries. Some examples of persuasion-level beliefs might be millennial views, the proper mode and meaning of baptism, and the place of tongues in the Christian life.

Opinions. Opinions are beliefs, desires, or even wishes which may not be clearly taught in Scripture or which may legitimately differ for various believers. Opinions may concern subjects on which we either have a preference but acknowledge that others may also be right in holding a different view, or we do not have any confidence that we yet know the truth of the matter. Some opinion-level subjects might be: How long will it be until Jesus' return? What kind of music should we use for worship? Which is the best Bible translation?

Boundary Statements. These are creeds, statements of faith, or doctrinal statements that may legitimately incorporate a combination of convictions, persuasions, and even opinions. I believe that denominations, institutions, and movements are entitled to limit their leadership, or even their entire membership, to a set of beliefs that may be more restrictive than those common to all true Christians.

In the rest of this chapter, I will use these concepts to analyze how the Campus Crusade Statement of Faith (which all staff sign yearly) functions within the movement.[2]

AFFIRMING HISTORIC CHRISTIAN BELIEFS

One of the functions of boundary statements in general, and Crusade's Statement in particular, is to define who may be included and who must be excluded based on their doctrinal beliefs. In the case of Campus Crusade for Christ, the statement helps articulate who may, and who may not, be members of the full-time staff.

The Statement of Faith (reproduced later in the chapter) is short enough to be printed on a single side of one sheet of paper. Following two introductory paragraphs, the statement is divided into seventeen numbered paragraphs, each consisting of one to three sentences. The second of the introductory paragraphs reflects Bill Bright's "hold strongly but be gracious" approach to doctrinal beliefs. It states, in part:

> We accept those areas of doctrinal teaching on which, historically, there has been general agreement among all true Christians... We desire to allow for freedom of conviction on other doctrinal matters...

I understand the reference to areas of "general agreement" to be similar to what I have called "convictions." The "other doctrinal matters" would include what I have termed "persuasions." A number of the points articulate classic doctrines of Christianity and are intended to distinguish between historic, evangelical belief and those positions which are heterodox. I would like to comment on several of these distinguishing articles.

Article 1: Trinity. This statement identifies Crusade with the historic creeds and church councils but would exclude the God concepts of non-

Christian world religions (Islam, Judaism, Hinduism) and most of the cults (Jehovah's Witnesses and all other non-Trinitarian groups such as Witness Lee's "Local Church" movement).

Articles 2–5: Christ's virgin birth, deity, resurrection, and ascension. These clauses separate Campus Crusade from Protestant (and some Catholic) theological liberalism that denies (or greatly redefines) the full deity of Christ. It also helps eliminate cultic beliefs that deny or redefine Christ's deity.

Article 8: Imputed righteousness by faith through grace alone. This statement is worded to exclude the traditional (Council of Trent) Roman Catholic view that grace is infused into believers as they cooperate through their own good works.[3]

Article 9: Assurance of salvation. This article was explicitly worded to include the beliefs of both Reformed and Methodist evangelical believers. Although the statement is often misread as an affirmation of eternal security (the fifth point of Calvinism—Perseverance of the Saints), it actually merely states that all who are born again can immediately be assured of their salvation by the internal witness of the Holy Spirit. It stops short of saying whether that assurance (and salvation itself) can ever be lost. The wording of this statement is a clear indication that, while salvation by grace is a conviction-level belief, the issue of whether that salvation can be lost is a matter of persuasion best left to the conscience of each believer.

Article 10: The Holy Spirit's indwelling and filling. This article states both that the Spirit indwells every believer from the moment of spiritual birth and that the filling of the Spirit is appropriated by faith. This wording would exclude the traditional Pentecostal teaching that the "Baptism of the Holy Spirit" is a second event, marked by speaking in tongues, which is a prerequisite to being filled and empowered by the Holy Spirit. The statement does leave room, however, for the less dogmatic views that often characterize those in movements such as Calvary Chapel and the Vineyard. Teachers in these groups, although often retaining the language of the "Baptism of the Spirit" referring to a second event, usually affirm that all believers are indwelt by the Holy Spirit and that any Christian can be Spirit-filled and empowered by faith.[4]

Articles 14–15: Death is immediately followed by conscious fellowship with the Lord or separation from Him. These articles exclude two of the traditional Seventh-Day Adventist teachings: soul sleep and annihilationism. Article 15, by affirming everlasting judgment and condemnation for unbelievers, also excludes the annihilationist and universalist tendencies of some contemporary evangelical thinkers.

TAKING SIDES ON INERRANCY

One doctrinal stance in the Statement of Faith might be viewed as an exception to the general "hold strongly but be gracious" approach of Bill Bright and the Campus Crusade for Christ Statement. In the second sentence of the first paragraph of the introduction, we find a clear statement that the Bible is inerrant. The question of whether it is appropriate to describe the Bible as "inerrant" or merely "infallible" was one of the major debates among evangelical Christians during the latter half of the twentieth century (particularly the seventies and eighties). Why take a stand on this controversial, persuasion-level belief?[5]

First, I would like to make a couple of points of historical clarification. The current Campus Crusade Statement of Faith was drafted in the late 1960s. In 1972, Dr. Bright's alma mater, Fuller Theological Seminary, changed its statement of faith, eliminating the idea of inerrancy from the clause about the Bible.[6] Subsequent to Fuller's decision to change its statement, Dr. Bright and the leadership of Campus Crusade inserted the word "inerrant" (in parentheses) into the second sentence of the first paragraph of Crusade's Statement of Faith. This was not a change of position, but rather a clarification of the position that was always intended. Even without the parenthetical addition, the language of the statement clearly affirmed inerrancy. It said that the Bible "was written without error in the original manuscripts." The word "inerrant" was added so there could be no doubt about the original meaning intended by the phrase.

Why was it important to Bill Bright and the other Campus Crusade leaders to take so clear a stand on an issue where prominent and respected evangelical leaders disagreed? Several years ago, I had a brief conversation with Dr. Bright which may shed some light on why he and Crusade have chosen so strong a position in this controversy.

In September 1998, I received a call from the President's Office of Campus Crusade saying that Bill would like to talk with me later in the week. My first reaction was a tensing in my stomach. *What have I done wrong that Bill needs to call me personally?* I wondered. Phone calls from our president have been rare in my thirty years on staff.

When the appointed hour came and I answered the phone, Bill's voice had a warm, grandfatherly tone, and I heard the words that I understand longtime staff members often hear from Bill. "My dear Alan, it's so good to speak with you again."

But it turned out my fears were not entirely unwarranted.

"NavPress has sent me the manuscript of your new book, asking me to endorse it," Bill continued, "and I intend to do so. But I have a concern with one statement you've made in chapter five."

I was immediately impressed and, frankly, amazed that Bill had taken the time to familiarize himself enough with my book to be concerned about a single statement buried a third of the way into the manuscript. As I scrambled to find my copy on the computer, I tried to imagine what I might have said that concerned him. After all, I had written the book primarily for our staff and was already using the manuscript as a basic text to train the new Campus staff!

"Alan, on page 79, you say that because of manuscript evidence 'we can have a high level of confidence in the integrity and reliability of our modern biblical texts.'"

"Yes," I said, still unable to fathom why that statement could be problematic for him.

"My concern," he said, "is with the phrase 'high level of confidence.' I'm afraid some people might read that to mean that you had something less than *complete* confidence in the Bible."

"Ooh," I said slowly. "I guess I can see how someone might read it that way. That's not what I meant, and I certainly don't want to communicate that I have doubts about the Bible."

"I was sure you didn't," Bill said. "Perhaps we could work out a wording that would communicate more clearly."

We spent the next couple of minutes hashing through the phraseology until both of us were satisfied. In the published version of the book, the sentence now affirms that "the science of manuscript evidence has progressed to the point where we can trust the integrity and reliability of our modern biblical texts." At the end of the next paragraph, I also added a sentence to conclude the discussion. "The fact that there are a few minor differences in ancient manuscripts does not undermine my confidence in the inerrancy of the original autographs or my trust in the Bible I hold in my hands."

I think Bill's conversation with me illustrates two crucial aspects of his approach to this issue. First, I think it shows how important this issue has been in the heart and ministry of Bill Bright. Although the rest of my book covered all the major doctrines of Christianity (including some other controversial ones), Bill had no concerns about the remainder of what I'd written.[7] I realize now that Bill was doing with my book something corollary to what was done with the inerrancy clause in the Campus Crusade Statement. In both cases, he wanted to make certain no one could misunderstand where Campus Crusade stands as a movement. He wanted it to be entirely clear that we harbor no doubts or hesitations of any kind concerning the truthfulness and accuracy of God's holy Word.

The second clue to Bill's approach to the inerrancy issue came a few minutes later in the conversation. We happened to mention Fuller Seminary, and he expressed his warm regard and respect for a number of longtime friends there, including Dan Fuller.[8] Clearly, Bill did not believe that these faculty members had ceased to be Christians or should be condemned as heretics. Bill was treating inerrancy as a persuasion-level issue. He recognized that sincere, godly Christians disagreed, but he nevertheless held inerrancy as a persuasion that was crucial for the ministry of Campus Crusade.

EVALUATING EFFECTIVENESS

How has this approach of "holding strongly but being gracious" served the ministry of Campus Crusade over the years? Have the boundaries been drawn too broadly or too tightly? Bill Bright and Crusade have received considerable criticism over the years (most frequently from Calvinists) for being too broad and inclusive. Often the charge has been that we've been too friendly with Wesleyans and with Charismatics. I was raised Presbyterian and would not consider myself to be either a Wesleyan or a Charismatic. Rather, I often identify myself as a moderate Calvinist. Yet my own judgment is that the theological boundary has been drawn in something very close to the right place.

Despite his own Presbyterian roots, Bill Bright founded Campus Crusade to be an interdenominational parachurch movement, not a Reformed missionary society. In my view, there would have been nothing wrong with his choosing to start a distinctively Presbyterian home mission society if he had felt God leading him to do so. But that was not what Bill felt God leading him to do. Rather, he was to start an evangelistic movement that would reach as many as possible with the simple gospel of Christ's love and forgiveness. To do so, Bill decided to attract as many genuine, dedicated Christians to the Crusade staff as possible. He wanted staff membership to be open to evangelical Wesleyans, Baptists, Lutherans, and Episcopalians, as well as Presbyterians, as long as all could wholeheartedly agree with Campus Crusade's doctrine and ministry distinctives. I believe this choice and the way it shaped the Statement of Faith have served the movement well.

But what about the opposite charge? Perhaps Bill has drawn the boundary too tightly, especially on the issue of inerrancy. After all, many sincere godly believers who love Christ and hold to the historic Christian doctrines do not feel they can honestly say that the Bible is without error. Wouldn't it be better for the movement if we welcomed them on staff as well? Certainly, there are other wonderful evangelistic movements (such as Young Life) which have chosen differently. Admittedly, this is a judgment call. However, it is my view that Dr. Bright and the other Crusade leaders have made the wiser choice. Perhaps a personal story will help illustrate why I'm glad our doctrinal statement clearly affirms inerrancy.

A number of years ago, I spent considerable time discussing this issue with a staff member whom I will call Ron (not his real name). When I met him, Ron had already spent many years as a faithful full-time, faith-supported Crusade staff member. It soon became clear to me that Ron loved the Lord deeply and sincerely desired to continue a ministry of evangelism, discipleship, and teaching for the rest of his life. To help prepare further, Ron was pursuing an advanced degree at a major seminary. At this school, he was attracted to a prominent professor who was part of a new movement called "Anglo-American Postmodernism." By the time I met him, Ron had become a strong disciple of this new approach to evangelical belief. In fact, he had the vision to return to full-time staff duties and spread his new understanding of Christianity throughout the Crusade ministry, believing that it would help us to better evangelize the current generation in Western culture.

When I raised the issue of inerrancy, Ron said, "From a postmodern perspective, I can't make any sense of the term."

"How then," I asked, "can you continue in good conscience to sign the statement of faith which clearly teaches inerrancy?"

His answer was a fascinating one. "Well, I understand the modern framework out of which that statement was drafted. And I also understand the heart and intent behind the words. And I can honor the intent even though, as a postmodernist, I can no longer find meaning for myself in the words themselves."

"Ron," I said, "that's simply not enough. You know the meaning that was intended by those words. You can't simply say that you honor and respect those who wrote them. You must, in good conscience, still believe them yourself, as you know they were intended to be understood. Or else you must leave staff."

Others on staff gave Ron similar counsel. Eventually, he chose to leave. Since that time, I have made a substantial study of postmodernism in general and of its conservative, evangelical branch in particular. My own eventual judgment was that it is a dangerous, though well-intentioned, distortion of Christianity.[9] In this instance, I believe the inerrancy clause in the Crusade statement saved the ministry from much greater future problems.

GUARANTEEING PROTECTION?

Is the Campus Crusade Statement of Faith an ironclad guarantee against doctrinal drift within the movement? Sometimes, as in the case of Ron, it can play a crucial role. But overall, my judgment would be "no." I do not believe that any statement, no matter how carefully worded, could ever be, by itself, a complete protection against doctrinal defection.

This point was powerfully expressed to me nearly twenty years ago during an evening I had the privilege of spending with theologian Charles Ryrie. Dr. Ryrie had graciously agreed to come to San Bernardino for several days to advise those of us in the newly established International School of Theology. One evening, I volunteered to take him to dinner where I enjoyed a fascinating conversation with him over salad and pasta.

At one point in the evening, I told him that I was the current chair of the faculty selection committee. Then I posed this question: "If you were in our position, just beginning a new evangelical school, what measures would you take to avoid the kind of doctrinal drift toward liberalism that has plagued so many formerly conservative seminaries?"

His answer surprised me. I expected that he might propose certain points for inclusion in the seminary's doctrinal statement. Or I thought he might suggest theological questions we should pose to prospective faculty. After all, he was a widely published and very influential American theologian. But his answer had little to do directly with theology. "The most important thing you can do to protect your seminary is to hire faculty who share their faith in Christ with others."

I am convinced that Dr. Ryrie was right. Nearly twenty years later, I'm convinced the practice of hiring faculty members who are active in practical ministries, including evangelism, is one of the most important distinctives, and greatest protections, for our various schools of theology around the world.

I would like to conclude with an expansion of the point Charles Ryrie made to me nearly two decades ago. I believe there are two emphases of the ministry of Bill Bright that have been vitally important in protecting the various ministries of Campus Crusade (including its educational arms) for the last fifty years. Significantly, both of these emphases are reflected in the statement of faith. Both are notable because neither are common subjects found in the historic creeds of Christendom nor in most contemporary doctrinal statements. I mentioned one of these distinctives earlier in this chapter. Article 10 speaks of various ministries of the Holy Spirit. The last sentence of the article says, "His fullness, power, and control are appropriated in the believer's life by faith." I believe that Bill Bright's emphasis on the importance of every staff member (and every Christian) living day by day filled and empowered by the Holy Spirit has been a significant boon and protection for the ministry.

The second emphasis that has served as an important protection for the ministry is the one highlighted by Dr. Ryrie, the stress that Bill has placed on evangelism and the Great Commission. The final article of Crusade's statement reads:

> The Lord Jesus Christ commanded all believers to proclaim the Gospel throughout the world and to disciple men of every nation. The fulfillment of that Great Commission requires that all worldly and personal ambitions be subordinated to a total commitment to "Him who loved us and gave Himself for us."

It is my belief that these two distinctives, the Spirit-filled life and fulfillment of the Great Commission, are perhaps the greatest lasting legacy of Bill Bright to the movement of Campus Crusade for Christ and to the Body of Christ throughout the world.

THE CAMPUS CRUSADE FOR CHRIST STATEMENT OF FAITH

The sole basis of our beliefs is the Bible, God's infallible written Word, the 66 books of the Old and New Testaments. We believe that it was uniquely, verbally and fully inspired by the Holy Spirit and that it was written without error (inerrant) in the original manuscripts. It is the supreme and final authority in all matters on which it speaks.

We accept those areas of doctrinal teaching on which, historically, there has been general agreement among all true Christians. Because of the specialized calling of our movement, we desire to allow for freedom of conviction on other doctrinal matters, provided that any interpretation is based upon the Bible alone, and that no such interpretation shall become an issue which hinders the ministry to which God has called us.

1. There is one true God, eternally existing in three persons—Father, Son, and Holy Spirit—each of whom possesses equally all the attributes of Deity and the characteristics of personality.
2. Jesus Christ is God, the living Word, who became flesh through His miraculous conception by the Holy Spirit and His virgin birth. Hence, He is perfect Deity and true humanity united in one person forever.

3. He lived a sinless life and voluntarily atoned for the sins of men by dying on the cross as their substitute, thus satisfying divine justice and accomplishing salvation for all who trust in Him alone.
4. He rose from the dead in the same body, though glorified, in which He lived and died.
5. He ascended bodily into heaven and sat down at the right hand of God the Father, where He, the only mediator between God and man, continually makes intercession for His own.
6. Man was originally created in the image of God. He sinned by disobeying God; thus, he was alienated from his Creator. That historic fall brought all mankind under divine condemnation.
7. Man's nature is corrupted, and he is thus totally unable to please God. Every man is in need of regeneration and renewal by the Holy Spirit.
8. The salvation of man is wholly a work of God's free grace and is not the work, in whole or in part, of human works or goodness or religious ceremony. God imputes His righteousness to those who put their faith in Christ alone for their salvation, and thereby justifies them in His sight.
9. It is the privilege of all who are born again of the Spirit to be assured of their salvation from the very moment in which they trust Christ as their Savior. This assurance is not based upon any kind of human merit, but is produced by the witness of the Holy Spirit, who confirms in the believer the testimony of God in His written Word.
10. The Holy Spirit has come into the world to reveal and glorify Christ and to apply the saving work of Christ to men. He convicts and draws sinners to Christ, imparts new life to them, continually indwells them from the moment of spiritual birth and seals them until the day of redemption. His fullness, power and control are appropriated in the believer's life by faith.
11. Every believer is called to live so in the power of the indwelling Spirit that he will not fulfill the lust of the flesh but will bear fruit to the glory of God.
12. Jesus Christ is the Head of the Church, His Body, which is composed of all men, living and dead, who have been joined to Him through saving faith.
13. God admonishes His people to assemble together regularly for worship, for participation in ordinances, for edification through the Scriptures

and for mutual encouragement.

14. At physical death, the believer enters immediately into eternal, conscious fellowship with the Lord and awaits the resurrection of his body to everlasting glory and blessing.
15. At physical death, the unbeliever enters immediately into eternal, conscious separation from the Lord and awaits the resurrection of his body to everlasting judgment and condemnation.
16. Jesus Christ will come again to the earth—personally, visibly and bodily—to consummate history and the eternal plan of God.
17. The Lord Jesus Christ commanded all believers to proclaim the Gospel throughout the world and to disciple men of every nation. The fulfillment of that Great Commission requires that all worldly and personal ambitions be subordinated to a total commitment to "Him who loved us and gave Himself for us."

NOTES

1. I first explored these technical terms for my Master of Divinity thesis at the International School of Theology in 1983 under the direction of Steven M. Clinton, my thesis chair. Dr. Clinton and I eventually published a revised and edited version of the thesis under the title, "Levels of Belief in the Pauline Epistles: A Paradigm of Evangelical Unity," *Bulletin of the Evangelical Philosophical Society* 1991, Vol. 14, No. 2, 70–84. A more popular version of the same concepts was elaborated in the first chapter of my book, *What Christianity Is All About: How You Can Know and Enjoy God* (Colorado Springs: NavPress, 1999). The book has been used as a basic text for the past five years in the Doctrine Survey course as a part of winter and summer Campus Crusade for Christ new-staff training in the United States.
2. In my view, the Campus Crusade for Christ Statement articulates several conviction- and persuasion-level beliefs. I do not think it speaks to any issues I have defined as "opinions."
3. What is not entirely clear to me is whether this statement also excludes all post-Vatican II Catholic thinkers. Bill Bright came under considerable criticism for endorsing the two Evangelicals & Catholics Together study documents. While this controversy is much too complex to address properly in this chapter, it should be noted that both documents clearly stated the remaining differences between the evangelical and Catholic signers. Specifically, the first statement acknowledged, "Evangelicals hold that the Catholic Church has gone beyond Scripture, adding teachings and practices that detract from or compromise the Gospel of God's saving grace in Christ." The second statement admitted that unresolved questions between the two groups included the issue of "the historic uses of the language of justification as it relates to imputed and transformative righteousness." The text of both statements (including a list of signers) can be found at www.onebody.org.

4. See, for example, Chuck Smith's discussion of these issues in "Empowered by the Spirit," chapter three of *Calvary Chapel Distinctives* (Costa Mesa, CA: The Word for Today Publishers, 2000), 29–35.
5. In *What Christianity*, I argue that the authority of the Bible, not inerrancy, is the cardinal conviction that separates believers from nonbelievers. I class inerrancy as a persuasion-level belief, one that I am certain is true but would not use as a basis of dividing fellowship with other believers. However, I also state that I "am glad that my own institutions (Campus Crusade for Christ and the International School of Theology) include inerrancy in their statements of faith and I, for one, would fight to retain that clause."
6. From the founding of the seminary in 1947, the relevant clause in the Fuller statement read: "The books which form the canon of the Old and New Testaments as originally given are plenarily inspired and free from all error in the whole and in the part. These books constitute the written Word of God, the only infallible rule of faith and practice." In the new statement adopted in 1972, the same clause now reads: "Scripture is an essential part and trustworthy record of this divine self-disclosure. All the books of the Old and New Testaments, given by divine inspiration, are the written word of God, the only infallible rule of faith and practice." Although the new statement retained the idea that the Bible is the "only infallible rule of faith and practice" (the reliable guide in matters of doctrine and morals), it eliminated the assertion that it was also free from all error (inerrant). One of the motivations for this change was to appeal to the seminary's large Presbyterian constituency, which Fuller has done with great success, seeing more than a thousand of its graduates ordained in the PCUSA denomination.
7. Bill's endorsement, which appears on the back cover of the book, reads "With great skill and insight, Dr. Scholes captures the very essence of God's loving message to the human race, and he does so in an easily understood way. I highly recommend this book for any and all who are seeking a more personal, intimate relationship with God."
8. Daniel Fuller, the son of the seminary's founder, was in the initial group of five staff who joined Bill and Vonette in the nascent ministry of Campus Crusade at UCLA in 1952.
9. Space will not allow a full analysis of the teachings of evangelical postmodernism. Briefly, all postmodernists have been influenced by Wittgenstein's concept that truth is established by (not merely learned through) the language game of a particular community. If this premise is accepted, it seems to me that the conclusion is inescapable that all Christian doctrines are produced by and relative to the Christian community (or even specific subgroups within Christianity). It does not seem possible for a postmodernist to consistently maintain that Jesus is *The Truth* for all people, no matter what their community and language game. This teaching, in my view, would eventually lead to Christians abandoning the urgency of the Great Commission.

CHAPTER 25

The Lordship Salvation Debate

RANDALL C. GLEASON
Working with Staff since 1992
Professor of Systematic Theology,
International School of Theology, Asia, Manila

My spiritual pilgrimage was typical of many raised in a Christian family. One of my earliest memories was of my older sister explaining to me at the age of five how to pray and invite Jesus to come into my heart. Although I prayed to receive Christ at that time, it was not until my sophomore year in high school that I began to understand the true meaning of discipleship. While attending a youth conference, I asked Christ to become the Lord and Master of my life. After that decision, I was baptized in our local church and began to have an intense hunger to study the Bible and a strong desire to share my faith with others. The dramatic change in my life caused me to doubt whether I was truly saved when I had prayed earlier as a child. I began to ask the question, "Does salvation require submission to Christ as Lord as well as trust in Christ as Savior?" I soon discovered that many have asked the same question, spawning one of the most hotly debated controversies within twentieth-century evangelicalism.[1]

The brief exchange in *Eternity* magazine in 1959 between two well-known evangelicals helped to define the key points of the "Lordship salvation" debate. To the question "Must Christ be Lord to be Savior?", Everett F. Harrison answered "NO" by demonstrating the difference between saving faith and discipleship, and the danger of basing assurance of salvation upon complete surrender.[2] On the other hand, John R. W. Stott maintained that Jesus must be accepted as both Lord and Savior by emphasizing the inseparable connection between saving faith and repentance, obedience, and newness of life.[3] The recent defense of the Lordship view by well-known Bible teacher John MacArthur brought new life to the controversy. The publication of his book, *The Gospel According to Jesus*,[4] in 1988 drew immediate responses from Charles C. Ryrie and Zane C. Hodges, both former professors of Dallas Theological Seminary, defending the non-Lordship position.[5] Since then, many have written on this controversial subject.[6] Along the way, a Campus Crusade for Christ booklet, *Have You Made the Wonderful Discovery of the Spirit-filled Life?*, has often been presented as an example of the non-Lordship view.[7] To commemorate Dr. Bright's worldwide impact through his Holy Spirit booklet, I offer this summary and critique of the Lordship debate. Rather than an endorsement of either side, Dr. Bright provides a helpful biblical balance that has often been missed in the rhetoric of the debate.

"LORDSHIP SALVATION" DEFINED

Advocates of Lordship salvation object to the preaching of a gospel that "encourages people to claim Jesus as Savior yet defer until later the commitment to obey Him as Lord."[8] They reject the assumption that faith is simply giving intellectual assent to "some basic facts about Christ," claiming that it has produced a generation of "professing Christians" with a false sense of assurance.[9] They renounce such a notion as a distortion of the gospel similar to that which Paul warns against in Galatians 1:6–8:

> I am amazed that you are so quickly deserting Him who called you by the grace of Christ, for a different gospel; which is really not another; only there are some who are disturbing you, and want to distort the gospel of Christ. But even though we, or an angel from heaven, should preach to you a gospel contrary to that which we have preached to you, let him be accursed (NASB).[10]

They call for a return to the true demands of the gospel, which includes a willingness to submit to the Lordship of Christ in every aspect of one's life. MacArthur states, "People who come to Christ for salvation must do so in obedience to Him, that is, with a willingness to surrender to Him as Lord."[11] Thus, saving faith should not be distinguished from the true marks of discipleship, including "repentance, surrender, and the supernatural eagerness to obey."[12] MacArthur concludes, "No promise of salvation is ever extended to those who refuse to accede to Christ's lordship. Thus, there is no salvation except 'lordship' salvation."[13]

Lordship advocates are often accused of promoting a salvation by works. Their opponents maintain that to make works of obedience the inevitable result of faith is to make works a condition of salvation. Hodges makes this allegation:

> It may even be said that lordship salvation throws a veil of obscurity over the entire New Testament revelation. In the process, the marvelous truth of justification by faith, apart from works, recedes into shadows not unlike those which darkened the days before the Reformation. What replaces this doctrine is a kind of faith/works synthesis which differs only insignificantly from official Roman Catholic dogma.[14]

However, MacArthur emphatically denies works-salvation:

> Let me say as clearly as possible right now that salvation is by God's sovereign grace and grace alone. Nothing a lost, degenerate, spiritually dead sinner can do will in any way contribute to salvation. Saving faith, repentance, commitment, and obedience are all divine works, wrought by the Holy Spirit in the heart of everyone who is saved. I have never taught that some pre-salvation works of righteousness are necessary to or part of salvation. But I do believe without apology that real salvation cannot and will not fail to produce works of righteousness in the life of a true believer.[15]

MacArthur claims that works of obedience are both the inevitable product and necessary evidence of genuine faith. Notice that the cause-and-effect relationship is in only one direction (i.e., faith producing works of obedience, not works of obedience resulting in salvation). To insist that any cause-and-effect relationship between faith and works necessarily implies a works-salvation is to commit the fallacy of mistaking the effect for the cause. Bock correctly observes that "for a person to hold to works-salvation he must say, 'Because I have done a specific act, God is obligated to save me.'"[16] This is clearly not what MacArthur and other Lordship advocates claim. Therefore, the accusation of works-salvation is unwarranted and a misrepresentation of the Lordship position.

THE MEANING OF SAVING FAITH

The nature of genuine faith is acknowledged by all as one of the most fundamental issues in the Lordship controversy. Those opposed to Lordship salvation emphasize saving faith as an intellectual response to the truth of the gospel. This is clearly seen in Zane Hodges' claim that saving faith is simply "believing the facts" about Christ.[17] Although Ryrie acknowledges a volitional aspect of faith, he explains it as "an act of the will to trust in the *truth* which one has come to know"[18] (emphasis added). Hence, his examples of faith call sinners to believe "that Christ can forgive his sins," "that He can remove the guilt of sin and give eternal life," and "that His death paid for all your sin."[19] In each case, his emphasis is clearly upon believing truths *about* Christ. Non-Lordship advocates also stress the simplicity of faith and reject the tendency to distinguish between authentic faith and insufficient faith (e.g., counterfeit faith, temporary faith, dead faith).[20] Moreover, the genuineness of a person's faith should not be questioned even if he comes "to the place of not believing."[21]

Lordship advocates offer a very different understanding of faith. They emphasize the enduring quality of saving faith in the person of Christ evidenced by submission and obedience to Him. Kenneth Gentry explains, "When one believes in Christ, he is bound to Him in an obedient, vital relationship. Commitment is an essential element in the act of believing. Faith is not merely intellectual assent."[22] Following Louis Berkhof's definition of faith, MacArthur reasons that genuine faith includes three components:

> An intellectual element (*notitia*), which is the understanding of truth; an emotional element (*assensus*), which is the conviction and affirmation of truth; and a volitional element (*fiducia*), which is the determination of the will to obey truth.[23]

The volitional element implies that "obedience is the inevitable manifestation of true faith."[24] MacArthur is correct to conclude that any faith failing to produce obedience is "dead" and therefore according to James insufficient for salvation (James 2:14–26).[25] However, his assertion that "Obedience is . . . an integral part of saving faith"[26] blurs the distinction between faith and obedience. His further claim that "faith encompasses obedience"[27] is clearly in conflict with Paul's point that we are justified by grace through faith—*not* through obedience (Romans 4:2–16). Unfortunately, it is necessary here to distinguish between what MacArthur says and what he really means. His point is that the "desire to obey" is the volitional part of faith and not obedience itself. He makes this distinction when he explains how the desire to obey can remain present in the believer even though he is disobedient:

> Because we all retain vestiges of sinful flesh, no one will obey perfectly (cf. 2 Corinthians 7:1; 1 Thessalonians 3:10), but the desire to do the will of God will be ever present in true believers (cf. Romans 7:18).[28]

Jonathan Edwards's concept of "Religious Affections" offers a proper emphasis upon the volitional element of faith. For Edwards, "true religious affections" include the inclination and will to obey God evidenced in obedience.[29] MacArthur echoes this when he clarifies, "Those who believe *will* desire to obey, however imperfectly they may follow through at times. So-called 'faith' in God that does not produce this yearning to submit to His will is not faith at all."[30]

Lordship proponents also insist on the enduring nature of true saving faith. They support this claim through the use of the present tense of the verb "believe" (*pisteuō*), indicating continuous action and the abiding quality of faith as a gift bestowed by God (Ephesians 2:8,9).[31] They are correct to conclude that the "orthodox faith" of the demons (James 2:19), "superficial faith" of the multitude (John 2:23–25), and "temporary faith" of the rocky soil (Luke 8:13) are insufficient for salvation. However, the complex lists of ingredients Lordship advocates include in genuine faith allow little room for immature faith. For example, MacArthur offers the following definition of "saving faith":

> It clings to no cherished sins, no treasured possessions, no secret self-indulgences. It is an unconditional surrender, a willingness to do anything the Lord demands... It is a total abandonment of self-will, like the grain of wheat that falls to the ground and dies so that is can bear much fruit (cf. John 12:24). It is an exchange of all that we are for all that Christ is. And it denotes obedience, full surrender to the lordship of Christ. Nothing less can qualify as saving faith.[32]

However, Scripture is filled with examples of believers with weak faith. Even to His disciples Jesus said, "You men of little faith" (Matthew 8:26, NASB). Faith is frequently presented in Scripture as something that grows and matures (James 1:2–4). Yet Lordship proponents often fail to include this idea in their understanding of faith. MacArthur uses the example of childlike faith (Matthew 18:3) to illustrate obedient humility[33] yet how mature and full-blown can the faith of a child be? A child is often disobedient and requires the training and discipline of a loving father to bring him to maturity. MacArthur asserts, "Faith obeys. Unbelief rebels... There is no middle ground."[34] Yet examples abound throughout Scripture of genuine faith mixed with unbelief. The genuine faith of the Israelites departing from Egypt (Exodus 4:30,31; 14:30,31; cf. Hebrews 11:29) is confirmed both by their worship (Exodus 15:1–18) and by their obedience (Exodus 12:28,50) yet they were still guilty of rebellion (Numbers 14:9; Deuteronomy 9:23,24) and unbelief (Numbers 14:11). Likewise, Moses was a man of great faith, yet he committed the same sins of unbelief and rebellion (Numbers 20:12,24), thereby forfeiting his right to enter the promised land with the others. Unfortunately, believers often do rebel. Initial faith is always less than perfect. However, God does not leave it there. He uses the process of discipline (Hebrews 12:4–13) and trials (1 Peter 1:6,7) throughout the believer's life to bring his faith to maturity.

REPENTANCE AND SALVATION

Some who oppose Lordship theology deny that repentance is necessary for salvation.[35] Others limit the meaning of repentance to "a change of mind" about Christ, thereby making it virtually synonymous with faith.[36] Ryrie affirms both approaches when he declares, "It is faith that saves, not repentance (unless repentance is understood as a synonym for faith or changing one's mind about Christ)."[37] Lordship advocates object to such a narrow definition of repentance. They define repentance as a turning to God from sin that "involves a change of heart and purpose" inevitably resulting "in a change of behavior."[38] MacArthur explains:

> *Intellectually*, repentance begins with a recognition of sin, understanding that we are sinners, that our sin is an affront to a holy God, and more precisely, that we are personally responsible for our own guilt... *Emotionally*, genuine repentance often accompanies an overwhelming sense of sorrow... *Volitionally*, repentance involves a change of direction, a transformation of the will.[39]

In other words, repentance requires a willingness to forsake sin in order to obey God. Furthermore, repentance is regarded as inseparable from saving faith. MacArthur explains, "Genuine repentance is *always* the flip side of faith; and true faith accompanies repentance."[40] Hence, repentance is no less essential for salvation than faith, and therefore must be included in the gospel message.

The Lordship understanding of repentance is essentially correct for the following reasons. First, though it is true that "repentance" (*metanoia*) literally means "a change of mind,"[41] its use throughout the New Testament often denotes a decision to change one's behavior (e.g., Acts 26:20; 2 Corinthians 12:21; Revelation 2:21,22). Most evangelical scholars acknowledge this understanding of repentance.[42] However, we should be careful to remember that repentance is the decision to change our life, not the actual behavior that results from the decision. Grudem clarifies:

> We cannot say that someone has to actually live that changed life over a period of time before repentance can be genuine, or else repentance would be turned into a kind of obedience that we could do to merit salvation for ourselves.[43]

Second, repentance is clearly a part of the gospel message throughout the New Testament. Jesus charged his disciples just before His ascension: "Repentance for forgiveness of sins should be proclaimed in His name to all the nations, beginning from Jerusalem" (Luke 24:47, NASB). Peter and

Paul responded by preaching repentance to unbelievers throughout the Book of Acts (Acts 2:38; 3:19; 5:31; 8:22; 11:18; 17:30; 20:21; 26:20). Therefore, repentance must be preached as part of the gospel at all times to all nations. Third, repentance is often linked with faith in the New Testament (Mark 1:15; Acts 11:17,18; 19:4; 20:21; Hebrews 6:1). Although sometimes only faith is mentioned as necessary for salvation (John 3:16; 6:28,29; Acts 16:31; Romans 10:9), other times only repentance is mentioned (Luke 24:47; Acts 2:38; 3:19; 5:31; Romans 2:4; 2 Corinthians 7:10; 2 Timothy 2:25). Often those who repent are considered believers (Acts 2:38–47; 3:19; 11:17,18). Hence, the biblical concept of repentance is no less important for salvation than faith.

Those opposed to a Lordship understanding of repentance often echo the claim of Lewis Sperry Chafer, the founder of Dallas Theological Seminary, that "the New Testament does not impose repentance upon the unsaved as a condition of salvation."[44] However, most fail to properly understand Chafer's comments in their historical context. Dallas Seminary professor Darrel Bock explains:

> What Chafer argued is that repentance alone, without the positive side of faith, is not good enough. Regret or sorrow for sin is not enough if it is not wedded to trust. When Chafer affirmed that repentance alone is inadequate for salvation, he had in mind the idea of sorrow associated with the "anxiety benches" in the tent revivals of his day.[45]

A true repentance tied to faith was indeed included in Chafer's understanding, for in writing the Dallas Seminary doctrinal statement, he stated, "We believe that the new birth of the believer comes only through faith in Christ and *that repentance is a vital part of believing*, and is in no way, in itself, a separate and independent condition of salvation."[46]

THE MEANING OF "LORD": GOD OR MASTER?

The Lordship of Christ is often tied to salvation in the New Testament. For example, "Everyone who calls on the name of the *Lord* will be saved" (Acts 2:21, emphasis added), and "If you confess with your mouth, 'Jesus is *Lord*,' and believe in your heart that God raised him from the dead, you will be saved" (Romans 10:9, emphasis added). Lordship teachers regard such passages as indisputable evidence that salvation requires the willingness to submit to Christ as "sovereign master."[47] However, opponents of Lordship salvation object, pointing to the fact that the term "Lord" (*kurios*) has a variety of meanings in the New Testament, including "God" (Acts 3:22), "owner" (Luke 19:33), or "sir" (John 4:11).[48] When used in passages dealing with salvation (e.g., Romans 10:9), they claim "Lord" functions primarily as a divine title meaning "God." As such, "Jesus is Lord" (1 Corinthians 12:3) is a confession of Jesus Christ's deity rather a commitment to submit to His rule.[49] It is true that the divine name *Yahweh* is frequently translated "Lord" (*kurios*), thereby providing an important proof for the deity of Christ when applied to Jesus (Acts 2:36; cf. Isaiah 40:3). This does not mean, however, that the divine meaning of "Lord" should be distinguished from His sovereign right to rule. The deity of Christ naturally includes His authority to rule as sovereign God. Therefore, to confess "Jesus as Lord" implicitly acknowledges His divine right to exercise dominion over one's life. Confusion arises, however, when the question of how much submission is enough to validate the genuineness of that confession. To demand that Christ be "Lord of all" as evidence of genuine faith diminishes the interplay between a commitment to Christ's Lordship and the lifelong process of "being transformed into his likeness with ever-increasing glory, which comes from the Lord" (2 Corinthians 3:18).

FAITH AND DISCIPLESHIP

Non-Lordship proponents are careful to distinguish between the gift of salvation and the cost of discipleship.[50] They insist that since discipleship requires great effort and salvation is a free gift, the two should not to be confused.[51] They conclude that discipleship is the responsibility of believers, not unbelievers, and therefore should not be included in the demands of the gospel.[52] Lordship theology makes no such distinction. MacArthur asserts that "every Christian is a disciple" by noting that the word "disciple" is used as a synonym for "believer" throughout the Book of Acts. Furthermore, the goal of evangelism according to the Great Commission (Matthew 28:19,20) is to make disciples not merely believers.[53] He is correct to stress that discipleship is not something to be entered into subsequent to conversion. However, when MacArthur claims that "the call to Christian discipleship explicitly demands . . . total dedication," he fails to make the important distinction between entrance into discipleship and the process of growth within discipleship.[54] Total dedication is the goal of discipleship and not a pre-condition to becoming a disciple. MacArthur often gives the impression that there are only committed disciples who practice total obedience to Christ.[55] Although he admits that true disciples sometimes do sin, he insists that they "inevitably return to the Lord to receive forgiveness and cleansing."[56] The Lordship portrait of a genuine disciple seems to ignore the biblical examples of those who did not always live lives worthy of a disciple.[57] Peter denied Christ and John Mark turned back on his first missionary journey, yet both remained true disciples. The Scriptures give other examples of poor disciples who were hesitant to follow Christ (e.g., Joseph of Arimathea, John 19:38). True believers will always struggle with the demands of discipleship, and therefore we should not doubt the genuineness of their faith when they do.

ASSURANCE OF SALVATION

While both sides of the Lordship debate equally affirm the unconditional security of all true believers, they offer two distinct approaches to assurance. Lordship teachers offer an assurance available to all believers based upon the promises of Scripture but conditioned upon the pursuit of holiness and the fruit of the Spirit.[58] They note that believers are commanded regularly to examine themselves (1 Corinthians 11:28) to see if they are "in the faith" (2 Corinthians 13:5). "Full assurance" (Hebrews 6:11; 10:22) is, therefore, not automatic but requires diligence "to make certain about His calling and choosing you" (2 Peter 1:10, NASB). This is achieved by making "every effort to add to your faith goodness,... knowledge,... self-control,... perseverance,... godliness,... brotherly kindness,... [and] love" (2 Peter 1:5–7). Some non-Lordship proponents reject any conditions to assurance. They claim that all believers should be completely assured of their salvation beginning the moment they believe apart from any evidence of a transformed life.[59] They argue that to tie assurance to obedience is to corrupt a salvation of grace by making it partly dependent upon works. Other non-Lordship teachers emphasize that assurance is based primarily upon the promises of God's Word but secondarily on the transformation of life.[60]

All are correct to affirm that all true believers can immediately be assured of their salvation based upon the promises in God's Word. However, this might not be "full assurance" (Hebrews 6:11), namely, an assurance completely absent of any doubt. Peter clearly states that growth in obedience and the practice of the spiritual disciplines can strengthen our assurance (2 Peter 1:5–11). Believers often grow in their assurance as they experience the grace of God worked out in their lives over a period of time. Those who divorce assurance from any change of life overlook the danger of false professions. Paul warns of those who "profess to know God, but by their deeds they deny Him" (Titus 1:16, NASB). To them the Lord will say, "I never knew you; depart from Me, you who practice lawlessness" (Matthew 7:23, NASB). Furthermore, while "assurance" is founded upon "eternal security," the two must be distinguished in meaning. On the one hand, eternal security speaks of the absolute certainty of the believer's salvation from God's perspective. Assurance, on the other hand, refers to the conscious awareness of salvation from the believer's perspective. As such, "full assurance" of salvation may not be the privilege of a believer living in deliberate disobedience to God. At the same time, to doubt the salvation of every believer who seriously struggles with disobedience in his life leaves him vulnerable to the accusing work of Satan (Romans 8:33–37; Revelation 12:10).[61]

THE POLEMIC TONE OF THE DEBATE

Many points of difference in the debate have been confused by the polemic style of the leading spokesmen on both sides. Both MacArthur and Hodges are guilty of two tendencies that have overheated the discussion.[62] The first is the creation of "straw men" that project inaccurate caricatures of opposing views. Ryrie wisely cautions against this:

> Realize that a straw man usually is not a total fabrication; it usually contains some truth, but truth that is exaggerated or distorted or incomplete. The truth element in a straw man makes it more difficult to argue against, while the distortion or incompleteness makes it easier to huff and puff and blow the man down.[63]

Such misrepresentation limits the possibility of mutual understanding and fruitful discussion. An example of this is Hodges' gross misrepresentation of the Lordship view when he writes, "Those who feel unable to inspire lives of obedience apart from questioning the salvation of those whom they seek to exhort, have much to learn from Paul!"[64] Such an unfair characterization overlooks the Lordship emphasis upon the confident assurance of victory rather than doubt as the primary inspiration for every Christian to obey God and overcome temptation. J. I. Packer expresses this best when he writes,

> Nobody has much heart for a fight he does not think he can win... But the Christian is forbidden such disastrous pessimism. God obliges him to expect success when he meets sin. For Scripture tells him that at conversion the Spirit united him to the living Christ. This was his regeneration. It made him a "new creation" (2 Corinthians 5:17), and ensured his permanent superiority in the conflict with sin.[65]

A second tendency creating misunderstanding is the widespread use of rhetorical hyperbole. Both sides are guilty of frequent overstatements designed primarily for rhetorical effect. For example, MacArthur states that "a place in the kingdom is not something to be earned." But later on the same page when speaking of the rich young ruler, he asserts, "Christ set the price for eternal life, but he refused the terms."[66] Such unguarded statements may grab the attention of the reader, but ultimately they confuse MacArthur's position. Bock correctly summarizes MacArthur's book as "a mixed bag of good observations and significant overstatements."[67] The negative fallout of such rhetorical hyperbole is that to properly understand the different viewpoints, the reader is often required to distinguish between their forceful rhetoric and what they actually mean. This not only adds needless friction to the dialogue, but also blurs their true points of differences.

THE CARNAL CHRISTIAN

The term "carnal Christian" has become a lightning rod issue within the debate. Non-Lordship proponents explain the diversity of spiritual maturity among Christians by appealing to Paul's contrast between the "spiritual" and "carnal" (1 Corinthians 3:1–3). For example, Ryrie declares,

> There were carnal or fleshly Christians in Paul's day... Paul says they walk as mere men (verse 3), this is like unsaved people. That does not mean that they were in fact not believers; Paul addresses them as believers. But it *does* indicate that believers may live like unsaved people.[68]

Lordship teachers strongly condemn Ryrie's notion of two categories of Christians. Anthony Hoekema warns, "The concept of the 'carnal Christian' as a separate category of believers is not only misleading but harmful."[69] Using even stronger terms, Reisinger denounces the theory as "one of the most perverse teachings in our generation."[70] This conflict is rooted in two distinct models of sanctification.

- **Reformed model** (Lordship view).[71] Although the believer's sanctification is perfect in Christ positionally, it is not perfect in this life experientially. After the believer accepts Jesus Christ as Savior and Lord, he continues to struggle with sin and temptation. However, because of the transforming effects of regeneration, the believer is free from sin's dominion and will progressively grow toward greater holiness throughout his life. Through the process of sanctification, the old sin nature is progressively subdued, but never entirely abolished in this life. Yet, due to his new identity in Christ and superiority over the sin nature, the believer will inevitably experience greater conformity to the image of Christ throughout his life until death.

- **Chaferian model** (non-Lordship view).[72] The believer is positionally sanctified when he is set apart from sin to God at the moment of conversion. However, experiential sanctification often does not begin until after a subsequent act of dedication when the believer commits himself to the Lordship of Christ. This single act of dedication initiates the growth process which occurs gradually through the counteraction of the new nature (new man) of the believer against his old nature (old man). The degree of growth is determined by the believer's yieldedness to God, confession of sin, and the practice of the spiritual disciplines empowered by the Holy Spirit. Those who do not take the step of dedication are "carnal Christians" and fail to grow.

A comparison reveals several important differences between these two models.[73] First, the Reformed model expects spiritual growth to spring forth immediately following conversion, while the Chaferian model allows for a delay of growth resulting in two types of Christians: spiritual and carnal. Second, the Reformed view anticipates gradual victory in the context of an ongoing struggle for all Christians while the Chaferian model stresses the need for an additional crisis of dedication necessary for "carnal Christians" to break their cycle of defeat. Third, contrary to the Lordship view, the Chaferian model suggests some believers may choose a lifelong pattern of carnality virtually no different from the unconverted.

Lordship proponents reject the Chaferian model for the following reasons.[74] First, they claim that the idea of a carnal Christian implies "a true believer can continue in unbroken disobedience from the moment of conversion."[75] Such a notion is incompatible with the unfailing work of God that transforms the life of every true believer. MacArthur explains,

> If...salvation is truly a work of God, it cannot be defective. It cannot fail to impact an individual's behavior. It cannot leave his desires unchanged or his conduct unaltered. It cannot result in a fruitless life. It is the work of God and will continue steadfastly from its inception to ultimate perfection (Philippians 1:6).[76]

Second, they claim that to promote a second distinct and necessary step (i.e., act of dedication) beyond conversion reveals a defective understanding of the unity of salvation. Namely, such an emphasis drives an unhealthy wedge between justification and progressive sanctification. Third, they reject the categorization of Christians into two types as harmful because such a notion opens the way for "depression on the part of those... on the lower level of the Christian life, and pride on the part of those who... have reached the higher levels."[77]

Lordship theology is correct to reject certain aspects of the Chaferian model of "carnal Christian." Although Paul declared the Corinthians were "still carnal" (1 Corinthians 3:3, NKJ), he did not mean that they constituted a distinct class of Christians whose lives were no different than unbelievers.[78] To divide Christians into categories of spirituality (i.e., carnal/spiritual) seems contrary to Paul's very point against making divisions in the body (1 Corinthians 1:10–12; 3:4). Even the "carnal" Corinthians were experiencing some measure of spiritual growth, for Paul later includes them in his claim, "We all... *are being transformed* into the same image from glory to glory" (2 Corinthians 3:18, NASB). To suggest that a believer can genuinely be a "new creation" (2 Corinthians 5:17) and yet remain a "carnal Christian" with little change of character diminishes the transforming effects of regeneration.[79] Paul exhorted the Corinthian believers to grow by "perfecting holiness in the fear of God" (2 Corinthians 7:1, NASB), not to move from one level of spirituality to another.

Lordship advocates are also right to challenge the Chaferian emphasis upon a distinct act of dedication. According to the Chaferian model, Paul's exhortation to "present yourselves to God as... instruments of righteousness" (Romans 6:13, NASB; cf. 12:1) refers to "the initial act of recognizing the Lordship of Christ and the right of the Holy Spirit to control and direct the life of a believer."[80] John Walvoord, Charles Ryrie, and Dwight Pentecost all claim with Chafer that this dedication is "accomplished once for all" by appealing to the aorist tense of the verb "present."[81] However, most Greek grammarians have disputed this use of the aorist.[82] Rather than a command for a once-for-all dedication of oneself to God, Paul's exhortation is better understood as a call to the continuous presentation of oneself for service in a manner similar to the repeated presentation of the free-will offerings in the Old Testament.[83] Many Christians experience sudden turning points that lead to dramatic changes in their lives (e.g., rediscovery of a neglected truth, greater awareness of the cost of discipleship, recovery from backsliding, unique fillings of the Holy Spirit). However, the Bible says nothing about a specific decision of commitment every believer must make subsequent to conversion to reach a new plane of Christian living categorically different from his life before.

However, the wholesale rejection of the notion of "carnal Christians" by Lordship advocates seriously underestimates the impact of sin in the lives of believers. Paul's words to the Corinthians undeniably teach that "carnal Christians" do exist (1 Corinthians 2:14–3:3, NASB). It is true that he is not suggesting grades of spirituality; however, he does accuse the Corinthians of immature and fleshly behavior (3:1–3). His point is that though they "have received... the Spirit" (2:12), he "could not speak to [them] as spiritual men" (3:1, NASB) because they were "walking like mere men" (3:3, NASB). They had the Spirit, but they were thinking and living like those who did not. That their carnal condition had continued for a long while is indicated by Paul's regret that they were "not *yet* able to receive" solid food (3:2, NASB) and were "*still* fleshly" (3:3, NASB). How long could they stay carnal? Long enough to "suffer loss" at the judgment seat of Christ and yet "be saved... as through fire" (3:15). Every believer will evidence some growth during his lifetime, yet that does not preclude the possibility that after conversion he may enter into a state of carnality that continues for an extended period, even to the end of his life. A notable example of this is Lot. In the Old Testament, Lot is always portrayed as a selfish, compromising individual. Ryrie ably explains:

> If we had only the Old Testament record concerning Lot, we would seriously question his spiritual relation to God. But the New Testament declares that he was a righteous man in God's sight even when he was living in Sodom (2 Peter 2:7,8 where the word *righteous*, translated "just" in v. 7, is used three times of Lot). So here is a man whose lifelong rejection of the sovereignty of God over his life did not prevent him from being righteous in God's sight.[84]

Therefore, it is critical for all who hold to Lordship salvation to account for extended periods of disobedience in the life of the believer.

Another serious omission in Lordship theology regards the issue of the "sin unto death" (1 John 5:16, KJV). The Bible is clear that disobedience in the life of the Christian will not go unnoticed by God. Hebrews 12:5–11 teaches that the Lord will always discipline those who truly belong to Him. Furthermore, divine discipline can ultimately result in the loss of physical life. According to 1 John 5:16, it is possible for a believer to commit a "sin unto death," which, due to God's judgment, results in the loss of physical life.[85] In the Old Testament, we have the example of the Exodus generation who rebelled at Kadesh Barnea. With the exception of Joshua and Caleb, they all died in the wilderness (Deuteronomy 2:14), including Moses and Aaron. This kind of temporal judgment which ultimately leads to physical death is also mentioned several times by Paul. He speaks of delivering certain ones within the church over to Satan "for the destruction of [their] flesh" in order that their "spirit may be saved" (1 Corinthians 5:5, NASB; cf. 1 Timothy 1:20). Also due to their disregard for the Lord's table, we are told that in the Corinthian church "a number sleep" (1 Corinthians 11:30). Indeed, God may judge a sinning Christian with physical death as a result of falling into a state of disobedience. This condition is so contrary to the believer's status as a "new creature" that the Lord removes such a one from the earth to prevent the continuation of such a state. The severe warnings against Christians living in disobedience indicate that it is indeed possible for a believer to be in this condition. However, MacArthur ignores all these facts with his insistence that the mark of a true disciple is that "when he does sin he *inevitably returns* to the Lord to receive forgiveness and cleansing"[86] (emphasis added). If such was truly the case, the Lord would never have made provision for "the sin unto death."

Lordship advocates are correct to be concerned about the serious problem of false profession within the Church today. However, their solution to this problem is flawed by overstatements and an inadequate account of sin in the life of the believer. Repentance, discipleship, and a willingness to obey are each a vital part of the gospel presentation. However, none require an exhaustive understanding of all that the Lord demands to be genuine. Furthermore, no matter how clearly the gospel is presented, false profession can never be totally avoided, for "even Jesus had a Judas."[87]

AN ALTERNATIVE TO THE LORDSHIP CONTROVERSY

In his booklet *Have You Made the Wonderful Discovery of the Spirit-Filled Life?*, Dr. Bright offers a needed alternative between the two-stage spirituality of the non-Lordship model and the denial of Christian carnality by Lordship theology. Dr. Bright's concept of the carnal Christian fits well Paul's teaching in 1 Corinthians 3:1–3. Never does he state that carnality is a stage that many will pass through before achieving spiritual victory. His distinction between Christians refers to two different spiritual conditions, not sequential categories or stages. His explanation of how to be filled with the Spirit contains no reference to a once-for-all act of dedication that initiates the believer into the new category of "spiritual man." His description of "spiritual breathing" clearly indicates that he is speaking of a lifelong spiritual discipline, not a once-for-all crisis experience. He calls believers not to "breathe" just once, but rather to daily practice personal confession of sin and the appreciation of the filling of the Spirit by faith. Furthermore, he acknowledges the danger of false profession when he warns, "The individual who professes to be a Christian but who continues to practice sin should realize that he may not be a Christian at all, according to 1 John 2:3; 3:6–9; Ephesians 5:5." When Lordship proponents object to the Holy Spirit booklet, they are primarily rejecting the Chaferian view of the "carnal Christian" and not an accurate understanding of Dr. Bright's teaching on the

Spirit-filled life.[88]

In *The Four Spiritual Laws* booklet, Bill Bright clearly makes Lordship a part of coming to Christ. He explains that "it is not enough just to know [the first] three laws" (i.e., the facts of the gospel). Law four declares, "We must individually receive Jesus Christ as Savior and Lord . . . Receiving Christ involves turning to God from self (repentance) and trusting Christ to come into our lives to forgive our sins and to make us what He wants us to be . . . We receive Jesus Christ, as an act of the will." In this booklet, he presents only two of his three circles: the self-directed life with Christ outside and self on the throne, and the Christ-centered life with Christ on the throne. Thus the invitation to sinners is clearly to become a believer with Christ on the throne directing all the interests of one's life. This is repeated in the prayer of invitation, "I . . . receive You as my Savior and Lord . . . Take control of the throne of my life. Make me the kind of person You want me to be." Bright considers the request to "take control" and "make me the kind of person You want me to be" a necessary part of the prayer of faith. Here he expresses agreement with Lordship proponents who insist that a "willingness" to obey and submit to Christ must be part of the initial act of saving faith. Nowhere in the booklet does he either blur the distinction between faith and obedience or suggest that a commitment to Christ's saving work is sufficient apart from a willingness to obey.

Regarding the genuineness of my decision to accept Christ at age five, I have come to realize that childlike faith is truly all that God requires of us to be born again. As I look back at those earlier years, there were signs of spiritual life and obedience to Christ that confirm the reality of the first decision. Recently, a childhood friend shared with me a forgotten memory from the distant past. He reminded me how I had led him to Christ at the age of nine. His words confirmed to me that God was indeed graciously at work long before my dramatic teenage crisis experience. Fortunately, since that time, many spiritual turning points have moved me along in my pursuit of Christ. One such milestone was my decision to join the ministry of Campus Crusade for Christ. I thank Dr. Bright for his careful and balanced statement of the biblical gospel that has left an unparalleled impact on the cause of world-evangelism for a generation. May the Lord raise up more like Dr. Bright who can show us what God can do with a man wholeheartedly devoted to the Lordship of Christ.

Dr. Bright, along with the staff of Campus Crusade for Christ, through his simple yet profound teaching on the ministry of the Holy Spirit, has helped many thousands of true believers from many religious and theological backgrounds confess their sins and surrender their lives to the Lordship of

Christ. This daily practice has revolutionized their lives and witness and has helped them experience victory in their spiritual lives and ministries. Unfortunately, many Christians continue to live in defeat because they still do not know how to live daily in the power of the Holy Spirit. No matter what church or Christian organization you might belong to, please consider taking up the challenge to make sure that all members of the Body of Christ personally understand how to overcome carnality and live by faith in the power of the Holy Spirit.[89]

NOTES

1. Earlier examples include B. B. Warfield's critical review of L. S. Chafer's book entitled *He That Is Spiritual* (New York: Our Hope, 1918) in the *Princeton Theological Review* 17, April 1919, 322–27. On the significance of this early clash in setting the tone for the Lordship debate, see Randall Gleason, "B. B. Warfield and Lewis S. Chafer on Sanctification," *Journal of the Evangelical Theological Society* 40, June 1997, 241–56. Other important examples include John Murray's review of Steven Barabas's book entitled *So Great Salvation: The History and Message of the Keswick Convention* (London: Marshall, Morgan, and Scott, 1952) reprinted in *The Collected Writings of John Murray* (Edinburgh: Banner of Truth, 1982), 4:281–86.
2. Everett F. Harrison, "Must Christ Be Lord to be Savior? NO!," *Eternity*, September 1959, 14,16,48.
3. John R. W. Stott, "Must Christ be Lord to be Savior? YES!," *Eternity*, September 1959, 15,17,18,36,37.
4. John F. MacArthur, Jr., *The Gospel According to Jesus* (Grand Rapids, MI: Zondervan, 1988). The enthusiastic forewords in his book by J. I. Packer and James Montgomery Boice identify him as the leading spokesman for the Lordship view (see pages ix–xii).
5. Charles C. Ryrie, *So Great Salvation: What It Means to Believe in Jesus Christ* (Wheaton, IL: Victor, 1989) and Zane C. Hodges, *Absolutely Free!: A Biblical Reply to Lordship Salvation* (Grand Rapids, MI: Zondervan, 1989). Also noteworthy is the *Journal of the Grace Evangelical Society*, published "to promote the clear proclamation of God's free salvation through faith alone in Christ alone, which is properly correlated with and distinguished from issues related to discipleship" (see vol. 3 [Spring 1989], 2).
6. Others advocating Lordship salvation include Kenneth L. Gentry, Jr., *Lord of the Saved: Getting to the Heart of the Lordship Debate* (Phillipsburg, NJ: Presbyterian and Reformed, 1992) and Ernest C. Reisinger, *Lord and Christ: The Implications of Lordship for Faith and Life* (Phillipsburg, NJ: Presbyterian and Reformed, 1994). Also, see MacArthur's important rejoinder to Ryrie and Hodges provocatively entitled *Faith Works: The Gospel According to the Apostles* (Dallas, TX: Word, 1993) and his article "Faith According to the Apostle James," *Journal of the Evangelical Theological Society* 33, March 1990, 13–34) with responses by Earl D. Radmacher (MacArthur, 35–41) and Robert L. Saucy (MacArthur, 43–47). For a detailed and gen-

erally balanced critique of the debate, see the multi-authored work edited by Michael Horton, *Christ the Lord: The Reformation and Lordship Salvation* (Grand Rapids, MI: Baker, 1992).

7. Anthony A. Hoekema, *Saved by Grace* (Grand Rapids, MI: Eerdmans, 1989), 20–23; Michael Horton, "Union with Christ," *Christ the Lord*, 112,13; Jonathan Gerstner, "Legalism and Antinomianism: Two Deadly Paths Off the Narrow Road," *Trust and Obey: Obedience and the Christian*, Don Kistler, ed. (Morgan, PA: Soli Deo Gloria, 1996), 144,45; Reisinger, *Lord and Christ*, 81–84.
8. MacArthur, *The Gospel According to Jesus*, 15.
9. Ibid. 17.
10. Ibid.
11. Ibid., 207.
12. Ibid., 30,31.
13. Ibid., 28,29, footnote 20.
14. Hodges, *Absolutely Free!*, 19,20.
15. MacArthur, *The Gospel According to Jesus*, xiii.
16. Darrell L. Bock, "A Review of *The Gospel According to Jesus*," *Bibliotheca Sacra* 146, Jan.–Mar. 1989, 24.
17. Hodges, *Absolutely Free!*, 37–39.
18. Ryrie, *So Great Salvation*, 121.
19. Ibid., 119–21.
20. Radmacher, 37,38.
21. Ryrie, 141. See also Hodges, *Absolutely Free!*, 107–11.
22. Gentry, *Lord of the Saved*, 20.
23. Gentry, 20. See also Louis Berkhof, *Systematic Theology* (Grand Rapids, MI: Eerdmans, 1939), 503–5; Henry Clarence Thiessen, *Lectures in Systematic Theology*, revised by Vernon D. Doerksen (Grand Rapids, MI: Eerdmans, 1979), 271–73.
24. MacArthur, *The Gospel According to Jesus*, 175.
25. MacArthur, "Faith according to the Apostle James," 26–28.
26. MacArthur, *The Gospel According to Jesus*, 174.
27. Ibid., 173.
28. Ibid.
29. Jonathan Edwards, *Religious Affections*, James M. Houston, ed. (Portland, OR: Multnomah Press, 1984), 8,9.
30. MacArthur, *The Gospel According to Jesus*, 176.
31. Ibid., 172,73.
32. Ibid., 140.
33. Ibid., 178.
34. Ibid.
35. For example, Zane Hodges declares, "Though genuine repentance *may* precede salvation . . . , it *need not* do so. And because it is not essential to the saving transaction as such, it is in no sense a condition for that transaction" (*Absolutely Free!*, 146).

36. Thomas L. Constable, "The Gospel Message," *Walvoord: A Tribute*, Donald Campbell, ed. (Chicago: Moody, 1982), 207,8; Livingston Blauvelt, Jr. "Does the Bible Teach Lordship Salvation?" *Bibliotheca Sacra* 143, Jan.–Mar. 1986, 41,42; and Robert P. Lightner, *Sin, the Savior, and Salvation* (Nashville: Thomas Nelson, 1991), 212.
37. Ryrie, *So Great Salvation*, 99.
38. MacArthur, *Faith Works*, 88. See also Gentry, *Lord of the Saved*, 46,47.
39. MacArthur, *The Gospel According to Jesus*, 164.
40. MacArthur, *Faith Works*, 90,91.
41. William F. Arndt and F. Wilbur Gingrich, *A Greek-English Lexicon of the New Testament* (Chicago: University of Chicago, 1979), 511,12.
42. E.g. Millard Erickson, *Christian Theology* (Grand Rapids, MI: Baker, 1987), 935ff; Wayne Grudem, *Systematic Theology* (Grand Rapids, MI: Zondervan, 1994), 713; Thiessen, *Lectures in Systematic Theology*, 269,70; and Bock, "A Review," 28.
43. Grudem, *Systematic Theology*, 713.
44. Lewis Sperry Chafer, *Systematic Theology* (Dallas, TX: Dallas Seminary, 1949), 3:376.
45. Bock, "A Review," 29. A careful reading of Chafer confirms this (*Systematic Theology*, 3:372,73).
46. James H. Thames, ed., *Dallas Seminary 1999–2000 Catalog* (Dallas, TX), 156.
47. MacArthur, *The Gospel According to Jesus*, 206–10; Gentry, *Lord of the Saved*, 59–65.
48. Ryrie, *So Great Salvation*, 70; Ryrie, *Balancing the Christian Life* (Chicago: Moody, 1969), 173–76.
49. Ryrie, *So Great Salvation*, 73; Lightner, 209.
50. J. Dwight Pentecost, *Design for Discipleship* (Grand Rapids, MI: Zondervan, 1971), 11,14.
51. Hodges, *Absolutely Free!*, 67–76.
52. Lightner, 211.
53. Lightner, 196ff.
54. MacArthur, *The Gospel According to Jesus*, 197.
55. In a footnote, MacArthur mentions the "disciple" distracted by his father's death (Matthew 8:21,22) and the "disciples" who withdrew (John 6:66), but maintains that they were not true Christians (MacArthur, 196). This would indicate that in the Gospels "disciple" does not always mean a true believer. However, MacArthur is correct in asserting that Jesus' call to discipleship (e.g., "Follow Me") was basically a call to believe in Him.
56. MacArthur, 104.
57. Paul's repeated exhortation in his epistles "to walk worthy of your calling" (Ephesians 4:1; Colossians 1:10; 1 Thessalonians 2:12) suggests some within those churches were not walking worthy.
58. MacArthur, *Faith Works*, 202–12.
59. Zane Hodges, *The Gospel Under Siege* (Dallas, TX: Redecion Viva, 1981), 10. See also Hodges, *Absolutely Free!*, 93–99.

60. Lightner, 244–47; Ryrie, *So Great Salvation*, 143,44.
61. In counseling a doubting believer, I would use 1 John 5:13 to show him that he can know "now" that he has eternal life based upon his profession of faith in Christ. However, I would also explain that doubts often accompany a sinful lifestyle. If he is living in sin, repentance is an effective way to remove those doubts.
62. See Bock, "A Review," 39,40 and Paul Schaefer, "A Royal Battle," in *Christ the Lord: The Reformation and the Lordship*, Michael Horton, ed. (Grand Rapids, MI: Baker, 1992), 179–93.
63. Ryrie, *So Great Salvation*, 29.
64. Hodges, *The Gospel Under Siege*, 97.
65. J. I. Packer, *God's Words: Studies of Key Bible Themes* (Downers Grove, IL: Inter-Varsity, 1981), 185.
66. MacArthur, *The Gospel According to Jesus*, 146.
67. Bock, "A Review," 37.
68. Ryrie, *So Great Salvation*, 31.
69. Hoekema, *Saved by Grace*, 21.
70. Reisinger, *Lord and Christ*, 79.
71. Reformed theologians, including B. B. Warfield, J. I. Packer, R. C. Sproul, and John R. W. Stott, commonly advocate this view.
72. This label is given to the position associated with Lewis S. Chafer by Charles C. Ryrie, "Contrasting Views on Sanctification," *Walvoord: A Tribute*, D. K. Campbell, ed. (Chicago: Moody, 1982), 191. See also Ryrie's chart in *Balancing the Christian Life*, 187.

73. For a comparison between the Reformed and Chaferian views, see Gleason, "B. B. Warfield and Lewis S. Chafer on Sanctification," 241–56.
74. MacArthur, *The Gospel According to Jesus*, 24,25; Gentry, *Lord of the Saved*, 6–8.
75. MacArthur, *The Gospel According to Jesus*, 178 (footnote 22).
76. MacArthur, 74.
77. Hoekema, *Saved by Grace*, 20.
78. For a helpful analysis of 1 Corinthians 3:1–3, see D. A. Carson, "Reflections on Assurance," *The Grace of God: The Bondage of the Will*, Thomas R. Schreiner and Bruce A. Ware, eds. (Grand Rapids, MI: Baker, 1995), 2:390–93.
79. Even Ryrie admits, "If a believer could be characterized as carnal all his life, that does not mean that he or she is carnal in all areas of life... Every believer will bear some fruit" (*So Great Salvation*, 31,32).
80. John F. Walvoord, "The Augustinian–Dispensational Perspective," *Five Views on Sanctification* (Grand Rapids, MI: Zondervan, 1987), 218.
81. John F. Walvoord, *The Holy Spirit* (Grand Rapids, MI: Zondervan, 1958), 197; Ryrie, *Balancing the Christian Life* (Chicago: Moody, 1969), 79,187; Dwight Pentecost, *Pattern for Maturity* (Chicago: Moody, 1966), 129,30; and Chafer, *Systematic Theology*, 6:254,55.
82. E.g., D. A. Carson, *Exegetical Fallacies* (Grand Rapids, MI: Baker, 1984), 69–72; Buist M. Fanning, *Verbal Aspect in New Testament Greek* (Oxford: Clarendon,

1990), 359–61; Daniel B. Wallace, *Greek Grammar Beyond the Basics: An Exegetical Syntax of the New Testament* (Grand Rapids, MI: Zondervan, 1996), 500.

83. Rather than a "once-for-all" dedication of oneself to God, the aorist active imperative "present" (*parastēsate*) in Romans 6:13 is best understood as an ingressive aorist expressing a command to commence or begin presenting ourselves alive to God. Hence, Romans 6:13 could be translated, "Do not continue yielding your members to sin..., but *start presenting yourselves* to God" (see Nigel Turner, *A Grammar of New Testament Greek*, 4 vols. [Edinburgh: T.&T. Clark, 1963], 3:74,76). Its force is similar to the aorist active infinitive "to present" (*parastēsai*) in 2 Timothy 2:15, "Be diligent to *present* yourself approved to God as a workman who does not need to be ashamed, handling accurately the word of truth." Compare this with the same form of the word (aorist active infinitive) used in Romans 12:1, "I urge you ...to present (*parastēsai*) your bodies a living and holy sacrifice." In each case, the ingressive idea of beginning an ongoing process fits well the context (Fanning, *Verbal Aspect*, 359–61).
84. Ryrie, *Balancing the Christian Life*, 173.
85. W. Robert Cook, *The Theology of John* (Chicago: Moody Press, 1979), 138,39.
86. MacArthur, *The Gospel According to Jesus*, 104 (my emphasis).
87. Bock, "A Review," 38.
88. Hoekema, *Saved by Grace*, 20–23; Gerstner, "Legalism and Antinomianism," 144–45; Reisinger, *Lord and Christ*, 81–84.
89. You will find Dr. Bright's book *The Holy Spirit: The Key to Supernatural Living* (Orlando, FL: New*Life* Publications, 1980) helpful to make these things practical to you and your ministry.

CHAPTER 26

A Brief History of Campus Crusade for Christ

JUDY DOUGLASS

On Staff since 1964

Women's Resources, President's Office

This is a story that truly began at birth. In October 1921, Mary Lee Rohl Bright was pregnant. The doctor said that her life was at risk and doubted that both she and the baby could make it. So she prayed, not for her own life, but that she would be able to give birth to a healthy child. She told God that her child would be His, dedicated to His service. On October 19, 1921, William Rohl Bright was born in Coweta, Oklahoma. Both he and his mother lived.

Although this is a brief history of Campus Crusade for Christ, the history of this ministry cannot be separated from the story of Bill Bright. His years growing up on a ranch in Oklahoma encompassed a loving family, hard work, high goals, and significant achievements, but there was no evidence of that spiritual commitment made by his mother. As a young man, he headed off to California to seek his fortune. There, God engineered an amazing set of circumstances that saw his mother's prayers answered, changed the course of Bill's life, and had an incredible impact on all of history.

As Bill drove into the Los Angeles area, he picked up a young hitchhiker who was living in the home of Dawson Trotman, the founder of The Navigators. So Bill had dinner with the Trotmans, attended a birthday party for Dan Fuller of the Fuller Theological Seminary family, and then spent his first night in California at the home of Dawson Trotman. Although that encounter was brief, it was the first step in a major change for Bill Bright. The next encounter was with his apartment landlords, who attended the First Presbyterian Church of Hollywood and repeatedly invited

Bill to join them. One Sunday afternoon, after a horseback ride in the Hollywood Hills, Bill stopped by the church and slipped in for the evening service. He left again just as quickly, but soon he received a call from a member of the college and career class, led by Dr. Henrietta Mears.

Bill accepted a party invitation and was so impressed with the young people he met there that he began to attend the class and then later worship services at the church. Over time, he "became convinced that Jesus was truly the most remarkable person who ever lived, there was no one like Him in all of history... The months passed, and the more I learned about him, the more excited I became."

Then one Wednesday evening in the spring of 1945, Dr. Mears spoke to the young adult group on the conversion of the apostle Paul. She challenged her students to ask, "Who art Thou Lord, and what wilt Thou have me to do?" That night, Bill knelt beside his bed and asked that question. "In a sense," he said, "that was my prayer for salvation. It wasn't very profound theologically, but the Lord knew my heart and He interpreted what was going on inside me."

After crossing that threshold, Bill began to seek God with all his heart, to learn all that he could, and to tell others about the wonderful Savior he had met.

Bill also began to pursue a childhood friend from Coweta, Vonette Zachary. They wrote frequently, and on their first real date, Bill proposed. Amazingly, Vonette accepted, and that began a three-year engagement. But Bill began to realize that Vonette probably didn't really know Christ as her personal Savior. She began to consider Bill a religious fanatic. It appeared that the intended marriage would be derailed, but Bill arranged for Vonette to meet with Dr. Mears. While the two women talked, Bill prayed, and during that time, Vonette understood her need for a Savior and committed her life to Christ.

In the meantime, Bill was attending seminary, first at Princeton and then at the new Fuller Seminary in Pasadena, seeking to learn all he could about his Lord and Savior. In June 1947, Bill, along with Louis Evans, Jr. and Dick Halverson, attended a conference at Forest Home Conference Center in Southern California where Dr. Mears was speaking. They were enveloped in a profound experience. "We were overwhelmed with the presence of God. It was something I had never before experienced," he said. From this came the Fellowship of the Burning Heart as each of them committed to consecrate themselves absolutely to Christ, to a life of expendability.

In December 1948, Bill returned to Coweta to marry Vonette. They set up their home in Hollywood, where Vonette accepted a teaching position, and Bill continued his confections business and attended seminary. Then one Sunday afternoon in 1951, after a disagreement, Bill and Vonette each went to the Lord and wrote down their expectations for their lives and their marriage. Then they signed those papers as an expression of the surrender of their lives to God. In this contract with God, they prayed, telling God that their lives were surrendered totally and irrevocably to Him—He could do anything He wanted to, in them and through them, for His glory. Wherever He wanted them to go, whatever He wanted them to do, whatever the cost, they wanted to be His bondslaves.

To this day, Bill and Vonette look at the signing of that contract with God as a turning point in their lives. Just a few nights later, Bill had an experience with God that would finalize his life-change from business executive to leader of a worldwide ministry to help fulfill the Great Commission. God visited Him and opened his mind and touched his heart: "There is no way I can describe it," Bill said. "Without apology, all I can say is that I met with God, and I have never been the same since that unforgettable encounter."

Bill had received a vision to help reach the world for Christ and fulfill the Great Commission in his lifetime. The calling was to the college campus. The slogan was: "Reach the campus for Christ today, reach the world for Christ tomorrow." The next morning, Bill shared his vision first with Vonette, who rejoiced, and then with Dr. Wilbur Smith, one of his professors. Smith was enthusiastic, saying, "This is of God, this is of God!" He gave Bill a name for his vision: *Campus Crusade for Christ*. Bill and Vonette's first step was to pray. They gathered friends at seminary and church and set up a 24-hour prayer chain, divided into 15-minute blocks. There was no strategy yet—only seeking God and His plan.

THE '50S

In the fall of 1951, Campus Crusade for Christ began on the UCLA campus. Bill and Vonette gathered students from church to make presentations of the Christian perspective of life on campus, beginning in the Kappa Alpha Theta sorority house. He asked the Lord to let there be at least one who would respond to confirm the vision that God had given. He spoke on the subject of Jesus, who He is and how we can know Him personally. Then he invited anyone who wanted to receive Christ as Savior and Lord to come and tell him personally.

A line formed. Of the 60 women present, more than half expressed an interest in knowing how they could receive Christ. Another meeting was announced for the following night at the Brights' home near the campus, and he challenged the women to bring their friends. Over the next few months, meetings were held in fraternities, sororities, and dormitories. More than 250 UCLA students—including the student body president, the student newspaper editor, and a number of top athletes—committed their lives to Christ. So great was their influence on the entire campus that the chimes began to play Christian hymns daily during the noon hour. That was the first year of the fulfillment of the vision given to one man and his wife, who were totally submitted to the Lord, slaves of Christ.

At the end of that year, more workers were needed as the desire to expand to more campuses grew. They didn't know where to find those staff, but they knew that the ministry must be carried out by Spirit-filled people who would say yes to God without reservation, who wanted to change the world.

The first recruit was Gordon Klenck, followed by Roe Brooks. Both of them are still on staff with Campus Crusade. By the beginning of the second year of Campus Crusade for Christ, six staff workers were sharing Christ on three local campuses.

In 1952, a strong commitment to training began around the Brights' table with these first staff. Today, staff training conferences are held for Campus Crusade staff around the world. These offer basic ministry training in evangelism and discipleship for new staff, as well as vision, inspiration, and advanced training for senior staff.

Within this decade, the foundations of the ministry were carefully laid. The concept of "win-build-send" became core to the ministry: winning people to Christ through initiative evangelism—going where people are, talking to them about Christ in a relevant way; building them up in their faith—providing initial follow-up and discipleship; and then sending them out to teach others what they have learned and to help fulfill the Great Commission. This application of Paul's instructions in 2 Timothy 2:2, "Teach these great truths to trustworthy people who are able to pass them on to others" (NLT), solidified the concept of spiritual multiplication that enabled the ministry of Campus Crusade to become a movement and to continue as a movement through these five decades.

One of the keys to the rapid development of the ministry was a very clear presentation of the gospel of Christ, one that people could understand, respond to, and share with others. As Bill Bright worked on this presentation over the years, it took the form of what became known as "God's Plan for Your Life," and then "The Four Spiritual Laws." These four points of the gospel were memorized by every staff member, who wrote them on the back of materials presenting the gospel or on paper napkins at a restaurant. With whatever was handy, they shared the truth from the Word of God that led a person to an understanding of his need for Christ and how he could receive Him. When God's Plan was further refined into *The Four Spiritual Laws*, Bill, under the prompting of the Holy Spirit, departed from the traditional gospel beginning of "man is sinful." Instead, he began where God began: "God loves you." "Man is sinful" became the second law. This change caused a lot of concern and consternation among many staff, but it soon became evident that beginning with God's love was the most powerful way to tell people about Jesus.

Another key development in that first decade was that every staff member would develop his or her own financial support. In the early days, the ministry was supported by proceeds from Bill's business. When he sold his business, he began to do fund-raising for the entire ministry. But it became evident that the only way the ministry could grow to a size that would begin to encompass the vision that God had given would be for each staff member to be in the fund-raising business. To this day, every full-time missionary staff personally develops a team of prayer and financial supporters, who are partners with him or her in the ministry God has given them as a part of this movement. This makes it possible for many, many more people to be employed by the ministry, and it makes the donor feel a much closer, more personal tie to the ministry. This undoubtedly encourages greater giving and certainly more prayer involvement.

The Lord kept laying foundational stones. One of the keys to the effectiveness and growth of the ministry of Campus Crusade is the emphasis on the Spirit-filled life. Bill increasingly understood that it was the Holy Sprit's filling and empowering of a Christian that enabled him to serve God effectively. As he sought to impart this concept to staff and to those they ministered to, God gave him again a simple but clear presentation that first took the form of an article called "Ye Shall Receive Power," and later a booklet, *Have You Made the Wonderful Discovery of the Spirit-filled Life?* Undoubtedly, one of the strengths of this ministry has been this practical, moment-by-moment emphasis on being led, filled, and empowered by the Holy Spirit. The concept of spiritual breathing—of exhaling, or confessing sin as soon as we are aware of it, and then inhaling, or being filled with the Spirit by faith—has enabled even the youngest Christian to have power for effective ministry and the oldest Christian to deal with sin as soon as he is aware of it.

This was also the decade of the development of many of the basic materials that have been used in the growth of the ministry, such as the *Ten Basic*

Steps Toward Christian Maturity. This Bible study series equipped staff members to teach the basics to new converts, whether they were students or laypeople or even high-powered executives.

The vision was always worldwide in scope, and in 1958, under the leadership of Dr. Joon Gon Kim, the ministry expanded to Korea and, soon thereafter, to Pakistan. Surely, the gospel had to go to the uttermost parts of the world.

(STATS at end of decade: more than 100 staff; 40 campuses in 15 states and 3 countries)

THE '60S

If the '50s was a decade of beginnings and foundations, the '60s was a decade of innovation and rapid growth. Even in the early years of this decade that became a revolution, literature was a key tool. The *Collegiate Challenge* magazine was designed as an evangelistic piece used to engage students in conversation on relevant topics and lead into a presentation of Jesus Christ. In *Revolution Now,* Bill Bright challenged students to live all-out for Christ and be wholly engaged in taking Him to the entire world.

The acquisition of Arrowhead Springs, a former hotel and resort in the foothills of the San Bernardino Mountains in Southern California, set the stage for a quantum leap. Arrowhead Springs was not only a beautiful headquarters for the expanding ministry, but a training center that enabled staff, students, and laypeople to be taught how to walk in the Spirit, how to share their faith in Christ, how to build disciples, and how to be part of a spiritual revolution.

Illusionist André Kole fires people's imaginations and challenges their perceptions of the New Age movement.

The commitment to solid, biblical training continued and expanded. In 1962 the Institute for Biblical Studies began offering formal biblical, theological, and special ministry training. Today, this continues throughout the world for staff and others who generally have not had previous formal biblical training.

Bill Bright's willingness to let people with creative ideas try them out led to

Athletes in Action makes national news when its men's basketball team crushes collegiate powers Nevada–Las Vegas and San Francisco. UNLV coach Jerry Tarkanian, referring to AIA's evangelistic presentations at halftime, quips, "They beat you up in the first half, pray for you at half time, then beat you up in the second half."

incredible diversity in the ways the ministry sought to reach people and the target audience as well. The Lay Institute for Evangelism became a key tool for reaching and training laypeople in churches and communities, so they could be a vital part in fulfilling the Great Commission. Reaching the campus for Christ began to include high school students, as the high school ministry—now known as Student Venture—was launched. And the Military Ministry began to reach and train personnel who could be missionaries for the Lord Jesus, truly to the uttermost parts of the world, with the help of the United States government.

André Kole, world-renowned illusionist, began to use his skill to draw thousands to see a magic show and hear about Christ, taking them from illusion to reality. The New Folk were the first of a long line of musical groups who have drawn crowds, entertained audiences, and freshly presented the message of Christ. Capitalizing on the great influence that athletes have, Campus Crusade developed Athletes in Action. This is a ministry to athletes and also uses athletes and their influence to share Christ. Teams have traveled throughout the U.S. and the world, playing their games and telling people about Jesus. In addition, Athletes in Action staff have worked on campuses and in communities with pro teams of many different sports. A fiery young man named Josh McDowell began to develop into a dynamic speaker for the Lord and a powerful advocate for the truth of the Word of God.

Committed to going where the students were, the Campus Ministry began to take groups to Spring Break at the beach, beginning first at Balboa Beach in California, and later to Daytona Beach in Florida. There trained students mingled among the spring breakers, starting conversations and talking about Jesus.

One of the most significant happenings of the '60s was the development of the "Four Spiritual Laws" into a booklet that could be used by anybody, anywhere. More than 2.5 billion of these booklets have been distributed and millions of believers are in the kingdom today because through these they have understood God's love for them and received His gift of salvation and forgiveness.

In 1967, all the U.S. Campus Crusade staff converged on the campus of the University of California at Berkeley, the seat of the radical student revolution spreading across the country and the world. This called for a radical presentation of the gospel. During this "blitz," 600 staff and students sought to share Christ, both personally and to groups, with every segment of the student population. Billy Graham delivered a message at the Greek theater on campus. Altogether, more than 700 students and faculty indicated decisions to receive Christ. A similar, but smaller, "blitz" was held at UCLA the following week.

God blessed these many different efforts and approaches to take the gospel broadly into the world, and the staff increase in 1967 was about 67 percent. By the end of the decade, the ministry was fully engaged in revolutionary approaches to reach a society caught up in a revolution.

(STATS: 2,200 staff; 25 countries)

THE '70S

Even as in the '60s, great innovation and rapid growth continued in the '70s, leading to increasing involvement around the world. The first of many major outreaches was Explo '72. More than 80,000 students, Campus Crusade staff members, and members of churches and youth groups converged on the Cotton Bowl in Dallas in June 1972. This unique conference included major rallies in the evenings, contemporary music concerts, messages by Billy Graham, extremes of hot and cold and rain and dry, and specific evangelism and discipleship training for all those attending. Many people were radicalized in their faith at this conference and made commitments to follow Christ into full-time service.

Explo '72 was followed in 1974 by Explo '74 in Seoul, Korea. More than 320,000 Koreans participated in evangelism and discipleship training. Large gatherings on Yoido Island in the evening reached more than a million in attendance. This conference was a catalyst to rapid growth of the Korean church, and Korea became one of the major missionary-sending countries of the world.

The first Great Commission Training Center (GCTC) began in Manila in 1971, where people from various countries of Asia came. Today, there are 70 GCTCs around the world, offering a six- to nine-month program designed to give ministry, biblical, and theological training in the classroom. The staff are also involved in actual supervised ministry throughout their training. In 1973, Agape International Training began at Arrowhead Springs, training staff who planned to minister in cross-cultural situations. These training programs continue in several locations throughout the world today, teaching principles of missions and cross-cultural communications and ministry, while the students carry on a cross-cultural ministry of evangelism and discipleship in the local community. Graduate-level seminary training also began at Arrowhead Springs in 1978 with the International School of Theology.

Worldwide Challenge magazine was begun during this time to tell donors what their prayers and dollars were accomplishing though this ministry and to allow them to experience to a greater degree the full life of walking in the Spirit and boldly sharing Christ with others. It continued in the award-winning traditions of *Collegiate Challenge.*

Spring-break projects led to summer projects at resort areas around the country. Students spent two to three months working at a resort to earn money for their education, while at the same time participating in training and outreach conferences. These projects proved to be one of the most effective ways to engage students in a long-term commitment to fulfilling the Great Commission. Even as they were effective in the United States, summer projects also became a major means of enabling students to go overseas. In many cases, the students would see how God could use them in another part of the world, and decide that God wanted them overseas long-term.

In Moscow for the premiere of the JESUS *film, Bill and Vonette stand inside the walls of the Kremlin, with the Cathedral Square in the background.*

"I Found It!" was a key phrase across North America and then around the world. TV ads, radio, billboards, bumper stickers —everywhere you looked Christians declared, "I Found It!" What did they find? New life in Jesus Christ. Churches across the country joined in this campaign, training their members to share the gospel, while those who responded to the ads were contacted by phone and in person and given an opportunity to receive Christ. There was an 85 percent exposure of the American public to the campaign, and thus to the message of Christ.

JESUS, *a film account of the life of Christ, premieres in 250 theaters in 1979. The film becomes the most-translated motion picture in history, and the single most important tool for accelerating the gospel worldwide.*

The decade of the '70s ended with the development of perhaps the most significant evangelistic tool ever seen apart from the Word of God. *JESUS*, an account of the life of Christ from the Book of Luke, was filmed at more than 200 locations in Israel and used a cast of more than 5,000. It premiered first in 250 theaters. Although the film has been an effective tool in the U.S., it has had far greater impact around the world. It is the most translated motion picture in history—currently translated into more than 600 languages with 3.7 billion viewers thus far. More than 1,180 denominations and mission agencies are using the *JESUS* film to bring the gospel to the world. Imagine the power for change of a person from an isolated tribe in Africa or Asia seeing his first film, in his own language, and hearing God speaking his language. To date, at least 121 million have recorded decisions for Jesus Christ, but it is known that there are many, many more beyond that.

Many hear about Jesus for the first time at a JESUS *film showing in Rwanda.*

(STATS: 11,500 staff; 71 countries)

THE '80S

The '80s became the decade of focused attention on how we would truly reach the entire world and fulfill the Great Commission. The development of the New Life 2000 plan gave hope to people that truly the Great Commission could be fulfilled in this generation. The population of the world was divided into million-population target areas, and our staff joined hands with denominations and groups around the world to reach the unreached.

One of the strengths of the Campus Crusade strategy has always been to use nationals. Whenever North Americans have gone into a country to begin a ministry, it has always been with the intention of finding and training nationals who would then take over the ministry. Unusual in its early days, this strategy is now broadly accepted as the best way to reach any people of the world. Those who live there—who are a part of the culture and know the language—are much better able to reach their own people than those coming from the outside. And yet those coming from the outside who go to another country are able to serve, encourage, train, and provide resources that would not otherwise be available to reach every person in every country.

In 1982, Campus Crusade sends its first team of students to the Soviet Union. Under the code name "Northstar," this summer mission project highlights an influx of covert ministry activity in Eastern Europe, which accelerates openly after the fall of the Iron Curtain.

Another means for reaching people in difficult places was the development of The Agape Movement, something like a Christian Peace Corps. People took their skills—teaching, farming, medicine, and many others—to remote parts of the world to use those skills to benefit people and seek opportunities to share Christ.

In 1983, 17,000 U.S. students, staff members, and other Christians met in Kansas City for KC '83. Billy Graham and Bill Bright spoke and challenged them. They went out into the community to meet physical needs, as well as to share Christ.

Two years later, Explo '85, a worldwide videoconference, linked an estimated 300,000 delegates at 98 conference sites on five continents with the help of eighteen satellites. Bill Bright flew from continent to continent to be a part of it with people in each area of the world. The use of satellite technology that made this conference possible has continued to develop and is a major component of efforts to reach people in every part of the world today.

The *JESUS* film translation continued and a shorter version was put on video to reach American audiences, taking the gospel right into homes, where it is increasingly difficult for ministering Christians to go.

(STATS: 8,434 full time and 1,576 associate staff; 93 countries)

THE '90S

The final decade of the millennium has marked the most rapid spread of the gospel in which this ministry has yet been involved.

After 30 years at Arrowhead Springs in San Bernardino, California, Campus Crusade relocates in 1991 to Orlando, Florida, moving into the Sunport Technological Center, a converted warehouse. Sunport serves for eight years as a temporary headquarters during development of land donated to Campus Crusade.

The decade began with a move of the Campus Crusade headquarters in 1991 from Arrowhead Springs in California, which it had outgrown, to Orlando, Florida. The ministry set up temporary headquarters in a renovated warehouse. Then in 1998, it moved to the Lake Hart campus, a beautiful site designed to make our staff as efficient as possible in supporting the field ministries, as well as to present a vision to the thousands of visitors, who are already coming, of how they can personally be involved in the Great Commission.

Representatives from 102 countries converged on Manila over a six-month period in 1990. During the New Life 2000: Manila project, more than 5,000 people (only 11 percent of them Americans) present the gospel to 3.3 million Filipinos, with 447,000 indicating decisions to receive Christ.

Campus Crusade joined with more than sixty other Christian organizations to form the CoMission, a united effort to take the gospel to the newly opened Soviet Union. This cooperation marked a new willingness among the many parts of the Body of Christ to work together, to share ideas, to enable each other to be more effective, to be willing to do anything to take the gospel to the whole world.

The CoMission unites more than 60 Christian organizations, including Campus Crusade, in the pursuit of making the most of the newfound spiritual openness in the former Soviet Union.

The Worldwide Student Network coordinated increasing efforts to draw students out of their comfort zones and into reaching the world. The Intercultural Resources team sought to help our staff see how they can be involved in breaking racial barriers and in working together to reach people of every ethnic background.

In 1994, Bill Bright called together 600 Christian leaders to meet in Orlando, Florida, for a Prayer & Fasting conference. Feeling a special anointing from God to call Christians to prayer and fasting, Dr. Bright has engaged in six 40-day fasts so far. He has also given leadership to six Prayer & Fasting conferences involving thousands of Christian leaders and lay people—bringing them together in large conferences as well as in satellite sites at churches, to pray and to fast for revival in our nation and the world.

Thousands participate in the annual Prayer & Fasting Conference, praying for revival in America.

"Dying to tell you." While battling AIDS, Steve Sawyer travels to tell college students about eternal hope (shown here at LA State University).

Even as AIDS spread illness and death throughout the world, God touched many people through the life of a young hemophiliac. Steve Sawyer contracted AIDS from a blood transfusion. While he was a student at Curry College in Boston, he became a Christian through the ministry of Campus Crusade for Christ. As AIDS began to take its toll, Steve wanted to tell people about Jesus. God kept him alive for five years longer than the doctors predicted, and during that time, Steve traveled from campus to campus around the United States, drawing large crowds of students as he shared the importance of knowing Jesus Christ and the eternal life that He offers.

Campus Crusade's response to a request from the Malawi Ministry of Education to help curb the spread of sexually transmitted diseases and promiscuity among African youth has bloomed into a proven worldwide

Campus Crusade's U.S. National Staff Conference becomes a world staff conference and a launching pad for fulfilling the Great Commission, as staff members representing 171 other nations attend and find their faith inspired.

strategy to spread the gospel through education. *CrossRoads* is a comprehensive strategy designed to teach Judeo-Christian values, character, and relationship development to students in and out of the classroom. Now in more than forty countries, parents, teachers, and students are being introduced to the *CrossRoads* curriculum, which addresses the root cause of all needs by providing an opportunity to establish personal faith in Jesus Christ.

During the Balkan crisis, Campus Crusade staff members helped bring God's love—by word and deed—to the refugees.

Ministry and theological training continued throughout the '90s and into the present. Campus Crusade for Christ's graduate-level seminary training, which began in the '70s, has expanded into a consortium consisting of nine schools in Africa, Asia, and the Americas. These schools offer two-, three-, and four-year seminary degree programs for pastors, potential pastors, Christian leadership, and full-time Christian workers on a post-college level, with a strong emphasis on both the practical and the academic. Non-graduate training is also offered to church planters, pastors, and other full-time Christian workers in Bible-school-type settings. Presently, about six such schools offer training in Bible, theology, and various ministry skills, with plans for more in the future.

New Life Training Centers, teaching the heart of the GCTC material, trained almost 13,000 staff and lay volunteers in 1999 alone. Finally, the International Leadership University recently began offering university degree education in various disciplines. Plans are being made to provide education in many places in the world, as well as extension training using the Internet, with the purpose of raising up Christians to provide leadership throughout the world.

Dr. Bright is awarded the Templeton Prize for Progress in Religion, given by investor John Templeton to recognize the spiritual dimension overlooked by the Nobel prizes.

In 1996, Bill Bright was honored for the incredible contribution he has made to spiritual life around the world. He received the Templeton Prize for Progress in Religion, the world's largest annual financial award—more than $1 million. It is given every year by investor John Templeton to recognize the spiritual dimension overlooked by Nobel prizes. Dr. Bright gave the money away to promote the spiritual benefits of prayer and fasting.

(STATS: 21,952 staff, 489,000 trained volunteers; 186 countries)

In 1999, Campus Crusade for Christ at Lake Hart opens its doors as the new home of Campus Crusade's world headquarters.

God has enabled Campus Crusade for Christ to provide a legacy of incredible diversity to the Body of Christ in many ways: the goal of the fulfillment of the Great Commission in this generation; *The Four Spiritual Laws*; the concepts of spiritual breathing, win-build-send, and initiative evangelism; the high value placed on innovation; the *JESUS* film, and much more. Each of these can be traced, directly or indirectly, to the faith and creativity of Bill Bright.

But a much greater legacy is reflected in his consistent answer when people ask what they can pray for him. Always, he answers: "Pray I don't lose my first love for the Lord Jesus." For him, all of this flows from being a slave to the Lord he loves. That is undoubtedly the root of the growth and fruitfulness of Campus Crusade for Christ.